MODERN STUDIES IN PHILOSOPHY

KANT

A Collection of Critical Essays

EDITED BY ROBERT PAUL WOLFF

UNIVERSITY OF NOTRE DAME PRESS

NOTRE DAME   LONDON

First Hardbound Edition: 1968

University of Notre Dame Press

Notre Dame, Indiana 46556

Printed by special arrangement with Doubleday & Company, Inc.

Anchor Books Edition: 1967
Doubleday & Company, Inc.
Garden City, New York

Manufactured in the United States of America

Modern Studies in Philosophy is a series of anthologies presenting contemporary interpretations and evaluations of the works of major philosophers. The editors have selected articles designed to show the systematic structure of the thought of these philosophers, and to reveal the relevance of their views to the problems of current interest. These volumes are intended to be contributions to contemporary debates as well as to the history of philosophy; they not only trace the origins of many problems important to modern philosophy, but also introduce major philosophers as interlocutors in current discussions.

Modern Studies in Philosophy is prepared under the general

CONTENTS

INTRODUCTION   ix

PART ONE. DISCUSSIONS OF THE *Critique of Pure Reason*

THE PREFACES AND INTRODUCTION

Can Kant's Synthetic Judgments Be Made Analytic?
   Lewis White Beck   3
Kant's Theory of Definition, *Lewis White Beck*   23

THE TRANSCENDENTAL AESTHETIC

Infinity and Kant's Conception of the "Possibility of
   Experience," *Charles D. Parsons*   37

THE TRANSCENDENTAL ANALYTIC

Categories, *W. H. Walsh*   54
Schematism, *W. H. Walsh*   71
A Reconstruction of the Argument of the Subjective
   Deduction, *Robert Paul Wolff*   88
Kant's Theory of Concepts, *George Schrader*   134
Knowledge and the Ego: Kant's Three Stages of Self-
   Evidence, *Samuel J. Todes*   156

THE TRANSCENDENTAL DIALECTIC

The Thing in Itself in Kantian Philosophy,
   George Schrader   172
Kant's 'Refutation' of the Ontological Argument,
   S. Morris Engel   189

PART TWO: DISCUSSIONS OF KANT'S ETHICAL THEORY

THE CATEGORICAL IMPERATIVE

Interpretation and Misinterpretation of the Categorical Imperative, *Julius Ebbinghaus*   211
Kant's Examples of the First Formulation of the Categorical Imperative, *Jonathan Harrison*   228
Kant's Examples of the Categorical Imperative,
   J. Kemp   246
The Categorical Imperative, *Jonathan Harrison*   259
The Copernican Revolution in Ethics: The Good Reexamined, *John R. Silber*   266
The Concept of Man as End-in-Himself,
   Pepita Haezrahi   291
What Does Kant Mean by 'Acting from Duty'?
   Paul Dietrichson   314
Kant as Casuist, *W. I. Matson*   331

PART THREE: DISCUSSIONS OF KANT'S AESTHETIC
      THEORY

Perception and Perfection in Kant's Aesthetics,
   Ingrid Stadler   339
Kant: The Aesthetic Judgment,
   Robert L. Zimmerman   385

BIBLIOGRAPHY

Bibliography of Works by and about Kant   409
Selected Bibliography of Articles on Kant, 1945 to
   the Present   412

INTRODUCTION

It is now only a few years short of two centuries since Immanuel Kant announced a revolution in philosophy, with his *Inaugural Dissertation* of 1770. The Critical Philosophy, as Kant came to call his system, received its definitive statement in the *Critique of Pure Reason*, published in 1781, and in the series of works that issued from his pen during the next two decades. Virtually singlehanded, Kant destroyed the discipline of rational theology, to which the greatest philosophers of the preceding two millennia had devoted their soberest attention. He transformed metaphysics, established the theory of knowledge on a firm theoretical foundation, discovered hitherto unrecognized problems in the philosophy of mathematics, and even gave moral philosophy a new direction. All philosophy before 1781 seems to flow into Kant's great system, and little that has appeared since cannot be traced back to his influence. It has been truly observed that in the modern world, one can philosophize against Kant or with him, but never without him.

It follows that a survey of the influence of Kant on recent philosophical literature would reduce simply to a survey of recent philosophical literature, and a book of readings of that sort would lose its focus and reason for being. Even if we were to restrict ourselves to the literature directly concerned with particular problems first posed by Kant, our nets would be thrown far too widely. For example, all the discussions of the distinction between analytic and synthetic judgments, and the wealth of books and articles on the universalizability of ethical judgments, would have to be included.

In this volume, I have restricted myself to a selection of papers which have appeared in some of the major journals during the two decades since the war. More than one hundred papers have been published, and it was a simple task to choose enough to fill a volume of this sort. I have tried to give some indication of the variety of work on Kant, as well as the variety of viewpoints from which that work has been done.

Several Kant scholars are represented by more than one selection. Among them are the dean of American Kant scholars, Lewis White Beck, whose recent commentary on the *Critique of Practical Reason* demonstrates his mastery of Kant's ethical philosophy as convincingly as his many papers have established his command of Kant's metaphysics and theory of knowledge. W. H. Walsh of England is represented by two important papers on difficult topics in the *Critique of Pure Reason*, and George Schrader of Yale demonstrates his command of the knotty issues surrounding the concept of the thing-in-itself in his piece on that subject. I might add that I am happy to reprint Professor Schrader's essay on Kant's theory of concepts, as I was in the audience of the Harvard Philosophy Club some years ago when it was first read as an address to that body.

The Harrison-Kemp interchange on the categorical imperative illustrates nicely the fascination which those famous four examples have held for students of Kant's moral philosophy. They rank with Descartes' lump of wax as topics of endless debate and analysis.

Two of the essays included in this volume were written especially for the occasion, and have not appeared elsewhere. Professor Todes' essay is part of a much larger work, systematic as well as historical, in which the phenomenology of the body plays a central role. Professor Stadler's essay on Kant's aesthetics is one of the very few extended treatments of that important branch of the Critical Philosophy to have been written in the past twenty years.

The essays in this book speak for themselves as interpretations of Kant and exemplifications of the work now being done on his philosophy. Rather than summarize and review them, therefore, I shall take the occasion of these introductory remarks to call attention to several important problems in Kant's philosophy which have *not* been much discussed in recent literature. It may be that in this way readers will be stimulated to broaden our understanding of Kant, and perhaps by the time the bicentenary of the *Inaugural Dissertation* arrives there will be a fresh crop of articles and books on topics hitherto untouched.

(i) The Critical Philosophy is a systematic inventory and certification of the powers, propensities, and possessions of the human mind. In every branch of thought and action Kant first seeks the contribution made by the mind and then attempts a critical evaluation of it. In science, mathematics, ethics, metaphysics, aesthetics, politics, some portion of the whole can be attributed to the activity of the observer or agent. Philosophy, for Kant, is the critique of that subjective contribution; Kant's philosophy is thus pre-eminently a philosophy of the self. Historically, we can view the *Critique of Pure Reason* as an answer to the Cartesian theory of the self enunciated in the *Meditations*. Kant himself indicates that he so interprets his enterprise by making the Cartesian "Cogito," or "I think," the first premise of his central argument. (See the opening passages of the Deduction of the Pure Concepts of Understanding, in the second edition of the *Critique*.)

Surprisingly, nowhere in the critical corpus do we find an extended, systematic discussion of the nature of the self, nor have modern students of Kant's philosophy concerned themselves especially with attempts to fill this gap by reconstructing a Kantian theory of the self. The reason for so striking a failure, I think it is fair to say, is the appalling difficulty of the task. Once we begin to itemize Kant's assertions about the self even within one work, such as the first *Critique*, we discover that there are endless contradictions, complications, and unclarities. Nevertheless, the effort must be made, for plainly we cannot hope to master Kant's philosophy and come to some judgment of its truth until we have synthesized his accounts of the activity of the mind, and made a coherent whole of his theory of the mind-dependent *a priori* element in experience.

In the theory of the first *Critique*, there are at least three different selves whose relations to one another must be established. First in the order of knowing is the empirical, or phenomenal, self, in whose empirical consciousness the manifold of perceptions is to be found. My empirical self has the best claim to being identified as *me*, for when I introspect, it is the contents of my empirical self that I encounter; when I act in the world, it is my empirical self that acts. It is the empirical self that can be said to doubt, hope, fear, love, expect, believe, desire, intend, approve and disapprove. When I take a walk, do a sum, give a speech, perform an experiment, make an observation, it is my empirical self that is acting. My virtues and vices, my strengths and weaknesses of character, the idiosyncrasies that make me the person I am, are all dispositions and characteristics of my empirical self.

But this empirical self is merely the appearance of my true, real, or noumenal self. The form of my empirical self is time, which is to say that empirical consciousness has a temporal order. My perceptions, thoughts, feelings, and actions are governed by causal laws, upon which a science of psychology (or anthropology, as Kant calls it) can be erected. My real self, on the other hand, is atemporal, and stands outside the causal order of nature. My empirical self is merely myself as it appears to myself, not as it is in itself. Hence, all the causal and other judgments that I can make about my character, experience, and activities, while necessarily and objectively true, stand under the limiting condition that they apply only to the self as appearance. The noumenal self is rational. Whether it has any distinguishing characteristics that set it off from other noumenal selves is, at best, a mystery. Indeed, it seems odd to speak of *my* noumenal self, although it is perfectly natural to speak of *my* empirical self, or personality. According to some of Kant's statements, the noumenal or real self is self-conscious, but its consciousness is "pure, original, and unchanging," unlike the variable flow of perceptions and feelings that makes up empirical consciousness.

According to Kant, the mind (noumenal self?) comes into relation with objects, and brings those objects under concepts, according to certain innate forms which lie ready in the mind and are imposed by the mind on its experience.

The active imposition of these *a priori* forms is called synthesis, and the locus of the activity of synthesis is the transcendental unity of apperception, or *transcendental ego*—the third self. The entire world order, including both the objects of nature and the empirical self that perceives them, is produced by the activity of synthesis. The active, knowing mind, or transcendental ego, knows things as they appear, not as they are in themselves, including of course itself, which also it knows only as appearance.

What are the relations among these three selves, in Kant's theory? The most natural answer is that the noumenal self *is* the transcendental ego, of which the empirical ego is the appearance. Countless passages in the *Critique of Pure Reason* support such an interpretation. Unfortunately, however, it creates many more problems than it solves. The transcendental ego is the source of the unity and order of the entire phenomenal world. The unity of nature is the objective reflection of the subjective unity of apperception. If the transcendental ego, to whom the synthesizing activity is attributed, were identical with the noumenal self, then there would be room in the world of nature for only one empirical self, namely myself. If two independent centers of consciousness were to appear in nature, myself and someone else, then we would be forced to one of two conclusions, both intrinsically absurd: either the two empirical selves would be appearances of the same noumenal self, in which case everybody in the world would really be one person; or else each empirical self would be the appearance of a separate noumenal self, or transcendental ego, and by some mysterious co-operation of noumenal agents the several independent centers of activity would simultaneously be synthesizing one and the same (numerically identical) order of nature. Neither of these alternatives makes any philosophical sense. When Kant wrote the *Critique*, he simply did not face the problem of the relationships among the many independent minds that populate the world. Much of the *Critique* is written either in the first person, or else in an impersonal style which abstracts from distinctions among different particular selves. So Kant speaks of *the* empirical self, *the* transcendental ego, and so forth. Sometimes Kant seeks to skirt the problem of many minds, as we may label this difficulty, by asserting that he is really exploring logical relationships rather than psychological mechanisms. When we come to his accounts of the activity of synthesis, however, we are forced to interpret them as descriptions of the activity of a genuine agent, and not merely as metaphorical accounts of the static logical relationships among propositions.

In the light of the difficulty of making sense out of the identification of the transcendental ego with the noumenal self, it is easy to understand why Hegel should have assigned the synthesizing functions to an impersonal world spirit, and reduced the distinction between noumenal and phenomenal self to a difference in degree of self-realization. It is easy, too, to understand the tendency of the sollipsistic idealists to accept the implausible conclusion that there is indeed only one genuine person in the universe, namely myself.

For Kant, however, the problem is yet more complex, for in his moral philosophy he makes essential use of the distinction between noumenal and phenomenal self in order to resolve the dilemma of freedom and determinism. To the empirical self, the noumenal self, and the transcendental ego, Kant adds yet a fourth self, the *moral self*. As appearance, I am sensuous, passionate, causally determined, a mere thing in the realm of things. But as noumenon, I am rational, free, a person worthy of respect and capable of according respect to other rational agents. When called upon to explain how freedom can be possible, Kant argues that the idea of a self-determined agent is not contradictory, because the entire causal order in which my actions take place is mere appearance, having the form of time and of causal sequence because of the creative activity of my mind. I can consistently assert that I could have acted differently, even though such an alternative action would have had to issue from a pre-existent sequence of causes, because it is my selfsame mind that has imposed that causal order on experience.

In short, Kant's moral philosophy depends essentially on the supposition that the synthesizing, nature-creating transcendental ego *is* the maxim-forming, morally acting noumenal agent, of which my empirical personality is the appearance. But now we see the full complexity of Kant's dilemma. My moral obligations are to other persons; I am bound to treat them as ends and not merely as means, to refrain from lying to them, to keep my promises to them, to further their happiness, and so forth. It follows that there *are* other persons appearing in the natural world—other persons, not simply bodies. Hence, there are other noumenal agents, other transcendental egos. But if we can resolve the conflict between freedom and determinism only by identifying the transcendental ego with the noumenal moral self, then we must try to make sense of the apparently absurd supposition that many independent noumenal selves are all simultaneously synthesizing the one nature in which they all appear, and doing so in such a way that to each one of them we may consistently ascribe freedom of the will.

Kant's moral philosophy exhibits yet other incoherences with regard to the self, for while maintaining that the causally determined empirical self is the appearance of an inaccessible noumenal self, Kant also repeatedly claims that there is a contest within each self between the sensuous and rational elements. The clear implication is that the noumenal self competes with the phenomenal self for control over the actions of the person whose components they are. Such a notion, of the conflict between duty and inclination, makes no sense whatsoever in terms of the first *Critique*, however much it may accurately reflect the phenomenology of moral experience. To be consistent, Kant would have to claim, as indeed he sometimes does, that every action is completely determined by our sensuous character, that every internal struggle is merely an opposition of sensuous, or phenomenal, forces, and that at the same time every action is the reflection or appearance of the noumenal self.

In his moral writings, Kant assumes that a moral agent, in the act of making a moral decision, is self-consciously present to himself. It would be impossible to understand deliberation, choice, moral concern, responsibility, or the sense of duty without that assumption, but in the first *Critique*, Kant makes it perfectly clear that the noumenal self is not present to itself, or at least that it has no *knowledge* of itself. Its self-awareness is, apparently, active rather than passive. However, Kant never adequately explores the nature of this distinction or explains how we can know ourselves *as* moral agents without knowing *that* we are moral agents.

These few inconclusive remarks should be enough to indicate the importance and complexity of the problem of developing a Kantian theory of the self. Contemporary discussions of the problems of free will, the universalizability of moral maxims, the nature of causal inference, and the possibility of knowledge of other minds, would all profit from a heightened awareness of the interdependence of these several subjects, and there is no better way to develop that awareness than by a systematic exploration of their relationship in the philosophy of Kant.

(ii) A second neglected topic in the study of the critical philosophy, closely related to the problem of the self, is the Kantian doctrine of the architectonic interconnectedness of the various portions of the Critical corpus. Kant was fond of claiming that his philosophy fit together so tightly that the truth of any one part depended on the truth of the rest. Indeed, he even succumbed to the idealistic fallacy of supposing that the coherence and completeness of the system was a proof of its validity. Nowadays critics and students of Kant tend to ignore the architectonic, treating it either as the forgivable hobby of a great man, or else as a reflection of the baroque propensity for systematic elaboration that gripped so many philosophers in the eighteenth and early nineteenth centuries. Kant's extravagant claims for the table of categories have been debunked by the discovery, among his unpublished papers and manuscripts, of various preliminary and experimental sketches in which he juggled categories and functions of judgment until he hit upon a neat, satisfying system of triads symmetrically arranged.

Nevertheless, the several major parts of Kant's philosophy are deliberately constructed by him to form an integrated whole, and one can, for example, neither understand nor evaluate the theory of regulative ideas in the first *Critique* without taking account of the theory of teleological judgment in the third *Critique*. Recent commentators have tended to treat Kant's works as though they were separate philosophical treatises, addressed to distinct problems and only superficially related. When discussing the *Groundwork of the Meta-*

physics of Morals, for instance, critics will usually say only a few words about phenomena and noumena in connection with the problem of freedom and determinism. Yet the central problem of interpreting Kant's theory of the universalizability of maxims is insoluble unless one pays close attention to the first *Critique* argument that concepts have the form of rules, and that all causal judgments about the world are implicitly general in character. Again, the suggestive but obscure discussions of the sublime in the *Critique of Judgment* must be brought into conjunction with the discussion of the pure *a priori* intuitions of space and time as infinite given wholes, and both must somehow be made to cohere with the doctrine of the impossibility of infinite synthesis that lies at the base of the antinomies in the Transcendental Dialectic.

It is not hard to explain why most commentators have focused exclusively on one segment or other of the Critical philosophy. The difficulty of Kant's doctrines makes mastering even one of the *Critiques* a mind-stretching task. To master them all in depth and then to trace out the underlying logical relationships among their principal theses is more than Kant himself was able to do. The result is that the literature on Kant has somewhat the air of a multitude of reports from the blind wise men who encountered the elephant. Each one tells of the part on which his hands happened to fall, but a careful reader might fail to recognize the beast from their descriptions.

Beyond mere difficulty, there is a more important reason for the resistance of Kant's philosophy to synoptic commentary. The Critical philosophy is written at two levels simultaneously, and Kant never succeeded in bringing them into satisfactory relation with one another. On the surface is the great architectonic exposition of the powers of the mind, with every faculty, capacity, activity, and content carefully fitted into place. The three great *Critiques* treat successively of the three intellectual faculties: understanding in the first *Critique*, practical reason in the second *Critique*, judgment in the third. These faculties stand to one another in the same relation as the first, second, and third category in each triad of the Table of Categories. Knowledge is limited in the first *Critique* to make room for morality and faith in the second, and the two are reunited through aesthetic judgment in the third.

So long as we are content to remain at this superficial level, the entire Critical philosophy hangs together reasonably well, although the exuberance of Kant's philosophical imagination generates classificatory problems even there. But to the great benefit of philosophy, and to his eternal credit, Kant himself was *not* satisfied to remain at the level of the architectonic. Again and again, he dove beneath its surface to plumb the depths of experience and action. In each of the *Critiques* he explores major problems in ways so revolutionary that he ends by transforming the very assumptions on which the original architectural structure was grounded. For example, Kant began by asserting that our concepts have problematic, or possible, application universally, to things in themselves as well as to appearances. The limitation of our knowledge is due to the forms of our sensibility, he claimed. This view, arrived at as early as the *Inaugural Dissertation*, led naturally to the doctrine that for purposes of moral philosophy we could believe in, or act on the supposition of, causal attributions to the noumenal self. Though the impossibility of perceiving the self in itself ruled out knowledge of free moral action, it was nevertheless open to us to *think* or conceive of such action, since the concept of cause and effect did not in itself suffer the limitations which our sensibility imposed upon it. In the course of exploring the nature of conception in the Analytic of the first *Critique*, however, Kant came to the conclusion that the categories, among them that of cause and effect, are actually rules for the synthesis of a sensuous manifold. As such, they do not have even *possible* application to anything but a sensuous manifold, and hence they cannot be problematically applied to things in themselves.

This revision in Kant's theory of conception should have led to a thorough reconstruction of his moral philosophy, for if we cannot even hypothetically posit causal efficacy of noumena—cannot, that is, give meaning to the assertion that the noumenal self acts—then we cannot speak of acting *as if* we knew that the self were noumenally free.

A similar problem is created by Kant's exploration of the

nature of moral experience, as I have already noted. For purposes of the first *Critique*, it was important to deny that the noumenal self had any direct access to its own functioning and consciousness. Kant well knew that his philosophy would appear to its early readers as yet another version of subjective idealism, and he went to great pains in the second edition of the *Critique* to dissociate himself from Berkeley. He stood as well in diametric opposition to the Cartesian doctrine that the self had privileged and primary knowledge of itself, and only secondary, indirect knowledge of the natural world. So in the passages added to the Aesthetic in the second edition, Kant insisted in the clearest possible language that even in the most intimate act of introspection, the self knew itself only as appearance, never as reality.

In his several works on moral philosophy, however, Kant wished to do justice to the experience of moral conflict, of the sense of duty, of the majesty of sovereign reason within the soul. He was forced therefore to speak as though introspection could reveal the moral agent to himself. To be sure, he carefully denied that we can ever know for certain whether we have acted from inclination or out of duty, but it would take a stern adherent to the strict letter of the first *Critique* to read Kant's moral works without interpreting them as an account of reason's self-conscious and deliberate struggle with sensuous inclination. In the first *Critique*, Kant was content to describe the synthesizing activity of the transcendental ego as a "blind but indispensable function of the soul, without which we should have no knowledge whatsoever, but of which we are scarcely ever conscious" (A 78). To give such a characterization of the activity of practical reason, however, would be grotesque. It would amount to saying that when men act morally, they do so absent-mindedly.

I think it is clear from even these two examples that any account of Kant's philosophy as a whole must penetrate the surface of the Critical system and seek out the relationships among the more profound doctrines that Kant espoused in his philosophically most original moments.

(iii) One of the few specific parts of the Critical philosophy to which very little attention has been paid in recent years is Kant's political philosophy. Although politics was not among Kant's principal interests, he wrote several essays and treatises about problems traditionally associated with that subject, including "On Everlasting Peace" and *The Metaphysical Elements of Justice*, the latter being the first part of the *Metaphysics of Morals*. Although a good deal of attention has been paid to the first of these, relatively little can be found in recent articles or books on the second, in which Kant's major political teachings are laid out.

The primary reason for this neglect is that on the surface, the *Rechtslehre* appears shallow and unpromising, and filled with discussions of particular problems peculiar to the continental legal tradition. It is hard, for example, to see what philosophical interest could be generated in the distinction between public and private law; and an *a priori* deduction of the concept of property simply looks like one of the more transparent manifestations of liberal bourgeois ideology in late eighteenth-century thought. Kant's political writings, we might be tempted to conclude, belong with his logical treatises in the histories of philosophy rather than among the philosophical classics that are eternally alive.

There are several facts, however, that should caution us against too hasty a rejection of Kant's political writings. First, it is well known that he was deeply influenced by the philosophy of Rousseau, and we might at least suspect that some relationship could be traced between the doctrine of the *Social Contract* and Kant's own views. Second, the *Metaphysical Elements of Justice* are treated by Kant as equal in importance to the *Metaphysical Elements of Virtue*; both are presented as derivative from, or dependent upon, the doctrine set forth in the *Groundwork of the Metaphysics of Morals*. If Kant himself placed so great an emphasis upon his theory of law and justice, we must at least try to discover his reasons. Finally, there is the intriguing fact that in the famous *Grundlegung*, Kant formulates one version of the categorical imperative in terms of what he calls a "kingdom of ends." The moral relationship among autonomous rational agents, we are told, is like that which would be borne to one another by members of an ideal political association. Kant speaks of a kingdom, whereas Rousseau speaks of a civil state or sovereign, but a careful comparison of the two would, I think, reveal that Kant's moral philosophy is actually at base a theory of an ideal republic of autonomous agents.

Such a conclusion would require a good deal of textual evidence and argumentation, but I have no doubt that investigation along these lines would prove fruitful. Kant's moral philosophy takes as its central theme the idea of a self-legislated law, and it is no mere verbal accident that democratic theory founds itself upon the same idea. The democratic community stands in the same relation to the laws it makes as the moral individual does to his own self-determined imperatives of action. Kant's absorption in the continental tradition of jurisprudence may have led him to conceal rather than reveal the connection between his moral and political philosophy.

PART ONE

DISCUSSIONS OF THE CRITIQUE OF PURE REASON

CAN KANT'S SYNTHETIC JUDGMENTS
BE MADE ANALYTIC?

LEWIS WHITE BECK

In the sixties, when Kant had first drawn his distinction between analytic and synthetic judgments, he made the following note: "If one had the entire concept of which the notions of the subject and predicate are *compars*, synthetic judgments would change into analytic. It is a question of how much arbitrariness there is."[1] This question has been asked repeatedly since that time, and the clear and unmistakable trend of the answers has been that the decision whether a specific judgment is analytic or synthetic is arbitrary or at least is dependent upon variable conditions of how much the judger knows about the subject of the judgment and on his arbitrary decision of the choice and formula of his definitions.

In recent discussions of the distinction, analytic judgments are those that follow from explicit definitions by the rules of logic; and, definitions are nominal or stipulative, to some degree arbitrary. If it is further argued, as is often done, that all *a priori* judgments are analytic, it follows that the distinction between *a priori* and *a posteriori* is likewise a shifting, arbitrary distinction.

Kant, who first asked the question, seems to have decided very early that the line of demarcation between these two types of judgment was *not* variable or arbitrary. The purpose

Reprinted with permission of the author and of the editors from *Kant-Studien*, Band 47 (1956), Kölner Universitäts-Verlag, in which it was first published.

[1] Reflexion 3928. The numbering of the *Reflexionen* and all page references to the works of Kant are, unless otherwise noted, those of the edition of the Prussian Academy.

of this essay is to inquire into the reasons for his decision
and to indicate some of its implications for his philosophy
as a whole.

I. ANALYTIC AND SYNTHETIC JUDGMENTS

Judgment, for Kant, is a synthesis of representations, having objective validity. The synthesis must be in accord with
some objective, normative rule, and not merely illustrate
some contingent law of association. A representation, functioning in the synthesis of judgment, is not just a brute given
mental content, but is a mark of an object, its meaning fixed
by a rule. Abstraction from the given complexity of representations in consciousness, and the generalization that a
particular kind of representation is the mark of a particular
kind of object, are necessary in converting raw representations
into marks which can be manipulated in knowing.[2] Concepts are such marks functioning in knowledge; they are
representations   under   an   analytical   (abstractive)   unity
through which they are discursive and not merely given sense
contents. As concepts, they are not given; they are made
concepts by being involved in a special attitude of intention and the interpretation of data. All that we directly have
of an object is such marks. Our original consciousness is a
congeries of raw materials for concepts, and the business of
consciousness is to refine and organize these representations,
assigning to some of them the role of subjects and to others
that of predicates in judgments which are their objectively
valid syntheses;[3] only as predicates of possible judgments do
Vorstellungen serve as concepts, and only as containing representations under themselves do concepts refer to objects.[4]

Besides the analytical unity by which *hic et nunc* representations are made to serve as marks under a discursive concept (e. g. this *quale* at this time is seen as an example of a
specific quality also instanced in another *quale* at another
time), in order that there be judgment there must also be a

---

[2] Reflexion 2881.
[3] Cf. Reflexionen 3920, 4634.
[4] *Critique of Pure Reason,* A 69=B 94.

synthetical unity through which the concepts (and their corresponding representations) are referred to the same object.

This object may not be given at all, or if given it is given as only a still further complex of representations which refer to "the same object" only by virtue of some precedent synthetical unity. The synthetical unity, which is a form and not a content of experience, is not given, but is prescribed to experience by a rule that requires a common focus of meaning of the several concepts that appear in a judgment; if one such object is not meant by the various concepts, the synthesis of the concepts is a comparison, a setting of them side by side, and not a judgment. This common object is called by Kant X, and the rule of synthetical unity means that the terms in a judgment (concepts derived through the analytical unity of representations), such as A and B, must be regarded as marks of X. Then through A and B we know X, and the cognition of X through A or B is a concept of X.[5] A and B are, epistemologically, predicates of X, but one of them is made to serve as the logical subject and the other as the logical predicate. The one called subject is directly related to X, the one called predicate is indirectly related to X in the judgment, though its occurrence in experience may be direct evidence of the existence of X (usually it is the wider concept, and is applied to a specific X only through the mediation of the subject concept).[6] Thus, to summarize and make specific: when X is known through two concepts related to each other in a synthetical unity, then a judgment whose form is given by a category or rule of this synthetical unity is established. If the rule is, for instance, the category of inherence and subsistence, the judgment reads, "There is an X such that X is A and X is B."

If B is related to A directly by being included as a part of its connotation, so that "X is A" implies logically "X is B," the judgment is analytic. In an analytic judgment, reference to X is otiose, and we say simply, "All A is B" where A and B are "partial concepts" of X, and B is a constitutive part of A. But "*All A is B*" is an elliptical expression,

[5] *Reflexion* 3920.
[6] *Fortschritte der Metaphysik, Immanuel Kants Werke,* ed. Ernst Cassirer, 11 vols. (Berlin, 1912–1922), VIII, 245.

since *A* is a complex concept containing *B*. Fully expanded, therefore, the analytic judgment is the tautology, "All *A.B* is *B*."

When *B* is a concept of *X* because it is a *nota notae* of *X*, i. e. a mark or constituent of *A*, we can speak of the judgment as one in which the certainty of the connection of subject and predicate is "through identity."[7] If the identity is explicit, the judgment is inconsequential. The important case is the one in which the identity is implicit, so that its explication "widens our knowledge *formaliter*" though not *materialiter*. *B* may be "covertly contained in the concept"[8] and not thought "so distinctly and with the same (full) consciousness" as *A*.[9] It is an "analytic attribute" of *A* contained in it and elicited from it by logical analysis.[10] But it is essential that it be "contained in" *A*, so that the judgment is explicative, not ampliative, and independent of further experience of the *X* of which both *A* and *B* are concepts.

Now if the decision on analyticity of a specific judgment could be based on a definition of the subject, it would be easy enough to determine whether the judgment is analytic. But Kant rejects this procedure, because he holds that "definability" is a stricter condition than "analyzability," and that we can therefore make analytical judgments with concepts we cannot define. It is, in fact, through organizing analytic judgments that we gradually approach to definition,[11] which is the end, not the beginning, of knowledge.

Since Kant has so restricted the scope and value of definition, these statements about the inclusion of one concept in another are exceedingly obscure. It seems that, without a stated definition, they can be understood in part only psy-

---

[7] *Vorlesungen über Logik*, § 36. Kant objects to calling them identical judgments, however; cf. *Über eine Entdeckung . . .* , p. 244.

[8] *Critique of Pure Reason* A 7=B 10.

[9] *Prolegomena*, § 2 a.

[10] *Über eine Entdeckung . . .* , pp. 228 f.

[11] *Prolegomena*, § 2 c 3; cf. *Vorlesungen über Logik*, § 109 Anmerkung; *Über die Deutlichkeit der Grundsätze*, p. 282 (tr. Beck, p. 262); *Falsche Spitzfindigkeit*, p. 61. I have studied the relation between Kant's theory of definition and the distinction between the analytic and synthetic in some detail in "Kant's Theory of Definition," to appear in *Philosophical Review* 65 (1956).

chologically or phenomenologically. Speaking for the phenomenological interpretation is the emphasis upon what is "actually thought" in the subject; speaking for a logical interpretation is the fact that analytic attributes may be uncovered and brought to light only by sustained inquiry, and are not present, in any phenomenological sense, in the thought of the concept of the subject.

If we investigate each phrase in these passages, the possible confusion of the two meanings is not removed. For instance, "contained in" (*enthalten in*) was a logical term used by Kant's contemporaries to describe predicates belonging to all individuals denoted by a concept.[12] But Kant obviously does not mean it only in a logical sense, for then synthetic attributes would be contained in the subject concept, which he denies; "contained in" seems to have reference to the subjective intension, and thus to have at least psychological overtones. But the words "actually thought in the concept of the subject" are elsewhere given a strictly logical meaning, since Kant says that what is really thought in a concept is "nothing other than its definition."[13]

I think we have to suspect here a fundamental failure on Kant's part to distinguish the logical from the phenomenological aspects of thought. Where definitions or fairly complete analyses are available, he thinks of the distinction between analytic and synthetic judgment as logical; where they are not, but are rather the objects of search, he has recourse to a phenomenological criterion, by virtue of which he seeks definitions through analysis of what, in the plainest sense, is "actually thought" in a concept or even "contained in" a complex experience subject to subsequent analysis.[14]

[12] Vaihinger, *Commentar zu Kants Kritik der reinen Vernunft*, I, 258. "Contained in" is contrasted with "contained under"—Reflexion 3043. The latter, used in describing synthetic judgments, seems to mean for Kant what Vaihinger says was commonly meant by "contained in." Cf. also Reflexionen 2896, 2902.

[13] *Critique of Pure Reason*, A 718=B 746.

[14] A recent paper by Robert S. Hartman, "Analytic and Synthetic as Categories of Inquiry" (*Perspectives in Philosophy*, Ohio State University, 1953, pp. 55–78), has the special merit of singling out the two kinds of analyticity, one of which it calls definitional and the other expositional, and distinguishing both from "analytic" in the

While we cannot speak of two definitions of the analytic, and can at most say that the analytic has both a logical and a phenomenological dimension, we can discern two criteria for analytic judgment. Kant, in apparent disregard of their differences, uses first one and then the other as it suits his purposes, perhaps in the conviction that their answers will in any specific case be the same.

(i) The logical criterion of analytic judgment is its conformity to the law of contradiction, a necessary condition of any judgment and a necessary and sufficient condition for an analytic judgment. The test is applied as follows: substitute in a judgment synonyms for synonyms, or an analysis or definition of the subject concept for the subject itself. Then the contradictory of this judgment will infringe the law of contradiction if the original judgment is analytic. And as the contradictory of a self-contradictory proposition is necessary, the original judgment is necessary.

In applying the logical criterion, a definition in the strict sense is not required, for it is from the analytic judgments in informal exposition that we first gain the definition. All that is needed is a partial analysis of the subject concept. The absence of definition may at most prevent only the decision that some specific judgment is *not* analytic,[15] for what is mentioned as the predicate may be an unnoticed analytic attribute that we would have noticed had we possessed a full definition. But no criterion is infallible; even given a strict definition, the pertinency of a specific attribute as analytical may be a discovery of the most difficult and surprising kind. It is in such cases that there will be the greatest divergence between decisions made on this and those made on the phenomenological criterion.

(ii) The phenomenological criterion is the issue of an in-

---

sense of descriptive of what is "contained in" an experience of an empirical object. Hartman's paper presents very clearly the processes by which analytic judgments lead to definitions, and definitions then establish a new and stricter criterion of analyticity. Another study of the process by which an analytic judgment may become synthetic is K. Sternberg, "Über die Unterscheidung von analytischen und synthetischen Urteilen," *Kant-Studien* 31 (1926), 171–201.

[15] Cf. *Vorlesungen über Logik,* § 109 Anm.

spection of what is found introspectively to be really thought in the concept of the subject. Though we have seen that what is "really thought" is said to be a definition, and that the mention of predicates not thought "with the same (full) consciousness" suggests a very wide range of predicates that might pass the logical but fail the phenomenological test, still it is clear that Kant was not free from a psychologizing, introspective tendency in his decisions on what is analytic and what is synthetic. The *Port Royal Logic*[16] demanded "moderate attention" to see whether the predicate is "truly contained in the idea of the subject," and not a completely articulated logical system as a criterion for this decision; the same kind of "moderate attention" seems to provide a criterion for Kant. He repeatedly asks himself and the reader what he thinks when he thinks a particular concept, and though undoubtedly one may think much, by casual association, which is not "contained in the concept," what he does *not* think is *not* included in the content of the concept.

Just as he has previously distinguished between what is contained in and what is contained under a concept, so also he distinguishes what "lies in" a concept and what "belongs to" it.[17] There seems to be here a tacit distinction between two kinds of concepts, one being a concept of a highly refined analytical or abstractive unity, subject to strict definition, and the other being a looser complex of representations, more or less loosely held together and expandable through the accretion of new experience or subject to restriction in content through the supervention of a definition.[18]

I now turn, for the space of one paragraph, to Kant's de-

[16] Part IV, ch. vi.

[17] *Critique of Pure Reason*, A 718=B 746; but cf. *Vorlesungen über Logik*, Einleitung viii, (IKW, VIII, 373) where attributes belong to the essence, so far as they are derived from it.

[18] The confusion between these two meanings of "concept" has been discussed by Koppelmann, "Kants Lehre vom analytischen Urteil," *Philosophische Monatshefte*, 21 (1885), 65–101; and by H. Ritzel, "Über analytische Urteile," *Jahrbuch f. Philosophie u. phänomenologische Forschung*, 3 (1916), 253–344, at 261–76, 324. The full significance of it, as representing the interpenetration of two stages of inquiry dominated respectively by the analytic and the synthetic method, is ably worked out by Hartman, *op. cit.*

scription of synthetic judgments, after which I shall come back to these two criteria of analytic judgment. The following material is essential for evaluating the issues raised by the two criteria.

B may be related to A indirectly by virtue of the fact that both are predicates of the same X. Then the concept A does not include the concept of B as a part of its logical essence, and to relate them to each other in judgment requires reference to the X of which each is a partial concept. There are three kinds of X which serve to mediate between A and B. (i) X may be a schema of an object in general (of a thing, cause, etc.). (ii) X may be a determinable intuition of space or time or both, which A and B both refer to and make determinate. (iii) X may be a datum or *concretum* of experience, "the complete experience of the object which I think through the concept A."[19] In the former two cases, the judgment will be valid regardless of the empirical content of the concepts, and in the first case there is established the kind of judgment which appears in "metaphysics as science." Failure to provide a schema without the conditions of space and time and to put the thing in itself in the role of the X makes synthetic judgments impossible except of objects of possible experience. The second is the situation with respect to mathematical judgments, where X is a construction. In the third alternative, the judgment is *a posteriori*. But in each case it is a synthetic judgment, since the predicate is not found by analysis of the logical subject. If X is (as is actually the case) a subjective condition for the synthesis of A and B, the resulting synthetic judgment is, in the transcendental sense, only subjectively valid; though we can say still that the predicate is a part of the real and not of the nominal essence. In the same sense, an analytic judgment is objectively and even transcendently valid, not being restricted to the conditions of synthesis placed upon the X.[20]

From this account of the origin of synthetic judgment, and from the two criteria mentioned above, it is clear that the distinction between analytic and synthetic judgment is

[19] *Critique of Pure Reason*, A 8; omitted in B.
[20] Reflexion 3950.

not one of formal logic, for formal logic abstracts from the meaning of all terms.

II. VARIABILITY OF THE DISTINCTION

Eberhard interpreted an analytic judgment as one the predicate of which is an *essentia* of the subject, and a synthetic judgment as one whose predicate is an attribute derived from an *essentia*. But Kant denies that this is his meaning, for he holds that "derived from" is equivocal. If the attribute is derived by logical analysis, the judgment is indeed analytic whether we *knew* that the attribute was "contained in" the subject concept or not; but there are other attributes, synthetic attributes (*Bestimmungen*), that are not contained in the logical essence, even though they might be associated with it in our minds, e. g. as weight with body. They are derived not by logical analysis but by construction or exhibition of a corresponding intuitive object. From such an experience the attribute can as it were be read off, though it is not a *nota notae* of the subject concept but a *nota* of the real object. It is this kind of synthetic predicate which is a part of the *ratio essendi* of the object, and it gives the concept of the subject and all its judgments whatever objective validity they have.

Though Eberhard was a mediocre thinker much of whose argument is vitiated by being based upon patent misunderstandings of Kant, he did nevertheless ask a difficult and important question, "How do we decide what is 'actually thought' in a concept?" Unless a definite and plausible criterion can be given that is exempt from the vagaries of the phenomenological criterion and of the logical criterion when Kant attempts to employ it unarmed with definitions, then an important member of the structure of his philosophy must be given up. Modern writers, reacting against both psychologism and phenomenology, wanting a behavioral rather than an introspectional criterion if a significant logical criterion cannot be given, have directed their main attack on the possibility of maintaining the distinction, in any particular instance, without a complement of definitions.

Rather than considering the views of those who give up or relativize the distinction for the reasons just mentioned, however, it will be more profitable to consider the views of a critic who admits a sharp distinction between analytic and synthetic, yet who does not base it on the test of nominal or stipulative definition. A critic this close to Kant is likely to be more instructive, at this juncture, than one more radically opposed to Kant. The criticism I shall consider is that by C. I. Lewis, which is in part an infinitely improved version of some debating points raised by Eberhard. Kant's cognizance of these arguments, admittedly in a more primitive form, makes a study of them especially worthwhile for an understanding of Kant himself.

Lewis argues as follows. The notion of a necessary but non-analytic proposition such as "Every event has a cause" is based on an equivocation. For 'event,' as a concept which does not contain 'having a cause' as a part of its meaning, is not the same as the concept of 'event' ·which does contain the concept 'having a cause.' Part of Kant's argument is based on the former and simpler concept, and here Kant rightly infers that the proposition is synthetic. But the argument that the proposition is *a priori* is based on the second, richer, concept. We can, according to Kant, think without contradiction an uncaused event; hence the relation expressed in the judgment is synthetic; but we cannot imagine, represent, or know an event as objective without relating it to another event by a rule of causation; hence the judgment is known *a priori*.

The equivocation is that 'event' in the second case means 'phenomenal event in objective space and time,' while in the first case it is not so restricted. If this restriction is made explicit, however, the relation between the restricted concepts is seen to be analytic. The second Analogy of Experience seems to be synthetic only because the word 'event' is not usually given the restricted meaning. The term needs to be fixed by definition before one can pronounce the judgment to be analytic or synthetic; and in defining it, we must be sure to include in its meaning everything needed to determine the objective applicability of the term in question: ". . . Anything which is essential to the temporal character of an event must be included in the adequate concept of it as a temporal event.

. . . A definition which does not logically entail all characters essential to what is defined, is faulty."[21]

Kant's reply to this kind of criticism, as it appeared in
its first crude form, or rather Schultz's reply written under
Kant's supervision, makes two responses.

(i) Two different propositions, one of which is analytic
and one synthetic, may be expressed by the same sentence,
for the same word in the sentences may refer to two different concepts, one narrower and one broader.

(ii) Closely related to this is the assertion of the "fixity"
of a concept. A concept cannot be arbitrarily widened
through the accumulation of information. It can be replaced
by another called by the same name; but of any given concept it can be decided what is implicit in it to be expli-
cated in analytical judgment and what does not lie in it at
all. When one changes a definition, which may change the
status of many judgments, the judgments are changed not
merely in status but in meaning and validity. Definitions should not, therefore, be arbitrarily changed; a new
one must pass the same kind of test of "realness" that the
old one originally passed and later failed, if it is not to be
merely stipulation without objective reference. We cannot con-
vert empirical knowledge into *a priori* knowledge simply by
refining our language:

> Let one put into the concept of the subject just so
> many attributes that the predicate which one wishes to
> prove of the subject can be derived from its concept
> merely by the law of contradiction. The critical philoso-
> phy permits him to make this kind of analytic judg-
> ment, but raises a question about the concept of the sub-
> ject itself. It asks: how did you come to include in this
> concept the different attributes so that it [now analyti-
> cally] entails synthetic propositions? First prove the ob-
> jective reality of your concept, i. e. first prove that any
> one of its attributes really belongs to a possible object,
> and when you have done that, then prove that the other
> attributes belong to the same thing that the first one be-

[21] C. I. Lewis, *An Analysis of Knowledge and Valuation*, pp. 161–
62. I have given a fuller exposition of Lewis' views (without discussion
of the point raised here) in "Die Kantkritik von C. I. Lewis und der
analytischen Schule," Kant-Studien 45 (1954), 3–20.

longs to, without themselves belonging to the first attribute. The whole question of how much or how little the
concept of the subject is to contain has not the least
bearing on the metaphysical question: How are synthetic
a priori judgments possible? It belongs merely in the
logical theory of definition. And the theory of definition
without doubt requires that one not introduce more attributes into a definition than are necessary to distinguish the defined thing from all others. Hence [in a good
definition] one excludes those attributes of which one
can demand a proof whether and on what grounds they
belong to the former attributes [that *are* included].[22]

Put in our own words, Kant is saying that a definition
which will change a synthetic into an analytic judgment must
be either nominal or real. If nominal, it does not in the least
affect the cognitive status of the original judgment; while it
may make the original sentence formally analytic, it does not
give to the knowledge it expresses any logical or epistemic
necessity it previously lacked.[23] And if the definition is a
real one, we must know the necessary conjunction of independent, coordinate attributes in order to make it; and this
conjunction is precisely what was stated in the synthetic judgment whose status is now being disputed. All that is effected
by such a procedure, we might say, is that the locus of *a
priori* synthesis is shifted.

III. INDEFINABILITY OF THE CATEGORIES

Thus far I have considered only Kant's explicit answers to
the criticism that the analytic-synthetic distinction is variable.
I now examine Kant's reply in its general philosophical
bearings.

[22] *Rezension von Eberhard's Magazin*, pp. 408–9.
[23] In this, Lewis is in agreement with Kant. In criticizing these who
identify the *a priori* and the analytic, and then define the analytic in
terms of linguistic rules or procedures, Lewis writes: "If implications
of conceptions of this sort should be well worked out, it must appear
that they are fatal to the thesis that what is *a priori* coincides with
what is analytic; since the notion that what may be known true without recourse to sense experience, is relative to vocabulary or dependent
on conventions of procedure, is not credible" (*op. cit.* p. 36).

I have already mentioned that there are in Kant's writings two quite different species of concept. In one case, like that of "water", the word is "more properly to be regarded as merely a designation than as a concept of the thing,"[24] and its meaning does vary with experience. In the other, the concept is fixed either by definition, or fixed because it is a *pure* concept which, while not subject to definition, is not subject to revision by the accumulation of experience. In the latter case, Kant believed that a fixed decision could be made concerning what was and what was not included in it, even at a time before a stated definition had been reached. The rationalistic tradition in which Kant wrote fixed many of the most important concepts by "implicit" definition and common use or by nominal definitions that had become well established.[25] Thus Kant could confidently decide that a given proposition is analytic without the necessity of referring to a "rule book" of stipulative definitions. We, in a more conventionalistic period, are usually puzzled by some of his decisions, and can only feel that Kant and his contemporaries were committing what Whitehead called the "fallacy of the perfect dictionary"—when the dictionary could not, in principle, exist for Kant at all. But the more important point is that the concepts with which Kant is most concerned, viz. the categories, are not fixed by definition and need not be fixed in this way. They are fixed because, as pure, they are not susceptible to experiential modification.

Let us consider what Kant was attempting to do with these concepts. It had been shown by Hume that they could not be given objective validity by definition, and though Kant might have given a richer, more determinate definition to such a concept as cause, a still more extended Humean argument would have been fatal again to its claims to objective validity. Definition and proof of objective validity are not the same except in mathematics, which, for quite peculiar reasons, does not have to meet the Humean type of criticism. Assuming a broader definition, a proof of the objective valid-

---

[24] *Critique of Pure Reason,* A 728=B 756.

[25] Cf. J. H. Hyslop, "Kant's Treatment of Analytic and Synthetic Judgment," *Monist,* 13 (1903), 331–51, which emphasizes Cartesian and Newtonian conclusions as they "infected" the concepts Kant used.

ity of its analytic consequences is still called for if Hume's criticisms of the rational structure of empirical knowledge are to be met. Given the broader definition, of course, antecedently synthetic judgments become analytic. So long as the definitional component is expanded *ad lib,* any *a priori* judgment can be shown to be analytic. But apriority is not dependent upon this kind of analyticity; the analyticity of such a judgment is not a condition of its apriority but a subsequent, factitious addendum to it. That is, there must be recognition of some special dignity of function of a specific proposition that makes it worthwhile to devise a language in which it will be necessary; but the linguistic necessity is established subsequent to this recognition.

Kant did not simply suppose that causality had objective meaning; he tried to show that it did, and in doing so he found that he had to add to the concept of sufficient reason determinations which neither Hume nor the rationalists had suspected; he had to give a new interpretation to "possible experience" as the mediator between the terms of such a judgment. To have suppressed this interpretation for the sake of a formal definition of cause which would render the second Analogy of Experience analytical would have distorted the whole procedure of the critical philosophy, and would have left unanswered the reiterated question, how can *this* judgment, based on definition, be valid objectively?

Kant thought that real definitions should come at the end of inquiry, not at the beginning. One might expect, therefore, that the contribution of the *Critique of Pure Reason* might have been seen as a new set of definitions subsequent to which *a priori* judgments previously called synthetic would now be called analytic. Why did Kant not see his work in this way, but obstinately regarded the Analogies as synthetic judgments—in spite of the fact that he might have seen the logical classification as tentative, dependent upon the richness of the concepts?

There were several reasons why Kant did not do this. Among them was his respect for tradition; more important was his recognition that Hume's objections to the rational foundations of empirical knowledge could not be met by new definitions. And a still more fundamental reason is to be found in his repeated denials of the definability of the categories: the definitions which some might think would serve for this reduction of all *a priori* knowledge to analytic knowledge cannot be given. Definitions, however elaborated, are still conceptual relations; but what is needed is some way to get a concept into relation with an object, and to do it in an *a priori* fashion. Concepts alone, however richly furnished with predicates, do not establish contact with things; only intuition can provide this contact. We can indeed conceptualize and name the requisite intuition; but in doing this, we treat it like a universal concept, and as such it fails to establish the objective reference. It always leaves open the question: does *this* complex universal apply? The category, whether it can be defined or not, must be schematized—must be provided, in Lewis' terminology, with a sense meaning as well as a linguistic meaning. Kant is profuse in his definitions of pure categories, but these definitions are nominal.[26] Schematizing a category is very different from defining it:

> There is something strange and even nonsensical in the notion that there should be a concept which must have a meaning but which cannot be defined. But the categories are in a unique position, for only by virtue of the *general condition of sensibility* can they have a definite meaning and relation to an object. This condition, however, is omitted in the pure category, for this can contain only the logical function of bringing the manifold under a concept,[27]

without specifying the concept or the condition of its application to a specific manifold.

No philosopher has emphasized more than Kant the fundamental difference between sense and understanding while at the same time asserting their complementary function. This fundamental difference is essential here. It is not the *concept* of an intuitive condition, which might be added to a concept or included in its definition, that gives full meaning to the category; it is the *condition of sensibility* itself,[28]

[26] *Critique of Pure Reason*, A 244=B 302.
[27] *Ibid*. A 244–245; omitted from B. Italics supplied.
[28] The difference between a concept of an intuitive condition and the intuitive condition itself is formally like that between the concept

the condition of its actual use in specific circumstances according to rule. This is a transcendental addendum, a real predicate, a synthetic predicate, a *Bestimmung*, an element in the *ratio essendi* as well as the *ratio cognoscendi*. It is not just another attribute without which the definition is "inadequate." Make the added condition a conceptual amendment to the definition, and the entire question is postponed: we would still have to ask, "How does *this concept* have *a priori* objective application?"[29]

IV. THE STATUS OF MATHEMATICAL JUDGMENTS

Because Kant does admit definitions, in the strictest sense, only in the field of mathematics,[30] it is easy to admit a sharp distinction between analytic and synthetic judgments here; in fact, mathematical definition has been taken as establishing the paradigm of the analytic-synthetic distinction.[31] Granting the sharpness of the distinction between analytic and synthetic here, most competent critics of Kant are in agreement that he was in error in saying that mathematical judgments are synthetic. It is said that what kept him from seeing that they are analytic was the lack of adequate mathematical definitions, definitions not available until much later. Professor Lewis characteristically writes: "It would be ungrateful and unjust to blame Kant for not foreseeing that, from

of existence and existence itself. Kant's criticism of the ontological argument, *mutatis mutandis*, could be used here against the view (expressed by Lewis, *op. cit.* p. 162, middle paragraph) that the *concept* of space suffices, if we assume, with Kant, that mathematics is knowledge of something real.

[29] There is still another argument in the *Critique* (A 245, absent from B) against the definability of categories, to wit, that such definitions are circular. I do not think the argument is valid; but inasmuch as it applies, if at all, to the pure as well as to the schematized categories, it is not relevant to our purposes here.

[30] *Critique of Pure Reason,* A 729=B 758.

[31] "Kant scheint bei der Einteilung der Urteile in analytisch und synthetisch von der Fiktion auszugehen, dass auch die nichtmathematischen Begriffe definiert werden können." —K. Marc-Wogau, "Kants Lehre vom analytischen Urteil," *Theoria,* 17 (1951), 140–54, at 150.

genuinely adequate mathematical definitions, the theorems of mathematics might be deducible."[32] Obviously, deducible from definition and analytic are here regarded as equivalent notions.

This however, as we have amply seen, is not what Kant meant by 'analytic.' In the *Prolegomena* he wrote:

> "As it was found that the conclusions of mathematics all proceed according to the law of contradiction . . . men persuaded themselves that the fundamental principles were known by the same law. This was a great mistake, for a synthetical proposition can indeed be understood [*eingesehen*] by the law of contradiction, but only by presupposing another synthetical proposition from which it follows, never by that law alone."[33]

From this we see the following: (i) Mathematical theorems may be synthetic even if proved by the law of contradiction, i. e. by strictly logical procedure. Deducibility is not a sufficient condition for analyticity. To be analytic, in Kant's meaning, a proposition would have to be proven by the law of contradiction *alone*, i. e. its contradictory would have to be *self*-contradictory; but in mathematical proof by strict logic, the contradictory of the proposition contradicts some *other* assumed propositions. (ii) A proposition will be called synthetic if among its premises is a synthetic proposition, such as an axiom, or a mathematical definition, i. e. a synthetical definition which can be exhibited in a construction. (iii) Mathematical axioms (fundamental principles) are synthetic since they are not established by the analysis of a given concept, but only by the intuitive construction of the concept, which will show the necessary presence of attributes not included in a logical definition of the subject.[34]

The theorems, therefore, can be called synthetic even though they are strictly (analytically, in modern usage) demonstrable. The famous discussion of the example, "$7 + 5 = 12$," two paragraphs later, is quite independent of

---

[32] *Op. cit.* p. 162.

[33] *Prolegomena*, § 2 c 1 = *Critique of Pure Reason*, B 14.

[34] *Über die Deutlichkeit* . . . , p. 277 (tr. Beck, p. 263); *Über eine Entdeckung* . . . , pp. 229 ff.; *Critique of Pure Reason*, A 730= B 758.

the grounds given in the quotation for calling the theorems synthetic. It is, in fact, inconsistent with it. In the quotation, Kant is conceding that a theorem does follow from premises by strict logic; whatever may be the nature of the premises, the internal structure of the proof is logical. But in the discussion of "7 + 5" Kant is arguing that a theorem does not follow logically even from synthetic axioms, but that intuitive construction enters into the theorem itself and its proof. These two theses—that an intuitive synthetic element is present in the primitive propositions, and that an intuitive synthetic process is present in demonstration—are independent of each other. Because a mathematical judgment is often synthetical by the phenomenological criterion, Kant seems to have supposed that there were good logical reasons for calling it synthetic. Of these two theses, only the first is of any moment in the epistemology (not the methodology) of mathematical knowledge, but it is only the second of the theses that could be corrected by the use of what Lewis calls "genuinely adequate mathematical definitions."

The real dispute between Kant and his critics is not whether the theorems are analytic in the sense of being strictly deducible, and not whether they should be called analytic now when it is admitted that they are deducible from definitions, but whether there are any primitive propositions which are synthetic and intuitive. Kant is arguing that the axioms cannot be analytic, both because they must establish a connection between concepts, just as definitions do, and because they must establish a connection that can be exhibited in intuition. And this is what is denied by the modern critic of Kant.

I think Kant is obviously right in saying that there cannot be a system of nothing but analytic propositions; there must be some complexes to analyze, and these must be stated synthetically. But if the postulates are not analytic, this does not mean that they are synthetic *propositions*, i. e. synthetic statements expressing truths. A stipulation can "establish" synthetic relations, but it does not thereby qualify as a proposition. If it be assumed that mathematics is a game, then the analytic-synthetic distinction is of no importance in discussing the postulates, because the premises are not propositions at all but are only stipulations or propositional functions.[35]

Kant did not espouse the game theory. Mathematics was for him objective knowledge. That is why he regarded the axioms as propositions, not proposals. Were they mere relations of ideas, in Hume's sense, they could be made as "adequate" as one wished, yet the question of how they could be objectively valid would remain untouched. But for Kant, real mathematical definitions are possible, because the definition creates the object. This sounds like stipulation again; but the object is not an arbitrary logical product of subjectively chosen independent properties. To define a mathematical concept is to prescribe rules for its construction in space and time. Such a definition is a synthetical proposition, because the spatial determination of the figure is not a logical consequence of the concept but is a real condition of its application. The real property is joined the logical properties synthetically, not analytically.

Objections to Kant's views of mathematics, therefore, cannot be removed merely by the substitution of more adequate sets of definitions and postulates, as if being a better mathematician would have corrected Kant's philosophy of mathematics. *The syntheticity of mathematical knowledge in Kant is not a consequence of the inadequacy of his definitions.* It is an essential feature of his entire theory of mathematical knowledge, by which the identity of mathematics and logic was denied. Mathematical knowledge in his view of the world has objective reference, and this is obtained not through definition but through intuition and construction. His mathematical definitions are real; what is deduced from them may be, in modern but not Kantian terminology, analytic propositions. But the propositions admitted as theorems

---

[35] Kant says that mathematical definitions are *willkürlich*, which is usually translated as "arbitrary." But the connotation of "random" present in "arbitrary" is not present in Kant's word "arbitrary," for Kant makes the antonym of "arbitrary" not "necessary" but "empirical." *Vorlesungen über Logik*, § 103 Anm. *Willkürlich* has reference to the volitional character of a synthetic definition, a rule for the synthesis of a concept; but a mathematical concept is synthesized only under given conditions of intuition, and is therefore not arbitrary in the modern sense of this word.

by Kant are not like the analytic propositions of modern mathematics or the relations of ideas of Hume, for they have a necessary relation to experience through the synthetic, intuitive character of the definitions and axioms. Even propositions which Kant admits are analytic belong to mathematics only if they can be exhibited in intuition.[36] Whatever improvements in Kant's definitions might have been introduced for the sake of making the theorems analytic in his sense would have cost a high price in setting mathematics apart from the discussion of the conditions of possible experience. And had they been seen as analytic, Kant's long and deep concern with mathematics would not have positively contributed to his interpretation of the problems of empirical knowledge. For Kant saw in mathematics a clue to the objectivity of all *a priori* knowledge, both analytic and what he considered to be synthetic. This is indeed the sense of the Copernican revolution: even empirical objects are constructions; and their necessary conditions are geometrical. Had Kant radically sundered mathematical knowledge from the intuitive *a priori* structures of empirical knowledge, as he criticizes Hume for doing,[37] both would have been rendered unintelligible to him. The question is thereby raised whether, in introducing modern amendments into Kant's theory of mathematics (perhaps for the purpose of "saving what is essential in the critical philosophy"), we do not at the same time overlook or destroy everything distinctive in his theory of empirical knowledge.

[36] *Critique of Pure Reason*, B 17 = *Prolegomena* § 2 c 2.
[37] *Prolegomena* § 2 c 2; *Kritik der praktischen Vernunft*, p. 51 (tr. Beck, pp. 161–62).

KANT'S THEORY OF DEFINITION

LEWIS WHITE BECK

I

In most contemporary writings on the distinction between analytic and synthetic propositions, an analytic proposition is defined as one that follows from an explicit definition by rules of formal logic. If, as is usual, it is assumed that all definitions are nominal or stipulative, and further that all *a priori* propositions are analytic, it follows that the necessity of an *a priori* proposition is linguistic in origin and scope.

The original distinction between analytic and synthetic propositions, however, was drawn by Kant, who did not make any of these three assumptions. Confusion arises through discussing, in Kantian terms, a distinction whose modern usage differs widely from that of the author of the distinction; discords are produced by Kantian tones in otherwise empiricistic harmonies. Sometimes one or more of the three doctrines mentioned above is attributed to Kant himself,[1] or more

Reprinted with permission of the author and of the editors from *Philosophical Review*, 65 (1956), 179-91.

[1] Three widely scattered specimens are: (a) "La notion kantienne du jugement analytique semble d'exiger que les concepts soient d'une part absolument susceptibles d'une définition unique, rigoreuse et sans aucune ambiguité, et que d'un autre côté leurs définitions soient susceptible d'être analysées sans qu'on aboutisse à des jugements synthétiques" (Paul Tannery, *Bulletin de la Société Française de Philosophie* [1903], 124); (b) "Kant scheint bei der Einteilung der Urteile in analytisch und synthetisch von der Fiktion auszugehen, dass auch die nicht-mathematischen Begriffe definiert werden können" (K. Marc-Wogau, *Theoria* 17 [1951], 150); (c) "The distinction . . . is easy and clear as long as we deal with merely stipulated or nominal definitions, as Kant seems to have supposed we could" (R. E. Gahringer, *Journal of Philosophy*, 51 [1954], 435).

often it is argued that the Kantian doctrine is important and plausible only when seen as anticipating and preparing the way for the more recent doctrines. Either of these tactics keeps Kant's own doctrines from teaching us anything important and distinctive by obscuring what was unique and original in them but has since been forgotten or neglected.

My purpose here is to try to show the relationship between Kant's own views of definition and of analytic judgment. I shall suggest that the interpretation of his analytic judgments as those based upon definitions is without historical warrant. This raises the question whether modern disputes about the possibility of *a priori* synthetic propositions, in which the theory of definition plays a decisive role in the formation of criteria for analyticity, are really discussions of the problem to which Kant devoted the first *Critique*.

II

To define, according to Kant, means to present the complete concept of a thing within its limits and in its primary or original character. A complete concept is one with a sufficiency of clear predicates for the entire concept to be distinct; and the predicates stated are primary or original in the sense that they are not derived from other predicates included in the definition. The predicates must, in other words, be primitive and co-ordinate; no derivative and subordinate predicates are admissible in a definition, for otherwise the definition would require proof.[2] If a definition does incorrectly contain derivative predicates—properties instead of *essentialia*—it is lacking in *precision*. Definition is a "sufficiently distinct and precise concept (*conceptus rei adaequatus in minimis terminis, complete determinatus*)."[3]

The definition of "definition" that Kant gives here leads him to deny the name "definition" to many sentences commonly so called. It is reached partly by an analysis of usage, and partly by a decision which makes the concept more pre-

[2] *Critique of Pure Reason*, A 727=B 755n.
[3] *Vorlesungen über Logik*, § 99.

cise: "There are definitions of concepts which we already have but which are not correctly named. In these cases, it is not that the meaning of a word is analyzed, but that a concept, which we already possess, is analyzed; and then it must be particularly shown what name properly expresses it."[4]

Kant distinguishes two major and independent divisions of definitions: into analytic and synthetic, and into nominal and real.

A definition is analytic if it is of a given concept; synthetic if of a concept made or synthesized by the definition itself.[5] The former makes a concept distinct, the latter makes a distinct concept.[6] Under each of these major divisions, there is a subdivision: the concept defined may be given or made *a priori* or *a posteriori*.[7]

An analytic definition states the original analytic predicates of the thing defined. An analytic predicate is a partial concept of a thing actually thought in the concept of the *definiendum*.[8] Thus an analytic definition is an analytic judgment containing no subordinate predicates. A synthetic definition, however, contains synthetic predicates, predicates whose union first establishes a distinct concept of the *definiendum*.

The other major division is between nominal and real definition. Kant does not draw this distinction as one between the definition of a word and the definition of a thing; because he regarded the concept, rather than thing or word, as the *definiendum* he was prevented from using this formula of the distinction. Rather the difference lies in the content of the *definiens* and in the methodological function of the two kinds of definition. A nominal definition states the logical essence of the concept of the thing, or serves merely to

---

[4] Reflexion 3003. (All references to the *Reflexionen* are by number, as established in the edition of the Prussian Academy, Vols. XIV–XVIII.)

[5] *Vorlesungen über Logik*, § 100.

[6] *Ibid.* Einleitung viii, *Immanuel Kants Werke*, ed. Ernst Cassirer, 11 vols. (Berlin, 1912–1922), (VIII, 376); Reflexion 2929. All subsequent references to pages in the *Vorlesungen* are to the Cassirer edition.

[7] *Vorlesungen über Logik*, § 101.

[8] *Ibid.* p. 372.

distinguish this thing from others. If it does only the latter, it is called a diagnostic definition in contrast to a definition stating essential primitive predicates.[9] The logical essence, stated in nominal definition, is the original primitive concept of all the *essentialia*;[10] the diagnostic definition may state only the irreducible minimum of some easily recognized attributes or properties, sufficient as a criterion in a dichotomous classification by a pass-fail test.

A real definition not only puts one word in place of others, but the *definiens* contains a clear mark by which the object can be recognized and by virtue of which the defined concept is shown to have "objective reality"—by which it is shown that there is a defined thing.[11] (The diagnostic definition does this, but not by stating the diagnostic symptom as an *essentia* of the thing.) Real definition, therefore, is a part and not merely a tool of knowledge. Real definition states the real essence constituted by real predicates, not merely by logical predicates included ("already thought in") the concept of the subject.

A synthetic predicate is a determination (*Bestimmung*) not contained in the subject-concept but enlarging it; it is not found by analysis. It determines a thing, not merely its concept. "Anything we please can be made to serve as a logical predicate; the subject can even be predicated of itself; for logic abstracts from all content. But a *determining* predicate is a predicate which is added to the concept of the subject and enlarges it. Consequently it must not be already contained in the concept."[12] A real definition, therefore, is always a synthetic judgment, even though the real definition, *as definition*, may be analytical and is analytical if the concept is given.[13]

Real predicates are never arbitrarily synthesized into a logical product called the essence; in every case the determinations are not purely conceptual but intuitive represen-

[9] Reflexionen 2994, 3003.
[10] *Vorlesungen über Logik*, Einl. viii, p. 374.
[11] *Critique of Pure Reason*, A 241–242n.
[12] *Critique of Pure Reason*, A 598=B 626 (tr. Kemp Smith); Reflexion 4055.
[13] Reflexionen 2955, 2994.

tations. General logic is concerned only with the logical essence or predicates; or, rather, in abstracting from all contents it treats determinations as if they were logical predicates. But knowledge of things requires knowledge of and through determinations, not merely the mouthing of their names, and this knowledge is knowledge of the real possibility of the object through a specific determination as both its *ratio essendi* and *ratio cognoscendi*.[14] We find the logical essence by reflecting on the predicates which constitute or are made to constitute the nominal definition; for real essence, we seek data from experience or intuition to determine whether and under what condition the object is really possible.[15]

This difficult and obscure matter is involved in the distinction between general and transcendental logic, and it cannot be made intelligible within the limits usually imposed on discussions of definition in formal logic. Kant is saying that in a real definition we do not merely equate a word with a logical product of arbitrarily chosen logical predicates, but we make at least a problematical existential judgment and state the conditions under which this judgment could be verified so that the *definiendum* will be seen to have "objective reference." There must be, in the *definiens*, some determination or compound of determinations that can be "cashed" in possible sensible (intuitive) experience. Its absence is the reason why all definitions in speculative meta-

[14] *Vorlesungen über Logik*, Einleitung, viii, p. 374. *Ratio essendi* is, of course, to be understood not as having a bearing on the thing itself, corresponding to the "real essence" in Locke; for Kant, like Locke, admits ignorance of that. But *ratio essendi* may be applied also to the object of knowledge; and when its *ratio cognoscendi* and *ratio essendi* in part coincide, there is *a priori* knowledge.

[15] *Critique of Pure Reason*, A 218=B 265. Kant insists on the distinction between the two meanings of possibility as early as the *Einzig möglicher Beweisgrund* . . . (Akademie ed.), II, 77–78, the most important point always being that existence is not a logical predicate. There are many things logically possible that are not really possible, because the non-conceptual condition that would show them to exist is not possible. Thus "a two-sided plane figure" is logically but not really possible, while a "two-sided triangle" is not logically possible (*Critique*, A 221=B 268). The only kind of possibility subject to formal definition is logical (*Critique*, A 244=B 302).

physics are only nominal. Its specific epistemological character is the reason also why general logic does not deal with
(or at least does not distinguish) real definitions, since
general logic disregards the transcendental difference between
a predicate and a determination; and neglect of this difference is, finally, the reason why logic, when used as an organon
in metaphysics, develops into dialectic.

The notion of real definition is not only excluded from
general logic by Kant (though he dealt with it in his Lectures, which far exceeded the bounds he set up around the
field of general logic), but is challenged on other grounds
by most modern writers who reject the ontological distinction between essence and property.[16] They admit, in any
specific case, the distinction between an essential and an
accidental definition, though on pragmatic not ontological
grounds. Kant, in accordance with a tradition going back at
least to the *Port Royal Logic*,[17] uses the distinction
between nominal and real definition to designate this other,
quite different, distinction: a real definition is one from
which other properties can be derived, while a nominal definition suffices only for "comparisons" and not for "deriva-
tions." Thus "The circle is a curved line all of whose parts
can be made to coincide" is described by Kant as a nominal
definition despite the fact that it prescribes an applicable
test; he means that it is a definition that contains a predicate
already derived, not an *essentia*; but instead of pointing this
out, he calls it nominal.[18]

Having now set up the major divisions, I turn to the specific types of definitions resulting from the two independent
divisions. They may be most easily seen from the following
table.

	Analytic *Logical definition*		Synthetic *Declaration*	
Nominal				
Real	A priori Exposition	A posteriori Description	A priori Construction	A posteriori Invention

[16] Cf. Richard Robinson, *Definition* (Oxford, 1950), pp. 154–55.
[17] Part I, ch. xii.
[18] Reflexion 2916; cf. Reflexion 2995. He does, however, point
out the real infirmity of this definition in the *Critique*, A 732=B 760.

1. *Analytic nominal definition.* Kant says little about this, and even that little is confusing. Because it is in any case of small importance to our inquiry, I shall not undertake to examine the various confusing statements he makes, but merely list the passages for the interested reader.[19]

2. *Synthetic nominal definition.* Such a definition is a stipulation or a "declaration" of an intended usage, the concept being created by the definition. Since they are not determined by experience or by analysis of a given concept, Kant says that such definitions are *a priori* synthetic, not realizing, perhaps, the inappropriateness of this adjective to what is not a proposition or judgment proper.[20]

3. *Analytic real definition.* A definition of this type states the defining predicates of a given concept known to have objective validity, and it contains the synthetic predicate (*Bestimmung*) which gives the defined concept this objective reference. Nevertheless, upon investigation it turns out that any attempt to state such a definition fails to meet the formal requirements of definition, with respect either to completeness or precision.

If the concept is given *a priori*, we cannot be sure that we have a complete analysis of it into its co-ordinate predicates. A concept given *a priori* may include "many obscure representations, which we overlook in our analysis, though we are constantly making use of them in our application of the concept." Therefore the completeness of a proffered definition is never more than probable, and rather than call such an indefinite analysis by the name "definition," Kant calls it an "exposition."[21]

If the concept is given *a posteriori*, its analysis suffers from the same infirmity mentioned above in discussing the definition of an *a priori* concept. Such a concept has no precise and complete analysis, for the concept itself is not a fixed union of predicates. It is variable, depending upon the scope

---

[19] *Vorlesungen über Logik*, § 106, Anmerkung 2; Reflexionen 2918, 2931, 2963, 3004.

[20] Reflexion 3007. Such a definition—in the case under discussion, it happens to be Kant's definition of analytic judgment—cannot be in error. *Über eine Entdeckung* (Akademie ed.), VIII, 232. All references to this essay are to pages in Vol. VIII of the Akademie edition.

[21] *Critique of Pure Reason*, A 729=B 757.

of the experience we classify under it. Kant in one place says that it cannot even be nominally defined.[22] A statement of the attributes and properties of a thing meant by an empirical concept is at most a description, which is not held to rules of precision and completeness; description provides many truths which serve as the "material for definition,"[23] the definition itself being only an ideal.

4. *Synthetic real definition.* It is obvious from the very name what falls here: such a definition must not only make a concept, but must show its real possibility by including the *Bestimmung* which is its *ratio essendi* and *cognoscendi*.

If the synthesis is of pure concepts, the real determination must be a character of pure intuition; if of empirical concepts, the real determination must be an empirical intuition. The synthesis of pure concepts is a construction. Construction is the presentation of a concept through the spontaneous production of its corresponding and verifying intuition. Concepts, if pure, can have an *a priori* representation only in pure intuition; and such representation is definition as this occurs in mathematics. If the concept is empirical in its components, we have the presentation of an actual empirical intuition not through the productive imagination alone but through a change effected in the real world. A definition of such a concept may be genetic, telling us how to make a corresponding object,[24] and the devising of the object is proof that the concept has real objective possibility and is not chimerical. Kant calls such a definition (as of a ship's chronometer) a "declaration of a project"[25] or an "exposition of appearances."[26] Since "exposition" and "declaration" are both used in other senses, I have called this, in the table, "invention."

In mathematics, we make a concept by synthesis. "The mathematician in his definitions says, *Sic volo, sic jubeo*."[27]

[22] *Reflexion* 2992.
[23] *Vorlesungen über Logik*, § 105, Anm. 3.
[24] *Reflexion* 3001.
[25] *Critique of Pure Reason*, A 729=B 757.
[26] *Vorlesungen über Logik*, § 102.
[27] *Reflexion* 2930; see also *Untersuchung über die Deutlichkeit der Grundsätze* . . . (Akademie ed.), II, § 1; (tr. Beck, p. 262)—here-

But in spite of the modern sound of this statement, mathematical definitions for Kant are real, not nominal. Mathematical entities are not arbitrary logical products of compatible logical predicates; the concepts have objective validity (in pure intuition) shown through the presentation of the corresponding determination. If the presentation is a product of the productive imagination, the construction is called schematic or pure, as of a figure (no matter how roughly drawn) used in a geometrical proof. Such a figure is not used empirically, and the actual drawing of it is not a part of the science of mathematics but belongs to art. Kant calls the empirically made sketch "technical construction"[28] and, indeed, it is like the "invention" of any empirical object. Mathematics is the only science able to construct its concepts *a priori*, and only by construction can we achieve completeness and precision in knowledge. Therefore mathematics is the only science which contains proper and strict definitions.[29]

Kant often speaks of synthetic definitions, including mathematical definitions, as *willkürlich*. The word *willkürlich*, ordinarily translated as "arbitrary," does not, however, suggest the caprice sometimes understood in the word "arbitrary"; "arbitrary" does not mean "random". Arbitrariness, as it is now commonly interpreted, is not a feature of mathematical knowledge as Kant interprets it; mathematical concepts are limited by the fixed conditions of intuition, just as empirical concepts are synthesized under the limits imposed by the actual content and order of empirical data. Kant contrasts *willkürlich* with *empirisch*, not, I think, with *notwendig*.[30]

III

I shall now consider the role that definitions play in the progress of knowledge, as this is described by Kant.

---

after referred to as *Prize Essay*, the first number referring to the page in the Akademie edition, the second, in parentheses, to my translation (Chicago, 1949).

[28] *Über eine Entdeckung*, 192n.
[29] *Critique of Pure Reason*, A 729=B 757.
[30] *Vorlesungen über Logik*, § 103 Anm.

The search for definitions of empirical concepts is justified by the technical demands for communication in relatively unambiguous language. We need to "fix" the meaning of a concept from time to time, and we do so by nominal definition or declaration. Such definitions, if made too soon or especially if taken too seriously as a part rather than as an instrument of knowledge, distort inquiry by permitting logical analysis to usurp the place of empirical amplification. "What useful purpose," Kant asks, "could be served by defining an empirical concept, such, for instance, as that of water? When we speak of water and its properties, we do not stop short at what is thought in the word 'water' but proceed to experiments."[31] Description suffices; definition which aims at being more than nominal is a useless presumption.

Turning from empirical to rational knowledge, Kant insists upon a sharp distinction between the methods proper to mathematics and those of philosophy. The mathematician begins with definitions and proceeds by a synthetic method (involving constructions) to his conclusions; his definitions cannot be false, and their only fault may be lack of precision, which is progressively corrected.[32] The philosopher, on the other hand, must begin with concepts already given to him, though confusedly and without sufficient determinateness. The thing meant is not intuitively clear in the sign, as in the concepts of mathematics,[33] all of which are subject to construction in intuition. The symbols, such as a set of points representing a number, have their meaning "on their face"; whereas the philosopher must use his symbols only as poor representations of richer concepts. These he must analyze in order to compare their segregated characteristics with those originally intended by a ready-made concept used to render unanalyzed experience intelligible. A definition reached by synthesis in philosophy could only by accident be a definition of a concept which originally posed the philosophical problem to us.

In mathematics there are few unanalyzable concepts, and

---

[31] *Critique of Pure Reason*, A 728=B 756 (tr. Kemp Smith).
[32] Reflexion 2979.
[33] *Critique of Pure Reason*, A 734=B 762; *Prize Essay*, 278 (264).

they can be used with assurance according to explicit rules without any need for analysis. Analyses of concepts, if made at all, belong to the philosophy of mathematics rather than to mathematics itself. In philosophy, on the contrary, there are many unanalyzable and indefinable concepts, but we do not begin our work with them. We discover what they are only by the analysis of given concepts, which are not entirely clear and distinct. Thus (if he is fortunate) the philosopher ends where the mathematician begins, to wit, with indefinable elementary concepts and definitions of the concepts given in the beginning. Definitions in philosophy, therefore, are not the conditions of knowledge; they are what we hope to conclude with, not the raw material with which we begin.

From these textual inquiries, we can conclude that definition does not play the dominant role in Kant's philosophy that it does in later theories of analytic judgment. In only one field, mathematics, does Kant admit strict definitions, and in mathematics it is possible to decide indubitably what is analytic and what is synthetic. In empirical knowledge, definition is only loose and informal, and we should expect what we do find, namely that decision on the character of specific judgments is variable and without great importance. It is *a priori* judgments outside of mathematics that Kant is chiefly concerned to establish, and of their concepts definition is impossible. Yet it is with respect to these judgments that it is of fundamental importance to distinguish the apriority of formal logic (analytic) from the apriority of transcendental logic (synthetic).

Definition is not essential to certainty in knowledge. Quite apart from Kant's belief that not all *a priori* knowledge is analytic, he does not even assert that analytic judgments are necessarily consequences of definitions. Though he indicates[34] that analytic judgments are deducible from definitions, this statement occurs in the reply to Eberhard, in a context supplied by his opponent; it is not his characteristic way of stating the nature of analytic judgments. Definition would be a sufficient, but is not a necessary, condition for analytic judgments; we may have *a priori* knowledge of

[34] *Über eine Entdeckung*, 229.

undefined concepts provided we can either exhibit the concept in pure intuition (schematize it to give a basis for synthetic judgments) or give a partial analysis of the concept.[35] And in three places,[36] at least, Kant describes the way logical certainty in knowledge is gained, showing clearly that definition is given a secondary role. He tells us that we begin by analyzing concepts, expressing the analyses in analytic judgments, and only then organize these analytic judgments into definitions. Even so, definition requires a completeness and precision that is often an unattainable ideal; yet its absence does not jeopardize the analytic judgments already made.

The *Critique of Pure Reason* is supposed to answer the question, How are synthetic judgments *a priori* possible? But if it is not possible to decide objectively whether a given judgment is synthetical or analytical, the entire *Critique* seems to be wasted effort. Can we make synthetic judgments and know that they will, as it were, remain synthetic while we examine their apriority? Or do not definitions grow and so extend their sway that a judgment once known only empirically can, under better definitions, come to be logically necessary? Can we not agree[37] that a "synthetic *a priori* judgment" is a judgment with an ambiguous term, and that when we remove the ambiguity by definition we either remove the apriority or the syntheticity?

This presupposes that analytic judgments are determined by definitions, and it at least suggests that definitions are arbitrary in such a manner that we have a choice as to whether the judgment in question will be made analytic or synthetic. Expressed in other ways, this is one of the oldest and probably the most common of all criticisms of Kant's theory. The difference which he thought was fundamental seems to be a subjective, shifting distinction, dependent upon how much one knows at a given time, and how one formulates what one knows. Very early in his use of the distinc-

---

[35] *Critique of Pure Reason*, A 731=B 759; *Prize Essay*, 285 (271); *Vorlesungen über Logik*, § 109 Anm.

[36] *Prize Essay* 282 (268); *Falsche Spitzfindigkeit der vier syllogistischen Figuren* (Akademie ed.), II, 61; *Prolegomena*, § 2 c 3 (ed. Beck, 18).

[37] With H. W. Chapman, *Mind*, n.s. 61 (1952), 391.

tion Kant seems to have anticipated this objection[38] though he gave no answer at that time, and for many years used the distinction as though completely oblivious of the objection.

He does not seem to have realized its full force until he prepared his reply to Eberhard. Even then, in the published reply he does not come to grips with the problem; but in the working paper prepared under his direction by Schultz there is a passage[39] which deals with the shifting of the line between the two types of judgments by the modification of definition. The passage is obscure, but I will try to describe what I think Kant would have said had he put it into shape for publication.

Kant invites his opponent to add any attributes he wishes to a concept, so that whatever it is he wishes to prove he can prove by deduction, i.e. analytically. But then Kant asks him: How did you come to include in the concept precisely those attributes you needed in order to render previously synthetic judgments analytic? He cannot reply that he is giving a definition of the concept unless he can show that he is obeying the rules of definition in formal logic. That is, he must be able to show that the newly introduced attributes are logically independent of the old, yet invariably attached to the subject in experience, so that the conjunction of the old and new attributes has the same denotation as the original concept. A narrower denotation will not do, for that means that a new concept has been introduced, not that an old one has been defined. Now in order to know the identity of the old and new denotation, he must know the connection of the independent attributes before stating them in a new definition; he must know this synthetically, for if they are analytically related the rule concerning the precision of definition is broken. Hence, definitions devised for the purpose of rendering synthetic judgments analytic are not real definitions, or in making them we must already know with certainty the synthetic judgment they were designed to establish as analytic. If they are not real but only nominal

[38] Reflexion 3928, dating from the late 'sixties.
[39] *Rezension von Eberhards Magazin* (Akademie ed.), XX, 408–9.

definitions, then the problem of synthetic *a priori* knowledge
(which Kant calls the metaphysical problem) is not touched
by this exercise in logic.[40]

IV

In contrast with the views mentioned at the beginning of
this paper, sometimes erroneously attributed to Kant, we
have found that Kant's views on the relation between definition and analytic judgment are as follows. While a judgment logically implied by a definition is analytic, analytical
judgments are not necessarily or even usually known or justified by deduction from definitions. Analytic judgments are
made by analysis of concepts which need not first be established by definition. Definition is a late stage in the progress
of knowledge, being preceded by the analysis of given concepts, expressed in analytic judgments. Because definition is
a secondary and more or less adventitious element in Kant's
theory of the criteria of analytic judgment, the view that
synthetic propositions can be rendered analytic by a change
in definition is foreign to the distinction as Kant established
and used it, and does not contribute to a solution of his
problem of justifying *a priori* judgments whose necessity is
not that of formal logic.

[40] I have translated this passage and discussed the issue of the
variability of the synthetic-analytic decision in "Can Kant's Synthetic
Judgments Be Made Analytic?" *Kant-Studien,* Band 47 (1955),
168–81.

THE TRANSCENDENTAL AESTHETIC

INFINITY AND KANT'S CONCEPTION
OF THE "POSSIBILITY OF EXPERIENCE"

CHARLES D. PARSONS

In this paper I intend to discuss Kant's theory that space is the "form" of our "outer intuition." This theory is intended, among other things, to explain what Kant took to be a fact, namely that we have synthetic *a priori* knowledge of certain basic properties of space and of the objects in space. In particular, Kant thought we knew *a priori* that space is in some respects infinite, for example infinitely divisible.

I shall not challenge Kant's claim that we have such synthetic *a priori* knowledge, but I shall attempt to show that Kant's theory of space must be taken in such a way that it does not explain this putative knowledge. For the intent of the whole of Kant's epistemology is to prove that our synthetic knowledge is limited to objects of "possible experience." Now when we try to give the notion of "possible experience" a concrete intuitive meaning, we shall find that the limits of possible experience must be narrower than what, according to Kant, is the extent of our geometrical knowledge of space.

The alternative to so limiting the possibility of experience is to define it by what, on mathematical grounds, we take to be the form of our intuition. But then the content of mathematics is not determined by any concrete knowledge of the form of intuition and the limits of possible experience associated with it. In this setting, the notion of "form of intuition" loses much of its force, and as an explanation becomes *ad hoc*.

The difficulty seems to me deeper than that which gives rise to the most common objections to Kant's theory of

Reprinted with permission of the author and of the editors from *Philosophical Review*, 73 (1964), 183–97.

space. These rest on a comparatively accidental feature of Kant's view, namely his belief that we can know *a priori* that space is Euclidean. It is then pointed out that there is no sufficient reason for believing this, and that there are physical reasons for preferring a theory in which space (more strictly, space-time) is not Euclidean. The Kantian might simply concede this point and reply that the form of our outer intuition might indeed not determine the answer to such a question as whether the parallel postulate is true, but it does determine more primitive properties of space, so that these can be known *a priori*. The infinite divisibility in particular is, so far as I know, not denied in any serious application of geometry to physics. The claim that we know properties of this order *a priori* is not absurd even in the contemporary context—and indeed I am not denying it, but only the adequacy of the Kantian explanation of it, if it is the case.

In order to carry our discussion further, we must say something by way of elucidation of the terms which Kant uses, and which we have used to state our problem. Our elucidation will not be completely thorough and satisfactory; to give such elucidation would be a larger and more difficult undertaking than the present paper, and there are probably some irresolvable obscurities. I hope, however, that my elucidation will be sufficient to make my own argument clear.

We shall begin with the notion of "form of intuition." According to Kant, intuitions, like anything "in the mind," are representations. A vital feature of representations is that they have what, after Brentano, is called intentionality. That is, they at least purport to refer to an object; moreover, they have a certain content which they represent as in some way belonging to the object. Kant defines intuition as a species of representation which is distinguished by being in immediate relation to objects, and by being in relation to, purporting to refer to, individual objects (A 19=B 33; lectures on logic § 1).[1] The implications of the word "immediate"

[1] I. e. *Critique of Pure Reason*, 1st ed., p. 19; 2d ed., p. 33. With a few minor modifications, all quotations will be from Kemp Smith's translation (2d ed., London, 1933).

will be considered below. Kant assumes that our faculty of intuition is *sensible*: that is, we have intuitions only as a result of being *affected* by objects. The primary instance of this is *sense perception*—seeing, hearing, and so forth.

Our intuitions have certain characteristics which belong to them by virtue of the nature of our capacity to be affected by objects, rather than by virtue of some characteristics of the specific occasions of affection which give rise to them. These characteristics are said to be the form of our intuition in general. Since spatiotemporality is among them, space and time are spoken of as *forms of intuition*.

This must be understood to mean that the nature of the mind determines that the objects we intuit should be spatial, and indeed intuited as spatial. Outer intuitions represent objects *as* in space. "By means of outer sense, a property of our mind, we represent to ourselves objects as outside us, and all without exception in space" (A 22=B 37). That its objects are in space is perhaps the definition of "outer" intuition, so that space is the form of outer intuition. Since inner intuition is characterized as of "ourselves and our inner state" (A 33=B 49), outer intuition is also distinguished by representing its objects as in some way outside our minds.

It might be remarked that from the fact "we represent to ourselves objects as . . . in space" it does not immediately follow that this is not an illusion. Since Kant characterizes phenomenal objects as "things to be met with in space," what the claim of non-illusoriness amounts to is that phenomenal objects really exist, such that perception puts us into immediate relation to them. That this is so is the claim of the Refutation of Idealism, which in turn (in the second edition at least) rests on the Transcendental Deduction.

Kant also supposed that space has certain mathematical properties which are reflected as properties and relations of the objects in space. It is of course the fact that they describe the *form* of our intuition which makes mathematical propositions *a priori*. Kant, of course, supposed that we know *a priori* that space is Euclidean. This means, in particular, that it is both infinite in extent and infinitely divisible. It is this which is the source of the difficulties which we shall develop.

A final preliminary remark concerns the concept of "possible experience." A main purpose of the *Critique* is to deduce the principles which describe the general nature of the objects given in experience by showing that they describe "necessary conditions of the possibility of experience." It follows, however, that these principles apply only to objects of possible experience. "The conditions of the *possibility of experience* in general are at the same time conditions of the *possibility of the objects of experience,* and . . . for this reason they have objective validity in a synthetic *a priori* judgment" (A 158=B 197).

If this analysis is to yield its result, the limitation of our knowledge to objects of possible experience must mean more than that the objects should be such as might present themselves in some way or other in a possible experience. For Kant allowed the possibility that the objects of experience should have an existence in themselves, apart from their relation to us in our perception and even apart from the general conditions of this relation. But of this we can know nothing; everything about the object which we can know must be able to show itself in experience and must therefore be limited by the general conditions of possible experience. We shall see that applying this dictum to the infinite properties of space produces difficulties for Kant.

THE "ANTINOMY" OF INTUITION

It follows from the fact that the empirical objects of perception are in an infinitely divisible space that they are *indefinitely complex.* For the spatial region which an object occupies can be divided into subregions, which again can be so divided, and so on. This is not to say that the object can be physically separated into parts indefinitely, although Kant does refer to what occupies a subregion of the region occupied by an object as a "part" of the object. Given two disjoint subregions of the region occupied by the object, the "parts" of the object occupying these subregions are distinguishable. One could know a great deal about the state of one "part" while knowing little or nothing about the state of the other.

We shall now develop some apparent implications of the definition of intuition as immediate representation, in such a way as to lead to an absurd conclusion. From the view that space is the form of our outer intuition, it seems to follow that the objects we perceive are represented in intuition as having the structure which objects in space have. Then it seems that they are perceived to be indefinitely complex. Indeed, Kant speaks constantly of a *manifold* of intuition, and says that every intuition contains a manifold.

We shall now take an extreme interpretation of this, and make the following argument. In intuition we have an immediate representation of a spatial extension. Such an extension contains subregions. It follows that we have an immediate representation of these subregions. Consider a particular one, say, one whose surface area is no more than half that of the original one. It follows that if we have an intuition of a region of surface area x, we have at the same time an intuition of a region of surface area $\leq \frac{1}{2} x$. By iterating this argument, we can show that we have an intuition of a region of surface area $\leq \dfrac{x}{2^n}$ for each n. In other words, we have *at the same time* intuitions of all the members of an infinite sequence of regions converging on a point. We must suppose that this is something Kant is denying when he says, in the solution to the Second Antinomy, "For although all parts are contained in the intuition of the whole, the *whole division* is not so contained, but consists only in the continuous decomposition" (A 524=B 552). But we do not have an interpretation of what it means for the parts to be "contained in the intuition of the whole."

We shall now make another deliberate misinterpretation of Kant. Kant also says that we can perceive the manifoldness of something given in intuition only by picking out its parts or aspects one by one:

> Every intuition contains in itself a manifold which can be represented as a manifold only in so far as the

mind distinguishes the time in the sequence of one impression upon another; for each representation, *in so far as it is contained in a single moment,* can never be anything but absolute unity.   [A 99]

Now what is suggested by the last part of this sentence is that what "representing as a manifold" means is apprehending a succession of simple parts one by one at different times. Then by the Threefold Synthesis which it is the purpose of the whole passage (A 97–104) to describe, the mind will impose certain relations on these simple entities so that the system of objects thus related will be a spatial whole. Some such interpretation as this is suggested by a number of statements by Kant to the effect that apprehension of a manifold is a successive act. "We cannot think a line without drawing it in thought" (B 154). It is hard to see what the simple entities might be in cases like this if not the points of the line. But then a "single moment" in the above passage would have to be an instant. Absurdities follow immediately. First, it contradicts Kant's repeated statements that the parts of space are not points but spaces, and that the successive synthesis in the apprehension of a space is a synthesis of these parts. Moreover, it is hard to see how the doctrine could be carried over to a two- or three-dimensional space. Of course the points of such a space can be placed in one-to-one correspondence with the instants of time in a time interval. But it would be fantastic to suppose that in thinking of, say, a square, we run through its points in the order deriving from such a correspondence. Indeed, since there is a one-to-one correspondence between the points of the whole of infinite space and the instants of a finite interval of time, it is hard to see why we should not be able to run through *it* in a finite time, contrary to the position of the First Antinomy.

I should not mention these absurd consequences if so distinguished a commentator as Vleeschauwer did not say that, according to this passage, apprehension involves absorbing a succession of simple instantaneous "impressions" which are *not* intuitions; this is the reason it requires a synthesis, so that these simple elements will be connected to form an "intuition."[2] Kemp Smith also reproaches Kant for failing to say what the simple elements are which are synthesized in the synthesis of apprehension.[3]

SOLUTION OF THE "ANTINOMY"

We have considered two interpretations which resemble the antithesis and the thesis of the Second Antinomy. The first was a naïve reading of the doctrine that space is a form of sensible intuition, the second a naïve reading of Kant's view that perception presupposes a synthesis. I think that neither of them is plausible either in itself or as an interpretation of Kant. Mentioning them ought to make clear that it is not so obvious what is meant by saying that space is a form of sensible intuition. The measures we take to reconcile the two tendencies expressed by the two sides of our antinomy will reveal the difficulties I mentioned at the beginning.

In order to interpret the passage from the synthesis of apprehension, we have to make a distinction which Kant does not explicitly make and which has some consequences which I am not sure that Kant would have accepted.

The most likely interpretation of the passage is that the manifoldness of an intuition can be apprehended *explicitly* only by going over the details one by one, in such a way that the times at which the different details are taken in are distinguished from one another. Although Kant may not be disputing that we can *in some sense* take in at least a limited complexity at a glance, it still appears that Kant is claiming something false. For in such cases as the perception of at least short written words, it seems that our perception of what the letters are can hardly be made more explicit by going over them one by one. The same is true of the divisions of a region of space provided that they are marked and the number of them is sufficiently small.

[2] *La déduction transcendentale dans l'œuvre de Kant* (Antwerp-Paris-The Hague, 1934–37), II, 242–44.
[3] *Commentary to Kant's "Critique of Pure Reason"* (2d ed.; London, 1923), p. 87.

This, however, allows us to save something of Kant's point. The amount of complexity and division which we thus take in is finite and in fact has an upper limit, even if this limit is indeterminate. We can take in the letters of a four-letter word at a glance, but not the letters of a printed page. If we consider a ten-letter word, we might find that some could, some could not, and others would not be sure whether to call what they did "taking the word in at a glance."

More generally, we observe that those details or parts of something which we perceive which we can apprehend are themselves given in perception, and therefore have the same indefinite complexity which the whole has. But this complexity is not as explicit to us as what we might call the "first-order" complexity. If it were in general, the antithesis of the above "antinomy" would follow, that is that *all* the complexity of the object is given to us at once. On Kant's grounds, this would imply the decidability of any mathematical question about the continuum, and in general it would imply that our senses are infinitely acute. It is not really possible to imagine what the world would be like if this were the case. A number of examples will show that it is not. Many of us can improve our perception of detail by putting on glasses, and it is likely that some (for example, Ted Williams) see better than we do even then. Our ability to perceive details decreases continuously with an increase in distance, from which it follows that it was not unlimited at optimum distance. The problems about submicroscopic entities arise because our senses cannot take in anything which occupies less than a certain amount of space.

It seems that Kant is not asserting that in momentary perception the complexity beyond what we take in explicitly (on his view *all* the complexity) is not given to us at all. Indeed, it is hard to see what this would mean. We could hardly say that the letters of a word which we look at look simple and undifferentiated. We might take the perception to be of an aggregate of "sense data" which are themselves simple, but then it could be only by virtue of external relations that they could be appearances of objects which are themselves complex (for example, the letters). This is simply the thesis of our antinomy.

The complexity which is given in a nonexplicit fashion can be perceived explicitly by taking a closer look directed specifically at some aspect of it. This seems to be what Kant calls, in the section on the synthesis of apprehension, running through the manifold.

We claim to have shown that the distinction between explicit and implicit givenness is necessary in order to save the doctrine of continuous space as a form of outer intuition from a contradiction with the fact of the limited acuteness of our senses, as is presented in the "antinomy" above sketched. In fact, the distinction is that which is made in Gestalt psychology between "figure" and "ground." The data of the senses at any given time are divided into that toward which the attention is primarily directed, called "figure," and that to which it is not, called "ground." In the simplest case of looking at a physical object the latter includes the "background." The figure appears more clearly and definitely. What needs to be noted is that within the spatial boundary of the figure, many aspects of the object appear as ground—subtle differentiations of its color, irregularities of its shape, all but a few of its spatial divisions. There is here, however, no definite line between appearing as ground and not appearing at all.

In the appearance of objects to us we can thus distinguish three levels: primary complexity or figure, which appears explicitly; secondary complexity or ground, which appears in a non-explicit way which is difficult to describe; and tertiary complexity, which does not appear at all but which might appear in some other perception of the same object.

RELATION TO KANT'S ACTUAL VIEWS

That Kant was not fully in possession of this distinction can, I think, be shown by analysis of the Threefold Synthesis and the Mathematical Antinomies.

In the Threefold Synthesis Kant argues that an intuition containing a manifold can be represented as manifold only by attending to its different aspects individually at different times (running through) and yet keeping them in mind as aspects of *one* intuition (holding together). This, however, presupposes a *reproduction* of the previous elements of the series and their *recognition* as "the same as what we thought a moment before" (A 103). In terms of the analysis I have given, there seems in the description of the threefold synthesis to be a striking omission: what is given *explicitly* to closer attention must be identified as what was given *implicitly* at an earlier stage of perception.

In the Second Antinomy, Kant speaks in what seems to me a not at all clear way about an object as a "spatial whole given in intuition" in such a way as to insure that a division of it (in the conceptual sense mentioned above) can continue without end. He is not clear as to why he asserts this and yet denies that "it is made up of infinitely many parts," on the grounds that "although all parts are contained in the whole, *the whole division* is not so contained" (A 524= B 552).

If Kant saw the matter clearly in the way we suggest, then he might very well not have made the distinction he makes between the solution of the First Antinomy and the solution of the Second. In the case of the Second, his solution might be taken to mean that if a part is given implicitly, and appears explicitly in a later perception, then this perception is of the same type as the preceding, so that the process can be repeated. There seems, however, to be no reason not to make the symmetrical assumption at least with respect to the infinity of the world in space. For the figure in our perceptual field is surrounded by ground. It is just as natural to assume that for any given direction, some element of the ground immediately in that direction can be made figure by a shift of attention, with a result of the same type as the previous perception, so that the result can always be repeated. This would mean that there would always be something outside any spatial region which we clearly perceived.

There is still a difference, but it is not the one in the text between a *regressus in infinitum*, where we know at the outset that at every point we shall be able to find some further term, and a *regressus in indefinitum*, where we can never know that we shall *not* be able to continue, but need not know that we always *can*. The difference is that the regions in the outward progression may be of objective size decreasing fast enough so that they can all be included in one bounded region. I am not quite convinced that this can be true while in the case of the division the objective size of the parts *must* tend to zero. It seems that in either case we might have some liberty in devising the measuring system so that the objective size of the whole does or does not become infinite in the first case, or so that the objective size of the parts does or does not tend to zero in the second.

INTUITION AND INFINITY

We can now return to the question we raised at the beginning, of the sense in which space and its properties are conditions of the possibility of experience, and in which the objects in space are objects of possible experience. Let us consider the assumption that justifies the continuation at every stage of the regress of the Mathematical Antinomies. This assumption is that whatever appears to us as ground can become figure, in such a way that it will have the same structural properties as the figure of the previous perception. We shall call this the Continuability Principle.

The expression "structural properties" is somewhat vague. By using it we require that the new figure should have a nonnull spatial extension (area) and that the new perception should have primary, secondary, and tertiary complexity. Of course, some of what belonged to the tertiary complexity will now be secondary.

That the objects in arbitrarily small or arbitrarily distant regions of space will be objects of possible perception, and therefore of possible experience, follows from iterated application of the Continuability Principle. The question arises what sort of possibility is in question. I shall argue that it cannot be practical possibility, and that it must be a sort of possibility which implies some circularity in Kant's explanations.

There are a number of circumstances which might prevent us from following out a part of the ground and making it figure. The object might change or be destroyed; *we* might die or be unable to make some necessary motion; we might have reached the limit of the acuteness of our senses.

The problem of change in the object is very complicated. In order to make a transition from ground to figure, it seems there must be some element of stability. For example, one could not look more closely at some part of a surface, and see clearly what one previously saw less clearly, if the surface changed in some wild way. How *much* continuity there has to be, however, depends on what one wants. In particular, I do not believe change gives rise on the macroscopic level to difficulties in principle about identifying subregions of the region occupied by the previous figure, or in identifying regions just outside it.

The limit of the acuteness of our senses seems to me more serious. Something which is too small or too distant cannot be seen as clearly as the things we see in everyday life. For this reason it is doubtful that the Continuability Principle applies in the sense of practical possibility to things which are so small or so distant that they appear as "dots." The range of application can be greatly extended with the aid of optical devices. But even with this latitude, physics would place a certain definite limit on our microscopic perception.[4]

In the case of great distance, we have to bring in the third limitation, that something might happen to *us*. In view of the fact that, according to present-day physics, our speed of motion must be less than that of light, if the object is very distant it will be a very long time before we can get close enough to it to see it much more clearly. But biology (or, perhaps, common sense) sets a definite limit on the amount of time we shall have to get there. If the question is not what one individual can perceive but what the species can perceive, then it seems that the second law of thermodynamics places an upper limit on the longevity of the species.

There is reason to believe, therefore, that (speaking

[4] In the case of the most powerful devices, a great deal of physical theory intervenes between our perception and our interpretation of it as of a certain very small object. And it is not clear that this interpretation will be true more than schematically; it may be that, as with a photograph, the fine structure of what we see no longer belongs to the object.

vaguely) every aspect of our perceptual powers is limited in a definite way by natural conditions. We could call a being of which this is true a *thoroughly finite* being. For such a being, there is an n such that he can have no perception of what is within any sphere of radius $1/n$, or outside a certain fixed sphere of radius n. I believe that in this statement we can replace "perception" by "empirical knowledge," if we limit empirical knowledge to what can be inferred from observations by induction. For by these means, we could not verify that the laws by which we might extrapolate to very distant or very small regions would not fail at these magnitudes.

Thus it appears that the "possibility of experience" for Kant must extend beyond what is practically possible for the sort of being we have reason to think we are. It would be possible to describe the perceptual powers of a being for whom the Continuability Principle would be true, but who would still be finite, in the sense that he would not need to have infinitely acute senses, or be immortal, or be able to perform infinitely many acts in a finite time, or anything similar. Such a creature (call him U) would be more bizarre than appears at first sight; for example, he would have to be able to increase the acuteness of his senses beyond any limit. The difficulty for Kant, however, is not so much one of forming an abstract conception of such a being, but of explaining how it can be that the *form of our sensibility* leads us to represent "appearances" as having the structure and relations which U's experience would reveal them to have. In the case of the Continuability Principle, this does not seem so unnatural, but if it is spelled out it seems unavoidably dogmatic: namely, the structure of ordinary macroscopic perception, in which the figure appears with its internal and external ground, is certainly compatible with the notion that the ground appears as something which "can become figure" in a sense in which this "possibility" is in some sense an aspect of the intuition and not, for example, something which would have to be inferred from general rules. Kant must, however, suppose that "intuition" must represent its objects as having the structure which is revealed in this most favorable situation, even those which are in fact presented only on the margins of our sense experience. As an extrapolation, this is quite natural. But when it is carried to infinity, far beyond the actual limits of our experience, it is not so clear that it is the only possible one. Even if it is, however, it is also not clear why it is to be regarded as a form in which objects must be "given" rather than as an imaginative or intellectual construction. Perhaps Kant came close to saying that it *was* imaginative.[5] The reason he did not regard it as intellectual seems to be that he thought that, apart from something nonconceptual, there was no source of any representation of infinity. That only the form of intuition can allow us to represent indefinite continuation in space seems to me to be the sense of the following dark saying: "If there were no limitlessness in the progression of intuitions, no concept of relations could yield a principle of their infinitude" (A 25).

The upshot of all this is that the "possibility of experience" must be a quite abstract kind of possibility, defined by the form of intuition. It is interesting to consider how it is related to contrary-to-fact possibility. If "object of possible experience" means "object of possible perception," then there must be objects which I *might have* perceived but did not. This is obvious without our earlier argument, if we bring in time and change. Since one cannot be in two places at once, everything about the state of the world *now* which I cannot perceive from my present vantage point must, on our assumption, be something I might have perceived but did not.

There is, however, an important difference between this sort of case and those of very distant and submicroscopic regions of space. Consider these three cases:

(1) I might have seen the Red Sox play yesterday if. . . .

(2) I might have seen the explosion (on a planet 10^{10} light years away) if. . . .

(3) I might have seen (something happening in a certain region of diameter 10^{-100} cm.) if. . . .

In (1) what might fill the blank would be something which could easily have been the case; for example, if the idea had occurred to me, if I had felt like it, if I had not had

[5] Cf. Heidegger, *Kant und das Problem der Metaphysik* (Bonn, 1929), esp. § 28.

to see my tutees, and so forth. What would fill the blank in
(2) would be something which could be the case only if my
origin and that of the whole human race were quite different
from what I take it to be, transposed to a quite different part
of the universe. What would fill the blank in (3) would be
something which could be the case only if our units of measure, and therefore we ourselves, were of a totally different
order of magnitude in relation to such physical quantities as
the size of atoms and electrons and the wave length of light.
It is not clear that we could even describe the circumstances
which, if they obtained, would be such that we could identify
some spatial region of diameter 10^{-100} cm., let alone find
out what is going on in it.

In any case, the possibilities (2) and (3) are of such a
sort as Kant would have regarded as idle and unverifiable,
for a reason which makes it difficult for him to make
any use of contrary-to-fact possibility. That reason is the
view expressed in the Postulates of Empirical Thought
(A 230–232=B 282–285) that we cannot know that there
is more than one possible experience, and that all our empirical knowledge must be brought under the unity of a single
experience. For this reason, he asserts that we cannot know
that there is anything really possible which is not actual.

It ought to be remarked that the extension of the possibility of perception to infinity depends on the *iterated* application of the Continuability Principle. Even with the assurance
that the Continuability Principle is true, we should not obtain the indefinite complexity of objects and the infinity and
infinite divisibility of space without this iteration; we should
not be able to deduce them without mathematical induction.
It appears that, for Kant, mathematical induction is in some
way founded on the form of our intuition, but Kant gives no
explicit statements to make clear how. I do not see that the
case is much better with the modern Kantians in mathematics
(for example, Brouwer and Hilbert).[6]

[6] Poincaré seems to me to shed more light on induction (*La
science et l'hypothèse* [Paris, 1908], ch. 1), but although he is called
an "intuitionist," I do not count him as a Kantian. He seems quite
uninfluenced by Kant's special conception of "pure intuition."

CONCLUSION

Kant's theory that space is a form of intuition has two conflicting pulls. On the one hand, it implies that the objects of outer intuition have certain characteristics, in particular that of being in some form of mathematical space. But in order to be an explanation of this fact, and in view of the fact that intuition is representation, nothing ought to be attributed to the form of intuition which is not revealed in the way objects present themselves to us in perception.

The first pull leads Kant to assume an aspect of the form of our intuition, namely the potential infinity of certain kinds of series of perceptions, which is beyond our actual powers of perception. He must hold that we represent objects as being in a space and time having parts which are beyond the experience of a thoroughly finite being, and that this arises from the form of our sensibility. But this cannot be justified phenomenologically. I should like to say that in this situation the term "form of sensibility" has no explanatory force. I am inclined to think that we cannot be justified in saying that our having a concept of the infinite is explained by the fact that the form of our sensibility contains the possibility of indefinite continuation and division.

Thus, if he is to maintain the view that the form of intuition is the *ratio essendi* of the mathematical infinite—in particular the infinite devisibility of space—Kant must take the uncomfortable position of saying that mathematical considerations are the *ratio cognoscendi* of the form of intuition, which in turn defines the possibility of experience. The content of mathematics is thus not determined by concrete knowledge of the form of intuition and the limits of possible experience associated with it. In addition to the difficulty about explanation, there are two further limitations of this position. First, it is hard to see how on this basis the notion of form of intuition can be used for critical purposes, to determine the boundaries of mathematical evidence. Second, this position has for the argument of the *Critique of Pure Reason* as a whole the implication that at some point the "synthetic" method which it purports to follow, of arguing directly from the nature of experience to the conclusions of transcendental philosophy, must be supplemented by the "analytic" method of the *Prolegomena*, of starting with the given content of science and arguing hypothetically to its *a priori* conditions, a method which Kant regarded as acceptable only as an expository device in a semi-popular work. (See *Prolegomena*, §§ 4–5.)

The situation we have described provides some explanation and justification of Heidegger's claim that Kant took the finiteness of our understanding more seriously than did his predecessors, but even he did not follow this through to the end. One reason he did not is that he also took seriously the fact that mathematics requires that there be some source in our cognitive apparatus for some sort of representation of infinity. And as he said, the possibility of mathematics is proved by the fact that it exists. But he did not fully succeed in reconciling this so often cited support of rationalism with the empiricism implicit in restricting the content of our knowledge to "possible experience."

THE TRANSCENDENTAL ANALYTIC

CATEGORIES

W. H. WALSH

It has often been assumed that, apart from the relatively unimportant case of the violation of grammatical rules, there are only two ways in which a man can talk nonsense:

(a) by saying something which patently conflicts with the well-attested findings of some recognised discipline or with what would be unquestionably accepted by common sense. This might be called material nonsense;

(b) by breaking rules of logic and so producing statements which are logically impossible. Statements of this kind (the simplest examples would answer to the logical schema "p.-p.") might be said to be formally nonsensical.

I want to show that there are important cases of what we should all recognise to be nonsense which are omitted in this dichotomy. And I want to connect these cases with the investigations certain philosophers have conducted into categories, producing thereby (as I hope) a clearer account than these philosophers have themselves given of the function and status of categorial concepts and of what differentiates them from other concepts. Briefly, my thesis is that categorial concepts serve to mark off, at a basic level, what makes sense from what makes nonsense, and in so doing provide a framework inside which the construction of empirical concepts must proceed. This way of putting the matter has the advantage of making immediately apparent the difference in logical type between categories and the empirical concepts which can be said, in a sense, to fall under them, and so

Reprinted with permission of the author and of the editors from *Kant-Studien*, Band 45 (1954), Kölner Universitäts-Verlag, in which it was first published.

obviates a persistent misunderstanding according to which the former are taken as merely bigger and better versions of the latter, designating more fundamental characteristics and known in some superior way.

I hope to show further that the thesis that there are categories, and even that there must be some concepts of this nature, carries with it no unwelcome consequences of the rationalist type. It certainly implies a limitation on the range of empirical possibilities, but this limitation is not necessarily fixed and unchanging. The bounds of categorial sense and nonsense may even shift as empirical knowledge accumulates, though the way in which this happens will need careful scrutiny if the special status of categorial principles is to be preserved.

Let me begin by giving a couple of examples.

(1) I am being driven by a friend in a motor-car when, without warning, the engine stops and the car comes to a standstill. I ask my friend what has happened. He replies that the car has stopped for no reason at all. I laugh politely at what I take to be his joke and wait for an explanation or for some activity on my friend's part to discover what has gone wrong; instead, he remains in his seat and neither says nor does anything more. Trying not to appear impolite, I presently ask my friend whether he knows much about motor-cars, the implication being that his failure to look for the cause of the breakdown must be explained by his just not knowing how to set about the job. He takes my point at once and tells me that it is not a question of knowledge or ignorance; there just was no reason for the stoppage. Puzzled, I ask him whether he means that it was a miracle, brought about by the intervention of what 18th-century writers called a "particular providence." Being philosophically sophisticated, he replies that to explain something as being due to an act of God is to give a reason, though not a natural reason, whereas what he said was that there was no reason for what occurred. At this point I lose my temper and tell him not to talk nonsense, for (I say) "Things just don't happen for no reason at all."

(2) A calls on B at an awkward moment when B has dropped his collar stud and cannot find it. "I had it in my hand a minute ago," he tells his friend, "so it can't be far off." The search goes on for some time without success, until A suddenly asks B what makes him think the stud is there to be found. Controlling himself, B explains that he had the stud in his hand and was trying to do up his collar when it slipped from his fingers; that there are no holes in the floor; that the windows of the room are unusually high; and that if the stud had come to pieces he must certainly have come across some bit of it after looking for so long. "Ah," says A, "but have you considered the possibility that it may have vanished without trace?" "Vanished without trace?" asks B: "do you mean turned into gaseous form, gone off like a puff of smoke or something of that sort? Collar-studs don't do things like that." "No, that isn't what I mean," A assures him gravely; "I mean literally vanished without trace, passed clean out of existence." Words fail B at this point, but it is clear from the look he gives his friend that he takes him either to be making an ill-timed joke or to be talking downright non-sense, a proceeding which only his being a philosopher will excuse.

What sort of nonsense is talked by someone who asserts seriously that events sometimes happen for no reason at all or that things sometimes vanish without trace, passing clean out of existence?

Is it *formal* nonsense as defined above? There is a very strong temptation for philosophers to say that it is, for the contradictories of the statements in question are often formu-lated in terms of necessity ("There *must* always be a reason for whatever occurs," "Things just *cannot* vanish without trace"), and it is very common to identify necessary with analytic statements. Some philosophers, indeed, make the identification a matter of definition; they hold that the only necessary statements entitled to the description are those whose truth depends on logical considerations. Of this dogma no more need be said now than that the statements with which we are concerned seem prima facie to count against it, for there is nothing logically impossible in the notion of an event happening for no reason at all or of a thing vanishing without trace and passing clean out of existence. Of course we could, if we chose, make it a matter of definition that nothing should be *called* an event unless we believed it happened for a reason, and similarly in the other case; but it should be plain that this subterfuge will not solve the problem. There is an important difference between saying "There are no events which happen for no reason at all" and saying "There are no 'events' which happen for no reason at all." What we decide to call things makes no difference to what happens in the world.

Is then to make the statements in question to talk nonsense in the *material* sense? To many philosophers this would seem the only possible thing to say, once the thesis that it was formal nonsense had been considered and rejected. Yet it is at least clear that if I say, for instance, that things may perfectly well sometimes go clean out of existence, vanishing without trace, I do not talk nonsense of the ordinary material sort. A man talks nonsense in the material sense, normally, if he fails to take account, or asserts the contradictory, of some obvious and well-established fact, or of some well-attested piece of theory; as for example if I say that you can put a kettle on the gas-stove, light the gas and find after ten minutes that the water has not changed its temperature. We know perfectly well, as a matter of common experience, that this is not how kettles behave when placed on lighted gas-stoves, and the politest thing we can say of someone who thinks that it is is that he has got his facts wrong. But in the examples given above mistakes of fact did not enter into the question. When my friend asserted that the car had stopped for no reason at all he was not putting forward an empirical hypothesis to the effect that this or that suggested explanation was false; he was asserting that there just was no explanation. It is true that if somebody said this sort of thing in real life he would be taken as asserting either that he did not know the explanation or that none of the obvious explanations for this kind of happening would fit; but this is only because we should be unwilling to take him at his word. It would not be flattering to the man to suppose that he was talking such nonsense.

This point can perhaps be made clearer if we turn our attention to the other example about a thing vanishing without trace. Of course there is a sense in which we regard it as perfectly sensible to say of something that it vanished without trace. Buildings or features of the landscape can be obliterated without trace by a hurricane or the dropping of an atomic bomb; if fortunately few of us have personal experience of events of this sort, we know perfectly well that they occur. But of course we also know that the expression "vanished without trace" is used somewhat loosely on these occasions, or rather is used with certain unspoken reservations in mind. When the team of scientists responsible for an atom-bomb experiment reports to its government that all the buildings on the island where the experiment took place vanished without trace, it is not meant that there is no answer to the question "What became of them?" They along with many other solid-looking objects were vaporised by the heat of the explosion and scattered to the four winds. But buildings which vaporise and scatter to the four winds do not vanish without trace in an unqualified sense of the term; they merely leave no trace of themselves on the spot where they stood. What A suggested to B in my example was that the collar-stud might have vanished without trace in an unqualified sense. That particular bit of matter might have gone clean out of existence, leaving no trace of itself in solid, liquid or gaseous form. If that had happened it would not be sense to ask the question what became of it, and this is what gives interest to the example for our purposes.

Hume in his essay on Miracles mentions the case of an "Indian" prince who refused to believe that water turned into ice in conditions of great cold (*Enquiry*, pp. 113–14, ed. Selby-Bigge). The position of someone who is incredulous about the report that solid buildings disappeared without trace when an atomic bomb was dropped is similar to that of this prince. Both have to learn that the boundaries of empirical possibility are not to be measured by any particular man's stock of empirical knowledge. Surprising as it may be, water turns into a solid in one set of circumstances and buildings vaporise in another. But however odd these events may seem to the unsophisticated, it would be even odder if water or buildings had vanished without trace, in the sense of having been not transmuted but annihilated. In fact, it would be another species of oddity altogether.

Doubts about the applicability on given occasions of questions like "What was the reason for this?" and "What became of that?" are not material doubts in the sense in which a doubt whether water will solidify if cooled is material. It is not facts or supposed facts which are challenged by such a doubt, but rather what I must call the framework of facts. The statements that nothing happens except for a reason and that nothing vanishes without trace in the unqualified sense of the phrase are, with the concepts which underlie them, of a higher logical order than are empirical statements and concepts; it is in terms of them that we present our empirical knowledge.[1] That is why any attempt to question them is felt to be far more serious than an attempt to question even a well-attested empirical truth. To discover that a statement we had believed to be materially true is false may come as a profound shock; but the shock is nothing like so great as would be that of discovering that there were events which occurred for no reason or things that went clean out of existence. Fortunately, we are not willing to let ourselves be readily exposed to the latter kind of shock: when the suggestion is made that we might here be in error, our instinct, as the examples show, is to repudiate it as absurd. And this reaction is a sound one, in so far as the statements in question serve to indicate bounds within which we can talk sense

[1] This point seems to have escaped many critics. For an interesting recent instance see Mr. G. J. Warnock's essay "Every event has a cause" in *Essays in Logic and Language*, 2d Series (Oxford, 1955), ed. A. G. N. Flew, pp. 95 ff. Warnock argues that the statement that every event has a cause, while not analytic, is empty of significance because it is of such a general character that there are no circumstances in which we should be justified in regarding it as false. To say that statements of this kind cannot be falsified is only to recognise that they are of a different logical character from everyday factual statements; but to go on and draw the conclusion that they are empty of significance is certainly not justified, for, as my examples show, we know very well what it would be like for such principles not to hold.

about the world. To ask whether it is sensible to observe what, in effect, functions as a rule for talking sensibly is not, on the face of it, a very sensible proceeding.

An alternative way of expressing what has just been said is this. If we were asked to write down as full a list as possible of true empirical statements, we should not (or ought not to) include the statements that nothing happens except for a reason and that nothing vanishes without trace in the sense of passing clean out of existence. These statements are rather presuppositions of empirical truths than empirical truths themselves. What is more (and this point is crucial), they are presuppositions of a very unusual kind. As Collingwood[2] made clear, every question has presuppositions in so far as asking the question implies (in the everyday, as opposed to the logician's, sense of the term) that something is true. Thus if I ask what is the name of the French Prime Minister I imply that someone is French Prime Minister. But most implications of this kind can be made the subject of further enquiry: we can ask, e. g. whether it is in fact true that there is a Prime Minister of France. Presuppositions of this sort, which are themselves answers to further questions, are called by Collingwood "relative presuppositions." The distinguishing mark of such presuppositions as that which underlay my question to my friend when the motor-car broke down, that there must be some reason for whatever happens, is that we cannot sensibly make them the subject of further questioning. There is no process by which we can establish them, comparable to the process by which we establish that there is (or is not) a Prime Minister of France. Hence, as Collingwood said, they are not "relative" but "absolute" presuppositions.

We need some convenient name for the class of statements of which the two statements in my examples are instances. Following Kant, I propose to call them "categorial principles" and the concepts which underlie them "categories." And I shall say that the man who disregards or questions categorial principles is talking categorial nonsense.

[2] R. G. Collingwood: *An Essay on Metaphysics* (Oxford, 1940), pp. 21 ff.

My argument so far has been an argument from fact. I have taken it as true that, if someone suggests that something might happen without any reason for its happening, or that a thing might pass clean out of existence, vanishing without trace, the suggestion will be dismissed as nonsense. Examining the logical character of such assertions, I conclude that the nonsense in question is of a special kind. Now the question might be raised whether it is not only true that we can find statements which indicate the bounds of sense in the way in which I have said categorial principles do, but further that there must be statements of this kind. To put the question in terms which will perhaps make it more familiar, was Kant right in holding not only that *a priori* concepts function in human experience but further that they must do so—that there would be no such thing as experience unless they did?

I propose to examine two arguments for what might be called the indispensability of categorial concepts and principles. The first is Kant's own argument in the Transcendental Deduction. Broadly, Kant may be taken as claiming that we could not have coherent experience without *a priori* concepts. Unity of consciousness is the ultimate prerequisite of experience; without it I could not say of my various experiences that they are all mine. Whatever falls within my experience must be capable of being connected with my other experiences; anything which fails to satisfy this condition could not be experience for me, or I should have, as Kant puts it in a striking phrase (B 134), "as many-coloured and diverse a self as I have representations." Hence whatever is necessary to unitary consciousness is a necessary condition of experience, and the categories are so necessary.

The sting of this argument is in its tail, and the difficulty is to see why the tail is needed. Would it not be possible to grant all Kant's main points without committing oneself to any assertion about *a priori* concepts? It is certainly true that unity of consciousness is a prerequisite of our having experiences. It is true again that, for unity of consciousness to obtain, it must be possible to connect diverse experiences together. If experiences are to be connected we must be able to bring them under concepts, i. e. to discover features which they or sets of them have in common with other experiences or sets of experience. But the concepts in question could perfectly well be, for all that has been shown to the contrary, *empirical* concepts. If I am to make something of a new experience and integrate it with my previous experiences it is enough that I should be able to bring it under some concept or other. Provided that I can pick out from it features of any kind which resemble what has fallen within my experience already, I shall be in a position to describe it in general terms and so to find it significant. In these conditions coherence of experience will be assured.

Yet Kant himself would not accept this conclusion. "Unity of consciousness according to empirical concepts," he wrote in the first edition version of the Deduction (A 111),

"would be altogether accidental, if these latter were not based on a transcendental ground of unity. Otherwise it would be possible for appearances to crowd in upon the soul, and yet to be such as would never allow of experience. Since connection in accordance with universal and necessary laws would be lacking, all relation of knowledge to objects would fall away. The appearances might, indeed, constitute intuition without thought, but not knowledge; and consequently would be for us as good as nothing."

This argument is largely a repetition of that we have considered already, but there is one new point: that unless we connected our experiences according to "universal and necessary laws" (i. e. according to categorial principles), "all relation of knowledge to objects would fall away." Without the categories there would be no such thing as objective knowledge. Behind this assertion lies Kant's conviction that we can distinguish between objective and subjective elements in our experience, items which have intersubjective validity and items which are purely private and personal, only if we define the objective as the regular and orderly, in contrast to the subjective which is arbitrary and irregular. The objective is what happens in accordance with rules. But the difficulty here, as before, is to know why it is necessary to bring in a reference to *a priori* rules. For the purposes of Kant's argument it would be enough that we should be able to bring our experiences under empirical rules in order to have objective knowledge of them. It is true that we could not make do with rules of any kind: if intersubjective discourse is to be possible our rules must be both consistently applied and acceptable to other people. There must in short be generally recognised criteria for accepting or rejecting them. But there seems to be no reason why such criteria should necessarily be identified with categorial principles.

I suspect that Kant may sometimes have thought (e. g. in his remarks about affinity in the first edition) that by bringing in the categories he could *guarantee* that appearances would stand under rules, and so answer Hume's scepticism by solving the problem of induction. If that was at any time his view (it clearly was not when he wrote the Appendix to the Dialectic), he was sadly mistaken: no amount of tightening up of the human conceptual apparatus will guarantee that whatever we experience must be such that it can be brought under concepts. Perhaps again he moved illegitimately from "The objective must be thought of as what happens according to rules" to "The objective is what happens according to necessary rules,"[3] a move to which he would in any case be inclined thanks to his belief that such rules were to be found in Newtonian physics, which for him was the prototype of objective knowledge. But however we explain this part of Kant's doctrine, it seems impossible to justify it. It should be made clear, however, that in saying that Kant was wrong in his general argument we are not committed to criticism of his detailed conclusions. He may have been perfectly correct in recognising the functioning of particular categorial principles, even though his case for the indispensability of such principles was unsuccessful. For my part I think he was: as should be obvious, the two categorial principles adduced above are only popular versions of Kant's principles of causality and substance, and if I were asked to produce further instances I should think first of Kant's other principles of the understanding ("No quality can be present except in a determinate degree" would be a good candidate). But this admission has no bearing on the main point under consideration.

[3] Compare the shift (e. g. A 116–118) from "Synthetic unity of consciousness is an *a priori* condition of experience" to "A *priori* synthesis is a necessary condition of experience."

Can an alternative way be found of showing that there must be categorial principles? What is in effect an alternative argument was developed by Collingwood in his *Essay on Metaphysics*. We have already stated some part of it in explaining his terminology of absolute and relative presuppositions, but the whole case can be put quite briefly.

The activity of asking questions, Collingwood held, is logically prior to that of making statements. We must enquire before we assert or deny, and hence every statement can be looked at as an answer to a possible question. Now questions, as we saw, each carry with them certain implications: one asks a question on the basis of a certain presupposition or of certain presuppositions. Most of these implications or presuppositions can in turn become the subject of further enquiry: we can devise further questions to which they are true or false answers. But because questioning precedes stating, there must always be some presuppositions which do not themselves become the subject of further enquiry, but are merely supposed or taken for granted. These are what Collingwood called "absolute presuppositions," and are identical with our categorial principles.

Formally this argument, which I myself regard as valid, establishes precisely what Kant tried and failed to establish in the Deduction: in Kant's language, that there must be categories. But Kant, no doubt because of the way in which he argued, took this conclusion to mean not merely that some of our concepts must be *a priori*, but further that there must be a fixed set of *a priori* concepts conditioning experience. The importance of substituting Collingwood's argument for Kant's (and incidentally the importance of showing that Kant's own argument is unsatisfactory) is to make clear that no such inference is justified. It is one thing to hold that there must be a level of categorial sense and nonsense, another to think that the bounds of categorial sense have been finally and irrevocably drawn. Collingwood's argument, at any rate, will certainly not justify this bolder conclusion. All that Collingwood established was that, at any given time, it is logically necessary that there should be presuppositions which are absolute for any particular enquirer. It does not follow from this that such presuppositions will remain constant or be shared by different enquirers, much less that they will be common to all men and fixed for all time. As a matter of fact it happens that categorial principles are widely shared and relatively constant; the case for their variability has been overstated by sceptically-minded philosophers, as has the parallel case for the variability of moral principles. But this is a contingent, not a necessary, fact. There is nothing to prevent me from giving up a presupposition which I now accept as absolute, or even from making it the subject of further enquiry if I can devise some means for doing this; though in each case it will be true that I shall be getting rid of one presupposition only to adopt another. To be free of presuppositions altogether is alone what is impossible.

What I have tried to show is that it is possible to accept the thesis that there are categories, and even that there must be categories, without committing oneself to consequences which are repugnant to all empirically-minded persons. Certainly the fact that we hold some things to be categorial nonsense implies a limitation on the range of empirical possibilities; it means, as my examples showed, that there are some possibilities which we refuse to entertain. But this is a less damaging admission than may at first appear. For it is not the case, as Kant thought it was, that we are provided with a permanent set of blinkers (part of the furniture of the mind, as it were) through which to contemplate the world. We build our empirical conceptual structures inside *a priori* frameworks, but the frameworks are not wholly static. We could change them, in whole or in part, and perhaps there are times when we do. It may even be that our attitude towards them is influenced by the nature of the material we meet with in experience.

Perhaps I may conclude this sketch with a brief discussion of this last point. A critic might argue that, in admitting that categorial principles are not fixed for all time, I have jeopardised their distinctive character. For if categorial principles are liable to change, it looks as if we have to say either that they are adopted and abandoned arbitrarily, or that they change with the progress of empirical knowledge. In the latter case, those categorial principles would be in force at any one time which seemed at that time to fit the facts best. Now of these alternatives it is scarcely possible to take the first seriously, and we are then, it would appear, driven back on the second. But since on that view our attitude to categorial principles depends on our empirical knowledge, it looks as if these principles are only empirical hypotheses of a very high order. If so, what becomes of the distinction between categorial and material nonsense which I have tried to draw?

That categorial principles should be adopted and abandoned arbitrarily, as a result of nothing more than changes in fashion, is, I agree, incredible; to say nothing more, it would be hard to see how to account for their relative stability if this view were taken of them. Nor could it be asserted with any plausibility that our attitude to such principles is quite unaffected by the progress of empirical knowledge; to give a familiar instance, our attitude to the principle that nothing happens except for a reason may well be affected in the long run by developments in quantum physics. Yet it does not follow that categorial principles are only empirical hypotheses of a very high order. Every empirical hypothesis must be such that it can at least be falsified; there must be possible evidence which would definitively count against it. But it is a property of categorial principles, as we have seen, that they cannot be falsified in this way; functioning as they do as rules, there is no evidence which can definitively count against them. If a man wants to stick to such a principle, he will be logically justified in doing so no matter what happens. How then do changes in empirical knowledge affect our attitude to categorial principles? Perhaps in this way. As empirical knowledge accumulates, we find that principles which we used to apply with ease become increasingly difficult to apply; we are confronted increasingly with situations to which they are inappropriate. We tend in these circumstances to drop categorial principles, not as having been shown to be false, but as having proved inapplicable. It is much as with a legal enactment which drops out of use not because it is repealed but because the circumstances for its application no longer obtain.

Perhaps the best analogy here is with moral principles. A Utilitarian might argue that moral principles must either be regarded as the product of caprice, or must be seen as reflecting social needs. The first alternative being impossible, the moral and the socially useful coincide, moral precepts expressing the most general rules of social utility. Now it is certainly true that the question whether a practice is socially useful has a bearing on our attitude towards it, and again that we tend to feel uneasy about moral principles when we see their adoption leading to results which are socially inexpedient. But the relation between morality and social utility is by no means so simple as this theory suggests. We sometimes stick to our principles even when doing so produces awkward results, not only for us personally, but for the community to which we belong as well (compare, for instance, the Roman Catholic attitude to contraception). We certainly do not automatically give them up in the face of socially unfavourable results. Yet the pressure of "the facts," here as in the instance of categorial principles, is steady, and the likelihood is that in the long run it will make itself felt. But when it does we do not declare that our former moral principles were mistaken; we drop them quietly as inapplicable, and turn to others which have a closer bearing on the actual state of affairs.

It may be useful by way of appendix to say something on the relation of the category-investigations I have been discussing to other enquiries which have gone, or go, by the same name. Mention of categories and category-mistakes has been frequent in British philosophical circles in recent years, thanks largely to the work of Professor Gilbert Ryle,[4] but it is not obvious what the contributions of Ryle and others have to do with the Kantian, or semi-Kantian, enquiries conducted above. I think myself that there is a connection, though not a very close one.

Ryle's investigations derive in essentials from the Aristotelian doctrine of categories. This doctrine has been variously interpreted; Ryle takes it as offering a catalogue of the funda-

[4] See (1) his paper on "Categories" in *Proceedings of the Aristotelian Society* (1938–39), now reprinted in *Essays in Logic and Language*, 2d Series, ed. Flew, pp. 65 ff.; (2) his inaugural lecture Philosophical Arguments, given in Oxford in 1945; (3) *The Concept of Mind* (London, 1949).

mentally different kinds of term which can figure in simple propositions. Some terms signify Substances, others Qualities, others Relations, and so on. Aristotle may have arrived at this classification, Ryle very plausibly suggests, by considering the various irreducibly different types of question which can be asked about any particular. Thus we have: What is it? (οὐσία); What-like is it? (ποιόν); What size is it? (ποσόν); Where is it? (ποῦ); How does it lie? (κεῖσθαι). The set of terms which would provide sensible (not necessarily true) answers to these and similar fundamental questions are said to belong to the same category. Many philosophical investigations consist for Aristotle in assigning a crucial term to its proper category, e. g. "number," "form."

Ryle proceeds to demand a generalisation of Aristotle's progamme. He wants to extend consideration from terms to "sentence-factors," defined[5] as "any partial expression which can enter into sentences otherwise dissimilar," and he will have nothing to do with Aristotle's restriction of the enquiry to the constituents of supposedly simple statements. He is inclined to think too that *all* philosophical problems reduce in the end to questions about categories. But his most important divergence from Aristotle comes out in the complaint[6] that the latter "relies, apparently, solely upon common sense and common parlance for evidence that a given factor is suited to fill a given gap" in a sentence. Against this, Ryle thinks it can be shown that when an attempt is made to work with an expression on the assumption that it belongs to one category when it in fact belongs to another, "logically intolerable results"[7] ensue. The business of philosophers is to bring out these logically intolerable results in crucial cases by using arguments of the reductio ad absurdum type. In the introduction to *The Concept of Mind*[8] Ryle writes: "I try to use *reductio ad absurdum* arguments both to disallow operations implicitly recommended by the Cartesian myth ((mind-body dualism)) and to indicate to what logical types the concepts under investigation ought to be allocated."

---

[5] "Categories," p. 68.
[6] *Ibid.* p. 70.
[7] Philosophical Arguments, p. 10.
[8] Page 8.

He adds, however, that he sometimes uses arguments of a less rigorous sort, and in these a good deal of reliance is placed on common sense and common parlance.

Ryle's fondness for the reductio ad absurdum springs from his connection of category-mistakes with type-fallacies. His article on categories begins with the assertion that "doctrines of categories and theories of types are explorations in the same field." Now the presence of a type-fallacy is shown by the appearance of antinomies; if somebody says "I am now lying" his statement has the peculiarity of seeming to be false if true and true if false. Ryle appears to think that this sort of situation will arise whenever anyone makes a mistake about the logical type or category to which an expression belongs. Hence for him the absurdity of a statement which trespasses against category rules is at bottom logical absurdity. As he puts it himself,[9] "what is absurd is unthinkable."

But this contention is patently false. To say nothing of the sort of instance with which we have been concerned earlier in this paper, what logical fallacy is committed if somebody says (to take one of Ryle's own examples) that Saturday is in bed? Ryle writes that " 'Saturday is in bed' is obviously absurd before any contradictions are seen to result from the hypothesis that it is true."[10] But is it clear that contradictions do result when we suppose the statement to be true? To take another instance: A asks B the time, and B gives the answer "It's a sort of bird, isn't it?" This answer involves a category-mistake, since a substance-expression is offered where only a temporal expression makes sense. But it does not appear to involve a contradiction, as would the answer (if meant in a straightforward way) "It's half past five on the day after to-morrow."

No doubt people who make category-mistakes can, and frequently do, also make logical mistakes in the narrow sense, but the two do not necessarily go together, nor is the absurdity of the one reducible to that of the other.

If this is granted we find a formal point of contact between investigations of the Kantian and Rylian types, or, if that is

[9] "Categories," p. 76.
[10] *Ibid.* pp. 75–76.

preferred, between Kant and Aristotle. Both parties are concerned in what they write about categories to examine a species of good sense and absurdity which is neither material nor formal as defined at the beginning of this paper. But here the resemblance ends. Categorial principles of the Kantian type approximate to material truths, in that they seem to be about the world, and are hence readily confused with empirical hypotheses. By contrast, the categorial injunctions which might be expected from Aristotle or Ryle (for instance, "Do not confuse substance-expressions with quality-expressions") look far more like rules of logic or grammar. It might be held, indeed, that even rules of this sort must find their justification in truths about the world: the reason why it is wrong to confuse substance-expressions with quality-expressions is that in fact substances and qualities differ. This is in effect to argue that any linguistic interpretation of Aristotle's doctrine of categories presupposes an ontological interpretation. But even if these contentions can be made out, there will still be obvious and important differences between saying "Saturday is in bed" and saying "My car broke down for no reason at all."

SCHEMATISM

W. H. WALSH

The chapter on Schematism probably presents more difficulty to the uncommitted but sympathetic reader than any
other part of the *Critique of Pure Reason*. Not only are the
details of the argument highly obscure (that, after all, is a
common enough experience in reading Kant, though one is
not often so baffled as one is here): it is hard to say in plain
terms what general point or points Kant is seeking to establish. Or if, accepting that the notion of a category has been
sufficiently clarified in the immediately preceding sections,
one says that the object of the Schematism chapter is to explain the circumstances under which categories can find concrete employment, it is difficult to go beyond that very
general statement. The terms in which Kant himself introduces his problem are notoriously unsatisfactory. Pure concepts of the understanding and empirical intuitions are, he
tells us (B 176=A 137), "quite heterogeneous," with the result that there is need of some "third thing," homogeneous
with both, if intuitions are to be subsumed under pure concepts. This third thing is found in the shape of the transcendental schema, which "mediating representation" is
alleged to be intellectual in one respect, sensible in another
(B 177=A 138). It is hard not to think of this as an artificial
solution, conceived in a crude pictorial manner, to a difficulty
which itself depends on an uncritical acceptance of faculty
psychology; and this conclusion draws support from the fact
that schematism does not appear to be discussed, either under that name or under any other, by philosophers other

Reprinted with permission of the author and of the editors from
Kant-Studien, Band 49 (1957), Kölner Universitäts-Verlag, in which
it was first published.

than Kant. Whatever the importance of schemata within the economy of the Kantian system, to pretend that they are of independent philosophical interest seems in these circumstances highly unplausible.

I want to try to show that, despite such impressions, Kant is occupied in this part of his work with questions which are by no means peculiar to himself, questions moreover which are of central importance in theory of knowledge generally. And I should like, if I could, to establish this thesis to the satisfaction not merely of Kantian scholars, whose judgment on it might conceivably be biassed, but also of philosophers who have no special axe to grind in the matter. I shall therefore in what follows express myself as far as possible in a nontechnical way, though I shall not be able to avoid frequent reference to Kant's own words and phrases.

A convenient way to begin is to locate the discussion of schematism in the broad context in which it arises. Kant himself puts the Schematism chapter near the beginning of the Analytic of Principles or Transcendental Doctrine of Judgment, which itself follows immediately on the Analytic of Concepts. The main divisions of transcendental logic, he holds, must follow those of general logic, whose "ground plan" (B 169=A 130) "exactly coincides" with the division of the higher cognitive faculties into understanding, judgment and reason. The Analytic of Concepts having dealt with the operations of the understanding so far as they concern the transcendental philosopher, he must now proceed to consider the use which judgment makes of the *a priori* concepts which are the product of those operations, examining first the general condition or conditions under which it can bring them into play, and then the particular judgments to which it proceeds on the basis of them. It is the object of the chapter on schematism to conduct the first of these examinations. As often happens with Kant, there is more in this seemingly pedantic set-up than immediately meets the eye. It may nonetheless be objected to on the ground that the various intellectual activities to which Kant is giving attention cannot be kept separate in this tidy-minded manner (it is by no means obvious that Kant manages to keep them separate himself), or again that it involves assumptions (about the higher cognitive faculties, for instance) which non-Kantian philosophers might be reluctant to grant. I shall therefore attempt to sketch the background of Kant's problem without formal reference to his own way of posing it.

The purpose of the opening sections of the Analytic of Concepts was to introduce us to the notion of a category; that of the later sections was to explain how such concepts function in thinking and to show that they are indispensable if we are to have objective knowledge. A category is a pure or non-empirical concept, by which is meant initially one supposed to derive from the nature of the understanding rather than to originate in reflection on the content of experience. It is perhaps necessary to remind ourselves that Kant, in contrast to Hume and the British empiricists, was disposed from the first to accept the existence of non-empirical concepts; despite his antipathy to the doctrine of innate ideas if taken literally, he might be said to continue the tradition of Descartes and Leibniz in this respect. But unlike earlier philosophers of a rationalist persuasion, he was under no illusions about the difficulty of accepting concepts of this nature. Holding firmly that the human intellect is a discursive rather than an intuitive instrument, he could not pretend that they were come by as the result of some special act of intellectual insight. They could not in consequence be material concepts of any kind. If we were to find an origin for concepts of this kind we must look to those activities of the intellect which it carried on without regard to the nature of the subject-matter with which it was dealing—the formal activities which are analysed by logicians. And if we were to find a use for them we must distinguish sharply between the functions they performed and those of empirical concepts, showing that they have to do not, as have the latter, with the matter of experience, but with its form.

These points are expounded, with greater or less clarity, in the Transcendental Deduction and preceding sections. We might sometimes wish not only that Kant had expressed himself in a less cryptic way, but even that he had put more emphasis on certain crucial distinctions. There is no possibility of appreciating the subtlety and force of his account of the "pure understanding" unless we recognise that categories

are altogether different in nature and function from empirical
concepts, or again that those principles which are said to be
based on the categories are of a widely different logical status
from empirical statements, even when these are of a high
degree of generality. Kant himself confuses the issue when
he speaks of the categories as giving rise to the highest of all
the laws of nature: as if *a priori* and *a posteriori* laws of
nature could be set side by side and differ only by the accident of origin. To make synthetic *a priori* and synthetic *a
posteriori* judgments species of a genus, and even to call the
former "judgments," were dangerous steps, which opened the
way to all sorts of misunderstandings, and may even have
misled Kant himself in his later years. But however that may
be, it could scarcely be said that his general attitude to the
possibility of *a priori* knowledge was uncritical. On the contrary, he was alive from the first to the suggestion that, even
if there were any pure concepts, they might well be without
"sense or significance." It was to deal with this problem of
the meaning and reference of *a priori* ideas, left conspicuously
vague in the inaugural *Dissertation*, that the doctrine of
schematism was devised. Kant's philosophical genius is nowhere more clearly shown than in his seizing on this crucial
subject, which, as M. Daval and others have argued, may well
be considered the central problem of the whole *Critique*.

Kant himself, as I have just indicated, tends to formulate
his problem as being that of how we can ensure that categories have "sense and significance." But this phrase, as anyone
familiar with recent discussions of meaning by analytic philosophers will readily appreciate, is ambiguous. In one sense
of the term, we can show that a category has significance if
we can find a way of framing intelligible sentences in which
the term or terms corresponding to it are used. Kant himself
admits throughout his discussion that categories have what
he calls "logical significance" (e. g. B 186=A 147). I take
him to mean by this that we can not only say such things as
that a monad is a spiritual substance, but could further, if
pressed, substitute for this sentence others which would claim
to explicate it, for example by saying that it is a self-subsistent
entity of an immaterial nature. That *a priori* concepts have
"sense and significance" in this minimal sense can be shown

in the simplest manner by pointing to the works of those metaphysical writers who have tried to use them: despite what positivists have said about metaphysicians talking nonsense, their books are not nonsense in the literal sense. There are rules for the use of even the most unpromising looking metaphysical term. But to establish this much is not in itself enough to vindicate the respectability of metaphysics, for the possibility remains that while metaphysical statements are meaningful in one sense of the term, they are not meaningful in another. To put the matter in Kant's terminology, though their key concepts have "logical significance" they may nevertheless lack "real significance"; or to put it in terms of the well-known distinction of Frege's, it may be that their words have meaning but lack reference. It may be that, for all their argument, they do not succeed in saying anything *about* anything. It is this possibility, as Professor Körner has argued in his recent work on Kant, that Kant has primarily in mind in the Schematism chapter. His aim is to show that categories, despite their non-empirical origin and remoteness from sense, can nevertheless be shown to have a sort of empirical reference and therefore to be capable of genuine application.

At this point it is necessary to introduce the complication of an apparent discrepancy in Kant's central arguments about schematism. Everything said so far suggests that the problem of schematism is one which arises only in the case of *a priori* concepts. This is the line taken at the beginning of the chapter on the subject in the *Critique,* where what is insisted on is the heterogeneity not of concepts and intuitions, but of pure concepts and intuitions, and followed in other passages in Kant's works where schematism is briefly referred to. Thus in the *Critique of Judgment* (§ 59) we read that to exhibit the reality of concepts "intuitions are always required. In the case of empirical concepts the intuitions in question are called examples, in that of pure concepts of the understanding they are called schemata." This suggests that there need be no question of schematising empirical concepts, since to show that these have genuine reference we need only point to the cases to which they apply. But elsewhere in the chapter on Schematism (B 180=A 141) Kant speaks as if empirical and mathematical concepts have schemata as well as pure intellectual concepts. Indeed, his definition of "schema" seems to apply only to concepts of the first two kinds, for when he says (B 179=A 140) "this representation of a universal procedure of the imagination in providing an image for a concept, I entitle the schema of this concept," he cannot be speaking of categories, since, as he says a little later (B 181=A 142), "the schema of a pure concept of understanding cannot be brought into any image whatsoever."

The explanation of this discrepancy is, I suggest, as follows. Kant begins with his own peculiar problem of whether real significance can be attached to the categories, and this is naturally uppermost in his mind whenever he considers the question of meaning. He rightly sees that there is a fundamental difference between categories and empirical concepts in this respect since, in the case of simple empirical concepts at any rate, you can point to the features of things or situations to which they refer, whereas you can do no such thing with concepts like "cause," "possibility" or "substance." He ought, no doubt, to have noticed that the matter is not quite so easy in the case of complex empirical concepts, in particular the highly abstract concepts used in advanced sciences, which involve special problems of interpretation; but his failure to do so does not affect his main point. What made him turn his back on his initial dichotomy was not reflection on this type of case, but rather a fresh concern with the whole question of what it is to possess or attach significance to a concept. Thinking about the matter further he saw that it will not really do to claim that a man is master of an idea when he can give an example of what it applies to; at the least he must be able to produce a series of examples covering the *range* of cases to which it applies. Kant himself expresses this, in a way which recalls the classical controversy on abstract ideas, by distinguishing schemata from images; to use a word with meaning it is not enough to have in mind what it applies to, in the sense of actually visualising something: we must be able to imagine the sorts of situation to which it applies, which means having the ability to produce a series of images. Having this ability is what Kant means by possessing the schema of the concept in question, and it is obvious that what he says here applies to concepts generally. Nor is this point affected if it is insisted, with Wittgenstein, that there are other ways of showing that you know what you are talking about than by visualising something, for example by producing a drawing or model of what you have in mind, for here again it is a question of producing not one model but a series. Whether or not these reflections assist Kant to make his main point in the Schematism chapter, it could scarcely be denied that they are of interest for their own sake.

Perhaps I might try to elucidate this point further by connecting it with another. Some of the difficulty of what Kant says in detail about schemata arises from his apparent tendency to think of a schema in two quite distinct ways. Sometimes, as at the beginning of his discussion, he speaks as if a schema were a feature of things which could be pointed to; it is this point of view which is to the fore in the not very satisfactory remarks about "mediation," where the schema serves as a "third thing" linking categories with appearances. But elsewhere a different attitude is taken up, in the passages where Kant speaks as if schematism were a procedure and, for example, describes the schema of a triangle as "a rule of synthesis of the imagination, in respect of pure figures in space" (B 180=A 141). The two points of view can perhaps be contrasted as static and dynamic. Now when Kant takes up the static point of view he sees no problem of schematism except in the case of categorial concepts (or *a priori* concepts generally), for here he has eyes only for the heterogeneity of these concepts and the material they are alleged to apply to. Empirical concepts, he boldly declares, are homogeneous with the cases which fall under them (as we have noticed, he might have had difficulty in defending this assertion in detail); it is only over pure concepts that a special problem arises. But when he transfers to the dynamic point of view he sees that the question of schematisation arises in a certain sense for all the types he has considered. In all such cases the question can be asked: what does a man have to do in order to show that he has grasped a certain idea and can make use of it? And in all the cases the answer will include the statement that he must be able to indicate the kind of situation to which the idea in question applies, which means that, in a broad sense of the words, he must be capable of a certain kind of imaginative activity.

It should not be difficult now to see that the problem of schematism is, despite the extraordinary terms in which he discussed it, by no means peculiar to Kant. In particular, it is not foreign to the thought of the empiricists. That this is true of what might be called the broader aspects of schematism would probably be allowed without dispute, but I think myself that it is also true of schematism as it applies only to *a priori* concepts. Kant's question "Can that concept be schematised?" corresponds closely to Hume's question "From what impression was that idea derived?"; or perhaps it would be more correct to describe it as a more subtle version of Hume's question. It is more subtle because Kant is not prepared, as Hume apparently is, to dismiss an idea as meaningless just because the person who seeks to make use of it cannot point straight off to some feature of the world to which it corresponds; he sees that the problem of meaning is more complicated than that. A deeper appreciation than Hume showed of the fact that not all concepts are of a single logical type no doubt contributed to this result: despite everything said above, Kant knew very well that categories and empirical concepts are widely different. Perhaps too the underlying sympathy with rationalism which Kant felt made him more patient with rationalist claims and so disposed him to think that *a priori* concepts have a function in knowledge despite their remoteness from sense. But when all differences are allowed for, the fact remains that Kant and the classical empiricists were in fundamental agreement over this matter. Both hold that an *a priori* concept which cannot, as it were, establish any empirical connections is a fraud, a mere *Gedankending* or *conceptus ratiocinans* to use Kant's own technical terms (cf. e. g. B 368=A 311, B 697=A 669). And the purpose of the Schematism chapter was to show that the categories at least do have satisfactory empirical connections.

My exposition and discussion of schematism have so far been couched entirely in general terms: I have tried to exhibit Kant's problem and to show its affiliations. But the Schematism chapter is of interest not merely for posing a problem, but also for its attempt to solve it, and I must now turn to a brief consideration of this aspect of the matter. Fortunately the nature and scope of this essay preclude anything like a detailed treatment, for which in any case reference can be made to the lucid and penetrating discussion in Professor Paton's commentary. What follows may even so be of use as a preliminary guide.

Let me begin by recapitulating the situation as Kant saw it. Categories are products of the pure understanding or are, in the language of the *Dissertation,* "pure intellectual concepts." I take these phrases as at once denying that experience will adequately account for these concepts and indicating an alternative view of their origin. Although only actualised on the occasion of experience, categories originate in and as it were embody operations which are native to the intellect. But since, for Kant as for the empiricists, the intellect has no intuitive powers, the only activities which are native to it are the formal activities on which it engages no matter what the subject-matter with which it is dealing. The root of the categories is thus to be found in pure logic, a science whose propositions are believed by Kant to be valid for every type of discursive consciousness, even if they are not quite true for all possible worlds.

I shall not enquire here whether this conception of a category, or even this conception of logic, can be defended, but shall proceed at once to Kant's problem and its solution. The purity of the categories, i. e. their non-empirical origin, is without doubt their distinctive feature, but equally it threatens to be their undoing. The difficulty is, in effect, one of bringing them down to earth. To put the point in terms other than Kant's own, it is being argued that knowledge has two wholly distinct components, *a priori* or linguistic and *a posteriori* or factual, and that categories belong to the former: the question which immediately arises is whether operating with the categories is anything other than playing with words. The danger can be expressed as a twofold one: the categories may turn out to be so pure that we do not succeed in saying anything by means of them, or so general in their application that we cannot use them to characterise anything in particular. Kant thinks he can guard against both possibilities by tracing a close connection between categories as they actually operate in human thinking and time, which is in his view the form of "inner sense" and therefore applies to everything we experience. The connection with time at once restricts the scope of the categories by making them specific as opposed to entirely general (logic, in Kant's view, holds for discursive consciousness generally, and discursive intellects with other forms of sensibility than our own are not unthinkable) and, in Kant's own phrase (B 186=A 146) "realises" them by giving them reference to features of concrete experience. Except under this condition they do not serve to determine any object, though Kant believes they might still be used to help make comprehensible the concept of a noumenon, so important for the purpose of his moral philosophy. It is not apparent, however, that they are sufficiently specific when all reference to time is removed to do even this.

The uncommitted reader may still find both problem and solution here artificial, and it must be admitted that they depend on the making of certain assumptions. It may be profitable to try to state briefly what these are. First, Kant is assuming that there are categories, and that an intelligible account can be given of the part these concepts play in human thinking. If challenged on these points he would presumably refer initially to the whole argument of the Analytic of Concepts, and beyond that to the existence of "pure physics" or more generally, the widespread acceptance of categorial principles like "Nothing ever happens except for a reason" and "Nothing vanishes without trace in the sense of passing clean out of existence" (on these see my article "Categories" in *Kant-Studien*, Band 45 [1953–54]). Secondly he is assuming, as already explained, that there can be nothing at the root of the categories but purely logical notions. His defence of this view would turn on the assertion that the human intelligence is a discursive and not an intuitive instrument; we can imagine him asking an opponent to show what is the source of the categories if it is not pure logic. Thirdly, he takes for granted that logic is something which does not vary with content and is in no sense empirical. This view has been questioned by modern writers like Quine and Waismann, but is still sufficiently widely accepted to be described as orthodox. So far as I know Kant makes no attempt either to support or defend it. Fourthly, Kant assumes that the proper way to get real content for the pure categories is to connect them with time, the status of which had, he thought, been sufficiently explored in the Aesthetic. As is well known, Kant himself stated, in a passage added in the second edition of the *Critique* (B 291), that to demonstrate the objective reality of the categories we need "not merely intuitions, but intuitions that are in all cases *outer intuitions*." This suggests that he may have thought at one point of recasting the Schematism argument in a fundamental way, by substituting space for time; but if he had this idea, he did not carry it out. From the point of view of those who cannot accept the arguments of the Aesthetic the change would in any case make little serious difference. And if it be said that Kant was not justified in trying to connect the categories with either time or space (or with both), it might be asked in return with what he should have connected them instead.

To say all this is, of course, still to say something highly general; to show that it is plausible to connect the categories with time is not to show how the connection is made. We are left asking what precisely Kant meant by describing schemata as "transcendental time-determinations" and how he thought his doctrine worked out in particular cases. An approach to an answer to the first of these questions might, I suggest, be made on the following lines. At the end of the Schematism chapter Kant writes: "The schema is properly only the phenomenon . . . in agreement with the category" and adds some Latin words which begin *"Numerus est quantitas phaenomenon"* (B 186=A 146). I interpret this to mean that the schema is in each case a sort of phenomenal counterpart to what is thought in the pure category, a feature of things which can at once be identified empirically and be taken to reflect the logical idea which is at pure category's root. Thus there corresponds to the logical notion of ground and consequent the schema invariable succession or, as Kant clumsily puts it, "the real upon which, whenever posited, something else always follows"; to the logical notion of that which is always a subject and never a predicate the schema permanence of the real in time ("*constans et perdurabile rerum,*" as Kant expresses it in his Latin version); to the logical notion of necessity the schema existence of an object at all times. It should be apparent from these examples that, despite Kant's tendency to distinguish sharply between schemata and concepts and to connect the former with intuition, the schema of a category is, in effect, a second concept which has the advantage over the category in its abstract form of being directly cashable in terms of sense-experiences, and can yet be plausibly thought to provide an interpretation of it. And in each case, as the examples show, the schema has to do with determining the temporal relations within which the objects of human experience stand.

I shall not attempt to work out this interpretation for all the schemata given by Kant, and indeed I cannot do so with any conviction for the categories of Quantity and Quality, where it would be generally agreed that Kant is at his most obscure. But I doubt if this deficiency is as serious as might at first sight appear. It is, after all, the principle of the schematism argument which is of philosophical interest, rather than its details which tend to reflect the author's particular preconceptions and assumptions. The central difficulty which troubles Kant is one which arises for any philosopher who is not prepared to accept a dogmatic empiricism. Granted that we have concepts such as cause and substance and necessity, how are we to find a real or empirical use for them? The most striking feature of such concepts is just that they are not immediately applicable in the way simple empirical concepts are: to put it crudely, you cannot show the meaning of substance (or even that of cause) in the way you can show the meaning of blue. That this is so should surprise no one who has followed Kant's account of the function of categories and seen that they are of a higher logical order than the everyday concepts which fall under them; but this reflection is not in itself sufficient to dissolve the problem. The fact remains that, if categories are to have a genuine use, we must be able to show how they make an empirical difference or have empirical effects or (which comes to the same thing) have an empirical cash-value. The importance of the doctrine of schematism is that it tries to do precisely this, and in a measure at least succeeds in doing it.

It should be noted that, as often, Kant pitches his claims over schematism high: he writes as if he had found not one possible way of finding an empirical employment for categories, but the one and only possible way. Each pure category, on his way of thinking, has its own particular schema, and it is assumed as obvious that it could have no other. Kant does not suggest, or even hint, that there might be anything provisional or subject to revision in the process of schematisation: if we say that the purpose of that process is to give an interpretation of concepts which are in their nature non-empirical, we must not think of such an interpretation as being precisely parallel to the interpretations which physicists offer of concepts of a high degree of abstraction. Such interpretations are, I take it, regarded as being no more than approximate: the possibility of finding a different "model," which will enable us to "picture" the concepts more effectively, is never ruled out. But there is no comparable modesty in Kant's otherwise not dissimilar account.

It may be useful in this connection to compare what Kant says about the schematisation, or quasi-schematisation, of ideas of reason with what he says about the schematisation of categories. The problem in the two cases is in essentials identical: how to make a concrete use of concepts which are by nature remote from sense. To show that such a use is possible we need, in Kant's technical terminology, to find intuitions corresponding to them. In the case of pure concepts of the understanding this can be done, since we can point to the appropriate schemata; the difficulty about ideas of reason is just that "absolutely no intuition commensurate with them can be given" (*Critique of Judgment*, § 59). To make sense of such ideas we must accordingly have recourse to an alternative procedure, in which use is made of "symbols" as opposed to schemata proper. What happens here is, roughly, that we find some empirically intuitable situation which can serve as a model by reference to which the idea can be made comprehensible. The idea of God, for example, is incapable of being schematised, but we can nevertheless make partial sense of it for certain purposes by making a father's relation-

ship to his children the symbol of God's relationship to the
world. Kant points out in an interesting way that this indirect
manner of "presenting" a concept (to use his own technical
term) is not confined to ideas in the strict sense: thus, as he
says, we apply it in a political context when we contrast a
constitutional monarchy as a living organism with a despotism as a mere machine. We do not mean to imply that a
despotism is literally a machine, but elucidate the concept
by stressing the identity of relation between a despotic ruler
and his subjects, on the one hand, and a machine operator
and the various parts of his machine on the other. Kant adds
that there are many such uses in everyday language, as when
we use words like "ground," "depend," "flow from" in a metaphorical way.

What is noteworthy in this discussion, for our present purposes, is not so much these intriguing *obiter dicta* as the sharp
contrast drawn between schema and symbol, and hence between the meaningfulness of categories and that of ideas.
Certainly Kant wishes to maintain against what he calls
"modern logicians" (i. e. Leibniz and his followers) that it is
wrong to oppose symbolic to intuitive; the symbolic and
schematic modes of representation are each species of the
intuitive genus. But the difference between them is even so
all-important. In a footnote to § 59 of the *Critique of Judgment* Kant writes: "The intuitive element in cognition must
be contrasted with the discursive, not the symbolic. The former is either schematic by demonstration, or symbolic as being a representation according to a mere analogy." The key
word here is, I think, "demonstration": where a concept can
be schematised you can point to what it stands for, where
you have to have recourse to symbolism a good deal less than
that is possible, so much less indeed that "symbolic *cognition*" is strictly speaking a misnomer. A little later, in the
passage mentioned above about certain words in common
language, Kant speaks of these as cases where "the expression does not contain the proper schema for the concept, but
only a symbol for reflection." The use of the words "the
proper schema" here plainly implies that every concept capable of schematisation can be schematised in one and only
one way. The account of symbolisation, by contrast, seems

to allow that the relationship between idea and symbol is altogether less intimate: symbolising is a relatively arbitrary process, and hence each idea can be symbolised in a variety of ways.

I have gone into these details at length to bring out the very substantial claims Kant made for his doctrine of schematism. It is true that the passage just discussed was written some time after the *Critique of Pure Reason* and makes no distinction between empirical concepts and categories; but I doubt if it contains anything of importance to which Kant would not have subscribed when he wrote his great work. Now the question might be asked whether Kant was right in thinking that the "correspondence" between category and schema was as unique as he took it to be. Granted that categories must be schematised, is it so certain that the process can be carried out in one way only? It is not immediately obvious that a system of pure concepts must get its cash value by being associated with rules for fixing the position of happenings in an objective time-order, and the difficulty does not disappear if the exclusive reference to time is dropped and space brought in as well. The familiar suspicion that Kant framed his system of categories with one eye (or indeed both eyes) on Newton readily revives at this point.

This question is clearly of crucial importance for the whole problem of metaphysical truth. Kant's case against traditional metaphysicians, to recapitulate, is that having only the pure categories on which to build they succeed neither in saying anything precise nor in saying anything about anything in particular. By contrast with this his own reformed metaphysics offers firm and unshakeable knowledge: thanks to the provision of schemata the pure concepts of the understanding get in it an undeniable empirical use. Moreover, since each pure concept has its appropriate schema, the system which emerges can be regarded as definitively true: the work of the metaphysician can be done once and for all. The problem of metaphysics is thus conclusively solved.

Now this argument can be attacked in two distinct ways. It might be said, in the first place, that Kant misrepresents traditional metaphysicians when he thinks of them as doing no more than move in a closed circle of words. Even the most abstract and scholastic system of metaphysics, on this way of thinking, has some basis in fact: every metaphysician seizes on some feature or aspect of the world which he proceeds to make central in the system he constructs. Thus notions like the notion of a monad are not, as Kant would have us suppose, nothing more than logical skeletons dressed up, but have real flesh on their bones thanks to the fact that they originate in particular experiences. And accepting them does not, as opponents of metaphysics allege, bring us news from nowhere, but enables us rather to see familiar objects and events in a new and illuminating way.

With this defence of traditional metaphysics I have myself considerable sympathy, though I think the connection between metaphysical concepts and their supposed empirical basis needs to be made far clearer than has hitherto been done. Instead of attempting to discuss it here, however, I should like to turn to the alternative criticism of Kant, which will, in fact, involve substantially the same points.

Suppose for argument's sake that we grant the truth of everything Kant says about the empty character of traditional metaphysics: this would not exempt his own reformed metaphysics from attack. Philosophers might be got to agree that, since the human mind has no intuitive powers, *a priori* concepts must at bottom be purely logical notions. But it does not follow that they will also agree that such concepts can gain significance only if they are schematised on the lines which Kant indicates. Even if they are sympathetic to the idea of schematism as such (and it is hard to see how they could not be, once Kant's formulation of the problem has been understood), they may well wonder whether alternative methods of schematising could not be come by. Admittedly, this suggestion is easier to make in the abstract than to substantiate in the concrete; to give real body to it we need to know what an alternative set of schemata would be like. Presumably, however, we could get some inkling of this, sufficient at least to make the whole suggestion less shadowy, if we considered the possibility of making sense of the categories in organic as opposed to mechanical terms. Elements in an organic complex would here take the place of elements in a temporal situation. Substance might be interpreted in terms of growth and form as opposed to what underlies mechanical change, and causality be thought of in terms of purpose and function.

If such a set of ideas could be worked out in detail, we should find ourselves with an alternative account of the pre-suppositions of experience, an alternative empirical use for the categories and thus in effect an alternative metaphysics. The difficulty is, however, that for all the fascination which the idea of conceiving of the universe in teleological terms has exercised from the time of Aristotle onwards, no one has yet succeeded in making the idea really precise. Certainly Kant himself, despite his apparent placing of mechanical and teleological principles on the same level in solving the an-tinomy of teleological judgment (*Critique of Judgment*, §§ 70–71), was never seriously tempted to embrace the over-all teleological attitude to nature whose possibility he clearly saw. In a revealing passage (*Critique of Judgment*, § 68) he explained that teleologie is normally relegated from natural science to theology because we are fundamentally unable to understand it; we have insight only into what we can produce, and while we can produce machines we cannot produce organisms by artificial means. The model in terms of which Kant sought to comprehend nature is here plain to see, but so also are the difficulties of a suggested alternative model. If neither this nor any further alternative can be given concrete form, the possibility that the categories might be connected with a different set of schemata will remain empty. And thus Kant's doctrine of schematism, if not altogether satis-factory at the theoretical level, will continue to stand on the strong empirical ground that the schemata offered do enable us to give real meaning to the categories and find for them a genuine use.

A RECONSTRUCTION OF THE ARGUMENT
OF THE SUBJECTIVE DEDUCTION

ROBERT PAUL WOLFF

The second section of the Deduction of the Pure Concepts of the Understanding in the first edition of the *Critique*, known familiarly as the Subjective Deduction, is at
once the most important, the most obscure, and the most
elaborately commented upon passage in Kant's great work.[1]
The controversial "patchwork theory" of the composition of
the *Critique*, first developed by Erich Adickes and Hans
Vaihinger, and later revised by Norman Kemp Smith, reaches
its interpretive heights in application to the barely twenty
pages of the Subjective Deduction. In that brief space, Kemp
Smith finds no fewer than four distinct passages representing
the earliest as well as the most developed stages of Kant's
thought, strung together in what he claims is a quite logically
inconsequent order. In opposition to Kemp Smith *et al.* H. J.
Paton ridicules the patchwork theory as an historical impossibility and an exegetical excess. The text, he insists, is quite
consistent and comprehensible without recourse to the incredible claim that Kant patched it together from pieces of
work dating from widely different times during the eleven
years of the composition of the *Critique*.
I have stated my views on this controversy elsewhere.[2]

Reprinted with permission of the publishers from Robert Paul
Wolff, *Kant's Theory of Mental Activity*, Harvard University Press,
Cambridge, Mass., 1963. Copyright 1963 by the President and
Fellows of Harvard College.
[1] This essay is taken from my commentary on the Analytic, *Kant's
Theory of Mental Activity*, Cambridge, Mass., 1963. The textual
evidence for the interpretation developed here can be found on pp.
134–54 of that work. I have omitted it here for reasons of space.
[2] See *Kant's Theory of Mental Activity*, pp. 78–85.

For the purposes of the present essay I offer my analysis only as a logical reconstruction of the argument contained in the text. However Kant may have actually composed the passage, he managed to include in it elements of four separate complete arguments beginning with a quite simple, even rudimentary, argument-sketch and proceeding through progressively more complex forms to a version that is sophisticated and quite subtle. By exhibiting the text in this manner, we can see what problems Kant faced in developing a deduction of the pure concepts, how he was forced to alter his theory to meet difficulties, why he abandoned the notion of the transcendental object $= X$, and what remained for him to accomplish in the later sections of the Analytic, in particular the Second Analogy of Experience.

Following the textual demarcations of Kemp Smith, but departing from his ordering and interpretation of them, I shall distinguish four stages in the development of the argument of the Subjective Deduction. At the completion of my analysis of each stage, I shall state the argument as a formal proof, so that the reader can see precisely what it is that I am attributing to Kant. The burden of my reconstruction, however, will not rest on these progressive versions of the argument; rather, my principal effort will be to analyze and clarify the notion of *synthesis,* together with the derivative notion of *synthetic unity.*

THE PREMISES OF THE ARGUMENT

In each of the versions of the argument of the Deduction the premise is the same. The starting point is the *cogito,* "I think," of Descartes. Or rather it is a revised form of the *cogito* which expresses what Kant believes to be the most general fact about any consciousness: its unity. A second and subsidiary premise concerning the contents of consciousness is implied by Kant's statements at various points. This enthymeme, which proves to be the key to the early stages of the Deduction proof, is the assertion that the representations contained in consciousness can be viewed in two ways, either as objects of awareness *simpliciter* or as *representations* of something other than themselves. Let us examine these premises in order.

The Unity of Consciousness. "It must be possible for the 'I think' to accompany all my representations; for otherwise something would be represented in me which could not be thought at all, and that is equivalent to saying that the representation would be impossible, or at least would be nothing to me" (B 131–132). In this way, Kant introduces in the revised version of the Deduction the idea of the unity of consciousness. Following Descartes, though with very different results, he adopts the "I think" as the absolutely first principle of all philosophical speculation. But Kant does not merely assert "I think." Rather he states that the "I think" can be attached to each of my mental contents. Thoughts are not like stones in a heap, or rabbits in a hat. They do not simply lie in the mind as an aggregate of unconnected contents. They are all bound up together as the thoughts of *one mind.* They are all *my thoughts,* and only mine.

The force of this statement, however, is not on the face of it obvious. "All my mental contents are my mental contents" is merely a tautology, and "an 'I think' attaches to all my mental contents" does not seem much better. What is the characteristic to which Kant is trying to call our attention? Light may be thrown on the problem if we make use of a trick first suggested by Brentano.[3] Imagine, then, that we have written a six-word sentence on two different pieces of paper. We tear up the first piece so that each scrap contains just one word. (Suppose, for example, that the sentence is "The unicorn is a mythical beast.") The other piece we leave intact. Then we line up six people on one side of the room, each with a scrap of the first piece, and opposite them we stand a seventh person, to whom we give the whole sentence written on the untorn paper. Each member of the group of six reads the word which he has been given. Jones reads "The," Brown reads "unicorn," and so on. Smith, the seventh man, reads "The unicorn is a mythical beast." Now,

[3] William James took it from Brentano, and Kemp Smith in turn quotes it from James. Cf. N. Kemp Smith, *A Commentary to Kant's 'Critique of Pure Reason'* (2d ed.; London, 1923), p. 459, note.

every word of the sentence is contained in the consciousness of some member or other of the group of six.[4] Similarly, every word of the sentence is contained in Smith's consciousness. But the two cases are absolutely different, for while in the former it is true that the separate parts of the sentence are contained in *some* consciousness, they are not contained in the *same* consciousness, and hence there is no *unity of consciousness* of them, as there is in the case of Smith. William James puts the point in the following way:

> Take a sentence of a dozen words, and take twelve men and tell to each one word. Then stand the men in a row or jam them in a bunch, and let each think of his word as intently as he will; nowhere will there be a consciousness of the whole sentence.[5]

The fact is that one consciousness of twelve words is not the same as twelve consciousnesses of one word each. Following Kant's terminology, we may characterize the difference by saying that the one consciousness of all twelve words binds them together, or conceives them as a unity. These descriptions are metaphorical, but whether or not they can be reduced to literal terms (as, in fact, will later be done), the state of affairs to which they point seems undeniable.

We can get a further insight into the unity of consciousness by showing that it is not merely a matter of association of ideas, as Hume had argued. This point is of great importance in understanding how Kant's position differs from Hume's. As we shall see, the relationship which Kant asserts to hold between the unity of consciousness and the association of the contents of consciousness is one of entailment rather than equivalence. Kant claims that if a manifold of representations are bound up in one consciousness, then it follows that they are related to one another by association. But he denies the converse: perceptions or concepts may stand in associative relations *without being part of the same consciousness.*

To say that two ideas are associated is to say that when

[4] If we can be permitted for the sake of the demonstration to ignore the difference between words and concepts.

[5] William James, *Principles of Psychology*, 2 vols. (New York, 1890), I, 160.

one of them is thought, the other is, or tends to be, thought also.[6] Thus, the idea of bread brings with it the idea of butter and pepper reminds us of salt. Somewhat more to the point, the image of the face of a friend calls to mind ideas of his stature and dress, his personal characteristics, and his past actions. Now it might be supposed that associations of this sort are what constitute the "unity of consciousness." Hume develops this view with characteristic deftness in the section of the *Treatise* entitled "Of personal identity."[7] The following lengthy extracts will put the whole theory before us:

> But setting aside some metaphysicians of this kind, I may venture to affirm of the rest of mankind, that they are nothing but a bundle or collection of different perceptions, which succeed each other with an inconceivable rapidity, and are in a perpetual flux and movement. . . . The mind is a kind of theatre, where several perceptions successively make their appearance; pass, re-pass, glide away, and mingle in an infinite variety of postures and situations. There is properly no *simplicity* in it at one time, nor *identity* in different; whatever natural propension we may have to imagine that simplicity and identity. The comparison of the theatre must not mislead us. They are the successive perceptions only, that constitute the mind. . . .
>
> What then gives us so great a propension to ascribe an identity to these successive perceptions, and to suppose ourselves possest of an invariable and uninterrupted existence thro' the whole course of our lives?[8]

After examining the matter, Hume asserts that:

> the true idea of the human mind, is to consider it as a system of different perceptions or different existences, which are link'd together by the relation of cause and

[6] Note that it won't do to add that they are thought *by the same mind*, for it is precisely this notion of one mind or one consciousness, which is supposed to be definable in terms of association.

[7] Hume does not raise directly the question of the unity, or as he would put it, the *identity* of consciousness, but rather that of the unity of personality or self. The two questions, however, would come to the same thing on both his view and Kant's.

[8] David Hume, *A Treatise of Human Nature*, ed. L. A. Selby-Bigge, pp. 252–53.

effect, and mutually produce, destroy, influence, and modify each other. Our impressions give rise to their correspondent ideas; and these ideas in their turn produce other impressions. One thought chaces another, and draws after it a third, by which it is expell'd in its turn. In this respect, I cannot compare the soul more properly to any thing than to a republic or commonwealth, in which the several members are united by the reciprocal ties of government and subordination, and give rise to other persons, who propagate the same republic in the incessant changes of its parts. And as the same individual republic may not only change its members, but also its laws and constitutions; in like manner the same person may vary his character and disposition, as well as his impressions and ideas, without losing his identity.

[*Treatise*, p. 261]

Thus, turning Plato's analogy around, Hume portrays the soul as a republic writ small. Is the image an appropriate one? Is a system of causal connections relating perceptions to one another all that we mean when we speak of the unity of the self? The answer is *no*, as can best be seen by considering cases in which the laws of association are operative, while yet we would refuse to say that the ideas are bound up in one consciousness.[9] Let us imagine two men, A and B, who exhibit the following curious relationship: every time A smells bacon frying, B, wherever he may be, finds himself thinking of eggs. If A sees a fire, B imagines heat. In short, the contents of B's mind are, as a matter of discoverable fact, causally associated with those of A's.

Such a situation would certainly raise questions about the nature of the causal relation between the minds of the two men. We might even be led to postulate some sort of psychic influence. But the one thing which we would *not* be led to suppose is that A and B were *one mind* in two bodies. Against such a suggestion is the fact that A does not think of eggs

[9] The variation in language from philosopher to philosopher makes it difficult to discuss these questions without a continual flow of terminological explanations. Thus Hume's most general word for any content of consciousness is "perception," while Locke's is "idea" and Kant's is "representation." I shall use these interchangeably, letting the context indicate the precise meaning.

when he smells bacon, and that B does not find himself thinking of bacon when the idea of eggs pops into his mind. In
short, the associated ideas are not all in the same mind. To
say this, however, is just to assert the existence of a self which
is something other than a mere aggregate of associated
thoughts and perceptions.

Kant struggled with the problem of consciousness throughout the period when he was writing and revising the first
Critique. The analysis of the unity of consciousness, though
it played an essential role in the Deduction, was never carried far enough to resolve its difficulties and obscurities. Even
the preliminary account given above is largely an inference
from statements which Kant did not fully explain. Nevertheless, Kant's realization of the complexity of consciousness
marks a major advance on the rationalist theories of Descartes
and Leibniz or the empiricist doctrine of Hume. Where they
concentrated their attention on the objects of awareness, he
sought the nature of awareness itself. Out of his analysis of
the structure of consciousness there developed the revolutionary argument of the Deduction.[10] In the end, Kant failed
to find a satisfactory theory of the self which could reconcile
the transcendental ego, the empirical ego, the moral self,
the noumenal self, and all the faculties of reason, will, judgment, imagination, understanding, feeling, and sensibility
which he attributed to them.

The Double Nature of Representations. In the terminology of the *Critique*, the generic name for all mental contents
is "representation" (*vorstellung*).[11] Categories, empirical
concepts, ideas, pure intuitions, and perceptions are all referred to in the *Critique* as *representations*. There is some
doubt as to the proper classification of feelings (*Gefühle*),
such as pleasure and pain; as Kant is not concerned with
them and considers them irrelevant to cognition, he leaves
the matter open.

[10] Cf. Kemp Smith, pp. xxxix–xlv.
[11] Cf. A 320=B 376–377. The other definitions given there do not
conform to Kant's customary usage. Compare with Hume's use of
"perception" (*Treatise*, opening sentence) and Locke's use of "idea"
(*Essay*, Book I, ch. 1, § 8).

Representations, viewed in one light, are merely the contents of our consciousness, the immediate objects of awareness. But at the same time they perform the function of referring beyond themselves to the objects which they purport to represent. Needless to say, this referential function exists whether or not there really is some object to be represented. It is precisely because the concept of a unicorn purports to represent that we can call it fictitious. As Kant puts it in the Deduction, "All representations have, as representations, their object, and can themselves in turn become objects of other representations."[12]

A. S. Pringle-Pattison, commenting on Locke's use of the analogous general term "idea," gives the following lucid account of the distinction between the two functions of mental contents:

> Endless controversy has gathered round this definition ["idea" = "whatsoever is the object of the understanding when a man thinks"] and round Locke's actual use of the term 'idea.' It is important to remember, in the first place, the distinction signalized by Descartes between an idea as a mental state, a psychical occurrence, and the same idea as functioning in knowledge and conveying a certain meaning. The former he called the *esse formale seu proprium* of an idea, and in this respect all ideas stand upon the same footing. . . . The treatment of ideas so regarded belongs to psychology. But ideas not only exist as facts in the mental history of this or that individual; they have also, in the modern phrase, a 'content' or meaning; they signify something other than themselves. We regard them, in Descartes's words, 'as images, of which one represents one thing and another a different thing', and this is the important aspect of ideas

---

[12] A 108. The sentence comes from Stage I of the Deduction. Note the reference to representations becoming the "objects of other representations." The point is that in order to treat representations as mental contents, we must make judgments about them by means of other representations (which are thereby employed *as representations*). Thus, I may say of my perception of a house that it is a vivid perception, a fleeting perception, a perception similar to one previous, a perception which I had last Tuesday, etc. Representations treated as contents of consciousness are events, and so have causes, effects, etc.

for us. He calls it their *esse obiectivum seu vicarium*. So regarded, ideas are the subject-matter of epistemology or theory of knowledge, and it is in this light that Locke appears to contemplate them in the definition.[13]

Kant's concern, as we shall see, is not with one aspect of representations rather than the other, but precisely with the fact that there are these two aspects.

Perhaps it would be well to add here that the distinction between perception as an object of consciousness and perception as consciousness of an object is valid even if one adopts a phenomenalist analysis of objects as constructs of perceptions. A visual perception of a table is not, on any reasonable phenomenalist theory, a piece of the table, like a leg or drawer. As Kant makes brilliantly clear in the Second Analogy, an object viewed as a perceptual construct is a collection of judgments, not a jigsaw puzzle of little bits of immaterial matter. An understanding of this fact would have saved us from some of the sillier sorts of sense-data phenomenalism with which this century has been afflicted.

STAGE I OF THE ARGUMENT:
THE TRANSCENDENTAL OBJECT = X

At this point, I begin the stage-by-stage development of the argument of the Analytic. The final version, in the form of a proof of the causal maxim, only appears in the Second Analogy. The four preliminary versions are all inadequate or incomplete in greater or less degree. Thus the first form of the argument, given a few pages further on, is little more than a skeleton of a proof. Each succeeding restatement embodies some clarification, addition, or advance in insight which Kant has put forward in order to overcome the failings of the preceding version. The second version substitutes the categories for the overly abstract concept of the object $= x$. The third version incorporates the analysis of "synthesis," thereby making a tremendous advance over the first and sec-

[13] Locke, *An Essay Concerning Human Understanding*, abridged and ed. by A. S. Pringle-Pattison, p. 15, note by editor.

ond versions. The fourth version revises the argument to bring out its relevance to Hume.

The task which Kant sets himself in the *Critique* is to prove rigorously that we have genuine empirical knowledge, assuming as his only premise the fact of the unity of consciousness. In other words, he wants to deduce the possibility of knowledge (and its actuality as well) from the unity of consciousness.[14] This is equivalent to showing that *the possibility of empirical knowledge is a necessary condition of consciousness*. In later stages, Kant makes this more specific by proving that *the* A PRIORI *validity of the categories is a necessary condition of consciousness*. At this point, however, he is not ready to introduce the categories and demonstrate their function in *a priori* knowledge.

The problem of the first stage, then, is to discover a chain of argument which will link the unity of consciousness with the possibility of knowledge. Kant can proceed in two ways, either by deducing consequences progressively from the unity of consciousness, or by ascending regressively to this premise from the possibility of knowledge. In fact he does both, meeting in the middle with the proposition that the concept of the Transcendental Object $= x$ must have universal applicability to the contents of consciousness. This proposition, he claims, can be deduced from the mere unity of consciousness, and in turn implies the possibility of knowledge. Hence it serves to establish the connection between the two and thereby complete the proof.[15]

[14] In order to avoid excessively clumsy expressions, I have stated this in a shorthand manner. Strictly, one deduces propositions from other propositions, not facts from facts. Thus, Kant is seeking to show that the proposition "I am conscious and my consciousness has a unity" implies the proposition "It must be possible for me to acquire genuine empirical knowledge." More strictly still, the latter should perhaps state: "It must be possible for me to formulate, and assert with justification, valid propositions concerning the experienced world."

[15] The proof which Kant offers is perfectly straightforward and deductive, but in expounding it he employs a partially regressive style. In a similar manner, one might state a geometrical proof of, say, eight steps by first *ascending* from step eight to step five, and then *descending* from step one to step five. In the present instance, the universal applicability of the concept of the Transcendental Object is *proved*

Let us begin "from below" with the conclusion which we wish to reach: the existence of knowledge. What is the defining mark of knowledge that sets it off from mere subjective fancy? The answer, as Hume recognized in his analysis of causal judgments, is *necessity*. Knowledge is the assertion of a necessary connection between the subject and the predicate of a judgment. When I state, for example, that all bodies are heavy, I am not merely reporting the fact that on past occasions I have found the property of weight to be conjoined with the properties of spatial extension and impenetrability. I am asserting that there is an objective connection among these properties, such that I *must* connect them in my judgment. Now it is sometimes the case that a merely logical connection exists between the subject and predicate of a judgment, as when I say that all bodies are extended. Here the necessity derives from the meanings of the subject and predicate terms alone, for "body" is defined as "that which fills space." But "all bodies are heavy" is not such an analytic judgment. Hence there must be some other kind of necessity of connection between "body" and "weight." Kant calls such a connection a *synthetic unity* and the problem thus becomes that of synthetic judgments *a priori*.[16]

What is it that enables us to connect with necessity two

from the original premise of the unity of consciousness. It therefore becomes (like step five) a mere step in the final proof. See the statement of the proof at the end of this section.

[16] Cf. A 6 ff. Note that the terms *"a priori"* and *"a posteriori"* do not refer to types of judgments but rather to *ways of knowing* a judgment. This point is frequently misunderstood by readers of the *Critique*. The two classes which between them include all judgments are *analytic judgments* and *synthetic judgments*. It is obvious, Kant thinks, that we can know all analytic judgments *a priori,* which is to say we can assert them as necessarily and universally true. His problem is to show that we can also know certain synthetic judgments *a priori,* and indeed that this possibility is a consequence of the mere fact of consciousness. The German for "synthetic *a priori* judgments" is "synthetische Urteile a priori," which indicates this distinction in meaning by placing the "a priori" after the noun. Kant never writes "synthetische *a priori* Urteile." Grammatically, "analytic" and "synthetic" are adjectives which modify the noun "judgment," while *"a priori"* and *"a posteriori"* are adverbs which modify the verb "know" and its cognates.

concepts which have no analytical unity? (At this point, remember, Kant is not arguing, but merely expounding regressively.) Consider for example the various perceptions I have of the desk in front of me. What binds these representations to one another and distinguishes them from any arbitrary selection of representations which I might make? What is the difference between asserting that this extended body is metallic, and saying (merely as a figment of my fancy) that it is made of stone? Kant, be it noted, is searching for the general characteristic which distinguishes any cognitively valid judgment from an arbitrary juxtaposition of representations. He is not concerned with the rules or actual evidence by which I decide that this particular desk is indeed metal rather than stone.

Kant agrees completely with Hume's insistence that there is nothing in the representations themselves linking them together. The sight of the top of the desk does not compel me to conclude that it feels hard; its shape does not entail its weight. (If such connections existed, the propositions asserting them would be analytic.) Speaking in the most general way, what binds these diverse representations together is simply the idea that they are all representations of the *same object*. The shape and solidity of the desk do not go together by virtue of some direct identity or similarity between them; they are the shape and solidity of *the* desk, and hence we can join them in the judgment, "the rectangular desk is solid." This is what we mean when we say that the judgment is true, and not just an idle fancy. As Kant says:

> The object is viewed as that which prevents our modes of knowledge from being haphazard or arbitrary, and which determines them *a priori* in some definite fashion. For in so far as they are to relate to an object, they must necessarily agree with one another, that is, must possess that unity which constitutes the concept of an object.
> [A 104–105]

If we reflect on this notion of an *object of representations*, we realize that it signifies something independent of our knowledge, standing over against the mind and serving as the objective anchor of our judgments. In Kant's language, it is a "ground of unity of representations," which means a ground of synthetic unity. But, Kant argues, "it is easily seen that this object must be thought only as something in general = x, since outside our knowledge we have nothing which we could set over against this knowledge as corresponding to it" (A 104). In fact, since we can never go beyond our representations, the source of their unity must be sought in the *concept* of an object = x, and not in the object itself.

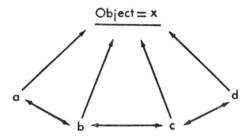

Object = x

Thus, the organizing and uniting principle of our representations in a mode of knowledge is the concept of an object = x. The diagram indicates the way in which relation to an object creates a connection among diverse representations.

This regressive exposition has established a relation between the applicability to representations of the concept of an object = x, and the possibility of valid modes of knowledge. It has shown, Kant believes, that *if* the concept of the Transcendental Object = x is applicable to all the contents of consciousness, *then* they will all be capable of being joined in valid empirical judgments. As Kant says in the last paragraph of Stage I of the Deduction:

> The pure concept of this transcendental object, which in reality throughout all our knowledge is always one and the same, is what can alone confer upon all our empirical concepts in general relation to an object, that is, objective reality. This concept cannot contain any determinate intuition, and therefore refers only to that unity which must be met with in any manifold of knowledge which stands in relation to an object.   [A 109]

We have discovered the second half of the proof by an analytic or regressive investigation. Now we shall attempt to complete it by a progressive argument, descending from the unity of consciousness to the universal applicability of the concept of an object = x. The discussion of the unity of consciousness earlier in this chapter served to demonstrate that it is more than a network of associative relationships, as Hume thought. But we have not yet explained what is meant by the term "unity of consciousness." Unity would seem to imply impossibility of separation, and yet Hume showed that any two distinguishable mental contents are capable of being separated. It does not help us much to use images like "in the mind" or "bound up in one consciousness," for they are all physical metaphors and obviously illegitimate as literal descriptions of the mind. Representations are not in the head, nor are they tied together like stalks of wheat in a sheaf.

Hume makes the point very acutely in his discussion of the concept of identity, or what Kant would call synthetic unity.

> One single object conveys the idea of unity, not that of identity. On the other hand, a multiplicity of objects can never convey this idea . . . The mind always pronounces the one not to be the other, and considers them as forming two, three, or any determinate number of objects. . . .
> Since then both number and unity are incompatible with the relation of identity, it must lie in something that is neither of them. But to tell the truth, at first sight this seems utterly impossible. Betwixt unity and number there can be no medium; no more than betwixt existence and non-existence. After one object is suppos'd to exist, we must either suppose another also to exist; in which case we have the idea of number: Or we must suppose it not to exist; in which case the first object remains at unity.
>
> [*Treatise*, p. 200]

It would seem that if we consider representations to be merely objects in consciousness, we will never find an explanation for this paradoxical synthetic unity, which in Hume's words falls "betwixt unity and number." But suppose we em-

ploy the subsidiary premise of our argument, and recall that
the contents of consciousness have a double nature: they are
representations as well as objects of consciousness. Now we
see that there is a way in which the contents of consciousness
can establish necessary relations with one another. This is
possible only if they are referred, *qua* representations, to an
object which serves as the ground of their unity. Furthermore,
since all the contents of consciousness are bound up in a
single unity, they must all be referred as representations to a
single ground of unity, which can be called the Transcendental Object = x.

Thus, the unity of consciousness is possible only if the
concept of the Transcendental Object = x is applicable to
all the contents of consciousness. And as the first part of our
analysis showed, the concept of the Transcendental Object = x is applicable to all the contents of consciousness
only if they are capable of being united in valid modes of
knowledge.[17] Combining the two, we get: "If I am conscious
and my consciousness has a unity, then it must be possible
for me to acquire valid empirical knowledge." Which is what
was to be proved.

The formal proof can be stated as follows:

FIRST VERSION OF THE DEDUCTION

To Prove: I possess valid synthetic judgments *a priori.*

Proof

1. All the contents of my consciousness are bound up in
   a unity. [Premise]
2. The contents of my consciousness have the double
   nature of representations. [Premise]
3. The only way to unify a diversity of mental contents
   is by referring them *qua* representations to an object
   as ground of their unity. [Premises 1 and 2 and analyses of unity of consciousness and concept of an object, above]
4. If all the contents of my consciousness are bound up
   in a unity, then they must all be referred *qua* repre-

---

[17] "P only if Q" is another way of saying "If P then Q."

sentations to a *single* object $= x$ as the ground of their unity [3, and analysis of object $= x$, above];

or, alternatively

5. If all the contents of my consciousness are bound up in a unity, then the concept of an object $= x$ applies to all the contents of my consciousness. [Analysis of concept of transcendental object $= x$, and 4]
6. Representations have objective reality conferred upon them, and thereby yield knowledge, by having applied to them the pure concept of an object in general $= x$ which they are thought as representing.

[Analysis of knowledge, above]

or, alternatively

7. If the concept of an object $= x$ applies to all the contents of my consciousness, then they yield knowledge in the form of judgments asserting a necessary connection among representations. [6, by conversion]
8. By 5, 7, 1, and the rules of logic, we get:
   The contents of my consciousness yield knowledge in the form of judgments asserting a necessary connection among representations.

["If P then Q, and If Q then R, and P" implies "R"]

which is to say:

I possess valid synthetic judgments *a priori*. Q.E.D.

STAGE II OF THE ARGUMENT: THE PURE CONCEPTS OF UNDERSTANDING

The first version of the argument, although it can be put in the guise of a formal proof, is quite obviously no more than a proof-sketch. It is condensed, opaque in certain key steps, and metaphorical where it should be literal. In succeeding stages of the Deduction Kant eliminates these flaws, one at a time, until finally the proof is completed in the Second Analogy.

The first difficulty which comes to view is the vagueness of Kant's statements about the relation between empirical concepts and the concept of the object $= x$. This latter is said to refer "only to the unity" of a manifold of representations. It also is described as "conferring relation to an object" on empirical concepts. But we are not told at all how this is done. Kant clearly must work out a more detailed and adequate account of the notion of objectivity, and connect it with an expanded theory of the concept of an object = x.

Furthermore, it is not at all evident how we can have *a priori* knowledge, if our concepts must either be empirical or else the vacuous concept of the transcendental object. From the former we can derive at best synthetic judgments *a posteriori*, and the latter by Kant's own insistence yields no knowledge whatsoever. Again the problem is to explain how an *a priori* but empty concept can shed an aura of necessity on content-ful but *a posteriori* empirical concepts.

More seriously still, Kant appears to be caught in the assertion that something can be the cause of itself. He claims that the unity of consciousness, and thereby consciousness itself, is possible only through the application to the given manifold of the pure concept of an object = x. But this pure concept, as it has no content itself, must work by means of empirical concepts, such as "body." Now empirical concepts are formed, according to Kant, by abstracting certain common characters from experience and putting them together into a class notion.[18] This can only be done after I am conscious, presumably. So it would appear that empirical concepts are ingredients in the very mental activity (unification of consciousness) whereby they first become possible. They both precede and depend upon consciousness.

The difficulty again stems from the inadequacy of the concept of an object = x. What Kant needs at this point is a theory of pure concepts which teaches that they (1) originate in the mind itself rather than in experience, (2) serve conjointly as the means for the synthesis or unification of the manifold of consciousness, and (3) constitute, as it were, a spelling out of the concept of an object of knowledge. Such a theory would explain the possibility of *a priori* knowledge,

---

[18] This is done through the logical employment of understanding. Cf. *Logic*, I, 1, § 3. "The empirical concept arises out of the senses through the comparison of objects of experience and contains through the understanding merely the form of universality."

for the pure concepts, like space and time, would be innate "conditions of the possibility of experience." It would also avoid the circularity of the stage I argument, for the pure concepts would precede consciousness and make it possible. They would not be abstracted from experience *a posteriori*. The pure concepts would also take the place of the overly abstract concept of an object $= x$, and hence would make it easier for Kant to explain precisely how objective reference is conferred on a manifold.

What Kant needs at this point is of course *the categories*. They serve all the purposes listed above, and in stage II of the Deduction Kant substitutes them for the concept of the transcendental object. Thereafter in the Deduction the object $= x$ is dropped from the argument and is not mentioned again.[19] The revised proof is as follows:

SECOND VERSION OF THE DEDUCTION

To Prove: I possess valid synthetic judgments *a priori*.

Proof

1. All the contents of my consciousness are bound up in a unity. [Premise]
2. The contents of my consciousness have the double nature of representations. [Premise]
3. The only way to unify a diversity of mental contents is by referring them *qua* representations to an object as ground of their unity. [Premises 1 and 2 and analyses of unity of consciousness and concept of an object, above]
4. If all the contents of my consciousness are bound up in a unity, then the concept of an object $= x$ applies *a priori* to them.
    [See steps 4–5 of First Version of Deduction]
5. The categories, or pure (i.e. *a priori*) concepts of understanding, are modes of the concept of an object $= x$. They spell out what is contained in it, and thereby serve as rules for the unification of consciousness. [Metaphysical Deduction and comments above]

[19] It is this fact which is used by Kemp Smith in dating A 104–110 as the first layer of the Deduction.

6. If all the contents of my consciousness are bound up in a unity, then the categories are *a priori* applicable to them.   [4 and 5, by substitution]
7. Representations have objective reality conferred upon them, and thereby yield knowledge, by being connected to one another with necessity by means of the concept of an object in general = x.

[See step 6, First Version]

or, alternatively

8. If the concept of an object = x is employed to synthesize all the contents of my consciousness, then they yield knowledge in the form of judgments asserting a necessary connection among representations.   [7]
9. If the categories are *a priori* applicable to the contents of my consciousness (i.e. are employed to synthesize the manifold of consciousness), then the contents of my consciousness yield knowledge in the form of judgments asserting a necessary connection among representations.   [5, 8, by substitution]
10. By 1, 6, 9, and the rules of logic:
The contents of my consciousness yield knowledge in the form of judgments asserting a necessary connection among representatives, which is to say:

I possess valid synthetic judgments *a priori*. Q.E.D.

STAGE III OF THE ARGUMENT: THE ANALYSIS OF SYNTHETIC UNITY

The substitution of the categories for the undefined concept of an object = x is an improvement in the argument of the Deduction, but it obviously leaves a good deal to be explained. No real reason has been offered for supposing that the categories are modes of objective reference. Indeed, if we set to one side the Metaphysical Deduction, we are still completely in the dark as to the identity and existence of any pure concepts of understanding. This failing in the argument is not made good anywhere in the Deduction proper. Not until the Analytic of Principles does Kant give us a genuine proof of the validity of the individual categories. We must therefore not expect more than a general reference to some pure concept or other in any of the versions of the Deduction.

More serious still is Kant's failure thus far to present a convincing analysis of the pivotal notion of *synthetic unity*. As Hume argued in the passages quoted earlier, it is an apparent contradiction to ascribe a unity (or "identity") to a diversity of impermanent mental contents. What then does it mean to say that the contents of consciousness have a synthetic unity?

Kant's first attempt at meeting this demand is his account of the role played in cognition by the concept of an object. The results of this analysis find expression in the first and second versions of the proof. But it is obvious that the matter has not been satisfactorily dealt with. The concept of an object does not literally draw representations to itself like pointed arrows; nor is an object in any literal sense a ground or base. Kant has not even told us yet *what* a pure concept is and *how* it functions.

In this next stage, Kant carries his theory a great distance forward by providing just such an analysis of synthetic unity. He does so by way of a description of the activity of synthesis. In the Metaphysical Deduction, Kant had said of synthesis that it was "a blind but indispensable function of the soul, without which we should have no knowledge whatsoever, but of which we are scarcely ever conscious" (B 103). Nevertheless, in the Subjective Deduction (A 97–104 = stage III) he analyzes in detail the several aspects of the synthesizing activity of imagination. The result is to give us our first real insight into the nature of synthetic unity.

The discussion which follows is the real heart of this interpretation of the Deduction. What I have attempted to do is to develop a complete theory of the mental activity of synthesis, basing my arguments on the suggestions in the Subjective Deduction. Out of the theory will come answers to such questions as, What is synthetic unity?, How can necessary connections be established among discrete elements of experience?; and a step will be taken toward answering Kant's recurrent question, What is an object (of knowledge)? Be-

cause the *Critique* only provides clues, but not a completely
elaborated theory of synthesis, I have been forced to employ
a certain amount of philosophical argument which can at
best be attributed to Kant by inference. Many passages support my interpretation, but I must nevertheless admit that
at times I exceed the customary limits of "reading into" a
text. My defense is that only by such a technique can one
succeed in making good sense and a reasonable argument out
of the Deduction. I shall begin the analysis of the activity
of synthesis with an examination of rules and rule-directed
activities.

Rules and Synthetic Unity. The clue to a complete understanding of synthetic unity is provided by a passage in Section 2 of the first-edition Deduction. Kant states:

> All knowledge demands a concept, though that concept
> may, indeed, be quite imperfect or obscure. *But a con-
> cept is always, as regards its form, something universal
> which serves as a rule.* The concept of body, for instance,
> as the unity of the manifold which is thought through it,
> serves as a rule in our knowledge of outer appearances.
> But it can be a rule for intuitions only in so far as it
> represents in any given appearances the necessary repro-
> duction of their manifold and thereby the synthetic
> unity in our consciousness of them.
>   [A 106, emphasis added]

The significant words for our purpose are contained in the
second sentence of the paragraph: "a concept is always, as
regards its form, something universal which serves as a rule."
Throughout the Analytic Kant speaks of rules of synthesis,
by which our intuition is generated or a manifold reproduced.

(1) *The Nature of Rule-Directed Activities.* As a first step
toward interpreting the statement that concepts have the
form of rules, let us consider some of the significant characteristics of the functioning of rules in general. An activity, of
whatever sort, may be either haphazard or else performed
according to a plan. In the latter case we can formulate a set
of prescriptions in conformity with which the activity is done.
If we compare a potter with a child slapping clay, for ex-

ample, we see that they differ not only in the products of their acts, but also in that we can state a rule which the potter follows. Roughly speaking, it might run something like this: (1) Place a large handful of clay on the wheel; (2) smooth it while slowly turning the wheel; (3) make a depression in the center of the clay with the thumbs, etc. etc. For the child no such rule would exist, though we might perfectly well give a blow-by-blow *description* of his mudpatting.

In like manner we can distinguish an aimless wanderer from a purposeful pedestrian by the latter's adherence to a walking plan or set of directions: "Go down Massachusetts Avenue, turn left on Trowbridge, etc." Here again, we can describe the itinerary of the wanderer, but cannot state a rule which he is following.

There are three characteristics of rule-grounded activities which are important for our purposes. In the first place, an activity performed according to a rule can legitimately be said to proceed correctly or incorrectly. It makes no sense to say that the child is properly or improperly slapping mud, for there is no rule or standard of mud-patting against which the action can be judged. But if the potter sprinkles sand on the turning clay, or probes it too soon with his thumb, or molds it asymetrically, we can say that he is not making the bowl *correctly*. That is, he is not following the rules of bowlmaking. Similarly, the rambler's twists and turns are all neither right and wrong, but simply right and left. Should the pedestrian turn off on Plympton Street, however, we say "He has taken the wrong turn. He has not followed the directions."

Secondly, in the case of at least some rule-directed activities, the order of the steps of the activity is not haphazard, but is determined by the rule: *first* the clay is placed on the wheel, *then* it is shaped, *then* it is baked. To paint the clay first would be to disobey the rules of pottery-making. This is not the case, notice, merely because of physical necessity, as one might say that the pedestrian cannot turn on Trowbridge before he has got there. Even in the case of interchangeable stages of a rule-directed activity, the first may occur first because the rule prescribes it so. A good example of this is a musical composition, which is distinguished from any number of other possible compositions solely by the order in which its component notes are to be played.

The third significant characteristic of a regulated action is its coherence. All the parts or stages of the activity belong together by virtue of the rule, and are set off from other activities which may be accidentally associated with it, for example by occurring at the same time. The sequence, furthermore, has a clearly defined beginning and end. Suppose, to dwell a bit longer on our simple example, that one is asked to describe the playing child. Lacking any notion of a plan or rule which the child is following, we are forced to make a random catalogue, guided perhaps by nothing more than temporal sequence: first he slaps the mud, then scratches his ear, then wiggles his toes, and finally lets out a cry. But in describing the potter's movements, a knowledgeable spectator will group together in one narrative chain all the stages in the making of a bowl, omitting whatever incidental actions may occur in the same span of time. The potter scratches his ear while making the bowl, but not as part of the bowl-making process. Thus, out of a kaleidoscope of events, certain ones are selected as forming a *single* activity by virtue of their concordance with a single rule. In like manner, a description of the pedestrian will include all the turnings of his walk, but will exclude his facial gestures, whistling, and breathing, which are not parts of the activity dictated by his sheet of directions.[20]

These three characteristics of rule-directed activities, and in particular the third of them, provide a solution to the

[20] Mrs. Ingrid Stadler has pointed out to me that one can distinguish between rules, strictly so called, and plans, techniques, standards, etc. Thus, the pedestrian in my example might better be described as following directions or following a plan than as acting according to a rule. Correspondingly, the potter is employing a technique or, in the Greek sense, practicing an art. Although this point is valid, I do not think it works against my analysis of rule-directed activities, for in the three respects which I have singled out for attention, all of these species of purposeful activities are alike. It would be a mistake, let me add, to make too much of the legalistic overtones of "rule" in Kant's statements. That metaphor leads us away from a literal explanation of "synthetic unity" and "necessary connection."

problem of synthetic unity. The paradox of a multiplicity which has unity without losing its diversity—the problem which the ancients called the one and the many—is resolved by the notion of a rule-directed activity. Its stages are several and separable, but they proceed according to a rule which serves to set them off and unify them. Thus is found, in Hume's words, "a medium betwixt unity and number" (*Treatise*, p. 201).[21]

A final point of great importance must be mentioned concerning the distinction between haphazard and rule-governed activities. Contrary to what might appear to be the implication of the examples cited above, there is in principle no activity which by the nature of its component stages either *must be*, or *cannot be*, rule-directed. The child might possibly do at random just the things laid down in the pottery manual, and the rambler might perfectly well wander along the path of the pedestrian. Equally, one might follow a rule which prescribed mud-slapping, ear-scratching and toe-wiggling, or apparently aimless wandering. This is not to suggest that an observer would be unable to distinguish rule-directed from non-rule-directed activities. In the case of the present examples, he could do so simply by asking the potter or walker. The point is that any sequence of steps could be built into a rule, or occur by sheer chance.[22]

(2) *Two types of rule-directed activities.* A distinction can now be drawn between two different types of rule-directed activities. The first sort are activities concerned

[21] There is yet some explaining to do, strictly speaking, for the notion of a rule-directed activity will at best explain the unity of a series of mental acts, not the unity of a manifold of mental contents. This extension can be completed only after we have analyzed the nature of synthesis itself. Then it will be seen that the contents of consciousness are unified by virtue of their being all reproducible in imagination according to a rule. In other words, their unity consists in the nature of their generation.

[22] The reader should by now have some glimmering of where this is all leading. The distinction between subjective association and objective causal connection, for example, will turn out to be a matter of rule-directedness. The first characteristic of rule-governed activities —that they are susceptible to criticism as correct or incorrect—will then be called upon to explain the distinctively normative feature of knowledge as opposed to mere apprehension.

with the working up of a product, as in the case of the potter
and the bowl, or with the carrying out of a planned sequence
of actions, as in the case of the pedestrian on his walk. These
we may call first-order rule-directed activities. The second
sort of rule-directed activity consists in the formulation of a
rule in accordance with which a working-up or a carrying-out
is done.

Not all such rule-determinings are themselves rule-
directed. Some of these second-order activities may themselves be performed haphazardly. A child, for example, may
select at random a set of rules and make them into a game.
Then, having convinced some friends to join him, he can play
his game—i.e. he can perform the activities enjoined by his
rules. This play will be governed by the rules, but the activity
of *choosing* the rules will have been unregulated. Some cases
of rule-determining activities, however, are themselves governed by rules. For example, suppose that a toy manufacturer
were to tell his office boy to create a new game. "Make up a
game," he says, "which will require four players, use a deck
of cards, take no more than an hour, and be playable only
with a special set put out by our firm." This second-order
rule-directed activity of game-making contrasts with the unregulated game-making of the child, analogously to the ways
in which pottery making (a first-order process) contrasts
with casual mud-slapping.

First, it would make no sense to criticize the child for
making up a bad game, for he has no standard by which to
judge. The office boy, on the other hand, can quite well be
said to have performed his task well or ill, according as he
has or has not followed his employer's stipulations. Second,
the office boy can explain why the steps of the game appear
in their assigned order (because they must accommodate
four players, or must consume less than an hour, for example). But the child has no particular reason for putting
the hop before the skip, rather than the other way round.[23]

[23] This is not to suggest that children always compose their games
haphazardly. Actually we can discern a good many rules of thumb
governing the selection of forms of play. With a little directed questioning of the sort that Socrates used with the slave boy in the *Meno*,
a child might be made to express quite a few criteria of a "good game."

Finally, the office boy has a preconceived notion of the extent and number of the steps in the rule (or game) which he is creating, while the child merely adds on steps till he grows weary, having no criterion by which to determine the unity and completeness of the game.

The Nature of Synthesis. Thus far I have discussed certain of the aspects of rule-directed activities in order to throw light on the problem of synthetic unity. We have seen that an activity performed according to a rule has a coherence and completeness which is precisely the unity of a diversity. It remains to consider directly that activity which Kant attributes to the mind, and whose guiding rule is contained in the concept of an object, namely *synthesis.* The doctrine of the Analytic would be considerably clarified by the foregoing, even if we continued to rely on the figurative descriptions of synthesis which Kant gives in the Metaphysical Deduction. With the suggestions provided by the analysis of rules, we are in a better position to understand how the mind can give unity to a manifold of perceptions by going through it, taking it up, and connecting it according to a concept which serves as a rule. Nevertheless, the theory must necessarily remain partially obscure until we can state in detail the nature of this going through and taking up, this grasping, this synthesis.

The inadequacies of such locutions as "holding together" and "connecting" are obvious, and need little comment. Perceptions do not move past the mind like parts on a conveyor belt, waiting to be picked off and fitted into a finished product. There is no workshop where a busy ego can put together the bits and snatches of sensory experience, hooking a color to a hardness, and balancing the two atop a shape. The whole picture of construction or arranging conjured up by Kant's phraseology is unsatisfactory if pressed even a little. A further difficulty, in its way more serious still, is introduced by the factor of the passage of time, for the manifold which is run through stretches out in time.[24]

[24] We touch here on some of the most complicated points in the interpretation of the *Critique.* According to certain versions of Kant's theory, the synthesizing process actually generates the temporal order, and hence cannot itself be spoken of as in time. This implication, for

Now a perception which is past lies beyond the reach even of this sort of displacement. Could we make sense of the idea of rearranging a presented visual field, we would still be unable to explain how the mind takes a color from last week, and groups it with a shape from yesterday and another perspectival view of just a moment ago. If Kant is to be understood as employing anything other than complex and untranslatable figures of speech, some way must be found to restate his theory which avoids these difficulties.

A first possibility, which Kant uses frequently in the *Critique,* is to substitute "thinks together" for "holds together" and "thinks as a unity" for "grasps as a unity." This move is naturally suggested by the two senses of the word "begreifen," but such a solution, unfortunately, leaves the problem unchanged. If there is an unreduced figurative content in "holds together," then the substitution of "thinks" merely squeezes it all into the second word. What we need here is a completely new description of synthesis which, so far as possible, remains completely literal.

The key to an understanding of synthesis lies in the mental activity which Kant calls *reproduction in imagination.* It is an observable fact about men that they are able to recall past experiences, reproducing in the present copies or memories of perceptions from some earlier time. How this is done is a mystery which Kant does not attempt to resolve, and we do not seem to be any clearer on this point today. Even if some causal explanation could be put forward involving the physiology of the brain, it is hard to see how it would make the fact of memory any less opaque.

---

example, is essential to the resolution of the Antinomy of freedom and determinism in the Dialectic. On the other hand, the description actually given of synthesis makes it a process *in time.* It might be argued, of course, that since our language permits us to speak coherently only of the phenomenal, any attempt to describe nontemporal activities is doomed to failure. However, this condemns the word "synthesis," as well as the process which it names, to complete obscurity. Since the argument of the *Critique* cannot finally be understood until its key terms are clear, it seems preferable to emphasize the passages in which Kant offers us some explanation of the nature of synthesis, even if his theory is thereby left open to attack.

As noted above, Kant's ambiguity permits several interpretations on this point. If synthesis is considered productive of time itself, then a very neat solution exists to the problem of memory. Instead of becoming entangled in the ever more constricting bonds of a solipsism of the present moment, Kant can claim that the mind is present to different moments of time precisely because it creates them. Nevertheless, a heavy price is paid for this convenient line of argument, for it deprives us of our sole insight into the nature of synthesis, namely reproduction in memory. Kant cannot have it both ways at once: either he must analyze synthesis independently, and then use it to explain the functioning of memory, or he must begin with memory as a familiar mental capacity and explain synthesis in terms of it. It was undoubtedly this dilemma which led Kant to speak so equivocally of the Subjective Deduction in the Preface to the first edition.[25]

Kant develops the notion of reproduction in imagination in Section 2 of the first-edition Deduction, A 97–104. The starting point of the synthesizing process is the given manifold of intuition, resulting from an affection of sensibility—in other words, a diversity of perceptions. This manifold of intuition, whatever its origin may be, must conform to the conditions of inner sense, and hence must have the form of time. In other words, sensibility presents a succession of representations. But this manifold cannot yet be *conceived* as a succession of representations, for to apply to it even so general a concept requires that it be thought as *a* manifold, and hence that it be unified. In short, the manifold must be synthesized before concepts can be applied to it.[26]

Now, if I kept forgetting the last representation of the manifold every time I came to a new one in the temporal order, I would not be thinking them together in one con-

[25] "The latter [i.e. the Subjective Deduction] is, as it were, the search for the cause of a given effect, and to that extent is somewhat hypothetical in character (though, as I shall show elsewhere, it is not really so) . . ." (A xvii).

[26] More accurately, synthesis is the application of concepts to the manifold. Kant tends to obscure this identity by distinguishing between imagination and understanding, or between reproduction and recognition.

sciousness. There would be merely a succession of unitary
and disjoint apprehensions, not a unity. If I look at a tree,
then forget it and look at another, then forget it also and look
at a third, and so on, I can not in any meaningful sense be
said to have seen the forest. What I must do, therefore, as I
proceed from one moment to the next, is to reproduce the
representation which has just been apprehended, carrying it
along in memory while I apprehend the next. In looking at a
forest, I must say to myself, "There is a birch; and there is an
elm, plus the birch which I remember, etc."[27] The result of
this repeated recollecting—or synthesis of reproduction in
imagination, as Kant calls it—is the apprehension in one consciousness of a variety of representations which were originally disjoint. By carrying them forward, the mind has made
it possible to think them as a unity.

But this is not yet enough. I must apprehend the succession by reproducing it, but I must also be aware that what I
have just reproduced is identical with what I apprehended
a moment ago. To put it crudely, I have to know what I'm
doing. Merely reproducing the earlier contents will not suffice (A 103). When I count a row of twelve stones, I look at
the first one and say "one." Then I look at the second, think
of the first, and say "two." In saying "two" I am aware that I
previously said "one" and I can recall that act, knowing as I
recall it that it was the *precursor* of this "two," not merely
prior to it. The process is repeated up to "twelve," at which
time I am aware of myself as having performed a series of
connected acts. If I merely found myself saying "twelve"
after a while, or if I could recall previous utterances of "one,"
etc. but didn't recognize them as the earlier stages of a
single activity whose culmination was the "twelve," then I
could not know that I had just counted twelve objects. In
general, when I apprehend a succession of representations by
reproducing them in imagination, I must become conscious
of two things: first, that the present representations exactly
resemble those which they reproduce, and second, that the
representations before my mind belong to one set or group,

[27] Needless to say, this is a rather flatfooted description. But then,
the mind works with such rapidity and deftness that any attempt to
spell out its activities must seem ponderous by comparison.

and hence are unified. The process whereby I become conscious of these two facts is called by Kant "the Synthesis of Recognition in a Concept" (A 103).

How does the mind perform this last synthesis? What is it to be aware of a group of representations (thoughts and perceptions) "as a unity"? What is the difference between calling an idea or image to mind at random and reproducing or recognizing it? The answer lies in the analysis of *rules*. The mind's activity in reproducing the successive intuitions of a manifold is not random, but regulated. It proceeds in accordance with a rule which determines the mind to act thus and in no other way. When I count the twelve stones, I do not recall any past representations which please my fancy. I am bound by the rules of counting to label the first stone "one." I must then recall that "one" while labelling the second, and I must recall it as "one," not as "three" or "fifteen." I must continue on, obeying the rules, until I have reached "twelve." I then recall the previous eleven steps, and I am aware at that point that those recollected steps were performed *in accordance with the rule*. This is what we meant when we said that the steps had to be remembered as a series of *connected* acts. They are connected by being successive stages of a single rule-directed activity. The whole process, which enables me to know that there are twelve stones, is governed by a rule—in this case, the rule of counting. To conceive of "twelve" is actually to be conscious of the rule by which the mind has reproduced the succession of representations. As Kant says, "a concept is always, as regards its form, something universal which serves as a rule" (A 106). To be exact, it is the rule for the reproduction in imagination of a manifold of intuition.

Kant is not always careful to distinguish a concept from the act of conception, but we may say with some confidence that he thinks a concept to be a rule, and conception to be the consciousness of the rule. As we have seen, a rule-directed activity has a unity which consists in its various stages conforming to the same rule. The synthetic unity of a manifold, therefore, is the characteristic possessed by a collection of mental contents by virtue of their having been reproduced by

the imagination in accordance with a single rule. The consciousness of that synthetic unity is the conception of the
rule by which it has been produced.

Thus far, the explanation of synthesis as a rule-directed
reproduction in imagination has proceeded as if the previous
analysis of rules applied literally and without distortion to it.
This is not the case, however, for in at least two extremely
important ways the mental activity of synthesis differs from
such rule-governed activities as the potter's bowl making and
pedestrian's walking described above. First of all, Kant does
not think that the mind has any choice in the sorts of rules
which it will apply to representations. The categories, which
are the second-order rules by which the mind forms its empirical concepts, are beyond a certain point inexplicable.[28]
To be sure, they can be deduced from the general characteristics of time-consciousness, but we can neither understand
why inner sense has the form of time, nor choose to synthesize the presented manifold in another way. All this contrasts with the potter and the pedestrian, who can choose to
follow many different rules, or none at all for that matter.[29]

A second difference between synthesis and the rule-directed
activities which we have examined is that the operation of
the mind is pre-conscious as well as unavoidable. The pedestrian, we may suppose, is aware of the rules he is following: he has them on a piece of paper, can recall them if
necessary, can repeat them when asked. But Kant does not
suppose that even the most self-aware among us is always
conscious of the rules by which perceptions are reproduced,
or the general types to which these rules conform. We may
at times become conscious of these rules; indeed, Kant defines a concept as the awareness of the unity of the rule by

[28] Cf. B 145–146, where Kant makes this point quite forcefully.
[29] This sort of problem frequently arises when a philosopher takes
a concept which is originally applicable to a limited, optional activity,
and extends it to a non-optional situation. Socrates' extension of
'virtue' from the virtue of sheepherding or shipbuilding to the virtue
of being a man is one example; the modern attempt to view moral
reasoning as a kind of game is another. These conceptual graftings
are productive, but one must be careful to avoid drawing conclusions
whose legitimacy is essentially dependent on a *limited* use of the
concept in question.

which the perceptions are reproduced. Nevertheless, since the activity of reproduction is what *produces* unity of consciousness and thereby makes concepts possible, awareness of the rules of synthesis must always be subsequent to the synthesizing itself.

We see reflected here a conflict which runs all through the *Critique* and which Kant never successfully resolved. On the one hand, his rationalist orientation and concern with the conditions of knowledge incline him toward an emphasis on concepts, judgments, reasoning, and the other conscious processes of cognition. On the other hand, his discovery of the problem of consciousness, and his distinction between appearance and reality, force him to assign the generative processes of the mind to a pre-conscious transcendental limbo. Kant obscures this ambiguity to a certain extent by attributing the non-conscious functions to faculties of the mind whose operations are customarily considered conscious, such as imagination. He also attempts to resolve the conflict by distinguishing synthesis itself from the bringing of synthesis to concepts (A 79). This won't do, however, for the concept is simply the rule according to which the synthesis is performed, and hence must precede, not follow, it.

The Argument of Stage III. We are now in a position to restate the argument of the Deduction, including in it the clarification of "synthetic unity" and the account of synthesis. Notice that the categories are still introduced arbitrarily, although their function is now much better understood.

THIRD VERSION OF THE DEDUCTION

To Prove: I possess valid synthetic judgments *a priori.*

Proof

1. All the contents of my consciousness are bound up in a unity. [Premise]
2. The only way to introduce synthetic unity into a manifold of contents of consciousness is by reproducing it in imagination according to a rule.
   [Analysis of synthetic unity, above]

3. The categories, taken as a whole, constitute the most
   general *a priori* rule of synthesis.
                              [Analysis of categories, above]
4. If all the contents of my consciousness are bound up
   in a unity, then they have been synthesized according
   to the categories.   [2, 3]
5. Contents of consciousness have objective reality conferred on them, and thereby yield knowledge, by being brought into necessary connection with one another *qua* representations, for necessity of connection
   is the defining mark of objectivity.
                              [Analysis of objectivity, above]
6. But synthesis according to rules confers a necessity of
   connection on a manifold.
                              [Analysis of synthesis, above]
7. If all the contents of my consciousness are synthesized according to the categories (*rules* of synthesis),
   then they yield knowledge in the form of judgments
   asserting a necessary connection among representations.   [3, 5, 6]
8. By 1, 4, 7 and the rules of logic:
   The contents of my consciousness yield knowledge in
   the form of judgments asserting a necessary connection among representations, which is to say:

   I possess valid synthetic judgments *a priori*. Q.E.D.

If this version of the argument is compared with the first
and second versions, it will be seen that the subsidiary premise concerning the double nature of representations has been
omitted. Somehow, the analysis of synthesis has at the same
time provided a means of incorporating that assumption into
the proof. This fact is actually one of the most interesting
consequences of the theory of synthesis just outlined, and
reflects the great advance which the third version marks over
its predecessors.

In explaining the notion that mental contents function as
representations, it was tacitly assumed that the object which
they represent is a separate entity. The problem therefore
arose of describing the relation between the object and its
representation. Kant at first followed Descartes and others
in adopting a general form of the copy theory of representa-

tion. The concept or perception was considered, either literally or metaphorically, to be a copy of its object. So Kant explained the synthetic unity of an assortment of mental contents by asserting that they must all, in their role as representations, represent one and the same object—their connection in the mind mirroring the connection of states or properties in the object. This is the meaning of the diagram in the discussion of stage I, above.

However, this is for Kant the beginning of his philosophical inquiry, not the end. The explanation as it stands is obviously unsatisfactory for several reasons. It is, firstly, a highly figurative account of mental operations. The relation of representing, indicated in the diagram by the arrow, is still unanalyzed. Secondly, and from Kant's viewpoint very much more importantly, the theory of representation as stated makes *a priori* knowledge of the phenomenal world seem impossible. If the object is separate from its representations, then we are again faced with the problem of *a priori* knowledge of the independently real. Instead of examining directly the relation of representing, Kant turns his attention to the nature of the object, and to the characteristic of synthetic unity which the manifold of representations seems to possess. In the course of his investigation, he comes indirectly upon a new answer to the question, What is it for a mental content to represent an object?

The first step in the solution of this problem is the recognition that it is the *concept* of the object, and not the object itself, that is the focus or ground of the unity of the representations. Somehow their relation, as mental contents, to the concept of the object confers upon them a necessary unity. Through the analysis of concepts as rules, and of synthetic unity as rule-conferred, it becomes clear that the unity of the manifold of representations is the unity of a variety which has been reproduced according to a rule.

Now we can see what has become of the relation of representing. *To say that mental content R represents object O is to say that R is one of a variety (= manifold) of mental contents which has been, or can be, reproduced in imagination according to the rule which is the concept of O.*

Some of the above may not be entirely clear, for only in the Second Analogy does Kant directly attack the problem of the relation between a phenomenal object and its representations. His solution there, although stated with almost cryptic terseness, is precisely that which I have outlined here. The following sentence, from A 197, contains the heart of his new theory:

> If we enquire what new character *relation to an object* confers upon our representations, what dignity they thereby acquire, we find that it results only in subjecting the representations to a rule, and so in necessitating us to connect them in some one specific manner . . .

This is the most advanced stage of development reached by the argument of the Deduction. Its lacunae and shortcomings are not remedied by Kant until the Second Analogy of the Analytic of Principles.

STAGE IV OF THE ARGUMENT:
KANT'S ANSWER TO HUME. A 110–114

Thus far the development of the Deduction argument has been determined entirely by what we may call the Herz considerations—that is to say, the difficulties and inadequacies of the *Dissertation* doctrine which Kant set forth in the 1772 letter to Marcus Herz. However, these form only one of the problems which Kant struggled to solve during the '70s. The second great problem was that posed by Hume's critique of *a priori* knowledge in general, and particularly by his devastating analysis of causal inference. In this passage, Kant finally introduces this long-deferred topic and takes the first steps towards a solution. As if in recognition of his debt to Hume, Kant confines the discussion to causation, even though later on he systematically broadens it to encompass all twelve categories.

Hume's attack on causal inference was designed to prove that both particular causal judgments and the causal maxim itself lack any rational justification. His argument depends on two principles: that what is distinguishable is separable, and that what is conceivable is possible. From the first principle it follows that since the impression of an object is distinguishable from the idea of its supposed cause, the two can be separated, and one imagined without the other. The second principle then allows us to infer that the object can at least possibly occur without its "cause," and hence that the two are not *necessarily* connected. So too, the concepts of event and cause are distinguishable, hence separable. But then the contrary of the proposition, "Every event has a cause," is conceivable, and so possible. Hence, the proposition itself is not a necessary one.[30] Having proved to his satisfaction that causal inferences are logically indemonstrable, Hume goes on to ask where they come from. In Kant's language, he undertakes to answer *quid facti*, having disposed of the question *quid juris*. His answer is the theory of association, according to which a constant conjunction of like objects creates a mental habit, and also generates an internal impression of necessary connection. The following paraphrase from Beattie's *Essay on Truth*, which Kant undoubtedly read, gives the skeleton of the theory quite adequately:

When we think we perceive our mind acting on matter, or one piece of matter acting upon another, we do in fact perceive only two objects or events contiguous and successive, the second of which is always found in experience to follow the first; but that we never perceive, either by external sense, or by consciousness, that power, energy, or efficacy, which connects the one event with the other. By observing that the two events do always accompany each other, the imagination acquires a habit of going readily from the first to the second, and from the second to the first; and hence we are led to conceive a

[30] There are tremendously significant differences between these two lines of argument, though Hume himself treats them as similar. To say that fire is distinguishable from heat and "event" from "cause," is to use the word "distinguish" in two rather dissimilar senses. The first leans heavily on a notion of imagination, while the second seems to involve definition and logical consistency. This confusion on Hume's part is compounded by the fact that his theory of association *only* explains particular causal inferences. He never gives in the *Treatise* an associative or other explanation of the belief in the causal maxim.

kind of necessary connection between them. But in fact there is neither necessity nor power in the objects we consider, but only in the mind that considers them; and even in the mind, this power or necessity is nothing but a determination of the fancy, acquired by habit, to pass from the idea of an object to that of its usual attendant.[31]

Kant accepts Hume's criticisms of the rationalists. In his language this amounts to saying that the causal maxim is synthetic, not analytic. He is also prepared to accept, or at least he has no desire to quarrel with, Hume's account of the psychological mechanisms of association. What he wants to prove is that the causal maxim is a necessary truth despite the fact that it is not a mere truth of logic; in short, that it is a synthetic judgment *a priori*. The materials for this proof are the arguments already developed in the earlier stages of the Deduction.

In the first three paragraphs of the passage, Kant recapitulates the theory of *a priori* conditions of experience thus far developed. While doing so, he slightly alters several points in order to prepare the way for the discussion of Hume's criticisms. The most important matter concerns the question whether perceptions could possibly enter consciousness without conforming to the categories. Earlier, in A 84–92, Kant appeared to state that it would be possible. He said there that "appearances might very well be so constituted that the understanding should not find them to be in accordance with the conditions of its unity" (A 90). Using the same example which occurs in the present passage, he went on to say that under such circumstances, the concept of cause and effect might find no application, and hence be "empty, null, and meaningless." Nevertheless, he added, making his meaning unambiguously clear, "appearances would present objects to our intuition."

Now, the very heart of the entire Deduction is the claim that perceptions must conform to the categories, and thus give knowledge of objects, in order even to be admitted to

[31] Quoted in my "Kant's Debt to Hume via Beattie," *Journal of the History of Ideas* (January–March 1960), 117–23. Cf. p. 119.

the unity of consciousness. In Kant's view, sense-datum languages and the uninterpreted given, those foundation-stones of contemporary phenomenalism, are sheer impossibilities. As I indicated in the preliminary exposition of the Deduction, Kant claims to prove that the validity of the categories is a necessary condition of consciousness itself.

It is clear, therefore, that Kant must give up the earlier position. He does so in a very finely graded series of steps stretching throughout the second and third sections of the Deduction in A. The almost wistful tenacity with which Kant clings to the notion of an unsynthesized manifold, despite its obvious incompatibility with his central argument, suggests some deep philosophical problem which has not been resolved.

The question of the possibility of an unsynthesized manifold is so important that it might be well to break the flow of the commentary here and deal with it systematically. I shall assemble a series of passages in which we can observe Kant slowly changing his mind. The end result, reached in Section 3 of the Deduction, is that no perception could ever enter consciousness save under the condition of having been synthesized according to the categories. We can distinguish five separate steps in the transition.

(1) In § 13, as we have seen, it is flatly stated that an unsynthesized manifold is possible:

> Objects may, therefore, appear to us without their being under the necessity of being related to the functions of understanding; and understanding need not, therefore, contain their *a priori* conditions. . . . For appearances can certainly be given in intuition independently of functions of the understanding. . . . Appearances might very well be so constituted that the understanding should not find them to be in accordance with the conditions of its unity. Everything might be in such confusion that, for instance, in the series of appearances nothing presented itself which might yield a rule of synthesis and so answer to the concept of cause and effect. This concept would then be altogether empty, null, and meaningless. But since intuition stands in no need what-

soever of the functions of thought, appearances would
none the less present objects to our intuition.

[A 89–91]

(2) In § 14, the first seeds of doubt are sown. Kant has
just finished saying that "understanding need not contain"
the *a priori* conditions of objects of experience. Now, however, he says that in fact understanding does contain such
conditions, in the form of the categories:

> [The categories] relate of necessity and *a priori* to objects
> of experience, for the reason that only by means of them
> can any object whatsoever of experience be thought. The
> transcendental deduction of all *a priori* concepts has thus
> a principle according to which the whole enquiry must
> be directed, namely, that they must be recognized as *a
> priori* conditions of the possibility of experience,
> whether of the intuition which is to be met with in it or
> of the thought. Concepts which yield the objective
> ground of the possibility of experience are for this very
> reason necessary.   [A 93–94]

(3) A decisive step is taken away from the initial position
in subsection 4 of Section 2, "Preliminary explanation of the
possibility of the categories," which I have called the fourth
stage of the Deduction. In paragraph 2, Kant asserts:

> Unity of synthesis according to empirical concepts would
> be altogether accidental, if these latter were not based
> on a transcendental ground of unity. Otherwise it would
> be possible for appearances to crowd in upon the soul,
> and yet to be such as would never allow of experience.
> Since connection in accordance with universal and nec-
> essary laws would be lacking, all relation of knowledge to
> objects would fall away. The appearances might, indeed,
> constitute intuition without thought [*gedankenlose Ans-
> chauung*, literally "thought-less intuition"], but not
> knowledge; and consequently would be for us as good as
> nothing.   [A 111]

We still cannot be certain whether Kant thinks that we would
be conscious of this thought-less intuition. With the tantalizing phrase, "as good as nothing," he pulls back from the flat
statement that the preceptions would not enter consciousness.

(4) Two paragraphs later, Kant returns to the subject, and again leaves the impression that we cannot be conscious of unsynthesized perceptions, without however actually saying so.

> Without such unity [of the synthesis according to the categories] . . . [no] unity of consciousness would be met with in the manifold of perceptions. These perceptions would not then belong to any experience, consequently would be without an object, merely a blind play of representations, less even than a dream.   [A 112]

(5) In the Objective Deduction in A, some ten pages after the last passage just quoted, Kant finally states in absolutely unambiguous language that we cannot be conscious of an unsynthesized manifold. Speaking of the distinction between subjective association and objective connection or affinity, Kant writes:

> Now if this unity of association had not also an objective ground which makes it impossible that appearances should be apprehended by the imagination otherwise than under the condition of a possible synthetic unity of this apprehension, it would be entirely accidental that appearances should fit into a connected whole of human knowledge. For even though we should have the power of associating perceptions, it would remain entirely undetermined and accidental whether they would themselves be associable; and should they not be associable, there might exist a multitude of perceptions, and indeed an entire sensibility, in which much empirical consciousness would arise in my mind, but in a state of separation, and without belonging to a consciousness of myself. This, however, is impossible. *For it is only because I ascribe all perceptions to one consciousness (original apperception) that I can say of all perceptions that I am conscious of them.*   [A 121–122, emphasis added]

In keeping with the principle of interpretation which I have adopted, I shall not attempt to judge whether this progression reveals a parallel alteration in Kant's thoughts or a chronology of composition. It is significant, however, that the completely unambivalent statement comes in a passage in which Kant is presenting the argument of the Deduction, for that argument will not work unless the categories are viewed as necessary conditions of any consciousness whatsoever.

In § 4, the confusion is compounded by Kant's cavalier use of his own special terms. In the second sentence of paragraph 2, for example, "experience" clearly means "empirical knowledge," as on Kant's definition (B 147) it should. But in the beginning of the first sentence of paragraph 3, it is used as a synonym for "consciousness." Since this latter sense is required for the argument, Kant may very well have intended it here. The confusion is especially unfortunate, for the Deduction turns on the argument that empirical knowledge is a necessary condition of consciousness itself (i.e. that we can deduce the possibility of empirical knowledge *from* the mere fact of consciousness). If Kant is going to use "experience" sometimes to mean empirical knowledge and sometimes to mean consciousness, his argument will take the form of the tautology that "experience is a necessary condition of experience." There are quite a few passages in the *Critique* which have an apparent air of triviality for just this reason.

Paragraph 4 introduces the example of causation. The concept of a cause is said to be "nothing but a synthesis [of that which follows in the time-series, with other appearances] *according to concepts.*" The full-scale discussion of causation in the Analogies makes it clear that Kant agrees with the so-called regularity theory of causation. In so far as appearances are concerned, regular succession is the only relation common to all instances of causal influence.

Finally, in paragraph 5, Kant prepares to answer Hume, without however mentioning him by name. The progression of thought is somewhat confusing, for Kant appears to use the very arguments which Hume had discovered and employed in his critique of the rationalists. Thus, Kant points out that "experience does indeed show that one appearance customarily follows upon another, but not that this sequence is necessary." Compare this with the following statement in the *Enquiry Concerning Human Understanding*, from which Kant drew his knowledge of Hume's philosophy: "When we look about us towards external objects . . . we are never able . . . to discover any power or necessary connexion; any qual-

ity, which binds the effect to the cause, and renders the one
an infallible consequence of the other. We only find, that
one does actually, in fact, follow the other." The two statements make the same point.

Kant goes on to assert that the empirical rule of association
—the constant conjunction of cause and effect—must itself rest
on some objective ground. In effect Kant says to Hume: You
are right to claim that necessity is not given in the succession
of appearances, but you are wrong to conclude that therefore
the only necessity is the subjective, accidental feeling of necessity produced by the habit of association. That very association is only possible because it is grounded in an objective
affinity. The perceptions of flame and heat are associated
in experience because the states which they represent are
united *in the object*. This is why we *must* conjoin them in
our judgments. What remains, then, is to explain *how* it can
be that appearances "stand and *must* stand under unchanging laws."

The most natural reaction to this paragraph is to turn
against Kant his complaint about Beattie and others, that
"they were ever taking for granted that which [Hume]
doubted, and demonstrating with zeal . . . that which he
never thought of doubting."[32] First Kant insists that necessity is not given in experience—which Hume never doubted—
and then he takes for granted that there is more to causal
necessity than a habit of association—which Hume most vigor-
ously denied. The trouble, here as elsewhere in the *Critique*,
is that Kant mixes up the regressive and progressive methods
of exposition. He is not going to show *how* appearances stand
under unchanging laws; he is going to show *that* they do and
must. And this really will be an answer to Hume, who only
professes to account for our belief, while denying that it can
be given a proof.

The proof is stated in the sixth paragraph. It follows directly from the arguments of paragraphs 1–4. Appearances,
in order to be anything for us, must enter into consciousness,
and hence be bound up in a synthetic unity with all other
appearances. This can come about only if appearances submit

[32] *Prolegomena*, tr. Beck, p. 6.

themselves to the *a priori* conditions of synthetic unity, namely, the categories. Now Kant concludes:

> The representation of a universal condition according to which a certain manifold can be posited in uniform fashion is called a *rule*, and, when it *must* be so posited, a *law*. Thus all appearances stand in thoroughgoing connection according to necessary laws, and therefore in a transcendental affinity, of which the empirical is a mere consequence.

The formal proof of the affinity of the manifold is merely a revision of the argument of stage III. It can be stated in the following manner:

FOURTH VERSION OF THE DEDUCTION

To Prove: All appearances stand in thoroughgoing connection according to necessary laws.

Proof

1. All the contents of my consciousness are bound up in a unity. [Premise]
2. The only way to introduce synthetic unity into a manifold of contents of consciousness is by reproducing it in imagination according to a rule.
   [Cf. Third Version of the Deduction]
3. The categories, taken as a whole, constitute the most general *a priori* rules of synthesis.
   [Cf. Third Version of the Deduction]
4. If all the contents of my consciousness are bound up in a unity, then they have been synthesized according to the categories.   [2, 3]
5. But, by 1, 4, and *modus ponens:*
   The manifold of contents of my consciousness must have been synthesized according to the categories,

   which is to say,
6. The manifold of contents of my consciousness must have been posited in uniform fashion according to a rule.   [5 and 3]
7. But the representation of a universal condition according to which a certain manifold *must* be posited in uniform fashion is a *law*.   [A 113]

8. Therefore, by 6 and 7,
All appearances (contents of consciousness) stand in
thoroughgoing connection according to necessary laws.
Q.E.D.

Thus Kant refutes Hume.

ANALYSIS OF STAGE IV:
HAS KANT ANSWERED HUME?

The argument of stage IV looks very much like an answer
to Hume. If we assume for the moment that its several steps
are valid, then Hume must apparently confess that his sceptical doubts have been removed for even he cannot deny the
premise of the proof, that he is conscious. However, if we
examine the proof more closely, and then go back to the arguments of the *Enquiry* and the *Treatise*, we discover that the
matter is a bit more complicated than it seems.

Hume actually casts doubt upon several distinct philosophical propositions which require separate justification. To
be sure, these propositions all refer to causal inference, and
they are related to one another quite closely, but it is still necessary to avoid confusing them. One of the propositions concerns the supposed necessity of connection between cause and
effect. Hume pointed out that when we examine pairs of
events or objects which are said to be causally connected, we
find nothing more in the objective situation than a constant
conjunction of resembling pairs. To these repeated relations
of contiguity and succession he gave the name *association*.
But obviously association by itself does not exhaust the notion
of causal connection, for frequently we refuse to assert that
repeatedly conjoined events are so related.[33] Hence we must
locate the "necessity of connexion" elsewhere—in a subjective
habit of mind induced by the constant conjunction, says
Hume.

But even if we give up the attempt to discover some *ob-*

---

[33] To cite a famous example, the noon whistle at a factory does
not cause the departure of the 12:01 train from a nearby station,
even though they may be so conjoined daily for years.

jective distinction between mere association and necessary connection, we might still be able to rely upon past associations as a clue to future ones, and thereby certify our causal inferences. To do so we must appeal to some form of the principle of the uniformity of nature, but as Hume quite quickly showed, this principle falls victim to the same criticisms which have refuted the claims for necessity of connection. In part 2 of Section IV of the *Enquiry* he writes:

> These two propositions are far from being the same, *I have found that such an object has always been attended with such an effect,* and *I foresee, that other objects, which are, in appearance, similar, will be attended with similar effects.* I shall allow, if you please, that the one proposition may justly be inferred from the other: I know, in fact, that it always is inferred. But if you insist that the inference is made by a chain of reasoning, I desire you to produce that reasoning. [*Enquiry,* p. 34]

Thus Hume can be viewed as issuing two challenges to the defenders of causal inference. Taking them in reverse order, inasmuch as the second is a weaker challenge than the first, they are: (1) to prove that the observable associations of events are invariable and universal, and hence constitute a sound basis for inferring the future from the past; and (2) to explain the difference between mere association and necessary connection, and to prove that every event has a necessary connection with some other which is its cause.

I think it is fair to say that Kant has met the first challenge with the argument of the Deduction as it is stated in the fourth version. All the representations of consciousness are there demonstrated to stand in thoroughgoing, or universal, connection according to rules, which is to say that they are bound together by universal associations.

Kant also believes that he has met the second challenge, which he describes in the Deduction as the problem of the *affinity of the manifold.* The conclusion of the proof is that "all appearances stand in thoroughgoing connection according to necessary laws." But in a curious way, Kant has actually proved too much by his argument. Every representation, it now turns out, is bound up in necessary connection with other representations, and this seems to be the only sort of connection possible. In short, Kant appears to have eliminated altogether the category of subjective association, just as Hume had attempted to eliminate the category of necessary (objective) connection.

This will not do, however. What Kant needs to be able to explain is the *distinction* between mere association and necessary connection. He must show that such a distinction exists within the bounds of experience, and that some subjective associations are backed up by, or "grounded in," objective connections. He does not want to prove that all subjective associations are so grounded, of course, for in fact some repeated associations of perceptions are merely accidental and do not reveal causal connections. Kant's problem, it should be noted, is to explain the difference between grounded and ungrounded association, *not* to give rules for telling which associations in particular are which.

Suggestions of a possible line of development have already appeared in the distinction between transcendental and empirical syntheses, which is first broached in the Subjective Deduction, and then is echoed in the penultimate paragraph of Section 2. The full working out of this new addition to theory is reserved for Section 3, the Objective Deduction. In the Second Analogy, however, we find Kant giving up the doctrine of transcendental synthesis, and proposing instead a new and more satisfactory distinction between association and objective connection.

KANT'S THEORY OF CONCEPTS*

GEORGE SCHRADER

In the earliest pages of the *Critique of Pure Reason* Kant tells us that it is not the *empirical* but the *a priori* with which he is concerned, and that his principal question is: how are synthetic *a priori* judgments possible? The discussion of Kant's epistemological theory has quite understandably focused on his theory of categories and *a priori* principles, and in the more recent literature the issue has centered on the synthetic and the analytic *a priori*. But the concentration on the *a priori* has caused us to lose sight of the fact that Kant offers us, also, a theory of empirical concepts and that it is of equal importance for his epistemology. His theory of *a priori* concepts or categories is quite explicit, and sufficiently delineated that its virtues or weaknesses can be easily assessed. Most philosophers are fairly confident that they understand what Kant's theory of *a priori* concepts involves and even more confident that it is mistaken. But I am not sure that any of us know precisely what Kant's theory of empirical concepts actually is. If this is so, it is difficult for us to be sure whether or not it is mistaken. It is difficult to know what the theory is for Kant never states it systematically in the *Critique*. He refers often enough to empirical concepts, but whatever consistent theory about them is contained in the *Critique of Pure Reason* must be formulated from scattered

Reprinted with permission of the author and of the editors from *Kant-Studien*, Band 49 (1958), Kölner Universitäts-Verlag, in which it was first published.

* This paper was read before the Harvard Philosophy Club in February 1956. I am indebted to my colleague, Rulon Wells, for discussion of various problems considered in this paper and for valuable suggestions which I have exploited.

references in the text. In the present paper I wish to make a beginning toward the formulation of this theory.

It is not uncommon for philosophers to use a common term to apply to meanings which have nothing in common save the term. I suspect that this is notably the case with the term 'truth' as it is currently employed. I am not at all sure that if we were to examine the various ways in which the term 'truth' is used that we would find anything common to all of its uses. We might very well find that there is no common genus by virtue of which all 'truths' are to be understood. Certainly there appears to be no guarantee that we should always find such a genus, form, or essence which provides the connotative meaning involved in all cases where general terms are employed. And this may obtain with respect to the term 'concept'. We might discover that as we employ the term or as Kant employed it there is nothing in common between *a priori* concepts and empirical concepts save the name. But in view of Kant's apparent belief that *a priori* and empirical concepts do have something in common, it may be useful to determine what the common element is.

As most generally defined by Kant, a concept is a rule of combination or synthesis.[1] All combination, he states, is the work of understanding.[2] It would follow from these two statements that both *a priori* and empirical concepts are rules of combination and, further, originate in the understanding. In fact we are left in no doubt at all on this point for Kant tells us frequently that this is the case.[3] There would be no

[1] "All knowledge demands a concept, though the concept may indeed, be quite imperfect or obscure. But a concept is *always*, as regards its form, something universal which serves as a rule" (*Critique of Pure Reason,* tr. Kemp Smith, A 106, my italics). All citations from this *Critique* are from the Smith edition.

[2] "Combination does not lie in objects but is an affair of the understanding alone." B 135, cf. B 154, 155, B 34=A 20, A 106.

[3] "Whereas all intuitions, as sensible, rest on affections, concepts rest on functions. By 'function' I mean the unity of the act of bringing various representations under one common representation. Concepts are based on the spontaneity of thought, sensible intuitions on the receptivity of impressions." A 68=B 93, cf. A 86=B 119. It is clear from the context that Kant means to include empirical concepts in this description. In fact, he employs the empirical concept 'body'

problem at all if it were not for other aspects of his theory which makes us wonder if he really means what he says. For one thing such a view of concepts which assigns them to the synthetic or spontaneous activity of the understanding calls into question the sharp distinction Kant has made between empirical and *a priori* concepts. If both have their origin in understanding and if both serve as rules for combining the manifold of intuition into unity, then what is the precise difference between them? We may be tempted to question whether it may not be the case either: (1) that all concepts are *a priori*, including the empirical, or (2) that all concepts are empirical, including the *a priori*. Could Kant offer the general definition of concepts as rules of combination originating in the understanding and still distinguish sharply between empirical and *a priori* concepts? In spite of an abundance of criticism of Kant's theory of the *a priori*, we may have too easily assumed that his epistemological theory was or could be consistent. Is his empiricism and his theory of intuition compatible with his theory of the *a priori?* Hegel and the idealists generally thought that it was not. They may not have proved that his theory was fundamentally wrong, but they may have demonstrated that as stated it is not consistent.

Some of Kant's interpreters have, I think, slurred over what seems to be a serious inconsistency. They treat *a priori* concepts such as quantity, quality, and substance as rules for the combination of empirical concepts, insisting quite properly that apart from such rules there would be no combination to be recognized. They accept Kant's claim that the categories are constitutive of experience. But at the same time they regard empirical concepts as *abstracted* from empirical intuition. Now it may be the case that empirical concepts are arrived at by a process of abstraction; not a few philosophers have insisted that this is the case. In his lectures on Logic Kant states quite explicitly that they are arrived at by abstraction from empirical intuition.[4] But is this not flatly in-

---

to illustrate his point. This is, I think, an admirably clear statement of Kant's view of concepts, whether empirical or *a priori*.

[4] "The empirical concept springs from the senses through comparison of the objects of experience and obtains through the under-

consistent with his contention that the understanding cannot and does not intuit? It is a virtual dogma with Kant that intellectual intuition of any sort is impossible.[5] He sought to give an account of knowledge solely in terms of empirical or sensible intuition and intellectual synthesis. If, as he argued in the case of categories, the possibility of intuiting forms requires that they be antecedently constituted by an act of understanding, the same thing would appear to hold for empirical concepts. If I can derive an empirical form which serves to unify any sensibly given manyfold by abstraction from the manifold, then I must already have effected a unity of the manifold.[6] If we are to rule out the intuition of forms or universals at one level in terms of a general principle, what entitles us to admit them at another level? Mere convenience in accounting for the contingency of empirical concepts will not justify such a procedure. If we are to reject the Platonic account of forms, we must throw out the little ones as well as the big ones. If not, then a different argument must be offered against intellectual intuition than that given by Kant.

In spite of the fact that they offer radically different theories to account for concepts, there is a considerable area of agreement between Plato and Kant. Both of them insist that cognition at any level requires forms to unify whatever content may be given. Kant could, I think, accept a major part of the argument of the *Theatetus*, without qualification. For Plato there must be a form of whiteness or the mind would not be able to apprehend it, and for Kant there must be an

standing merely the form of universality" (*Logik, Immanuel Kants Werke*, ed. Ernst Cassirer, 11 vols. [Berlin, 1912–1922], VIII, 400); "The origin of concepts with respect merely to their form, rests upon reflection and abstraction from the difference of the objects which are specified by a certain representation" (p. 401). But he qualifies this by pointing out that "no concept would be possible through abstraction alone." Abstraction merely perfects and delimits the concept (p. 403). Kant makes it clear that the form of the concept is not abstracted from sensible data. "The form of a concept, as a discursive representation, is always constructed (gemacht)" (p. 401).

[5] Cf. B 72, B 307.

[6] "This unity of intuitions always includes in itself a synthesis of the manifold given for an intuition, and so already contains the relation of the manifold to the unity of apperception." B 144n.

empirical concept of whiteness which alone enables the understanding to recognize it. For both Plato and Kant, the form serves to unify a set of data, though for Plato the form is present to and given with the data whereas for Kant the form is imposed upon the data in the process of apprehension. This is only another way of saying that for Plato the unity is intuited whereas for Kant it is constructed. If we assume that Plato's theory is consistent, which I think it is for the most part, then we have a form for every conceptually cognizable unity at whatever level of generality or concreteness. Plato offers us a rich and complex system of forms which is designed to take care of every actual and possible combination of the manifold. Now if Kant's theory constitutes a rejection of the Platonic theory of forms and if it is consistent, we would expect a reversal of the whole field of forms. If we had not read the entire *Critique* but only the criticism of the doctrine of intellective intuition, we would expect Kant to offer us a complex theory of *a priori* concepts ranging from the simplest universal to the most general and abstract idea. We would then be somewhat surprised if not astonished to find that we were given twelve *a priori* categories plus whatever concepts could result from the combination of them, and an indefinite number of empirical concepts. It would strike us that the revolution had not been nearly so radical as we had been led to expect.

Empirical concepts share at least this much in common with *a priori* concepts in Kant's theory, namely that both are forms of unity. They reflect the spontaneous and synthetic function of the understanding.[7] The chief difference between them appears to be that empirical concepts refer directly to intuitively given data whereas *a priori* concepts refer to data only by way of empirical concepts. Empirical concepts may be regarded as the first level of intellectual synthesis which effects the most elementary ordering of the sensible manifold. A *priori* concepts, on the other hand, achieve a higher order combination by providing an objective and co-

[7] ". . . All combination—be we conscious of it or not, be it a combination of the manifold of intuition, empirical or non-empirical, or of various concepts—is an act of understanding." B 130, cf. B 160 ff.

herent unity of empirical concepts.[8] Thus redness may be taken as typical of empirical concepts. It enables us to apprehend a qualitative and quantitative unity within an immediately given space time field. In the exposition of the Principles of the Understanding Kant distinguishes between the categories of quantity and quality and the relational and modal categories on the basis that the former alone refer directly to the intuitively given.[9] This distinction suggests that there is actually a logical order among the categories such that the relational categories, for example, presuppose the categories of quantity and quality. The recognition of any set of data as constituting a phenomenal object, for example, involves the combination of qualities and temporal states in conformity with the categories of substance and causality. The empirical concept 'chair' involves the combination of a variety of simple concepts and, hence, is of a higher logical order than the concepts 'hardness' or 'redness'. In as much as the category of causality is a requirement for the recognition of an empirical object it, too, seems to be of a higher logical order than the concepts of simple qualities. Kant's argument appears to be that the categories of quantity and quality are constitutive of the space-time manifold as such, while the relational categories are constitutive of objects in space and time. He has this in mind in calling the former 'mathematical categories' and the latter 'dynamical categories'. He further characterized the distinction as that between constitutive and regulative principles, indicating that he considered the categories of quantity and quality to be more basic than the relational categories. But Kant did not abide by the latter distinction, though many of his readers would evidently have been far happier if he had. He reserved it for the distinction between the categories and the principles of reason. Nonetheless, even Kant's tentative entertainment of such a dis-

---

[8] "Although we learn many laws through experience, they are only special determinations of still higher laws, and the highest of these, under which all others stand, issue *a priori* from the understanding itself." A 128, cf. A 114, *Kritik der Urteilskraft, IKW,* V, 11, 23. "*Über die Fortschritte der Metaphysik seit Leibniz und Wolff, IKW,* VIII, 253.

[9] Cf. B 200=A 161, A 180=B 223.

tinction within the field of categories is significant in its recognition that they are not all of the same logical order.

It is important to note that the categories of quality are implicit in and required for the empirical concept 'redness'. Thus we cannot distinguish between *a priori* and empirical concepts on the basis that the former are merely rules for the combination of the latter. In the case of quality and quantity, at least, the categories serve as rules for the formation of empirical concepts. But still they do not relate immediately to the data of intuition. The empirical concept 'redness' is a rule for the unification of a concrete set of sensible data. The categories of quality, on the other hand, are rules for the formation of such simple concepts.[10] The three categories of quality constitute a unity in and of themselves. Quality is not one of the twelve categories but rather a class of categories. The four types of categories are differentiated into the twelve categories and the twelve categories serve as principles for the formation of an indefinite set of empirical concepts. Above the four types of categories is the transcendental unity of apperception which represents the original epistemological unity. Kant observes that the categories can be further combined to provide us with derivative *a priori* concepts. Presumably a complete account of the formal structure of experience would provide us with a fully articulated conceptual system. A fully adequate deduction of concepts should exhibit the logical interrelationship of all concepts. It should enable us to move from the simplest empirical concepts to concepts of the highest logical order. It would be too much to expect, of course, that any theory should perform this task in complete detail. But it should at least provide us with a principle for filling in the outline to the degree that our inclination and our patience permit.

Kant remarks that this task should be comparatively easy once the general principles of transcendental logic have been established. He was obviously quite confident that he had provided us with a sufficient guide for tracing out the logical connection between the pure categories and empirical concepts. He criticizes Aristotle for not having provided a prin-

[10] A 126.

ciple for the selection and justification of categories and
claims to have provided such a principle for his own derivation.[11] It is the transcendental unity of apperception which
serves as the highest principle of judgment.[12] But just how
we move from the pure and undifferentiated unity of apperception to the four types of categorial judgment or to the
twelve specific categories is not at all clear. As a matter of
fact Kant does not actually move from the pure unity of
apperception to the categories but from the multiplicity of
categories to the pure unity of apperception. Kant does not
deduce the categories from the unity of apperception either
logically or epistemologically. He argues with considerable
force and, in my judgment, persuasiveness that the categories
presuppose such an original unity. But he does not explain
how or why the unity of apperception differentiated itself
into twelve moments. This is not in itself a criticism of Kant,
for it may indicate only that his theory is incomplete—a point
which he fully realized. Nonetheless it leaves us in the position of not knowing how seriously we are to take Kant's remark that we cannot explain why it is that there are twelve
categories, no more and no less, and precisely these twelve
categories.[13] It might be the case that the categories necessarily presuppose the unity of apperception in that they are
derivative from and expressive of it, whereas the unity of
apperception might not require just this set of categories. If
this were so, then we could justifiably argue from categories
to an original unity of apperception even though we could
not derive the categories from the original unity.

But we must be careful that we do not completely miscon-
strue Kant's whole theory of concepts. In raising the question
whether or not concepts at one level are logically derivable
from concepts at a higher level and whether pure concepts
are derivable from an original unity or identity we are in
effect hypostatizing them and treating them as if they were
analogous to Platonic forms. A similar error has caused endless confusion in the understanding of Kant's ethical theory,
Kant never intended that particular moral laws should be

11 A 67=B 92; cf. A 81=B 107.
12 A 107 ff.
13 B 146.

logically derivable from the supreme principle of morality any more than particular logical rules can be derived from the principle of identity or non-contradiction. Even an analytically true statement is not derived from the principle of identity alone. Either it merely formulates the principle itself or it illustrates it. No tautology is logically derived or deduced from the principle of identity or non-contradiction alone, though this would not be counted as an argument against the soundness or usefulness of one of the so-called 'laws of thought'. As logical principles they do not constitute the source of all propositional truths; they serve rather to inform thought as it formulates and combines propositions. If certain logical principles are necessarily implicit in all thought, their validity does not rest upon the possibility of deducing a single proposition from them. Kant's ethics has often been interpreted on the assumption that the categorical imperative was intended to serve as an axiom or a postulate in a deductive system. Hegel, who should have known better, since his own theory of logic borrows so heavily from Kant, points out that you cannot infer from the imperative whether to steal or not to steal, to lie or not to lie.[14] And his criticism is telling if the categorical imperative is a postulate. If it is not a postulate but a principle to govern ethical judgment, then it would be foolish to expect to derive moral rules from it. Kant's argument is not that we should *deduce* our maxims from the categorical imperative, but that our maxims should conform to or express the imperative.

There is, I think, a fairly close analogy between Kant's ethics and his epistemology in this respect. We should not expect to be able to deduce the categories from a higher principle, or empirical concepts from categories.[15] The categories must conform to the unity of apperception since their primary function is to effect an objective unity in experience. Empirical concepts are, I think, somewhat analogous to moral maxims. They are not derivable from the categories but must

[14] Hegel, *Phenomenology of Mind,* Reason as Testing Laws, tr. Baille, pp. 453 ff.

[15] "Special laws, as concerning those appearances which are empirically determined cannot in their specific character be *derived* from the categories. Although they are one and all subject to them." B 165.

conform to them. I say *somewhat* analogous, for maxims do not necessarily conform to the imperative, whereas, empirical concepts must conform to the categories of the understanding. They are analogous in that they are subject to though not logically deducible from a higher formal principle. In the ethics we must distinguish between the moral law, moral rules, and maxims. Moral rules are not derivable from the moral law any more than maxims are logically derivable from moral rules. Maxims presuppose rules and rules a principle of law, but it is the maxims alone which relate directly to the content of will. Kant makes a similar distinction between *a priori* and empirical concepts, regarding the former as laws and the latter as rules.[16] This distinction recognizes that both involve logical functions of judgment. When viewed in this light the principal difference between empirical concepts and categories is that categories are of a higher logical order. Both are rules of synthesis, but the categories function as normative principles for the formation of empirical rules. It seems to me that in distinguishing between rules and laws Kant has provided us with a valuable principle for distinguishing between the empirical and the *a priori*. Both are rules of procedure for empirical judgment, but the latter alone are logical rules and, thus, *a priori*.

But this does not as yet provide us with a sufficient basis for distinguishing sharply between empirical and *a priori* concepts. If there is a logical order of priority even among the *pure* concepts, why is it not possible to regard empirical concepts as *a priori* though at a lower logical level? There are, I think, two important questions to be considered here: (1) are all concepts the product of the understanding? and (2) in what sense are empirical concepts contingent? If Kant's theory is consistent, which I think it is, he must maintain that all concepts are the product of understanding. I am prepared to regard the suggestion that empirical concepts are abstracted from empirical intuition as a non-critical doctrine.[17] It can be sufficiently demonstrated, I think, that it

[16] A 127.
[17] Cf. note 4 above. Although Kant's account of the formation of empirical concepts is somewhat ambiguous, he makes it quite clear

has no place in the *Critique of Pure Reason*. Even the simplest empirical concept is, on Kant's theory, a function or rule for effecting a unity in the sensible manifold. The essential difference between empirical and *a priori* concepts in the *Critique* is not that the former are *abstracted* from intuition whereas the latter are *contributed* by understanding, but rather that the former are contingent while the latter are necessary. For Kant the contingent is the empirical and the necessary the *a priori*. Our problem, then, is to determine whether or not empirical concepts are contingent and in what sense they are contingent.

But first we should note that the distinction between the necessary and the contingent is by no means absolute for Kant. The categories of understanding are contingent in that they are valid only for experience. They are presumably derived from the forms of logical judgment which do not stand under this limitation. But the categories are different from the forms of judgment in that the categories have no meaning and no function apart from space and time.[18] The deduction of the categories consists in showing that they are formal conditions of the possibility of space and time. Apart from *possible experience* we have no justification for claiming that the categories have an application or even a meaning, since their meaning consists in their function as principles for the unification of experience. The metaphysical deduction of categories is notoriously unsatisfactory and there is, I think, fairly general agreement that it does not constitute an integral part of the argument of the *Critique*. The table of categories is not logically derivable from the table of judgments, nor does the validity of the categories depend upon such derivation. The metaphysical deduction is important not for what it proves but for the problems it suggests about

that empirical concepts depend for their form and generality upon the spontaneity of the understanding. Cf. *Logik, IKW*, VIII, 376 ff., 445.

[18] Cf. B 148, B 306: "As a matter of fact they are nothing but *forms of thought*, which contain the merely logical faculty of uniting *a priori* in one consciousness the manifold given in intuition; and apart, therefore from the only intuition that is possible to us, they have even less meaning than the pure sensible forms." In other passages Kant assigns to the Categories a more exalted status. Cf. B 149.

the relation of general and transcendental logic. Kant thought that the principles of empirical judgment must reflect higher principles of logical judgment and that the latter should be made explicit in general logic. It was a perfectly reasonable assumption on Kant's part that transcendental logic should be subordinate to a formal logic which specifies the necessary principles of thought as such. The chief difficulty with the metaphysical deduction is that, even if successful, it rests upon a logic which is itself only contingently valid and for which some sort of deduction or justification would be required. It has been suggested by some interpreters that Kant's argument actually requires that general logic be subordinated to transcendental logic. But it would be more accurate to say that Kant's transcendental exposition of judgment requires a re-examination and reinterpretation of general logic. Transcendental logic would need to be considerably expanded if it were to include the content of general or formal logic.

Whatever may be said about the metaphysical deduction, and a lot can be and has been said about it, the categories of the understanding are only contingently necessary. They are laws of thought which govern empirical judgment. As has been noted, apart from this context they have no function and no meaning. They are not laws of *pure* thought but rather laws of empirical thought. They cannot be understood by reference to the empirical manifold alone for they exhibit the demands of thought as much as the requirements of intuition. Kant calls them *pure* categories but actually they are not pure. It is only the so-called unschematized categories which are pure and they are not real categories at all but only forms of logical judgment.[19] Those rules or principles for which a deduction is provided are designed to serve a restricted purpose. If the human mind did not depend upon intuition and, further, if intuition were different than it is, the categories might not be valid at all. Even if we assume that the metaphysical deduction is sound, we cannot regard the categories as mere applications of *pure* forms of logical

[19] "The Categories, therefore, without schemata, are merely functions of the understanding for concepts; and represent no object. This [objective] meaning they acquire from sensibility, *which realizes the understanding in the very process* of restricting it." B 187, my italics.

judgment. *Something* happens to the forms of judgment when applied to space and time. They undergo a transformation. The logical relation of ground and consequent becomes that of cause and effect and although the logical form is not altogether lost, it is considerably modified. And the same thing is true of the category of substance. The importance of the change that takes place as we move from general logic is sufficiently noted by Kant himself. And it is even more marked as we turn to the other categories whose resemblance to their formal counterpart is less apparent. It appears that mind is and must be sufficiently plastic to adapt its forms to the situation with which it is confronted. It can cope with a space time manifold because it is not so rigid as to insist upon employing a set of irrelevant categories. The understanding is spontaneous and creative with a mind of its own, as it were, but it is also flexible and adaptive. It maintains its autonomy by submitting itself to the demands of intuition.

In the introduction to the *Analytic* Kant tells us that the difference between general and transcendental logic is that the former involves no reference to objects and, hence, is unlimited in its scope, while transcendental logic is restricted to a range of objects and, hence, furnishes us with formal criteria of empirical truth.[20] Transcendental logic is restricted to possible experience and, thus, to objects in space and time. He tells us further that we cannot determine the principles of transcendental logic until the understanding has actually been at work under the stimulus of intuition. The mind opens up on the occasion of experience and gradually reveals to us the principles and rules it employs.[21] It does not thereby disclose to us *pure* rules or laws of synthesis as such, but rules for the synthesis of the space time manifold. We may have reason to believe that the rules of empirical thought are but specifications of still higher rules, but the important point is that they are specifications. Thought loses whatever original purity it may have had as soon as it plunges into the midst of experience. It demonstrates not only its *creative spontaneity* but also its *prudence.* Empirical cogni-

[20] Cf. B 80=A 56 ff.
[21] Cf. A 66=B 91.

tion is a *compromise* from the start. We never encounter a *pure* given, that omnipresent fiction of contemporary epistemology, nor *pure* forms of thought. Pure thought has already compromised itself in the specification of categories. It compromises itself still further as it moves toward a more intimate contact with the sensible manifold. Empirical concepts may represent the ultimate compromise which the understanding makes with intuition. The compromise is so great that we are hard pressed to distinguish the conceptual form from the intuited content. But if Kant is correct, the form is there and the fundamental distinction between intuition and conception must be maintained.

The categories are contingent though necessary, or put less confusingly, they are contingently necessary. They are necessary as conditions for the possibility of experience and contingent in that they are valid only for possible experience. There can be no real question about the contingency of empirical concepts. They either refer directly to what is immediately given or they have no reference at all. But are they merely contingent? That is the more interesting question. We have noted already that empirical concepts illustrate categorial principles. Empirical rules stand under *a priori* rules, though both are functions of the understanding. Why then are they not *a priori*? If not derivable from experience by abstraction and if not intuited, what choice is there but to regard them as *a priori*? There is none, I think, and we are bound to regard them as *a priori* if we look upon Kant's theory of concepts as consistent.

There are two apparent difficulties which may have prevented Kant from designating them as *a priori*. In the first place, it would be a colossal task to catalogue all empirical concepts. They are tailor made and custom fitted and indefinitely large in number. But more importantly, they are so intimately related to intuition that it is next to impossible to isolate the conceptual form involved. It is perhaps the latter reason that weighed most heavily in Kant's mind in his decision to count them as empirical rather than *a priori*. The contingency of empirical concepts is more apparent and more decisive than the manifestation of any necessary rules; they can easily be counted as merely contingent. As one approaches pure intuition the necessity involved in concepts seems to shift radically. At the level of pure categories the necessity is largely dependent upon the character of mind. It is the rule which stands out and the content which hovers in the background. But at the level of empirical concepts it is the content which is prominent, pushing the rule off to one side. The necessity lies more on the side of the data than on the side of the concept. We may easily persuade ourselves that our intuition requires no rule, that it is a case of pure sensing. We are never conscious of the employment of a rule and certainly not of forming a rule for the apprehension of immediately given data. The synthetic processes of imagination whereby empirical concepts are generated lie hidden in the depths of the human soul, Kant informs us.[22] They can more accurately be termed unconscious than conscious processes. Kant's doctrine of imagination plays an important role in his epistemology and on the subjective side serves to bridge the gap between intuition and conception. In fact, understanding itself may be viewed as a function of imagination operative at the conscious level and in accordance with explicitly formulated rules and laws. But the imagination is not blind or random even at the unconscious level, for the possibility of empirical cognition depends upon the fact that imagination follows the laws of the understanding.

In the Deduction of the Categories Kant offers us an elaborate account of the processes of synthesis from apprehension to recognition in concepts. The clear suggestion is that the process of empirical cognition is a continuous and graduated one, from the most elementary and immediate level of intuition to the recognition of objects in a system of relations. In the First Edition version of the Deduction he delineates a two-fold process of synthesis, the empirical and the transcendental. These are treated as strictly parallel, though the former operates under the constraint of rules imposed by the latter. This is not a very happy way of putting the matter and Kant later revised his formulation of it. There is only one process of synthesis at any level. It is empirical in that it operates with intuited data, but *a priori* in that it is not

22 *Anthropologie, IKW,* VIII, 88, 89; cf. A 15=B 29.

blind or random. At the level of apprehension of the manifold, the imagination is more passive than spontaneous. It is predominantly receptive, but already operating in the service of the understanding. It makes minimal demands upon what it receives, but is quietly insistent even so. The passivity of imagination at this level requires that it be exceedingly plastic and flexible. It demands only that whatever is given must fit into a unitary matrix. The forms of sensibility represent the most basic operation of the imagination as it effects a unity of the manifold. It is only in the *Analytic* in terms of the exposition of the synthesis of apprehension that we are able to understand the forms of sensibility.[23] They serve as rules governing intuition and are initially implemented by the imagination. The possibility of an objective unity of experience in time and space requires that imagination has done its work and done it well. Otherwise there can be no schematization or deduction of categories. As soon as we recognize that sensible intuition itself depends upon rules of apprehension, and that the latter are governed by the categories, we see that intuition and conception are more intimately related than we had been led to believe in the *Aesthetic*. We discover further, that the intuition of the sensible manifold rests ultimately upon the transcendental unity of apperception. Intuition and conception are so intertwined that it becomes increasingly difficult to see what room for play there is between them.

Yet, Kant is insistent upon maintaining the distinction between them. They are distinguishable but not separable elements in perception. We never intuit blindly, nor is empirical thought ever completely empty. Intuition without conception would be blind *if* it were possible. But it is not possible, if we are to accept the argument of the *Analytic*. In the famous treatment of sense certainty in the *Phenomenology of Spirit* Hegel attempts to show that sensation is not what it claims to be, namely pure immediacy. And he is surely correct on Kantian grounds, though Hegel sometimes

[23] "It is one and the same spontaneity, which in the one case, under the title of imagination, and in the other case, under the title of understanding, brings combination into the manifold of intuition." B 161*n*.

appears to have drawn mistaken conclusions from this premise. The fact that conceptual rules are necessarily present to
empirical intuition does not warrant the conclusion that intuition contains no immediate or irreducible sensuous element. That thought is implicit in intuition is a Kantian
doctrine. But it is so predominately *implicit* that it may be
impossible ever to separate it from the sensuous content in
which it is imbedded.

I have spoken already of compromise which I take to be an
important factor both in Kant's ethics and his epistemology.
Kant neglects to treat it fully in his ethical writings; he
hardly mentions it, in fact. Yet, he had a remarkably good
doctrine of compromise in the *Critique of Pure Reason.* If he
had brought it into play in his treatment of the will in his
ethics, he would have been far less open to the charge of un-
relenting rigorism. It should be apparent that the will is involved in compromise from the moment that it has anything
whatever to do with maxims or inclinations. Ethical decision
and action would be altogether impossible on Kant's theory
if the will were not flexible enough to mediate between its
a priori and *a posteriori* parts. It is one of the great virtues of
Kant's epistemology that he recognizes the necessity of compromise and attempts to analyze the factors involved. As an
epistemologist Kant not only accepted the necessity of compromise but embraced it as one of the most laudable powers
of the human understanding. As a moralist he is reluctant
even to admit its necessity.

Kant has a technical and forbidding term to designate the
process of compromise in the *Critique.* He refers to it as the
schematism of categories. To schematize a category or a concept is to relate it to intuition. And the task of schematization is assigned to the imagination.[24] Kant can afford to
maintain the irreducibility of sensible intuition only because
he has this marvelous faculty of imagination which is both
receptive and spontaneous. In his ethics it is the will which,
as the faculty of desire, contributes both the material content of maxims and the law to govern maxims. As Kant puts
it, the will stands mid-way between its *a posteriori* and its

[24] B 179=A 140.

a priori parts. The counterpart of the will in the *Critique of Pure Reason* is the faculty of imagination, which Kant sometimes refers to as the understanding. The term "understanding" is employed in both a restricted and a loose sense. In the strict employment it refers to the faculty of logical rules only; in the more inclusive employment it refers to the whole faculty of empirical cognition. But whatever term is used, it is evident that Kant had in mind a faculty which is responsible for the three levels of synthesis and which, in effect, furnishes itself with its own laws. Imagination operates both heteronomously and autonomously; it is as impressionable as an adolescent girl, but has all the cunning of a Socrates. Its lawgiving reflects the modes of its passivity; its intuition reveals its spontaneity. Unlike the will, it does not supply its own content, nor are its laws constituted without regard to the content with which it operates. But it manages in ways that must remain to a considerable degree mysterious to transform the raw material of sensation into a thoroughly respectable body of empirical knowledge.

Unfortunately we shall not be able to consider more closely this very interesting feature of Kant's epistemology, for we must return more directly to the matter at hand. What the understanding requires of experience is, to put the matter crudely, that it be able to find its way around in it. It insists that it should find its own original unity reflected in the systematic relatedness of experience. The categories, the forms of intuition, and empirical concepts constitute the principal strategic devices by which this end is attained. To regard any principles or rules as *a priori* is to assert that their primary function is to serve the understanding. They must be understood intentionally and, also, dispositionally.[25] The categories represent general dispositional tendencies on the part of the understanding. Stated most generally, they represent the attempt to establish necessary connections in experience.

[25] "We shall therefore follow up the pure concepts to their first *seeds* and *dispositions* in the human understanding in which they lie prepared, till at last on the occasion of experience, they are developed, and by the same understanding are exhibited in their purity freed from the empirical conditions then attaching to them." A 66=B 91, my italics.

But necessary connection is instrumental to the achievement of a stable framework in terms of which the understanding can orient itself in the midst of confusion. The difficulty of providing a precise definition of causality in the *Critique* indicates, I think, the extent to which Kant is seeking to give expression to a dispositional property of mind. He insists upon specific categories, but if we are to understand the categories we must understand the conception of mind to which they relate. The categories are *functions* and are designed to serve an end. The function itself is necessary with respect to understanding, but it is also general. That this is the case with respect to causality is made even clearer in the *Critique of Judgment*. In the latter work Kant refuses to limit it to any fixed interpretation of causal relations.[26] Causality means necessary connection, but this requires and is capable of interpretation. It is *a priori* in that it has its origin in the understanding and serves to give expression to a fundamental dispositional property of mind.

Empirical concepts are, also, *a priori* with respect to their form. They represent the attenuation of thought, as it were, though they serve no less significantly than the categories to satisfy the requirements of the understanding. As we have noted, the formal necessity which they exhibit is almost completely overshadowed by the empirical necessity imposed by intuition. The *a priori* necessity of empirical concepts is to fit the data, to fit it closely and snugly. And they accomplish their job remarkably well, so well in fact that we hardly expect ever to find a mis-fit. We may even be seduced into believing that in this mode of its operation the imagination is *infallible*. Whether or not it is infallible, a point which seems open to debate, the infallibility does not testify to the *absence* of conceptual rules but rather to their phenomenal success. On the interpretation I am advancing, and which I feel one is forced to accept if he follows the argument of the *Critique*, the difference between empirical and *a priori* concepts must be construed as one of degree rather than of kind. Categorial rules are no more *necessary* and no more *a priori* than empirical rules. It is only that they are more general

[26] Cf. §§ 69, 71.

and more abstract. In many respects empirical rules are more certain and more determinate than the categorial rules they implement.

But this analysis of concepts seems to lead us to an unwelcome conclusion, namely that the mind has more fixed rules than Calvin's Geneva. We seem to have gotten rid of the elaborate system of Platonic forms only to supplant it by a set of rules designed to meet every contingency. Have we not overreached ourselves in treating all concepts as *a priori?* Does this not sacrifice one of the chief virtues of the Kantian epistemology, namely that it can operate with a limited set of *a priori* principles? I am sure that this is the case, which leads me to believe that our formulation, though generally sound, is not complete. That Kant was troubled by this problem is indicated by the fact that he was not always certain what to count as *a priori* and what to count as empirical. In the *Metaphysical Foundations of Natural Science* and in the *Opus Postumum* he seems to have extended the range of the *a priori* in such a way as to include concepts and judgments which in the *Critique of Pure Reason* would have been regarded as empirical. This development in Kant's thought has sometimes been attributed to his senility or to an intemperate zeal for the *a priori.* But this is, I think, a mistake. This development may be regarded as a quite legitimate and consistent elaboration of his theory of concepts and, particularly, the recognition that the line between the empirical and the *a priori* is not so sharp as he had drawn it in the *Critique.*

It may be relevant to note that in contemporary epistemology the situation has been almost reversed so far as the Kantian theory is concerned. *A priori* concepts have been increasingly regarded as contingent, whereas empirical concepts, at least those which relate directly to intuition, have been tacitly accepted as necessary. In other words, the *a priori* has become the *contingent* and the empirical the *necessary.* But the terms contingent and necessary are highly ambiguous, as we have seen. A concept is always contingent or necessary with respect to something or other. In Kant's theory it may be necessary or contingent with respect either to sensible intuition or to understanding. We would expect that the less involved the understanding is with what is sensibly given, the freer it would be with respect to the rules it employed. It cannot be unconditionally free, but its most general rules are subject only to the limitations of its own nature. Kant seems to have thought that the understanding enjoys this sort of freedom only when it operates beyond the limits of possible experience. In the latter instance it suffers no constraint, but neither does it attain knowledge of anything. The crucial necessity pertaining to categories in the *Critique* is due to the constraint imposed by intuition. They are necessary rules of thought, but only of *empirical thought*. And this qualification is all important.

If my interpretation is at all plausible, we can regard Kant's theory of concepts as consistent, though only if we are willing to reformulate it. It is necessary, in the first place, to reject the view that empirical concepts are arrived at by abstraction. They must be regarded as on a par with the categories in issuing from the understanding. They are contingent in relation to sensible content, but they exhibit necessary demands of the understanding. A *priori* concepts must also be regarded as contingent and for the same reason. The chief difference between them is the degree of generality. At the level of empirical concepts the understanding has only the slightest degree of freedom or autonomy. Its autonomy is most pronounced and most apparent at the level of ideas. Knowledge is a compromise of thought with intuition throughout experience. In its capacity to hold on to its own principles even in the most compromising situation, the understanding discloses one of its greatest powers. So far as the understanding is concerned, empirical concepts make the minimum possible demand upon what is given. Thus, any change in rules that might occur at this level would be only of trivial importance to the understanding. But as we move from empirical rules to *a priori* laws and, finally, to regulative principles, we retreat, as it were, more and more into the fortress of the understanding. We have thrown up a line of entrenchments, most of which we are prepared to sacrifice if need be. But there is a final line of defense where the last stand must be made. Kant saw this well enough, but he may have put too little value on his outposts and too great importance on the penultimate bastions. The understanding can't afford to stake everything on the categories any more than it can afford to dispose of empirical concepts wantonly.

KNOWLEDGE AND THE EGO: KANT'S THREE STAGES OF SELF-EVIDENCE

SAMUEL J. TODES

Knowledge, according to Kant, is justified belief in necessary connections of experience. These necessary connections may be demonstrable either *a priori* or *a posteriori*; they may concern, respectively, either the form or the content of our knowledge. But in either case, according to Kant, to know something, as distinct from merely feeling something, is to make a judgment containing a "ground for necessary universal validity and thereby for a relation to the object."[1] Whether or not a judgment represents necessary connections among sensations is what distinguishes objectively valid "judgments of experience" from subjectively valid "judgments of perception."[2] In this paper I shall try to show that for Kant knowledge is, in the last analysis, self-knowledge; that it is based on evidence of ourselves to ourself; that it is in this sense based on "self-evidence."

Kant writes,

. . . we cannot represent to ourselves anything as combined in the object which we have not ourselves previously combined . . . [Such combination, or synthesis, is] an act of the self-activity of the subject.[3]

And, according to Kant, *all* our knowledge consists of representing something to ourself as formally or materially synthesized in the object. Therefore according to Kant all our knowledge consists of representing to ourselves some "self-

[1] *Prolegomena*, p. 299*n.*
[2] *Ibid.* p. 298.
[3] *Critique of Pure Reason*, B 130. ". . . ein Aktus seiner Selbsttätigkeit . . ."

activity" of our own. Kant thus regards the intelligibility of everything as a function of the intelligibility of our own self-activity. He regards our self-activity, however, as perfectly intelligible, for he takes it as axiomatic that,

> What reason produces entirely out of itself cannot be concealed, but is brought to light by reason itself immediately the common principle has been discovered.
> [A xx]

By "reason" here, Kant means our self-activity as thinking subjects in general, whether occupied with logical, mathematical, or empirical thought. For he holds in the same vein,

> That logic should have been thus successful is an advantage which it owes to its limitations . . . leaving the understanding nothing to deal with save itself and its form. [B ix]

Likewise, writing of the mathematician,

> If he is to know anything with *a priori* certainty he must not ascribe to the figure anything save what necessarily follows from what he has himself set into it in accordance with his concept. [B xii]

And similarly, writing of classic scientific experiments such as Galileo's and Torricelli's,

> . . . reason has insight only into that which it produces after a plan of its own . . . constraining nature to give answer to questions of reason's own determining.
> [B xiii]

All our knowledge, according to Kant, is a product of our self-activity as thinking subjects spontaneously responding to received sensations. This self-activity takes the form of synthesizing representations (for which sensations provide the ultimate filling); it takes the form of unifying them in accordance with synthetic (non-analytic) rules. The product of this synthesis is what Kant means by "experience." According to him our minds are such that for us only "experience" in this sense is intelligible. What we can know is limited by the range of our possible experience. "Things-in-themselves," that is, things considered independently of all successively received, fragmentary appearances which affect us and of which we make sense by spontaneous synthesis, are in principle unknowable by us. And that factor in experience which makes it knowable by us is our own rational self-activity which goes into it. Experience is intelligible to us because we know what we think merely by thinking it, and experience is in part what we think.

But though Kant holds that our self-*activity* as thinker is perfectly intelligible to us, he denies that our thinking *self* is intelligible to us. We know *that* we exist as a thinking subject because we are aware of the spontaneity (the self-activity) of our thought. But we do not know *what* we are as a thinking subject. We have no intuition into the source of our thoughtful activity. We know ourself as think*ing*, but not as think*er*. What then do we know ourself to be thinking? According to Kant, we do not think ourself, as, for example, Aristotle says the Prime Mover does, and as Kant supposes God does. We are not capable of rational intuition. No explanation of this incapacity is possible; it is simply so, a kind of *a priori* fact. We rather think *about* our passive self. As a passive consciousness we have an "inner sense," a time field in which we receive sensation. We are aware of ourself as spontaneous thinker by being aware of how we apply our active intelligence to the problem of making sense out of the contents of our own field of passive sensibility. By succeeding in this attempt, we come to know both the objects by which we have been externally affected and ourself as the passive creature who has been affected by these objects in his characteristic temporal way. Kant thus holds that "we intuit ourselves only as we are inwardly affected *by ourselves*" (B 156, Kant's emphasis). And that "time . . . is the mode of representation of myself as object" (B 52). A condensed, if rather cryptic, summation of his view is given as follows:

> Since I do not have another self-intuition which gives the *determining* in me . . . prior to the act of *determination,* as time does in the case of the determinable, I cannot determine my existence as that of a self-active being . . . (but only) as that of an appearance.
>   [B 158*n*, Kant's italics]

We are considering Kant's view of the sense we have of ourself, of our own ego. We have seen that for Kant our logically initial sense of ourself is in the form more of a question than of an answer. As passive sensibility we are incapable of knowledge; we undergo sensation without understanding it. Kant does not speak this way, but it seems consonant with his account to add that as passive sensibility we are utterly at a loss, aware only of *ignorance*.

We have an additional sense of ourself, as actively thinking, only on condition of having a sense of ourself as passive sensibility. For thinking is essentially our way of responding to ourself as sensibility; it is our way of making sense out of what is initially given to us. Even in this second stage, "I am conscious of myself, not as I appear to myself, nor as I am in myself, but only *that* I am" (B 157, my italics). I first become conscious of *who* I appear to be by actually and successfully exercising my spontaneous thought upon the materials of my passive sensibility. But according to Kant, the very form of my knowledge is such that I cannot rest rationally content with any partial knowledge of myself as appearance, which is all I can ever achieve by the actual exercise of my understanding. Even my ability partially to understand myself as actual appearance presupposes a further measure, viz. that I project before my mind's eye an *ideal* understanding of my experience made wholly determinate.

Our sense of ourself, according to Kant, is bound up with our sense of knowledge. Our sense of knowledge is the sense of a quest beginning with the awareness of self-ignorance and directed toward knowledge which implies self-knowledge. Throughout this quest, according to Kant, our goal is to understand the contents of our *own* field of experience which is not itself knowably contained in any larger world. Our goal is to understand the world of our experience whose unity is provided by ourself as thinking subject. Now the practical percipient *in* the world generally understands himself as giving unity or identity only to his local, body-centered perceptual field identified as "his surroundings" and to *his actual* experience in the world. The world itself and *all possible* experience in the world appear to be unified for him rather than by him. But Kant's thinking subject is an imaginative subject who *provides* the unity of his world rather than finding himself in it. As such he provides the unifying context of *all possible* experience in his world. Thus the fundamental problem for Kant's thinking subject is to understand himself in terms of the unity of all possible experience.

We shall now attempt to trace the three stages of the solution of this problem.[4] These three stages follow the order of Kant's categories of modality. (1) The first condition of any knowledge is knowledge of all possible experience in respect to its *possibility*, in respect to it as determin*able*. Such knowledge is of our self-activity as thinker. It is knowledge of ourself as the formal "transcendental unity of apperception." (2) The second condition of any knowledge is knowledge of all possible experience in respect to its *actuality*, in respect to our incompletable determin*ing* of it. Such knowledge is of the partial effects actually produced by the intelligent self-activity we direct upon our passive sensibility. Such knowledge is in terms of ourself as an actual "empirical ego." (3) The third condition of any knowledge is knowledge of all possible experience in respect to its *necessity*, in respect to it as wholly determin*ate*. Such knowledge is of the total effects ideally producible by the intelligent self-activity we direct upon our passive sensibility. It is knowledge of the ideal "transcendental object $= X$," which is the objective correlate of our self-activity as thinker, just as our empirical ego is the objective correlate of our passive sensibility.

If any "judgment of experience" is analyzed, and the elements of its complex sense given the order in which they presuppose one another, the first sense, according to Kant, will be of our active thinking self as capable of knowing our passive sensing self. The second sense will be of some empirical knowledge we actually do have of our passive sensing self, that is, of ourself as object, in virtue of the activity of our thinking self. In these first two stages, our knowledge is *reflexive*. That is to say, it is knowledge *of* ourself in one respect, *by* ourself in another respect; it is knowledge of our-

---

[4] Our first sense of ourself, as a purely passive sensibility, is a stage of pure ignorance; it *produces* the entwined problems of knowledge and self-knowledge, but is not a stage of its *solution*, so we will henceforth ignore it.

self as object, by ourself as subject; of ourself as known, by ourself as knower; of ourself as receptive, by ourself as spontaneous. As such it is intrinsically imperfect knowledge. For ourself in one respect, ourself as spontaneous knowing subject, remains unknown.[5] Despite Kant's "faculty psychology," he never loses sight of the fact that we are somehow *one* ego merely appearing in two ways. Full knowledge would accordingly be knowledge of the one ego closing the gap between the two halves of the split ego of our appearance to ourself. This gap is reflected in the difference between Space and Time. The spatialization of our experience is, according to Kant, the work of our spontaneous thought, while the temporal character of our experience attests to its source in our passivity. The fact that all our experience is both spatial and temporal thus attests to its "reflexive" character and to our active-passive ego split. The unachievable ideal of knowledge would be to know ourself as a purely spontaneous subject. The objective correlate of such knowledge would be to know our experience as entirely the work of our spontaneous self, that is, to know our experience as entirely spatial and non-temporal. Such knowledge would represent an active interpretation of passive experience so complete as to remove any traces of the original passivity. It would represent a work of thought on sensibility so complete as to restore thought to itself; thereby undoing, so to speak, that original exercise of our thought upon something *else* which limits us to the knowledge of our mere appearance. Now the "transcendental object $= X$" is in fact just such an ideal of an exclusively spatial understanding of our experience. Hence it represents an immediate understanding of ourself as active thinker by ourself as active thinker, whereas our empirical ego represents a mediate understanding of ourself as passive sensibility by ourself as active thinker.

Kant believes, thus, that these three stages characterize all knowledge as a quest of the following sort. (1) We begin with a sense that our true nature as a single ego is hidden from us; that we are, as a split ego, in search of ourselves and

---

[5] To know it, would be to know ourself in ourself, to have the rational intuition which we in fact lack.

capable of discovering ourselves. (2) We go on partially to
mend this split by empirically discovering something which
is in fact true about ourselves. (3) But such discoveries make
sense only in the context of a greater hope, viz. that we can
discover ourselves completely, and so become outwardly and
manifestly one with ourselves just as we are somehow inwardly and hiddenly one with ourselves. (1) We thus start
with a split ego; a sense of self-alienation, self-concealment,
loss of self. (2) We are then objectively impelled (in order
to know anything) to gain a merely *de facto reflexive self-
awareness*. (3) This, in turn, objectively impels us to hope,
albeit unrealistically, for a thoroughly necessary *manifest
unity of the self*. As Kant holds necessity to be that actuality
produced by its possibility alone (B 111), so he holds in
effect that the transcendental object = X is the representation of an ideal, necessarily existent ego (of stage 3) whose
actuality, unlike that of stage 2, is produced by its possibility (of stage 1) alone. The transcendental object = X also
represents Kant's goal of knowledge in general, viz. the understanding of the necessity in experience. In the transcendental object = X, Kant's goal of knowledge coincides with
his goal of self-knowledge.

(1) The first condition implicit in all knowledge is knowledge of the *a priori* conditions of the possibility of experience.
All such conditions, as conditions of the possibility of synthesis, depend upon the transcendental unity of apperception,
which has the function of giving unity to all syntheses. This
transcendental unity is the master unity of our ability to
have "experience" (in Kant's sense of that term) because it is
the source of our ability to form judgments, that is, to give
unity to diverse representations in accordance with a rule. It
is presupposed even by the categories, including the category
of Unity (B 130). For the twelve categories form a diverse set
that can be entertained in our single consciousness only in
virtue of our ability to judge each of them a "category," and
thus to unify the set of categories in accordance with the rule
giving the concept of a category, viz. the rule that a category
is a kind of unity exemplified by all intelligible judgments of
matters of fact. "We must ascribe all employment of the
understanding, even the whole of logic [to this transcen-

dental unity of apperception]" (B 134). This transcendental unity also makes possible our *knowledge* (as distinct from global intuition) of Space and Time, for such knowledge is possible only by a synthesis of productive imagination (B 137). Our transcendental unity of apperception "is that self-consciousness which, while generating the representation 'I think' . . . cannot itself be accompanied by any further representation" (B 132). Considered as a form of self-knowledge, it is the sense of our identity as subject, as one consciousness (B 133).

For Kant, thus, the spontaneity of our activity as thinking subject makes us self-conscious of the unity of our consciousness, and is thereby the fount of the possibility of all our knowledge. The self-movement of the percipient seems to play a similar role in practical perception, and the role Kant assigns to the self-activity of the thinking subject may be brought out by comparison. Kant holds that we produce the *a priori forms* of intelligibility by a spontaneous act of the self *not elicited by anything other than the self*. Similarly, all practical perception presupposes our ability to move ourselves by ourselves alone—in a (perhaps merely restless) response made, in the last analysis, to our internal needs rather than to any external objects *by* which we may hope to satisfy these needs. Kant holds that it is only on condition of our self-activity as thinker that objects of experience are *made* conceptually *determinable* for us. It is similarly only on condition of our self-movement as percipient that objects of experience are made perceptually determinable for us—as accessible in the near-far field generated by this movement.

Contrasts are also instructive. Since the self-activity of the Kantian subject is entirely formal, it does not imply the (spatial and temporal) sensuous fields upon which it happens to be directed. On the Kantian view, it is simply a kind of "*a priori* fact," so to speak, that our intuition takes these rather than some other forms. The self-activity of the percipient, however, is felt as the self-movement of his substantive body. The circumstantial fields in which this self-movement is directed are therefore felt as the fields of direction of the very body which is self-moving. The structure of the body, which is both self-active and in-the-perceptual-field, mediates between our self-activity and the field in which that activity is directed and expressed; it makes the one conformable to the other. Our spatial and temporal fields of practical perception have their characteristics in terms of the front-back, left-right, up-down characteristics of our self-active body.

(2) The second condition of knowledge is that of some actuality. Regarded as a condition of self-knowledge, it is knowledge in terms of our empirical ego. Knowledge in terms of our empirical ego is the actual, though uncompletable determining of what our transcendental unity of apperception first makes determinable. The distinguishing feature of the empirical ego is that all empirical knowledge must be in terms of it. Among all empirical objects, it and it alone *must* be to some extent understood if *any* object of experience is at all understood; and further, if it is at all understood, some other object of experience must also be to some extent understood. This is so because the empirical ego is the representation of inner sense as an object (B 54). It is to some extent understood if and only if any temporal perceptions are lawfully ordered. All other objects of experience are objects of outer sense. They are understood if and only if certain spatial events are lawfully ordered. But the perceptual material of *all* experience, spatial as well as temporal experience, is itself temporal and thereby a content of the empirical ego. This material is lawfully ordered in a temporal way if ordered by a rule of succession; and in a spatial way if ordered by a rule of reciprocal succession. It is thus plain that, for Kant, all spatial ordering implies a temporal ordering. He also believes that all temporal ordering implies a spatial ordering. For he writes,

> [My empirical ego] is determinable only through relation to something which, while bound up with my existence, is outside me . . . [it] is bound up in the way of *identity* with the consciousness of a relation to something outside me. . . .   [B xln, my italics]

This implication is more complicated to demonstrate. It is perhaps most simply done by reference to the *Anthropology* where Kant indicates, in effect, his belief that psychological understanding is psycho-physiological understanding. The temporal perceptions of an empirical ego are understood (i.e. unified under a rule) when they are understood as causes or effects of events in spatial sense organs. In sum, Kant seems to hold that all spatial understanding implies some psychological understanding (of regular sequences possible for the empirical ego) of perception; and all psychological understanding implies some spatial understanding (at least in the form of physiological understanding).

Let us now turn to a comparison between Kant's analysis of the role of self-knowledge in the thinking subject's actual determining of some object of experience, and the apparent role of self-knowledge in the percipient's actual determining of some object of experience. Kant holds that an empirical determination of ourself by ourself as thinking subject implies and is implied by some empirical determination of an object outside us. A similar conclusion seems warranted for perceptual experience. In practical perception, the determining of an object proceeds by way of some effective response to that object, and culminates by determining it as circumstantially outside us. This response, however, determines not merely the perceptual object upon which it is directed, but also the percipient from whom it issues. The effectiveness of the response institutes or develops in the percipient a certain perceptual skill which characterizes him empirically, that is, as having become a particular kind of percipient as a result of his experience. The determinations of the object and the percipient imply one another because they both stem from the sense of the same effective response.

Kant holds that the actual determining of objects of experience by a thinking subject is in principle interminable, due to the temporal character of our experience—which makes our actual experience receptive, successive, and fragmentary in respect to its matter, and always less than all possible experience. The case is similar with the perceiving subject. All possible experience is contained in the world-field. But actual perceptual experience is limited by the horizon of our hori- · zontal field in the world—and first of all by the front-back temporal character of that field in virtue of which content appears to enter our horizontal field as "forthcoming." The horizonality of our horizontal field appears, furthermore, to be ineliminable. It characterizes our circumstantial way of being in the world. We can never come *to* the horizon of the temporal field beyond which lies the unforeseeable future. We can only advance *toward* it while it recedes from us in a compensating way. The very structure of our forward-oriented active body always produces a future-field in which objects may appear ahead of us as still-to-be-encountered—no matter how much we have already experienced.

For Kant, as we have seen, inner sense (the time-field) is "the mode in which the mind is affected through its own activity" (B 67). In actually determining any object of experience, we know something of the empirical ego, "the subject, which is the object of the inner sense" (B 68). In all empirical determination, therefore, we somehow make ourselves passive objects of our own spontaneity. According to Kant, the common root of our split ego is inaccessible to us, and we can never understand the generation of our epistemological schizophrenia. But in terms of a phenomenology of practical perception, some understanding of how our spontaneous activity makes us passive does seem possible. By *active* self-movement the percipient first generates his forward-directed spatio-temporal field correlative with his own functional asymmetry. But as soon as he does so, he is *passively* thrown into the middle of it as an arena in which he must fend for himself, as vulnerable, and seek to find himself, by orienting himself with respect to something around him, though subject to failure.

(3) The third condition of knowledge is that of necessity. What our transcendental unity of apperception makes determinable, and what we actually though partially determine in relation to our empirical ego, we must represent to ourselves as ideally completely determinate. The conditions of the determinability of experience are necessary, and their necessity can be known beyond doubt. But they provide the necessity only of the form, and not of the content of experience. Actual empirical determinations concern the content as well as the form of experience, but they are only *presumably* necessary. Further experience may always falsify them. Kant believes he has shown that there must be *some* universal

and necessary empirical laws; but he does not believe we can ever know that the particular laws we believe necessary are necessarily the necessary ones. This distinction between the certainty with which we can know the necessary form of our experience, and the uncertainty to which we are limited in knowledge of the necessary content of experience, raises, according to Kant, an objective need for its eradication. That is to say, considered purely as knowers (disregarding psychological interests) we cannot rest content with this distinction. For this distinction represents our ego-split as knowers.[6] We can know the form of our experience with certainty because it is given by our spontaneity. But we cannot know the content of our experience with certainty because it is given by our receptivity. Hence the distinction between the certainty of form and the uncertainty of content represents the distinction between our spontaneity and receptivity as knower. This distinction, as we saw, implies our ignorance concerning ourself; it implies that the subject we *are* is hidden from us, and that we can know ourself only as we *appear* to ourself.

Since this ignorance affects the form of our knowledge we cannot, considered purely as knower, deny or disregard the need for its removal. Accordingly we always project before ourself as knower the ideal of "the complete experience of the object" (A 8), such as we can never in practice obtain. This is necessary in order to "prevent our modes of knowledge from being haphazard or arbitrary" (A 104). For what makes experience knowledge, according to Kant, is the necessary agreement with one another of the representations synthesized in this experience. And since our actual experience can be no more than partially synthesized it can lay claim to knowledge only by being understood in relation to its completion, that is, as presumptively completed. This representation of the complete experience of the object is what Kant calls the "transcendental object = X." This transcendental object is, on the object side, what the transcendental unity of apperception is on the subject side. Each represents, from

___

[6] It is not a merely psychological ego-split, because our character as having a "psyche" (i.e. an empirical ego) is only a *result* of this split.

its respective side, the unity of our experience—which is, according to Kant, the fundamental condition of its intelligibility. Each is "transcendental" because each, from its respective side, is the unintuitable condition of the possibility of intelligible intuition.

Kant's notion of the transcendental object suffers from an ambiguity deeply rooted in his philosophy. On the one hand, he sometimes writes as if his notion were intelligible in terms of *perceptual* experience, as if what he meant by the "transcendental object" were the whole comprised of particular objects which we can only intuit in successive snatches. For example, Kant holds that the transcendental object is what a judgment of experience is about. It is the unity of the subject matter of the judgment; that to which both the subject and the predicate of the judgment apply, even though the subject and predicate are logically independent of one another. He notes that we may refer to objects by concepts (e.g. "body") which do not imply all the characteristics (e.g. "weight") of these objects. Yet in doing so we mean to refer to the objects as wholes, including all their characteristics. In such a case, he holds, "the [subject] concept indicates the complete experience through one of its parts [sic!]; and to this part, as belonging to it, I can therefore add other parts of the same experience" (A 8). But Kant's stronger tendency is to write of the transcendental object in terms of *imaginative* experience. In these contexts, the "transcendental object" means the represented unity of all possible experience. This is the unity of a single object in which all separate, perceptual objects are merged. Kant writes in this vein that the transcendental object "in reality throughout all our knowledge is always one and the same" (A 109). Intuitable objects "in turn have their object which cannot be intuited by us . . . the transcendental object = X" (A 109). The transcendental object is then the single object of all separately intuitable objects. The transcendental unity of apperception gives unity to the transcendental object. But Kant cannot account in this way for the unity of a *local* object, also somehow known to be more than we know of it. Kant can make sense of the global determinability of intuition, characteristic of imagination, but he cannot make sense of the local determinability of intuition, characteristic of perception. He cannot in the last analysis distinguish particular objects, each having the transcendental object as its object.

Basic to Kant's discussion of the ego at all stages of its self-evidence is a view deserving some concluding remarks, viz. the denial that action has any formative influence *on the active agent,* that practice in any way makes the practitioner. Kant has a keen sense of some ways in which activity may be formative. For he holds that by our self-activity as thinker we make the whole knowable world and all objects in it. But he interprets our making this world of experience as simply our way of holding a mirror before our mind, so that we can see a representation of ourself as we are "in-ourself" *independently* of that representation. For Kant, in short, *we discover ourself by making our world.* This is an accurate analysis of objective imaginative experience. For we create the world of our imagination; and if we do so in an objective way, we thereby achieve self-expression and self-discovery. But this is plainly not true of the circumstantial self and world of practical perception. As skillful percipient, on the contrary, *we make ourself by discovering our world.* Kant's view that *all* our knowledge has the form of self-discovery by the making of our world shows that he has in this respect too, as in others noted earlier, imaginized the perceptual factor in our self-knowledge.

Kant holds that "I cannot determine my existence as that of a self-active being . . . (but only) as that of an appearance" (B 158). He implies that we *have* some perfectly determinate and intelligible nature "in-ourself," but cannot *know* more than an imperfect representation of it. Even the purely "spontaneous" activity of our understanding, as we can know it, is only the actualization of an antecedently determinate disposition. The categories are

> . . . dispositions in the human understanding, in which they lie prepared, till at last, on the occasion of experience, they are developed, and by the same understanding are exhibited in their purity, freed from the empirical conditions attaching to them.   [B 91]

Kant sees that self-discovery comes only as the result of considerable activity. But he believes as much as Aristotle that activity cannot be formative in respect to its source. The statement "That which produces the form is always something which possesses it"[7] might just as well have been Kant's. No matter how spontaneous the activity may be, whatever it produces must "lie prepared" to begin with as a wholly determinate disposition in the agent of this activity. Kant writes, for example,

> Before the artist can produce a bodily form he must have finished it in imagination.   [*Anthropology*, § 31]

Kant has no sense that the work of art is not finally planned to begin with, but is only worked out *in the act* of producing it. Some such Aristotelian view seems to be one reason for Kant's conviction that our whole activity of knowing, by which we make the whole world of our experience, is merely a way of approaching knowledge of the self we already determinately are in-ourself independently of all this activity.

But there seems to be another ground for this conviction—a specifically Kantian ground, which should perhaps be taken as more fundamental. Kant holds that the "absolute unity" (B 92) of the understanding is a condition of the possibility of knowledge. Knowing *is* simply our way of representing in intuition this unity of understanding. But this unity of understanding presupposed by all our understanding cannot itself be intuited in the world of our understanding. The most we can do is to represent it by the 'I think' which can accompany all judgments. Our understanding, in short, *presumes* a unity of ourself as subject, but cannot *present* this unity; it can do no more than represent it. If the very form of our understanding makes it evident that we have a unity as subject not presentable in our understanding, and if, as with Kant, one believes all experience is that of our understanding (our theoretical imagination), then one has no choice but to believe that we have a unity as subject not presentable in our experience *at all*. Our theoretical imagination does indeed presuppose a unity of ourself as subject, representable but not presentable in imagination itself. But this presupposed

[7] Aristotle *Physics* VIII. 5.

unity of ourself as subject *is* presentable in the perceptual world as the felt unity of our active body.

Kant holds that

> creation . . . cannot be admitted as an event among appearances, since its mere possibility would destroy the unity of experience. [B 251]

This is quite true in a given world of our imagination. But the contrary is true of the perceptual world. A condition of the possibility of the unity of our perceptual experience is that we *do* create ourself in the course of exploring and discovering our world. Our self-activity in doing so determines us not for the *second* time, as appearance, in recognition of determinations antecedently in us as subject, but for the *first* time, as subject who has made himself determinate by his active perception. By self-activity, we do not merely first *know* who we are by knowing what we are doing; we first *become* who we are by doing it. For exercise does not merely *employ* the skills which give us determinacy as subject; it also *develops* them in the first place.

THE TRANSCENDENTAL DIALECTIC

THE THING IN ITSELF IN
KANTIAN PHILOSOPHY

GEORGE SCHRADER

THE THING IN ITSELF AS A LIMITING CONCEPT

The charge has often been made against Kant that it is meaningless to talk about an unknowable thing-in-itself.[1] If the thing-in-itself is totally unknown and intrinsically unknowable, it cannot be known that it exists. One may posit the thing-in-itself as the cause of appearances which are known, but then one is guilty of extending the category of causality beyond the realm of appearances, a procedure which he had explicitly repudiated.[2] The validity of the thing-in-itself for the critical philosophy cannot depend upon its being posited as a separate and distinct entity which stands in the relation of cause to phenomena. Only if the thing-in-itself is also the thing which appears, is Kant's position consistent and defensible.

So far as his critical employment of the concept is concerned, the thing-in-itself is *not* a second object. The thing-in-itself is given in its appearances; it *is* the object which

Reprinted with permission of the author and of the editors from *Review of Metaphysics* (March 1949), 30–44. Copyright, 1949, by the *Review of Metaphysics*.

[1] Kemp Smith, *Commentary to Kant's Critique of Pure Reason*, pp. 206, 216 ff. Cohen, *Kants Theorie der Erfahrung*, p. 248. Smith is quite correct in holding that this terminology implies that appearances are merely subjective representations. However, it is not a vacillation between subjectivism and phenomenalism that is in evidence here, but between dogmatic realism and critical phenomenalism. The term 'appearance' in this context has no critical significance. Cf. *Prolegomena*, par. 49.

[2] A 190=B 235, A 533=B 561, A 562=B 590.

appears.[3] In other words, the object is taken in a twofold
sense. There is no contradiction, Kant maintained, in supposing that one and the same will is, as an appearance, determined by the laws of nature and yet, as a thing-in-itself, is
free.[4] He never meant to hold that the self of the theoretical
reason and the self of the practical reason are two separate
and distinct entities. It is one and the same object considered
from two perspectives. In this sense the thing-in-itself is
purely a limiting concept. So far as the critical method is
concerned, objects are always considered from a particular
and *limited* perspective, e.g. science, morality, art, et cetera.[5]
This is the central meaning of his theory of appearances. In
this employment of the concept it is completely meaningless
to speak of the thing-in-itself as a *cause* of appearances. The
critical distinction between appearances and things in themselves is not intended to be a distinction between subjective
sense data and public objects, but between public objects as
given according to two or more modes. This involves no extension of the category of causality beyond appearances.
Moreover, it is not open to the charge that an unknown object is given the attribute of existence. The thing-in-itself is
known as an appearance. By definition that is the only way
that it could be known. To say that we know only appearances
and not things in themselves is to state an obvious tautology,
namely that objects are known only as they are known.

This is, I am convinced, the critical meaning of the concept
of the thing-in-itself; yet Kant employs it in quite another
way. He sometimes refers to the thing-in-itself as the cause
of appearances.[6] On this view appearances are regarded as

---

[3] B xxvii, B 55, B 69, A 250=B 306, A 380; *Vorlesungen über Metaphysik*, p. 38; Paton, *Kant's Metaphysic of Experience*, II, 70; Adickes,
Kant und das Ding an Sich, pp. 8, 20, 35, 94; Fischer, *Geschichte
der neuern Philosophie*, II, 235; Erdmann, *Kant's Kriticismus in der
ersten und in der zweiten Auflage*, p. 19.

[4] B xxviii; cf. A 547=B 575.

[5] A 841=B 869, *Critique of Practical Reason, Immanuel Kants
Werke*, ed. Ernst Cassirer, 11 vols. (Berlin, 1912–1922), V, 63, 98;
Critique of Judgment, IKW, V, 225, 245; cf. Heyse, *Der Begriff der
Ganzheit und die Kantische Philosophie*, pp. 136 ff.

[6] A 37, A 190=B 235, A 288=B 344, A 494=B 523, A 614=B 642;
Prol., par. 32.

subjective sense data and things in themselves as independent objects, stripped of all primary and secondary qualities. It is obvious that on this basis the thing-in-itself is a superfluous and meaningless entity. If Kant were to make his critical theory consistent with this exposition, it would be necessary for him to abandon the concept of the thing-in-itself altogether.[7] It is this employment of the concept of the thing-in-itself to establish the existence of unknowable objects which has occasioned so much criticism of Kant's position.

Whatever interpretation of Kant's theory is advanced, it is evident that the concept of the thing-in-itself as the cause of appearances has nothing whatever in common with his critical distinction between appearances and things in themselves. This twofold employment of the thing-in-itself represents one of the fundamental inconsistencies in the *Critique of Pure Reason*. Kant was apparently unaware of the inconsistency even as he effected a revision of the first edition of the *Critique*.[8] If one considers Kant's private views, it is not difficult to understand the reason for this inconsistency. In his private views, he was a confirmed realist throughout the critical period.[9] Apparently he could not resist the temptation to offer a defence of realism, and employed the concept of the thing-in-itself to that end. However, this represents a dogmatic employment of the concept. Such passages must be dismissed as reflecting Kant's private views, but as of little significance for his critical position. In concerning himself with the problem of the perception of objects he was dealing with a secondary problem that is not at all essential to his

[7] Kant stated the matter clearly enough, but failed to recognise the full implications of his assertion: "The true correlate of sensibility, the thing in itself, is not known, and cannot be known; and in experience no question is ever asked in regard to it." A 30; cf. A 44=B 62.

[8] B 345, B 523, B 567; *Prol.*, par. 32.

[9] B xlin., A 191=B 236, A 51, A 380, B 524=A 496; cf. Adickes, *Kant und das Ding an Sich*, pp. 9, 64 ff.; *Kant und die als ob Philosophie*, pp. 4 ff., 59; Heimsoeth, *Metaphysiche Motive in der Ausbildung der kritischen Idealismus*, Kant-Studien, Band 29; Paton, *op. cit.* p. 70. Adickes' defence of Kant as a realist in his two volumes devoted to that end is beyond challenge.

critical objective.[10] This was the sort of problem which had occupied Locke and Berkeley but which Kant had deliberately avoided. Objectivity does not depend, on Kant's analysis, upon the independent existence of unperceivable entities.

The seriousness of Kant's inconsistency is easily seen when one recognises that, on a critical basis, it is only appearances which are objects.[11] In his references to the thing-in-itself as a cause of appearances, Kant reverses himself, regarding appearances as subjective and the thing-in-itself as the object. Objectivity, in this sense, has none of its critical meaning. Kant's position in maintaining that things in themselves are the cause of appearances, is altogether untenable. However, this clearly does not represent his critical view and should not be regarded as central to his position. Appearances are objects, but not *because* they exist independently. Things in themselves are intrinsically unknowable: hence, they are not *objects*, independent or otherwise.

Kant frequently employs the concept of the transcendental object in such a way as to make it synonomous with the concept of the thing-in-itself. Not only is this obvious from the general context, but Kant himself uses the terms interchangeably.[12] As in the case of the thing-in-itself, the transcendental object has both a critical and dogmatic meaning. In its critical employment it is strictly a limiting concept,[13] while in its dogmatic usage it is regarded as the cause or ground of appearances.[14] In this two-fold meaning, the transcendental object may be regarded as identical with the thing itself. It poses no additional problems of interpretation.

As employed in other contexts the concept of the transcendental object has no relation to the thing-in-itself. As

[10] A x ff., B 119=A 87; cf. Kemp Smith, *op. cit.* p. xlvi.

[11] "The concept of the noumenon is, therefore, not the concept of an object, but is a problem unavoidably bound up with the limitation of our sensibility. . . ." B 344=A 288; cf. A 255; A 289, B 309, B 311; cf. A 93=B 126; Cassirer, *op. cit.* pp. 371 ff., Erdmann, *Kants Kriticismus*, p. 639, Cohen, *op. cit.* pp. 239, 248, 253 ff.

[12] A 366.

[13] B 345=A 289.

[14] A 391, A 494=B 523, A 539=B 567, A 545=B 573, A 557= B 585.

the concept of an object in general which serves to unify the manifold of intuition, it is *a priori* and transcendental.[15] The meaning and function of the *a priori* object is never precisely determined in the *Critique*. In fact, Kant tended to abandon it altogether in the second edition. However, his statements that the transcendental object as an *a priori* concept is *unknowable* have no significance for the knowability of the thing-in-itself. No *a priori* concept or principle is *knowable*, for the determinate empirical content is lacking that is required for knowledge. In discarding the *a priori* concept of the transcendental object Kant was in no way giving up his notion of the thing-in-itself.

Another serious inconsistency in Kant's exposition concerns the possibility of applying the categories to the things in themselves. On the one hand he suggests the possibility of 'thinking' things-in-themselves through the categories, even though no intuition can be given to furnish the necessary empirical content.[16] In other connections he holds that the categories are absolutely without meaning when applied beyond the realm of appearances.[17] Some of his interpreters have concluded that in denying the possibility of applying the categories to things in themselves, Kant was, for all practical purposes, repudiating the notion of the thing-in-itself altogether. There would appear to be a serious dilemma involved in his position at this point. If the categories can be applied to things in themselves, Kant is fundamentally inconsistent with his critical position; if the categories cannot be applied to them, the things in themselves are completely meaningless.[18] The confusion results from Kant's twofold deduction of space, time, and the categories, and his

[15] A 109 ff., A 191=B 523, A 248=B 304, A 251, A 280=B 336, A 374.

[16] ". . . They relate to objects universally, that is apart from all conditions of sensibility." B 120=A 88; cf. B 149, B 167n. *Über die Fortschritte*, IKW, VIII, 251; Letter to Beck, 20th January, 1792, IKW, X, 115.

[17] "Even if we were willing to assume a kind of intuition other than this our sensible kind, the functions of our thought would still be without meaning in respect to it." B 343; cf. B 300=A 281 ff., B 308, A 256=B 31; *Prol.*, par. 32.

[18] Cf. Erdmann, *Kants Kriticismus*, pp. 144 ff.

effort to find a critical basis for his private metaphysical views. His ambivalent position results from his continuing struggle between rationalism and empiricism, between his private metaphysics and his metaphysic of experience.

Although Kant sometimes refers to space and time as the only forms of intuition of which human minds are capable, he never justified or needed to justify any such assertion. On the contrary, his position is intelligible only if that is not actually capable of being proved.[19] The objective deduction of space and time depends upon their being shown to be the necessary *a priori* conditions of mathematics, and, hence, of any mathematical science of nature.[20] If this was not clear in the first edition of the *Critique*, Kant made it explicit enough in the *Prolegomena* and the second edition of the *Critique*. Synthetic *a priori* judgments are held to be possible because of the reality of space and time, the logical conditions of mathematics. If any mathematical knowledge of nature is to be possible, these same logical conditions will be required.[21] In the objective deduction, Kant does not show that space and time are *psychologically* prior to experience, or even that they are *psychologically* necessary in the intuition of objects. It is the existence of mathematical physics which demonstrates the possibility of such synthetic *a priori* judgments of nature.[22] On this basis the forms of intuition are valid only for mathematical knowledge. Beyond that sphere no application whatever can be claimed for them. They cannot be regarded as the exclusive forms of intuition or as the logical conditions for all knowledge, but only for that intuition and knowledge which patterns itself after mathematical physics.

Kant also offered a psychological deduction of space and time, which has little in common with the objective deduction so far as method is concerned.[23] If his method is to be

[19] A 39=B 56, A 252.

[20] *Prol.*, par. 10; B xvi, B 21, B 41.

[21] B 23, A 94=B 126; *Prol.*, par. 14; Reflexion 983.

[22] *Prol.*, par. 15. The validity of the categories depends entirely upon their being shown to be the formal conditions of objective experience. Cf. A 94, B 294.

[23] A 22, A 26=B 42, A 31=B 47. The psychological analysis of space and time would establish only a psychological priority, which

the selective principle, one must choose between these deductions. In view of Kant's explicit statement that the objective deduction alone is essential,[24] this presents no real difficulty. It is unfortunate that the psychological deduction is frequently assumed as the archimedean point for the understanding of Kant's method. The two deductions have quite different implications, particularly for the meaning of the thing-in-itself. Whereas the objective deduction leaves the way open for other modes of intuition and is valid only for mathematical knowledge of nature, the psychological deduction would establish these forms as the only possible modes of human intuition. In the latter instance, either things in themselves must be capable of being intuited under the forms of space and time, or they can never be given in any experience whatever. The only alternative would be that objects which cannot be perceived might still be conceived. At times Kant was not averse to holding this view, unsatisfactory as it proved to be.

The deduction of the categories presents a similar difficulty. On the one hand, Kant presents the categories as the only possible forms of judgment.[25] But he never demonstrates this anywhere in the *Critique* or elsewhere in his writings. This is, in fact, one of the most dogmatic and rationalistic parts of the *Critique of Pure Reason*. The critical or transcendental deduction of the categories consists in their being shown to be the necessary presuppositional concepts of pure science of nature.[26] In the latter instance it cannot be claimed that they are the only forms of judgment, but only that they are required concepts for natural science. Only in so far as knowledge is patterned after mathematical science is the validity of the categories guaranteed. Again these two deductions have different and inconsistent implications. The

---

would be of no transcendental or logical significance whatever. It is the psychological deduction which motivates Kant to make the dogmatic claim that space and time are the *only possible forms* of human intuition. A 252.

[24] "Although this latter exposition is of great importance for my chief purpose, it does not form an essential part of it." A xvii. This applies to the categories as well as to space and time. Cf. B 167.

[25] A 80.

[26] Cf. n. 22.

more dogmatic deduction would postulate the categories as the necessary concepts of any human thought whatever. In this instance either they would have to be applicable to things in themselves, or else things in themselves could not be conceptualised. The critical deduction, on the other hand, would allow for the possibility of other categories for other types of experience. It would even imply the possibility of such concepts. From this standpoint it would be quite dogmatic and altogether uncritical to attempt an extension of the categories beyond appearances—unless some other basis were provided.

Kant had originally held that we can think things in themselves through the categories because of his conviction that the categories are the forms of human thought in general, applicable to any objects whatever. He was not inconsistent in holding that they might be applicable to objects apart from the forms of space and time. Since he admitted that they would be empty apart from some other mode of intuition which remained to be discovered, he was not contradicting himself. However, in maintaining that things in themselves actually could be thought through the categories, indeed must be thought through them, Kant was asserting more than his position would allow.[27] Thus, he was only correcting his position in the direction of greater consistency in amending his statements regarding the application of the categories to things in themselves. So far as the *Critique of Pure Reason* is concerned, one has no right to assert that things in themselves are even thinkable through the categories.

His further concern was to avoid any appearance of holding to the rationalist position. If the thing-in-itself is thinkable, that would seem to put Kant in the Leibnizian camp. He was exceedingly anxious to avoid any such semblance.[28] To say that we can have an intelligible concept of something that cannot be empirically given in intuition would seem to be saying that we can know objects by reason alone. The point is that the categories are *derived* from experience and without experience can have no meaning so far as knowledge

[27] B xvii; cf. n. 17 above.
[28] A 242, A 245, B 307.

is concerned. But this is true only in so far as the validity of
the categories is dependent upon the objective deduction.
They cannot be declared to be meaningless in an absolute
sense. It is only that no basis for an extension of their application has been provided in the case of the theoretical
reason.

Here Kant was drawn between two poles. His empiricism
prompted him to declare the meaninglessness of the categories when extended to things in themselves. Yet, at the
same time, he was attempting to provide a basis for just that
extension of them in the case of the practical reason. Although no intuition is available for the theoretical reason,
the categories might receive empirical meaning through
moral experience.[29] Thus the self might be regarded as a
substance that is spatial and determined in time for the
theoretical reason, and as a simple substance that is free for
the practical reason. In holding that things in themselves
are thinkable, e.g. God, the free moral self, the world as
totality, Kant had the moral part of his philosophy clearly in
mind.[30] It is evident that he was not willing to affirm the
reality of noumena merely on the basis of their being conceptually intelligible. Nonetheless, it is significant that he
speaks of noumena as intelligible cause, as thinkable, if not
theoretically knowable.[31] In the pre-critical period he had

[29] B xxii, B xxiii n., A 796=B 824, A 823=B 852; *Critique of Practical Reason*, IKW, V, 57 ff., 61, 63. *Vorlesungen über Religion*,
p. 77.

[30] Letter to Lambert, 2d September, 1770, IKW, IX, 74; B xxx;
Reflexionen 6317, 6349, 6353, Ber.; Heimsoeth, *op. cit.* pp. 145,
153 ff. In his exposition of the ideas of reason Kant attempted to
provide a theoretical foundation for the postulates of morality. A
transcendental function is claimed for them, but they are held to be
'regulative' only. Either they are constitutive of experience, conditions of its possibility, or they are not transcendental principles.
Kant's vacillation between his private metaphysics and his critical
position is clearly in evidence here. Cf. A 614=B 642, A 642=B 670,
A 826=B 854; *Was heisst: sich im Denken orientieren? IKW, IV,*
357; *Vorlesungen über Metaphysik*, pp. 72 ff., 265; Smith, *op. cit.*
pp. 525, 592; Guttmann, *Kant's Gottesbegriff in seiner positiven
Entwicklung*, pp. 35 ff.

[31] Reflexion 6280, Ber.; A 252, A 538=B 566, A 545=B 573;
A 566=B 594; *Prol.*, par. 32; *Grundlegung zur Metaphysik der Sitten*,

been convinced that they could be known intelligibly by reason alone. In the critical period he modified this position to hold that they are theoretically intelligible but not theoretically knowable. A further modification is to be found in his rejection of the theoretical significance of the categories beyond the area of experience from which they are derived. Apart from this experience their application is altogether problematic.

The dilemma with respect to the application of the categories to things in themselves is not insuperable. The first part of the dilemma is cleared up by admitting that no claim can be made for the application of the categories to things in themselves so far as theoretical knowledge is concerned. The limitations of the categories is implied in the very method by which they are derived. The inconsistency in Kant's exposition at this point results from a transition in his thought from a dogmatic to a more critical position. The second part of the dilemma is false. The meaning and validity of the concept of the thing-in-itself in no way depends upon an extension of the categories beyond appearances. The thing-in-itself is not actually the *cause* of appearances. Hence, nothing is lost if it is found to be impossible to apply the category of causality to the thing-in-itself. The thing-in-itself is primarily a limiting concept.[32] As such it has no positive or determinate meaning.

THE PRACTICAL REASON AND NOUMENAL REALITY

Kant's contention that moral experience gives us things in themselves involves an unfortunate use of language.[33] The

---

IKW, IV, 310 ff.; *Critique of Practical Reason*, IKW, V, 62, 98, 114 ff.

[32] "The concept of a noumenon is thus merely a limiting concept, the function of which is to curb the pretensions of sensibility; and it is therefore only of a negative employment." B 311. In this sense the concept of a noumenon is identical with the concept of the thing in itself.

[33] *Critique of Practical Reason*, IKW, V, 6, 55, 57, 114 ff.; *Von einem neuerdings erhobenen vornehem Ton in der Philosophie*, IKW,

objects of moral experience are no less phenomenal, on critical grounds, than the objects of theoretical knowledge. If the concepts of the practical reason are transcendentally ideal, which is required if they are *a priori*, their validity is limited to the experience from which they are derived. In this respect they are no different from the *a priori* concepts of the theoretical reason. Actually, it is two sets of phenomenal objects that are involved, rather than appearances and things in themselves. In so far as Kant employed the concept of the noumenon positively to designate objects which belong to an 'intelligible world' he was departing widely from his critical position. There is in evidence here a carry-over of pre-critical language. The question is whether it is merely the language of his rationalistic period that is retained. There can hardly be any doubt that Kant believed that the world postulated by the practical reason is the 'real' world. In holding that it is 'thinkable' he was clinging to an important element of his pre-critical metaphysics. His denial that it can be *known* theoretically only partially suffices to free his position of rationalistic overtones.

Although he insisted that the practical reason is fully autonomous, he apparently believed it necessary to provide a theoretical foundation for the postulates of morality. This dogmatic and rationalistic tendency in Kant's philosophy makes it appear that the practical reason serves only to validate a theoretical metaphysics which was required but not schematised by the theoretical reason. Kant's fondness for architechtonic, his continuing commitment to the fundamental principles of his pre-critical metaphysics accounts for this development. Actually, the practical validity of the postulates of morality in no way depends upon such a theoretical undergirding. Kant's position was ambivalent. He insisted upon the autonomy of the practical reason, declaring that the postulates of morality have no theoretical validity whatever. At the same time, he provided a theoretical foundation for the metaphysics postulated by the practical reason, maintaining that the realm of the practical reason is the 'intelligible' or

VI, 484, Anmerkung; *Grundlegung zur Metaphysik der Sitten, IKW,* IV, 310 ff.

'noumenal' world. This is a fundamental inconsistency in his position. The implicit rationalism of his philosophy is only partially concealed by his insistence that the metaphysics of morality is based upon faith rather than knowledge.[34] The term faith is not used in any conventional sense and serves to confuse the function of the critical method as applied to moral experience. Kant was attempting to make a theoretical claim for metaphysical concepts without being willing to accept all of the implications involved.

Only if it is assumed that there are just two modes of knowledge, the theoretical and the practical, is it proper to speak of moral experience as affording access to things in themselves. But even then it is only from the perspective of *science* that the concepts of the practical reason can be said to refer to noumena. Moreover, it would be equally legitimate to refer to the objects of scientific knowledge as noumena when speaking from the standpoint of moral experience. On this assumption, phenomena and noumena, appearances and things in themselves, become complementary terms. Objects as they appear in any other way than in space and time are then regarded as noumenal. Even though Kant appears to have made this assumption, the language is still misleading. Things in themselves can never be known or positively defined either theoretically or practically. In holding that they are given in moral experience, Kant beclouded the whole distinction between appearances and things in themselves.

Kant is, of course, permitted his own use of language. The objection here is not that he employs the term noumena to mean the phenomenal objects of moral experience, but that he means by noumena something other than appearances. It is not at all consistent or justifiable to equate noumena in this sense with things in themselves. The *a priori* concepts of moral experience are valid only for moral experience.[35] That is the central doctrine of the ethics. In insisting that moral experience provides an access, even indirectly,

---

[34] B xxx, A 471=B 499; *Critique of Practical Reason, IKW*, V, 12n.
[35] *Critique of Practical Reason, IKW*, V, 130, 143; *Grundlegung, IKW*, IV, 294; *Was heisst: sich im Denken orientieren? IKW*, IV, 349, 360, 364 ff.; *Über die Fortschritte, IKW*, VIII, 280.

to things in themselves, Kant is over-extending the application of these concepts. To say that the real self, the self *an sich* is a free self, is to make a claim which is altogether unjustified on the basis of Kant's method. The same thing is true of his postulation of God and a purposeful world as noumena. The positivistic metaphysics of the critical philosophy, the metaphysic of experience, embraces morality as well as science. Kant's attempts to give positive meaning to the concept of the thing-in-itself in whatever context represents a compromise with dogmatism and rationalism, a concession to his private metaphysics.

As Kant uses the term faith in referring to the concepts of moral experience, it has little of the traditional meaning and certainly none of the religious meaning which is usually associated with the concept. It is not an irrational faith, a faith that is blind or mystical to which Kant refers. He is at great pains to point out that the faith presupposed by morality is a rational faith (Vernunftglaube).[36] For Kant as a person I suspect that more than rational faith was involved. Thus the term faith has a double meaning for him. It refers to the critical or transcendental meaning and to Kant's private meaning, which was not at all dependent upon his critical analysis. He really tried to say two things which are incompatible: (1) that things in themselves are given in the case of the practical reason; (2) that the concepts of the practical reason have no theoretical validity when extended beyond the moral realm.

[36] *Critique of Practical Reason*, IKW, V, 12n; *Critique of Judgment*, IKW, V, 549 ff.; *Über das Misslingen aller philos. Versuche in der Theodicee*, IKW, VI, 134 ff.; *Über die Fortschritte*, IKW, VIII, 181 ff.; *Grundlegung*, IKW, IV, 131 ff.; A 828=B 846; Reflexion 6219, Ber.; *Vorlesungen über Religion*, p. 223. Adickes' contention that Kant later abandoned his 'Vernunftglaube' or indirect proof of God for personal faith based on direct witness of the moral law as 'die Stimme Gottes' is completely without foundation. (*Kant-Studien*, Band 50 [1958–59], 720 ff.) Kant had used identical language in many of his earlier writings. Cf. *Vorlesungen über Religion*, p. 219; *Über das Misslingen*, IKW, VI, 131; *Grundlegung*, IKW, IV, 302; *Religion Innerhalb*, IKW, VI, 143 ff. Moreover, Kant frequently uses the term as if (gleich als), in the *Opus postumum*; cf. Vols. XXI, 15, 20, 22, 28, 30, 74, 92; XXII, 51, 53, 56, 104, 112 ff., 117 ff., 127.

There can be little doubt that Kant actually believed that the practical reason gets at the heart of reality, that in a literal sense it presents us with things as they really are. It is the latter aspect of the practical reason, the latter type of faith, which has been most influential in modern theology. One can, if one will, choose to accept Kant's private view as the more significant of the two, but the two views must not be confused. So far as the critical method is concerned, it cannot be maintained that things in themselves are given, positively, unless one means to equate things in themselves with a specific order of phenomena. One may offer the rejoinder that so far as moral experience is concerned it is *as if* things in themselves are given. And I suspect that this is the case. There is an existential element involved in religious faith, perhaps even in religious faith that is based exclusively upon morality. But this proves nothing! Kant should have been the last to conclude from this fact that things *are* actually given as they are in themselves. It is not *psychological* certainty or belief with which Kant is concerned.[37] It is rather the *a priori* principles required by reason in order to account for objective moral experience that are involved. Some post-Kantians have attempted to specify the formal conditions of psychological belief, the *a priori* conditions of religious experience in the subjective sense. But there is little in common between such psychological conditions and the *a priori* principles of the critical philosophy. This is only to restate the point that the Kantian *a priori* is not intended to be psychological in character, whether for science or morality.

PHENOMENALISM AND METAPHYSICS

There are at least three important ways in which Kant employs the concept of the thing-in-itself dogmatically: (1) in positing the thing-in-itself as the cause of appearances; (2) in holding that the categories are applicable to things in themselves; (3) in maintaining that the practical reason

[37] Cf. *Die Religion Innerhalb der Grenzen der Blossen Vernunft*, IKW, VI, 193 ff.; *Critique of Practical Reason*, IKW, V, 12n.

affords an access to things in themselves. This threefold dogmatic employment of the concept is indicative of the metaphysical undercurrent which runs through the critical writings. Kant was personally convinced of the reality of God as a transcendent being, of the world as teleologically ordered, and of the soul as free.[38] He struggled to avoid any confusion of his private views with his critical position, but was not always successful in keeping them separate. Whereas the concept of the thing-in-itself is always negative and empty, a limiting concept, in its critical meaning, in its dogmatic employment it has positive metaphysical content. The conflict for Kant was not between subjectivism and phenomenalism, but between ontological realism and phenomenalism. If he had ever had the opportunity to reconsider the continuity of his critical writings, there is good reason to believe that he would have found occasion to effect certain changes in order to bring them into greater self-consistency. He would, I am convinced, have found it necessary to eliminate altogether: (1) those passages in which he refers to the thing-in-itself as the cause of appearances; (2) those passages in which he attempts to find a theoretical foundation for the concepts of traditional metaphysics; (3) those passages in which he holds that any one faculty or area of experience affords an access to things in themselves.

Kant might well have written a further treatise on metaphysics in order to consider the positive character of things in themselves. Kantian phenomenalism and metaphysics are not incompatible. Phenomenalism itself becomes dogmatic when it insists that it is *meaningless* to raise questions about the nature of things in themselves. In suggesting the possibility of analogical knowledge as a basis for metaphysical judgments, Kant explicitly recognised this alternative.[39]

[38] A 466=B 494, A 631=B 659 ff.; *Vorlesungen über Religion*, pp. 18, 96, 138, 224 ff.; Reflexionen 6155, 6214, 6451, 6237, Ber.; *Prol.*, par. 57; Adickes, *Die bewegende Kräfte*, pp. 358 ff.; Heman, "Kants Platonismus und Theismus," *Kant-Studien*, Band 8, pp. 68 ff., 73, 81 ff.

[39] A 567=B 595, A 829=B 857, A 697=B 725; *Prol.*, par. 58; *Critique of Judgment*, IKW, V, 48 ff.; *Über die Fortschritte*, IKW, VIII, 260, 289, 305.

Moreover, Kant might have attempted to consider experience in its wholeness, taking into account the transcendental principles of the various modes of experience. This would involve the explication of the transcendental concepts which are presupposed by science, morality and art.[40] The critical philosophy always presupposes a rational faculty which is capable of just such an effort. It is not the theoretical reason which criticises the theoretical reason, nor the practical reason which criticises the practical reason, but the philosophical reason which accomplishes both tasks. It is this same faculty which might achieve some synthesis or reconciliation of the theoretical, practical, and aesthetic modes of experience. In the *Critique of Judgment*, Kant attempted something of this sort. By his own admission, he was seeking to find a bridge between the theoretical and the practical reason.[41] However, only a beginning was made; the task remains altogether incomplete. At best one gets some indication of the way in which Kant might have gone about the business of dealing with the various areas of experience synoptically.

The logical development and extension of the critical philosophy in this respect would be an all-inclusive phenomenalism. To the extent that certain of the neo-Kantians have attempted to accomplish this, they have been true to the Kantian methodology. However, if that is one legitimate extension of the critical method it is not the only one permitted. Kant himself was a metaphysician at heart. He was never satisfied to ignore the questions of metaphysics, and it is doubtful if he could ever have been content with an account of experience that was merely phenomenalistic in character. There is no basis whatever, on Kantian grounds, for the assertion that nonphenomenalistic metaphysics is meaningless. It is only dogmatic and rationalistic metaphysics

[40] Cf. the First Introduction to Kant's *Critique of Judgment*, IKW, V, 184 ff., 221 ff. Kant discarded this introduction only because of its excessive length. Cf. Kant's letter to Beck, 4th December, 1792, IKW, X, 181; letter to Herz, 24th November, 1776, IKW, IX, 152.

[41] *Critique of Judgment*, IKW, V, 185, 198, 226; cf. Dorner, *Kants Kritik der Urteilsraft in ihrer Beziehung zu den beiden anderen Kritiken*, pp. 250 ff.

which is declared to be futile.[42] The implication of the critical philosophy is not to rule out hypothetical metaphysics, to deny the meaning of speculation as to the nature of things in themselves, but only to deny the possibility of certainty in obtaining answers to such questions.[43]

Phenomenalism is impossible as a permanent position for philosophy in that it cuts the nerve of philosophical inquiry. Philosophy, unlike the sciences, is concerned to raise questions about the ultimate. That it may be unable to obtain ultimate answers is no reason in itself to ban such inquiry. On Kantian grounds *certain* knowledge of things in themselves is impossible. Yet even Kant could not avoid raising such questions. How can the notion of a phenomenal self be reconciled with the notion of a free self? How can the concept of a mechanically determined world be reconciled with the concept of an organic and teleological world.[44] These are questions which Kant could not avoid. That he arrived at no conclusive answers is no justification for the conclusion that such inquiry is meaningless. On the contrary, it further establishes the importance and urgency of such inquiry. It may be questioned whether the critical method itself could ever suffice to deal with such questions. It may even be doubted whether Kant was, in attempting to answer these questions, operating as a critical philosopher rather than as a traditional metaphysician. The important point is that while Kant flatly declared that reality in itself is theoretically unknowable, he could not escape trying to formulate meaningful theoretical concepts of it.

[42] A 563=B 591; A 740=B 768 ff.; *Über die Fortschritte*, IKW, VIII, 269 ff., 275, 317.
[43] *Über die Fortschritte*, IKW, VIII, 250 ff., 260; *Critique of Practical Reason*, IKW, V, 63 ff., 147 ff.; *Was heisst: sich im Denken orientieren*, IKW, IV, 354 ff.; B 307 ff.
[44] *Critique of Judgment*, IKW, V, 244, 265, 479, 483.

KANT'S 'REFUTATION' OF THE
ONTOLOGICAL ARGUMENT

S. MORRIS ENGEL

Kant's compressed and tightly knit analysis of the ontological argument in the Transcendental Dialectic (Chapter III, Section 4) contains fourteen paragraphs. The first paragraph is introductory and summarizes his general position as to the relative functions of Understanding and Reason and acts as a link between his preceding argument and what follows. The last two paragraphs contain his conclusions. The eleven paragraphs in between have usually been divided into four groups, and each group has been taken to represent a different phase or stage in his case against the ontological proof.[1] Although Kant's Section does lend itself to this kind of division, the groups of four criticisms so obtained admit of a still further division into a set of three criticisms of a polemical and negative character and one of a more direct and positive character, separated by a highly significant transitional paragraph (usually, but mistakenly, counted as the last paragraph of the third criticism).

Of the set of three objections so isolated, the first (*that it is far from clear how it is possible to think the concept of an unconditionally necessary being, let alone prove its objective validity*) is given by Kant in the second paragraph of the Section; the second (*that to think of the unconditionally necessary being in terms of examples is both misleading and fruitless*) follows immediately upon that and is handled in

Reprinted with permission of the author and of the editors from *Philosophy and Phenomenological Research* (1963–64), 20–35.
[1] See, e.g. *Kant Selections*, ed. Theodore M. Greene (New York, 1957), p. 244n.

the next three paragraphs; the third (*that there is no subject which cannot be thought away, regardless of its predicates*) covers the next three paragraphs and completes that part of his programme.

At this point there follows in the text the transitional paragraph in which Kant seems to apologize for the polemical nature of the preceding discussion which, he fears, may appear unnecessarily severe and prolonged. He had hoped to be able to put an end to these idle and fruitless disputes in a few words by means of a precise exposition of the concept of existence, but his experience in these matters, especially with regard to the inveterate confusion of a logical with a real predicate, has convinced him of the futility of such a direct assault. A real predicate, he says here, is a predicate which determines a thing. It is a predicate which, when added to the concept of a subject, enlarges it (adds something to it) and does not merely explicate it. A logical predicate, on the other hand, is not a determining predicate, for logic abstracts from all real content, and anything at all can serve as a logical predicate. And by that I suppose he means that any symbol whatever can equally well serve as a logical predicate, since it is not, unlike the real predicate, a reflection or product of some external experience and is not limited by any of the external conditions of experience. Such a predicate adds nothing, and can add nothing, to what is already contained in the concept of the subject. The paragraph in its entirety runs as follows:

Ich würde zwar hoffen, diese grüblerische Argumentation, ohne allen Umschweif, durch eine genaue Bestimmung des Begriffs der Existenz zunichte zu machen, wenn ich nicht gefunden hätte, dass die Illusion, in Verwechslung eines logischen Prädikats mit einem realen, (d.i. der Bestimmung eines Dinges,) beinahe alle Belehrung ausschlage. Zum logischen Prädikate kann alles dienen, was man will, sogar das Subjekt kann von sich selbst prädiziert werden; denn die Logik abstrahiert von allem Inhalte. Aber die Bestimmung ist ein Prädikat, welches über den Begriff des Subjekts hinzukommt und ihn vergrössert. Sie muss also nicht in ihm schon enthalten sein.[2]

To the confusion of these two distinct kinds of predicates, then, is due all those illusions and deceptions, the exposure of which has occupied him thus far. The source of the confusion and its resulting illusions having now been laid bare, he can proceed with the direct statement, or to the fourth and final objection (*that the cause of all this confusion is the mistaken belief that existence is a real predicate when it is nothing of the kind*) which is given in the remaining three paragraphs (excluding the conclusion) of the Section.[3]

There is obviously a kind of cumulative progression in Kant's argument (the stages of which I have put into italics and enclosed in brackets), which increases in force as it proceeds. Taken as a whole, what Kant seems to be saying is this: The attempt has been made to derive the existence of an unconditionally necessary being merely from the concept of a most real being. But it is far from clear how it is possible even to think the concept of an unconditionally necessary being, let alone prove its existence. To try to think of it (as has sometimes been the practice in the past) in terms of examples (such as, for instance, triangles and angles) is of no help at all and proves nothing, for there is no subject which cannot be thought away, regardless of its predicates. (I cannot deny that a triangle has three angles and yet affirm the existence of a triangle. But there is no contradiction in denying both subject and predicate; there is no contradiction in saying there is no triangle and no three angles). Besides, existence or 'being' is not a real predicate, *i.e.* it is not the kind of predicate which can add anything to a subject, and so even if it did make sense to say of an unconditionally necessary being that it exists, the ground for so doing could not be that *only thus* would our concept of its perfection be complete!

[2] *Kritik der Reinen Vernunft*, ed. Raymund Schmidt (Hamburg, 1956), pp. 571–72.

[3] At this point readers of Kant have usually gone on to conclude, prematurely, that what follows is an attempt to show that 'existence' is a logical predicate. But this is, as I shall soon try to show, a mistake.

This abstract of Kant's argument makes it clear, I think, why he should have thought that a direct analysis of this concept of existence was all that is needed in order to dispose of the ontological proof, as well as of all those arguments which have traditionally been advanced in support of it; for if it can be shown that existence is not a perfection or a real predicate, then all arguments in support of the proof which presupposes that it is must fall to the ground. In what follows, therefore, Kant proceeds to make this direct assault on the proposition that existence is a real predicate. He first defines the nature of a real predicate, tries to show why existence does not belong to this class of predicates, and (as is his usual practice) why it has been mistakenly thought to be a real predicate. Unfortunately, Kant allows himself only three (comparatively) short paragraphs in which to do all this. Not unexpectedly, the result is somewhat less than satisfactory. Just how unsatisfactory and where, is what I should like to explore in this paper.

II

Of the three paragraphs which deal in this direct fashion with the ontological proof, the first is by far the most important and contains nearly everything Kant has to say on this matter. I shall therefore quote it in its entirety and confine my discussion almost entirely to it. In order to make my subsequent exposition somewhat more fluent and less cumbersome I give it here in Norman Kemp Smith's translation, supported, wherever necessary, by the original text.

'*Being*' is obviously not a real predicate; that is, it is not a concept of something which could be added to the concept of a thing. It is merely the positing of a thing, or of certain determinations, as existing in themselves. Logically, it is merely the copula of a judgment. The proposition, 'God is omnipotent', contains two concepts, each of which has its object—God and omnipotence. The small word 'is' adds no new predicate, but only serves to posit the predicate *in its relation* to the subject. If, now, we take the subject (God) with all its predicates (among which is omnipotence), and say 'God is', or 'There is a God', we attach no new predicate to the concept of God, but only posit the subject in itself with all its predicates, and indeed posit it as being an *object* that stands in relation to my *concept*. The content of both must be one and the same; nothing can have been added to the concept, which expresses merely what is possible, by my thinking its object (through the expression 'it is') as given absolutely. Otherwise stated, the real contains no more than the merely possible. A hundred real thalers do not contain the least coin more than a hundred possible thalers. For as the latter signify the concept, and the former the object and the positing of the object, should the former contain more than the latter, my concept would not, in that case, express the whole object, and would not therefore be an adequate concept of it. My financial position is, however, affected very differently by a hundred real thalers than it is by the mere concept of them (that is, of their possibility). For the object, as it actually exists, is not analytically contained in my concept, but is added to my concept (which is a determination of my state) synthetically; and yet the conceived hundred thalers are not themselves in the least increased through thus acquiring existence outside my concept.[4]

I will now take up Kant's analysis sentence by sentence (but not necessarily in the order in which they appear). The first thing to notice about Kant's opening sentence is that he does not say "*Being* is not a predicate", he says that "*Being* is not a real predicate." Those who are in the habit of ascribing to Kant the former statement either believe Kant is using the word "real" not in a technical but in a metaphorical sense, *i.e.* in the sense of "really", so that the sentence is made to read "*Being* is not a predicate at all"; or believe that Kant is expressing himself loosely and cannot possibly be implying that 'Being' is some other kind of predicate, although not a 'real' one, for he later goes on to say that logically the word has only one function and that is to serve as a copula in a judgment. But here too he is being misinterpreted, for

[4] *The Critique of Pure Reason*, tr. Norman Kemp Smith (London, 1929), pp. 504–5.

Kant does not say its sole function is a logical one, but merely that *from a logical point of view* it has this particular function. In his own words: "Logically, it is merely the copula of a judgment"[5] (*"Im logischen Gebrauche ist es lediglich die Copula eines Urteils"*).

But if Kant is using the word 'real', as he obviously is, in a technical sense, then what kind of predicate is 'Being', seeing it is not a 'real' one? In other words, if it is true that from a logical point of view 'Being' or 'is' functions simply as a copula, and from a 'real' point of view it is not a predicate which stands for something real, then what kind of predicate is it? It must be *some* kind of predicate, for Kant does not say "Being is not a predicate," he only says it is not a *real* predicate. And the answer to this question is not that 'being' is a logical predicate, for from a logical point of view not only is 'being' not a real predicate, it is not a predicate at all. If then 'being' is not a real predicate and not a logical predicate, what kind of predicate is it? What, in other words, is the implication of Kant's remark that " '*Being*' is not a real predicate"?

Kant's answer to this question is that "it is merely the positing of a thing, or of certain determinations, as existing

[5] Now Kant is partly responsible for this misreading of his thought, for in the transition paragraph which immediately precedes this one, a summary of which I gave above, he distinguishes between a logical and a real predicate and leads the reader to believe that these two predicates are not only mutually exclusive but jointly exhaustive of all possibilities. The reader not unnaturally proceeds to read the rest of the Section in terms of this strict dichotomy. But this is not Kant's intention. In fact in his transitional paragraph Kant is not speaking about a logical predicate as such but about a predicate, logical or real, used for logical purposes—for purposes of illustrating some logical rule or proposition—for, as he says, "anything we please can be made to serve as a logical predicate" and this would not, presumably, exclude real predicates. Thus to illustrate the nature of an analytic proposition (and it is the analytic proposition with which he is mainly concerned here) and bring into relief the *logic* of such propositions we might make use of all kinds of predicates, real or not. It is for this reason, of course, that this paragraph has usually been attached to the foregoing group which deals with analytic propositions every one of which, Kant's argument there asserts, can be thought away, but since it also reads as a summary of the whole set of three objections it would be best to regard it as transitional in nature.

in themselves" ("*Es ist bloss die Position eines Dinges, oder gewisser Bestimmungen an sich selbst*"). This is, of course, not very clear, but Kant will go on to explain later what he means. Before, however, we follow him in this it might be helpful to note the structure or logic of these first three sentences of the paragraph I am presently examining. The first states that "being" is not a real predicate and goes on to explain what a real predicate would be, *viz.* "a concept of something which could be added to the concept of a thing" ("*ein Begriff von irgend etwas, was zu dem Begriffe eines Dinges hinzukommen könnte*"). The emphasis here is not upon the common word 'concept' but upon 'thing'. To be a real predicate of a subject a predicate must do or add some thing to the subject and widen it in some way. The second sentence tells us something about the function of a predicate which is not a real predicate, *viz.* that it is one which merely posits a thing, or certain determinations, without adding 'anything' to them or extending them in any way. The important question here is, of course, where does such purported positing take place, and what status does the posited thing have? This question we may for the time being lay aside. The third sentence requires little expansion: it merely states that logically 'being' is merely the copula of a judgment. These three opening sentences, then, represent *three* distinct theses: one with regard to real predicates; one with regard to non-real predicates; and one with regard to logical predicates.

I have taken the trouble, and perhaps the reader's patience, to put this matter is such detail because these three sentences have usually been read as positing two theses only: one with regard to real predicates, the other with regard to logical predicates. The rest of the paragraph has then been read as an exposition of *these* two kinds of predicates. Now this reading of the paragraph is somewhat of an oversimplification and does not do justice to the real complexity of the argument. In the first part of the paragraph Kant gives an example of the logical predicate functioning as a copula and compares it to its counterpart, functioning as a nonreal predicate. When the parallel function of these two kinds of predicates (the logical and the nonreal) are established he proceeds to examine the functions of the nonreal predicate with *its* counterpart, the real predicate. The pivot upon which the whole thing seems to turn is the nonreal predicate whose use is compared with the logical predicate and contrasted with the real predicate.

(A)

I should now like to go on to examine the first part of this programme (in which the logical predicate is compared with the nonreal predicate) and attempt to discover what, in Kant's view, the function of a nonreal predicate is and how it discharges that function. "The proposition, 'God is omnipotent'," he says, "contains two concepts, each of which has its object—God and omnipotence. The small word 'is' adds no new predicate, but only serves to posit the predicate *in its relation* to the subject." There is nothing particularly striking or new in these remarks, although, perhaps, it may seem somewhat odd to speak of the concept of God as having an object when this is precisely what is at issue here. That Kant, however, does not mean by 'object' what the term ordinarily conveys becomes clear in the very next sentence. "If, now, we take the subject (God) with all its predicates (among which is omnipotence), and say 'God is', or 'There is a God', we attach no new predicate to the concept of God, but only posit the subject in itself with all its predicates, and indeed posit it as being an *object* that stands in relation to my *concept*." By recalling the use of the phrase "in relation to" in the previous sentence and its repetition here it becomes apparent that what Kant means is that in the nonreal use of the predicate 'Being' we posit a relationship among elements not unlike the kind of relationship which is established by the logical use of this predicate in judgments.

What is that relationship? This question is not easy to answer. Kant does not offer much guidance, and he tends to be—as is so often the case with him—technical without being precise. Still it is possible to make some sense of his all too brief remarks. What he seems to be saying, if not explicitly then at least by implication, is that the predicate 'is' has as its major function the job of asserting, establishing, or positing the subject. Although such positing can take various forms (depending upon what is posited or asserted) it is never an isolated or disconnected act. What is posited (or entertained) is, he says, an 'object' and by this I gather he means some conceptual entity or 'meaning'. This 'object' or 'meaning' is conveyed by means of some linguistic entity or 'concept'. The function of the word 'is' is to connect or relate the 'object' of the 'concept' of the predicate to the 'object' of the 'concept' of the subject—it is not ('is' is not, that is) in itself a 'concept' which has its own 'object'. This is, at least, the case with such propositions as 'God is omnipotent' which, he says, to use his own words this time, "*enthält zwei Begriffe, die ihre Objekte haben: Gott und Allmacht; das Wörtchen: ist, ist nicht noch ein Prädikat obenein, sondern nur das, was das Prädikat beziehungsweise aufs Subjekt setzt.*"

In a simple proposition of this type which has a subject, copula, and predicate, it is the function of the copula, according to Kant, to relate the 'meaning' of the concept-term of the predicate to the 'meaning' of the concept-term of the subject. What, however, happens in cases of those propositions which seem to have no predicate and in which the word 'is' appears to be itself a 'concept' having *its own* 'object' as, for example, in the proposition 'God is'? Here Kant's analysis becomes somewhat more complicated. In the case of the proposition 'God is' we seem to be missing a predicate; the sentence seems to be incomplete. 'God is' what? one is tempted to ask. This question, Kant implies, need not arise. The sentence is complete and intelligible. And not only is it complete and perfectly intelligible but the word 'is' in this proposition has a parallel function to that which it has in the proposition 'God is omnipotent'. How is that possible? Kant answers that the missing predicate-term here is the 'object' (unit of meaning) conveyed by the concept-term 'God' in the proposition. The term 'God' which appears in the subject-position in this proposition, that is, is projected by the speaker into the predicate-position. The predicate-position is now filled, but it appears we have done so by disposing of the subject and the sentence now appears to be devoid of a subject. This however is not the case. The subject position, according to Kant, is now occupied by the Subject (the speaker) himself. The proposition 'God is', in other words, has an *external* subject—the speaker himself who by means of the 'is' posits, or entertains, the object 'God' and entertains it as the 'object' of *his* 'concept'.

Kant's remark, therefore, that in the proposition "*Gott ist, oder es ist ein Gott, so setze ich kein neues Prädikat zum Begriffe von Gott, sondern nur das Subjekt an sich selbst mit allen seinen Prädikaten, und zwar den Gegenstand in Beziehung auf meinen Begriff*" seems to me to most readily lend itself (to summarize) to the following reading: from a logical point of view the word "is" merely posits the predicate in its relation to the subject; in those propositions in which the word "is" is not followed by a predicate and thus has no predicate which it could posit in relation to a subject and therefore seems to function in an entirely different way —functions as if it were asserting or positing an 'object' of *its own*—a little analysis will show that this is mistaken, that its function is still to posit (not itself, i.e. some mythical 'object' answering to 'is') but the predicate (in this case the subject-turned-predicate) in its relation to the subject (in this case me or my concept). In the proposition 'God is', therefore, the word "is" has a parallel function to that which it has in the proposition 'God is omnipotent' in that it connects or posits the subject (God) as the object of my concept, or posits it *in relation to* me—its *external* subject. In the proposition 'God is omnipotent', in short, the subject (God) is within the proposition; in the proposition 'God is' the subject (God) becomes an object which has as *its* subject the "I" which does the positing.

Now this may seem as if Kant were here implying that in addition to entertaining the class of predicates (real predicates) which issue in synthetic and ampliative propositions, and the class of predicates (logical predicates) which issue in analytic and explicative propositions, he is now supposing the existence of a third class, one which is distinct from either of these, but I do not believe that these are his intentions here. On the other hand, it is clear that his analysis which, among other things, involves speaking of subjects turning into objects is intended to draw its strength from a certain theory of linguistic processes upon which that analysis rests and of which it is a function. And I don't know how else one could make intelligible to oneself this dichotomy into subject and object, each with its own content, one posited by the other, and both in the one linguistic or conceptual stream other than by supposing that the doctrine rests upon a kind of conceptualistic or *two*-stream theory of language in terms of which alone the doctrine can be defended, if defended at all. And in terms of this theory of language, what Kant seems to be saying is that in making the statement "God exists," what I am asserting to exist is not God but, first of all, a certain conceptual entity or unit of 'meaning' which accompanies the expression of the word 'God' (and which Kant calls the object of the concept) and, secondly, the assertion that this 'object' or 'unit of meaning' is the objective correlative, so to speak, of the concept—is what I am thinking, is what I am entertaining.

I believe it is precisely this sort of view of language and thought which makes Kant's case seem so plausible at first sight. It is also this sort of view of language and thought which, as I hope to show, has tended to induce some people to accept Kant's conclusions and to give their assent to more than the argument actually succeeds in proving. At the moment, however, all I should like to indicate is that although most people would nowadays claim that nothing accompanies the expression of a word (for there are not two streams, a conceptual and a linguistic, but only one) this view of linguistic processes nevertheless is what makes it possible for Kant to make a prima facie case for saying that 'is' is not a real predicate and, in the second half of this paragraph, that a hundred real dollars do not contain one cent more than a hundred possible dollars—a remark which many still find to be most paradoxical. But the point is this: if there are two such streams in the use of language, and if in saying of anything that it exists we simply mean that the one stream is commensurate with the other, then of course it follows that not only is nothing added to our concept by saying of its objective correlative that it exists (and that to *deny* it would be absurd) but it is obviously even fatuous to assert it—since on the linguistic theory here presupposed the particular objective correlative could never be posited as the concept's objective correlative if it were not perfectly congruent with it!

And this is just the point of Kant's statement at the very beginning of the next paragraph. (I have not completed my examination of the first paragraph, but I cannot avoid bringing in this last point before moving on to consider the second half of the paragraph quoted above.) Kant says: "By whatever and by however many predicates we may think a thing —even if we completely determine it—we do not make the least addition to the thing when we further declare that this thing *is*. Otherwise, it would not be exactly the same thing that exists, but something more than we had thought in the concept; and we could not, therefore, say that the exact object of my concept exists." On the basis of the theory of language presupposed by Kant's analysis of the nonreal predicate, this follows with perfect necessity.

It becomes more and more apparent, as one examines these remarks carefully, that what Kant's analysis amounts to is this: when I say "God is omnipotent" there is, first of all, a linguistic stream represented by the characters on this paper or the particular sounds made when these are vocalized, and secondly, a conceptual stream of which these sounds are linguistic translations. The function of the copula here is to relate the conceptual entity represented by the word "omnipotent" to the conceptual entity expressed or represented by the word "God." In the proposition "God is," however, "is" has not got its own conceptual counterpart; it is a nonreal predicate whose function it is to relate the conceptual entity represented by the word "God" to the person entertaining it, as the 'object' of his thought (or, as Kant puts it, the object of his concept)—just as its function as a logical predicate is to relate or posit the predicate in its relation to the subject (of the proposition).

On the basis of this interpretation it becomes also clear what Kant's statement that 'Being' "is merely the positing of a thing, or of certain determinations, as existing in themselves" means, and what answers he would have given to the questions raised above as to where such positing takes place and what status the thing so posited is assumed to have. But the question one is still tempted to raise is, What makes Kant think the word "is" has not got its own conceptual "charge" or counterpart?

Now I believe it is possible that Kant was led to think this by confusing the two senses of the word "is" and forgetting that while the word "is" as a logical connective is devoid of its own semantic content, the word "is" (in the sense of "exists") may still possess such a content. Whether he was or was not so confused, it is clear that what he was trying to do was to develop a linguistic situation in which the word "is" (in the sense of "exists") could, without completely distorting its primary meaning, be shown to be reducible or to function in a way comparable or parallel to that which it has as a logical connective. If he could do that, then there would be no need to assume that "is" (in the sense of "exists") has a conceptual content of its own; there would be no need to assume that is to say, that "is" is a real predicate (and thus in one blow dispose of the ontological proof). Since, however, its function is not simply to connect elements on the one semantic plane but isomorphic elements from two separate planes (the conceptual and the linguistic) it is also not, he was forced to say, an ordinary logical predicate either, but rather a nonreal, nonadditive predicate which neither amplifies or explicates the subject, but simply *posits* it.

I cannot help feeling that this was Kant's plan; a repeated reading of the entire chapter has left me in no doubt that some such process of reasoning lies imbedded in its construction.

(B)

But although Kant's analysis, resting as I believe it does upon this two-stream theory of language, may seem plausible enough at the logical and conceptual level, it begins to show signs of strain when he turns in the second half of the paragraph to consider the relation of the nonreal predicate to its counterpart, the real predicate. Here the linguistic theory upon which he seems to depend serves him less well. But the transition from the nonreal to the real is handled so deftly that most readers probably never suspect anything amiss here. Their consent is forced from them, and almost before they realize it they are saddled with the paradox of the hundred real dollars which contain not a cent more than the hundred possible dollars. By this time it is already too late, for they now feel that the burden of proof lies on their shoulders and not on Kant's. They are even led to forget that Kant only some five or six paragraphs back criticized and censured the use of examples or analogies which, in this connection, are far more misleading than helpful, only to make use of one (this one) himself.

The content of my concept and its conceptual object (or its objective correlative), Kant had just finished saying, must be one and the same, for nothing is added to the concept, which expresses merely the possibility of the object, by *thinking* its object as existing. "Otherwise stated," he now adds ingenuously, "the real contains no more than the merely possible." And with that remark one is bodily transported to the realm of the real and very quickly confronted with the paradox of the hundred dollars. But the trouble with the argument as it stands now is that the linguistic structure which was able to carry it to this point has now been overloaded and can no longer support the extra weight put on it. For the *real* is an additional element which is not a product of my thought and therefore its correspondence with my concept can no longer be taken for granted as *a priori* certain. In other words, it might be quite reasonable to maintain that in entertaining a concept we at the same time posit its object which, being the concept's objective correlative, must coincide or be congruent with it. In positing, however, a concept of an existing thing what we posit is not some conceptual element of which we could say *a priori* that it is completely congruent with it, but the thing itself whose congruence with the concept is a matter to be proved or established and which cannot therefore be taken for granted. Kant's theory of language, that is to say, no longer proves to be an adequate instrument in dealing with this more complicated linguistic situation. It was serviceable enough when restricted to the conceptual plane, but is a good deal less so when confronted with a real world of objects, one which language seems to reflect in a direct and not in the indirect way presupposed by Kant.

Kant's answer to the objection I am raising—that if the concept were not congruent with the thing and should the thing contain more than the concept, the concept would not express the whole object and would therefore not be an adequate concept of it—is hardly satisfactory, for a person might still argue that we can never be sure that our concepts *are* adequate expressions of things or perfectly conform to their archetypes. It would also be a mistake to regard Kant's remarks at the end of the paragraph (that my financial position is "affected very differently by a hundred real thalers than it is by the mere concept of them") as in any way an answer to the objection raised here, for the same could be said of God's existence which also makes a good deal of difference to those who believe in Him. But both remarks are really irrelevant, for the question is simply whether existence adds something to a concept *per se* and to this question Kant gives an unequivocal answer that it does not. It is this thesis which remains to be examined.

III

Even if Kant were able to prove, despite the external (and therefore in some ways unfair) criticisms which I have made, that his analysis is nevertheless correct, it would still not establish what he wants it to establish, namely, that existence is not a predicate which adds anything to the concept of a thing, but something much less than this. In fact, all that his theory of language, upon which his analysis is based, will permit him to establish, I should now like to show, is that existence is not a predicate which can add anything to a concept of a thing *which already has it*.

Now it is not *obviously* true that existence is not a real predicate or perfection. Most people, if they are candid, will still admit that it requires some discipline and persuasion to give their assent to the thesis. On the other hand there is something "remarkably queer," as one recent writer has put it, in the doctrine that existence *is* a perfection. "It makes

sense," Malcolm has recently written, "and is true to say that
my future house will be a better one if it is insulated than
if it is not insulated; but what could it mean to say that it
will be a better house if it exists than if it does not?"[6]

I think it is possible now to give an answer to the question which will fully account for this feeling of queerness
and show why Kant's argument does not quite prove what
it sets out to prove. The point I want to make is that on the
theory of linguistic processes (or some theory close to it),
to say of a future house that it would be a better one if it
is insulated than if it is not insulated makes sense because
the house in question, although it already exists in thought,
exists simply as a house and nothing is therefore contradicted
by adding to this thought (as we move in imagination to
the predicate) the further thought that it is insulated. Nor
is there anything trifling or fatuous about this remark since
the original thought is an indeterminate one and the second
determines it. On the other hand, to say of the house *which
exists already* (that it exists in thought only as a future possibility makes no difference here, for, as Hobbes would say,
'thought is quick' and furthermore, for it, only the present
is real) that it will be a better house *if* it exists (meaning
that it *does not yet exist*) than if it does not, is at once
both absurd and fatuous—absurd because it involves a contradiction, and fatuous because one only gathers much later
(after having fallen into the trap of expecting that which
should not have been expected) that the statement was intended as a mere tautology and a trifling one at that.[7]

The same analysis applies to Malcolm's other examples
which like the one above were designed by him to illustrate
and support Kant's thesis. They can all be shown to be examples of either contradictory or fatuous propositions because to
posit anything is to entertain it in thought and this automat-

[6] Norman Malcolm, "Anselm's Ontological Arguments," *Philosophical Review*, 69 (1960), 41–62, p. 43.

[7] As a manufactured example this is not a particularly good one
since it is possible to account for its absurdity on more ordinary
lines, ones having nothing to do with the problem at hand. There
is always, as in this case, an element of comedy in speculations about
the relative merits concerning things not yet in existence.

ically sets the tone of the proposition and limits the range of its possible predicates. "A king might desire that his next chancellor," to take another of Malcolm's examples, "should have knowledge, wit, and resolution; but it is ludicrous to add that the king's desire is to have a chancellor who exists".[8] What is ludicrous here is *not* that the king would like to endow his chancellor with a property (existence) which he cannot possibly have (seeing that existence is not a property or a real predicate) but the fact that he *already has* the property with which he wishes to endow him. And this is just the point, I should like to suggest, about predicates such as 'existence'.[9]

According to Kant, the function of a real predicate is to increase or enlarge the domain or holdings, so to speak, of the subject term. He envisages the subject term as already in possession of a certain area over which it 'dominates' and it is the function of the predicate term to enlarge that domain and thus increase the 'denomination' of its subject term. But 'Being', he argues, is not that kind of predicate. Aside from its logical use, it merely posits or asserts that the part of the whole or domain which the subject occupies is the part of the whole of which, in fact, it is in possession. On the other hand, to think of 'being' (on these lines) as a real predicate would be to entertain the possibility of being able to predicate of a subject (to *add* to a subject), which occupies a part of this whole, not this same part and not some other part but the *quality* of the whole itself—only a part of which it possesses. And there is something either fallacious or odd about this, as is illustrated by the example of the king whose desire it is that his next chancellor should have knowledge, wit, resolution, *and existence*. Far from adding anything to the subject by the addition of such a predicate, this kind of predicate even tends to produce the contrary effect.

Now although Kant realized well enough that there was something odd about proceeding in this way, I don't believe he had any clear idea why this was so. The point, however,

[8] *Ibid.*
[9] But here again this example lends itself to a more ordinary interpretation which yields as much, if not more, humor.

is not difficult to state: if a subject is already in possession of
a part of a whole, it possesses at the same time all the qualities of that part—among which, in this case, existence must
be counted. Now since 'existence' is a kind of predicate whose
quantity can neither increase nor diminish with the addition
of further parts, nothing is accomplished by predicating of
the part the quality which it is believed the whole itself has
—either in virtue of its greater number of parts or simply
in virtue of it being a whole. In the case of such predicates
as 'existence', that is to say, the test of division or composition is inapplicable, for to have them at all is to have all there
is to have. One cannot, in other words, have other properties
and still not have 'being', and one cannot lose 'being' and
still retain other properties. Now although this is all perfectly reasonable and explains the oddity of predicating
existence of some things in some contexts, it does not follow
from this—as Kant mistakenly thinks it does—that existence is
not a real predicate or a real property. What does follow is
that in some contexts it is absurd to predicate of a thing
certain qualities, not because these are qualities that can add
nothing to the subject, but because the subject already has
the qualities which are predicated of it. To do so, despite
all this, is either to bring the predicate which it already has
into question or to commit the 'fallacy of double predication'—if I may be permitted to so call it. In the case,
however, of those things which do not have this quality, it
would still be possible to argue, I should think, that to predicate it of them would be to add something to them.

It is for this reason that there is something hollow and
inconsecutive in Kant's further argument in the paragraph
following the one I have been looking at where he states if
we think in a thing every mode of reality except one, the
missing mode is not supplied by my saying that this defective thing exists; for, on the contrary, it exists with the same
defect with which I have thought it. Now Kant cannot have
it both ways: either the missing quality or mode is not
'existence' but something else (in which case it follows, of
course, that the thing will continue to exist with the same
defect as before and nothing is accomplished by saying it
exists—that property it already has or had), or the thing is

not defective, for if existence is not a property then it is not a property the want of which could make it defective. Kant's example, in other words, is an impossible one.

Kant, nevertheless, goes on to conclude from this that when I, therefore, think a Being as the highest reality, without any defect, the question still remains whether it exists or not— that is, whether (as he goes on to explain) it exists as some *part* of this (whole) world of my experience. Now the obvious answer to this question (one usually resorted to by those who, like Malcolm, are still inclined to see something in the ontological argument) is that of course God does not exist in *that* way. God is not a part of this world and is not an object of my experience. But this simply means that God lacks *contingent* existence. But in the case of God this is hardly a defect, for if he had contingent existence he would not be God, or what we ordinarily understand by that term.[10]

To bring the various threads of my argument together. An examination of Kant's theory of predication shows that it rests upon certain presuppositions and assumptions regard-

[10] But even Kant, it should be noted, at the end of his third paragraph of the group of three I have been commenting upon, does not exclude the possibility that God might have an existence outside the field of our experience. He only adds that any such alleged existence, "while not indeed such as we can declare to be absolutely impossible, is of the nature of an assumption which we can never be in a position to justify." I don't think this remark can be interpreted as simply expressing the belief that despite everything said thus far it is still possible that God exists. Kant had never questioned *that*. Rather what I think it means is that it is possible that there is something which stands to God in the same way in which existence stands to things in this world. And this, if I am not mistaken, is what Malcolm (whose paper on Anselm has occasioned so much discussion) is trying to say as well. This is not, however, the point of my discussion, which is mainly or solely concerned with showing what Kant's argument proves and what it only purports but fails to prove. It has been my intention (perhaps it might be wise to add) neither to affirm that existence is a real predicate nor, still less, argue for the validity or truth of the ontological argument; for as far as the former matter is concerned I am no longer sure whether it is or not, and as to the latter all I have tried to suggest is that if the ontological argument fails to prove what it sets out to prove, the reasons for its failure must be other than those given by Kant. It would not have been part of my purpose to state what those reasons might be—even were I to know them, which I do not.

ing linguistic processes, presuppositions and assumptions which enable him to give a fairly plausible account of the three-fold function of the word "is": as copula in judgments; as a linguistic device identifying items in one linguistic stream with their congruent counterparts in the other; and as a nonadditive predicate. I have said nothing, in this paper, in criticism of 'is' functioning as a copula, but I have tried to show that Kant's account of the word functioning as a mechanism of identification breaks down when confronted with the world of real things, one not posited by us and therefore one not necessarily congruent with our concepts of it. To say something 'existential' about things in this world, it has seemed to me, is not to utter something uninteresting about them. But even if it were, even, that is to say, if it were true that 'existence' is not a real predicate, given these linguistic conditions, we could never be in a position to prove it; for anything we entertain in thought—according to this linguistic view—already shares that property and thus the most one could prove, given this frame of reference, is that 'existence' is not a predicate or a property which can add something to a concept of a thing which already—it is somehow assumed— has it, and not that it is not a property which can be added to things which, should it be somehow supposed, have not got it.

PART TWO

DISCUSSIONS OF
KANT'S ETHICAL THEORY

THE CATEGORICAL IMPERATIVE

INTERPRETATION AND MISINTERPRETATION OF THE CATEGORICAL IMPERATIVE*

JULIUS EBBINGHAUS

The concept connected by Kant with the phrase 'categorical imperative' seems easy to explain. It means a law valid for the will of every rational being and therefore valid unconditionally. This is in no need of interpretation: it can hardly be misinterpreted. Kant has stated it in the clearest and most intelligible terms. Understanding becomes much more difficult if we are concerned, not merely with the verbal definition, but with the content of the categorical command and with the inferences to be drawn from it. Even specialists have fallen into confusion about these questions and have, as it were, begun to see ghosts in quarters where reason prevails: but, quite apart from this, the doctrine of a categorical imperative inherent in the will of man himself appears at present to meet with most unexpected and most unwanted repercussions in the common opinion, not merely of Germany, but almost of the whole world. To lovers of humanity it may seem a lofty and worthy aim that doctrines elaborated by science and claiming to determine the conduct of every man should gradually spread wider and wider until at last every cottage is illuminated by the light this labour gen-

Reprinted with permission of the author and of the editors from *Philosophical Quarterly*, 4 (1954), 97–108.

* This article was originally published, under the title *Deutung und Missdeutung des kategorischen Imperativs*, in *Studium Generale*, 1 Jahrgang (1948), Heft 7. This translation, by Professor H. J. Paton, is printed here by kind permission of Professor Ebbinghaus and the Springer-Verlag of Berlin, Goettingen, and Heidelberg, the publishers of *Studium Generale*.

erates. But it also seems as if precisely this welcome process, which has gained greatly in intensity since the eighteenth century, has merely added one more to those evils of civilisation by which mankind is afflicted. When we argue with experts in our own subject, we can pretty well manage at least to be correctly understood and not to be saddled with conclusions in direct contradiction of our own thought; but we are, so to speak, robbed of all protection when matters of controversy among the learned are thrust, through the efforts of more or less unfriendly publicists, upon the wide masses of the educated or half-educated, are there passed from hand to hand, and are finally hurled into a sea of surging passion. This happens most of all when we are concerned with the propositions of a science which—like philosophy— is still having to *fight* for its existence so that attacks upon any doctrinal structure attempted in its name will never fail to find authorities prepared to back them. No matter how ludicrous men may consider the claim of philosophy as a guide to life, they are always ready, when they have reduced their affairs to utter disorder, to listen to those who find its cause in some philosophy they dislike.

No one need be surprised if in the present miseries of the world voices are raised expressing all too clearly the view that the susceptibility to National Socialism displayed by wide ranges of the German people springs properly from that readiness for unconditioned obedience, that spirit of unconditioned sacrifice, which is undoubtedly demanded by Kant in his law of duty; or at least—not going quite so far— the view that Kant's law voices precisely that Prussian or German inclination for discipline and subjection, that readiness for harshness and rigour, that insensitiveness to all the gentler movements of the spirit, which celebrated their frightful triumphs in the years of Terror. 'All that is worthy of respect in me is my capacity to obey—and the same must hold for you as it does for me'. In these words Friedrich Nietzsche already gave utterance to an interpretation of Kant's ethics in which the above view is anticipated. The morality of the categorical imperative as the morality of the correct Prussian official, who regards his superiors as gods or demi-gods and disdains the pleasures of life as sour grapes—

this is one of the travesties into which the greatest achievement in the field of ethics since Plato has been distorted by
a sociological treatment that has lost its bearings.

I

If we turn its own methods upon this treatment itself, we
discover behind it a tendency to interpret statements, not
by the real necessities which led to them, but by some sort
of assumed subjective motive. The law formulated by Kant
in his categorical imperative is not one by which any principle whatever to which a man may find himself drawn under
conditions of experience—such as obedience to potentates or
abstention from the pleasures of life—can be imposed on him
categorically. Kant's law is rather a way of expressing the
conditions under which alone a principle can have the character of a categorical demand. The categorical imperative is
thus conceived as the fundamental principle determining
which possible principles can be objectively valid for the decisions of our will as such. When we say it is our duty to
do something or to refrain from doing it, we manifestly have
in mind such a categorical demand or such an objectively
valid principle. Hence we can also say that on Kant's view
the categorical imperative contains nothing but the concept
of being under a possible moral obligation as such. If he
was wrong in maintaining that such a command is binding
upon our will, it is not to be inferred that duty must be
determined by some other law; what it would mean is that
there are no universally valid demands on human behaviour,
so far as this depends on our will, and consequently that
nothing whatever can be our duty and that we are entirely
free to do whatever we may happen to want. We might indeed by acting in this way get entangled in all sorts of disagreeable consequences, or we might be astute enough to
find means of escaping these disagreeable consequences; but
what Kant maintains is this: The sum total of these means
could never have the character of a system of precepts for
the will such that men would be under an objective obligation to obey them; nor could a necessary harmony of these

means be discovered (independently of a categorical imperative) such that it would be free from all possible conflict of the will with itself and with the will of others.

We can sum all this up in the proposition that the categorical imperative determines the concept of duty *solely as regards its form*. It states only what duty as such is and consequently what all duties have in common; but it contains nothing to show how the particular duties determined by it are materially different from one another. Yet we ought not to imagine that this purely formal character of the categorical imperative as the law of duty is identical with the property envisaged by those who describe as 'formal' both the principle of Kant's ethical theory and consequently this theory itself in distinction from other systems of morality. Here we find the first misinterpretation of the categorical imperative—the view that this necessarily confines moral philosophy to stating what the concept of duty is simply as regards its form and makes impossible the articulation of particular duties that are materially different. Every doctrine of duties, if it is based on any principle at all, must begin by stating in what duty consists—that is, by stating what is the concept of duty simply as regards its form. If we say, for example, that duty consists in performing the actions required to realise the happiness of the greatest number, we have determined the concept of duty simply as regards its form—that is, without specifying the content of the actions that are thus required. If Kant's principle has a still further special characteristic of formality, this is to be found in the *way* he determines the concept of duty simply as regards its form. This special characteristic may be described—negatively —as the assertion that if we are to discover the concept of duty, we must abstract, not merely from all the matter of duty, as is obvious, but also—as is not so obvious—from all the matter of the *will*; that is, from all purposes or ends.

Naturally, if anyone intends to realise something that he has made the end of his action, it is necessary that he should adopt the means adequate to realise it. But such necessity is a conditioned one (hypothetical, not categorical); and it contains no immediate law for his will since he must already will something definite before he can become subject to this necessity. 'Yes'—it may be replied—'we must naturally begin with some final end; this is already stated by Aristotle. And just as naturally such an end must possess some kind of necessity for the human will'. 'We are not to infer', says John Stuart Mill, 'that its acceptance or rejection must depend on blind impulse or arbitrary choice' (*Utilitarianism,* Ch. 1). But if, with Aristotle and Mill, we take happiness as the final end on which we may hope to find all men agreed, can we then say that there is for man an unconditioned command to make his own happiness his end? Even if he may in fact always make this his end, no one can say that this inevitability to be found in experience is the necessity characterising a *demand* in virtue of which man has the duty of adopting this end. And is it not at least conceivable that it may be both possible and necessary for the will of man to subordinate the end of his own happiness to a higher condition of his actions?

Suppose one answers: 'Yes, admittedly there must be an end necessary in and for itself—that is, necessary for the will of every rational being independently of all subjective conditions—an end which alone can supply the ground for an unconditioned demand that it be adopted'. The question then arises: In what way is it possible for us to have such an end? If we assume that man by nature can have no ends conflicting with the end that is necessary in itself, then clearly he can be subject to no command at all about the decisions of his will: his will must always of itself have this highest good as its object. In that case there can be no question of duty. If we admit, on the other hand, that he can decide to act contrary to this end which is necessary in and for itself, there must be, even beyond this highest end, a motive which can move him to do what he does not already do of himself— namely, to make this end his own. He would then need to have, above this highest end, a still prior end by which he would be required to take as his end what was good in and for itself. But such a prior end contains a contradiction; for all possible ends must naturally be subordinated to the end which is by definition the highest. Hence along this line we could produce neither a categorical nor a hypothetical imperative for adopting the end on which the whole necessity of human action is supposed to be dependent. We should be left merely with a choice between a will that was infallibly good and a will that could not even be asked to be good at all.

It is purely analytic considerations like these that ought to be adduced if we want to understand the real motive which led Kant to what constitutes the strictly formal character of his ethics. This character is to be found in the fact that in place of some previously given end—that is, in place of some matter of the will—Kant asserts that the mere form of maxims (that is, of the subjective principles of our arbitrary choice), so far as this fits them for the making of universal law, is what determines duty as regards its form. After what has been said, there should be no need to explain further why in this statement the word 'form' occurs twice. The form which fits maxims for the making of universal law —whatever may be their matter, that is, their end—is here identified with that demand by which alone an imperative can have the character of being categorical, or—in other words—by which duty is determined as regards its form. If in the language of abbreviation we call this imperative 'formal', this does not mean that *it* has no content. It has precisely the content we have just adduced; and we cannot infer conversely that because the categorical imperative has in fact a content, therefore Kant must be in error when he maintains that only the form which fits maxims for the making of laws can supply a universally valid ground for determining our will. Yet this is precisely the inference which one of the more recent writers on ethics has in fact drawn.

Apart from objections of this kind, which rest merely on a play of words, the fact that Kant has calmly built up a whole system of commands and prohibitions on the basis of his moral law has been looked on with the utmost suspicion and indeed with open scorn. 'When he begins', says John Stuart Mill again of Kant, 'to deduce from this precept any of the actual duties of morality, he fails, almost grotesquely, to show that there would be any contradiction, any logical impossibility, in the adoption by all rational beings of the most outrageously immoral rules of conduct' (*op. cit.*). This charge has its history. It is already present in Hegel's assertion that when Kant deduces particular duties, he goes continually round in circles since in order to show a contradiction between a maxim and the possibility of willing it as a universal law he has always to presuppose as necessary the very volition whose necessity it is his business to prove. By this method it would be open to us to put forward any kind of arbitrary conduct as a demand of duty. This seems to confirm one view of the history of moral evaluation. 'It can almost be said', writes one recent moralist (E. Becher, *Die Grundfrage der Ethik*, pp. 88 ff.), 'that there is no atrocity and no crime which has not been enjoined at some time and some place by conscience and duty or which is not still enjoined today. Murder, scorching and laying waste, the slaughter of the defenceless, of women and children without regard to guilt or innocence, robbery and betrayal, debauchery and orgies count as in accord with duty or at least as not against conscience; and so too actions that appear to us as morally quite indifferent are enjoined by this strict command'. Yet we cannot say in Kant's sense that the atrocities cited have been commanded 'at some time and some place' by conscience and duty, or are still commanded, unless we have first shown that such conduct is contained in the demand of his moral law. Obviously in the opinion of the author the formalism of Kant's ethics consists in this—that his concept of duty can be applied to any arbitrary behaviour, so far as man believes himself constrained to it *by any will* beyond which, for some subjective reason, he recognises no higher.

It is only one step from this to the sensational reasoning we find in a recently resurrected book of Dewey's—*German Philosophy and Politics* (2d ed., 1944), p. 87. 'The gospel of a duty devoid of content (!) naturally lent itself to the consecration and idealisation of such specific duties as the existing national order might prescribe'. Even if any one should be found who believes himself entitled by the formalism of Kant's moral law to declare the prescriptions of an existing national order to be prescriptions imposed upon the subjects of that order by the moral law itself, it is still barely comprehensible how Dewey could take such an interpretation of the 'gospel of duty' as a proceeding to which this gospel 'naturally lent itself'. If, as Dewey imagines, the thought of duty in Kant is 'devoid of content'—and so cannot contain any possibility of recognising any definite rule as either lawful or unlawful for human action—it is *quite impossible* to suppose that any definite prescription of the existing national order is 'consecrated' by the moral law; for in that case we should have to be able to show either that this prescription itself or that the competence of the national will to lay down such a prescription arbitrarily was required by the moral law. But if, in the opinion of the pseudo-Kantian who fills up the moral law with national prescriptions, the national order has to be sovereign in *arbitrary* ordinances, how can this rank as a categorical imperative (a law of duty)? If national prescriptions are such as are subject to absolutely no law in their volition, we can at least say this much with certainty—that we can be subject to them only *in contradiction* with the moral law of Kant. Otherwise this moral law itself would have to be able to agree with subjection to an arbitrary will that in and for itself was lawless.

Yet this is precisely what Dewey in fact thinks. He goes so far as to say: 'Idealism and personality separated from empirical analysis and experimental utilization of concrete social situations are worse than vague mouthings. They stand for realities, but these realities are the plans and desires of those who wish to gain control, under the alleged cloak of high ends, of the activities of other human beings' (pp. 29–30). If this is to be applied to Kant's Ideas of duty and personality, we are faced with the contention that these Ideas can serve to disguise any form of arbitrary despotism. On Dewey's view it would manifestly be possible for any tyrant to supply the content alleged to be lacking in these Ideas of Kant by telling those in his power that the unconditional obedience required by the command of duty was obedience to himself, and that their personality was manifested in a purity of will which in the interests of this obedience would shrink from no sacrifice of life or happiness. Such an abuse of *words* may be possible—but certainly not to any one who connects with the words 'duty' and 'person' the meanings attached to them by Kant. If the will of the tyrant himself is to have the character of a categorical imperative, this means that his subjects must be subject to him *in every possible exercise of their will.* But how can they be subjected to him *as regards their will* except on the ground that their own will determines them to this subjection? No one will wish to maintain that in virtue of some necessity independent of the exercise of his own will (and so by a law of nature) a man's will can, as it were, be transferred to the willing of another man. But the *maxim* by means of which a man makes this transference, if he subjects himself in every possible exercise of his own will to the arbitrary will of another, cannot possibly have the character of a law for *his* will, and therefore cannot possibly be a categorical imperative; for such a law would make him have no will of his own at all—and consequently he would also cease to be a person.

This is the answer, in the spirit and letter of Kant's moral doctrine, that should have been given to the despot when he sought to prescribe to persons his own arbitrary lawless will as the law of their duty. For the formalism of this doctrine does not, as Dewey imagines and a host of empiricists before him, contain a warrant for man *to select at random absolutely any will as his supreme lawgiver.* On the contrary: with the greatest possible determinateness of content this doctrine forbids man to subject himself to any will other than his own will so far as its maxims are capable of being laws. It forbids this because the maxim of such subjection, if taken as a law, is in necessary and irremovable conflict with his own will. Such a law cannot in the strict sense of the word be willed by him; for it is self-contradictory that a will should be able to will its own annulment with the necessity of law in every possible exercise of its own volition.

II

We have at least established this—that the obedience required by the categorical imperative is the direct opposite of an obedience by which a man could subject himself at random to any arbitrary power. If anybody is looking for definite precepts contained in the categorical imperative, he can put this down as the first—that such subjection is forbidden. The

ban admittedly is only another way of saying that the categorical imperative is in fact nothing but the law of the will's
autonomy (its making of its own laws). But with this view
of it are we not plunged into a difficulty of the opposite kind?
Instead of inferring that our will must be unconditionally
fettered to the will of another are we not bound to infer that
our own arbitrary will must be unconditionally unfettered?
Must not a will subjected solely to its own legislation be able
to pass any law it likes? Must it not be able in virtue of its
autonomy 'to will as a law' any arbitrary maxim it sees fit to
use in regulating its choice of ends? At any rate Kant—as we
have already heard—fails 'almost grotesquely' in the eyes of
his critics when he tries to persuade us that we must will any
particular maxim as a law or that we cannot will it as a law.
This failure is obviously called 'grotesque' because, in the examples he gives of such necessities and impossibilities, it
looks as if he casually introduces, in order to reach a decision,
that very consideration of the agent's personal advantage
which the categorical imperative professes to set aside as a
principle of moral evaluation. Suppose, for example, he wants
to show that nobody can will as a law the maxim of not
bothering about the distress of others: 'For', he says, 'a will
which decided in this way would be in conflict with itself,
since many a situation might arise in which the man needed
love and sympathy from others, and in which by such a law
of nature sprung from his own will, he would rob himself of
all hope of the help he wants for himself'. A clear case, it
might seem. 'This type of reason', says G. Simmel (*Kant*,
1904, pp. 97–98), 'will satisfy no one today, and indeed I
must admit that in Kant it is to me quite incomprehensible.
Why should an appeal to personal interest, which he nowhere
else recognises as a moral criterion, be all of a sudden taken
here as decisive?' This is a repetition of John Stuart Mill's
criticism—except that the forecast is reversed. Kant cannot
possibly be free to appeal to personal interest (in happiness),
says Simmel. He must inevitably appeal to happiness, says
Mill, when he wants to come down to concrete events; and
Mill's follower, Fr. Jodl (*Geschichte der Ethik*, II, 1889,
p. 18), repeats: 'In alleging reasons that make the universalisation of immoral maxims impossible, the decisive word in

Kant's own exposition is kept for "empirically material" principles—not, however, the principle of general happiness, but rather of the most commonplace egoism'.

Do such principles really have the last word? The opinion that they do rests manifestly on Kant's argument that we cannot will hard-heartedness as a law because we should then rob ourselves of all hope of (possible) help even when we stood in need of it. Naturally, this can be a reason only for an agent to whom personal happiness is an end. But certainly it cannot be said that personal happiness *to the exclusion of the happiness of others* must be his end, and therefore that his interest in happiness must be a *selfish* interest if it is to prevent him from making his own possible need irremediable by a decision of his own will. What can be said is this. Whether he subordinates his whole interest to his own happiness as a supreme principle or considers also the happiness of others, he cannot possibly will, *so far as his happiness is an end for him,* to be abandoned in his need by all who could save him, and consequently he cannot will his own unhappiness. This is a purely analytic proposition: its truth is in no way affected by questions about the principle on which he acts. Hence Jodl's contention—that here 'the most commonplace egoism' has the decisive word—is false.

Nevertheless—it may be insisted—the whole business still leaves a disagreeable aftertaste. The reason why we cannot will hard-heartedness as a law is simply that we must be afraid of damaging ourselves if we do so. 'Here it is stated as plainly as can be', says Schopenhauer in his prize essay *Über die Grundlage der Moral,* § 7, 'that moral obligation rests entirely on a presupposed reciprocity. Hence it is completely egoistic and is to be understood as a form of egoism that prudently commits itself to a compromise on the condition of reciprocity'. If we abandon this condition and imagine a man who assumes (rightly or wrongly) that he will never get into a position where he is in need of help, such a man can perfectly well agree that everybody should act on the maxim of hard-heartedness. Admittedly, if a man is prepared to act on the maxim of kindness only so far as he can in this way purchase the kindness of others, and if he would immediately withdraw his assent to this maxim as soon as he believed himself immune from need—such a man would be an egoist. But if he wills kindness only under such reservations, can he be said to will it *as a law*? Obviously he will never once show kindness himself except in so far as readiness on the part of others to help him will be its outcome. This is precisely the 'reciprocity' that Schopenhauer has in mind; but he fails to notice that if a man shows kindness only on condition that others are kind to him, his maxim of kindness is such that, if it were made into a law, it would remove the possibility of kindness altogether. For if every one makes his kindness depend on another's being kind to him, it is obvious that there is no possibility of anyone being kind at all.

Equally astray is the contention that if we feel ourselves immune from need, we can perfectly well will *the maxim of indifference* as a law. This maxim *as a law* would run as follows—Every one who feels himself immune from need may be deaf to the need of others. It is manifest that however immune from need we may imagine ourselves to be, we *cannot* will this law. The reason is that the universalised maxim of the hard-hearted, let him turn and twist as he will—and indeed every case in which no help is given to him—does not hold subject to the condition on which he agreed to do it, namely, that *he* should be immune from need. *Everybody* is authorised by the maxim to refuse help so far as he himself is immune from need—without regard to the position of the man to whom help is refused. Consequently a will which wills the maxim of hard-heartedness as a law necessarily contains in itself a will to be abandoned in the not absolutely impossible case of the agent's own need, and therefore it is a will in conflict with itself.

Naturally this is based on 'reciprocity'—not, however, as Schopenhauer thinks, on the arbitrarily arranged reciprocity of a deal in cattle, but on a situation entirely withdrawn from human choice, namely, that 'help' is a human relation with two terms: there is always one partner who gives help and another who receives it. Consequently nothing can alter the fact that if we lay down conditions for giving help, we also lay down conditions for receiving help. Hence if I wish the condition under which I can agree to the impossibility of receiving help to remain in force when my maxim about giving help is made universal, I must incorporate this condition in the maxim itself. The maxim will then take this form: I will never help any one who is immune from need. That such a maxim can be willed as a law without the slightest difficulty is certainly not a proposition that Kant would have been anxious to deny.

The series of fallacies into which Kant's critics fall again and again could never have been constructed but for a failure to observe that in a decisive passage in the *Groundwork of the Metaphysic of Morals* Kant has given the categorical imperative this form—Act only on that maxim *through* which you can at the same time will that it should become a universal law. The word 'through' has not only been disregarded: there has been such a failure to understand it that the patch-work theorists (to use a phrase coined by Professor Paton) have proposed to see in it a textual corruption and to cut it out. This would mean cutting out the very word that first gives the formula its greatest precision. You must be able to will the character of law 'through' the maxim; that is to say, the reason for the possibility of willing the maxim as a law must be found in the maxim itself—not in any external circumstances of the agent which are in no way determined by the maxim. If any one agrees to make the maxim of hardheartedness universally valid merely because he believes himself to need no help, he makes the possibility of his agreement depend on circumstances which on their side are not determinable by his maxim. For in the principle 'Help yourself' there is no warrant for the ground on which he assents to the universality of the maxim—namely, that he should be free from the need of others' help. Thus he cannot will *through* his maxim that it should become a law; and consequently he cannot conform to the conditions laid down by Kant.

After all this what remains of the charge of egoism? All that remains is this—Kant rests his argument on the supposition that a man cannot in harmony with his own will choose to be abandoned in misfortune by those who could give him help. We have already said that this has nothing to do with egoism. If I have fallen into the water without being able to swim, and champion swimmers are all around me in lifeboats some twenty yards away, is my wish that they should pull me out to be explained only on the ground that I am an egoist—that is, a man who bothers about the need of others only when he can count on getting some advantage out of it for himself? And how is this to be distinguished in principle from any other arbitrary case where a man is in need of help and other people have the power to help him?

But—it will be said—Kant does insist that for the sake of a higher interest we must be prepared to make unlimited sacrifices of our own happiness. He undoubtedly does require this; but what he has certainly never claimed is that we must therefore be prepared to sacrifice our own happiness *as a possible end altogether*. This is precisely the claim he would have had to make if it were to be inferred from his principles that a man must be able to will his own abandonment in need. In that case the categorical imperative would have to forbid a man to make his own happiness an end. How could we possibly find a reason for any such prohibition? One's own happiness as an end is admittedly not the *ground* on which a will can be in law-abiding harmony with itself and with the will of all others; but it does not follow that *by having this end* the will is split in such a way that there could never be any conditions under which the maxim of making one's happiness an end might be willed as a law. If we wanted to take the contrary view, we should have to be able to say that man can make his own happiness an end only by reference to the unhappiness of others or even of himself— only if he is made unhappy by the happiness of others or perhaps by his own happiness at some past or future time. Under special conditions something like this may perhaps actually happen. But no one can say that this is among the universal and necessary conditions of human happiness as such. And consequently we cannot say that the categorical imperative forbids us to make our own happiness an end. We are therefore in error if we take Kant's statement—that a man cannot will his own unhappiness—to be false on the ground that on Kant's own principles a man ought never to make happiness his end and consequently that on these same principles he must be able to will his own unhappiness.

Not only does Kant's statement not contradict the categorical imperative: it is in itself completely justified. Man cannot renounce happiness altogether as a possible end: to have or not to have this end in no way depends on his own choice. Nature forces this end upon him as soon as he begins to have ends at all. We cannot even conceive beyond this end any further motive which might induce him to make this end his own. This is why Aristotle declared happiness to be the final end of man; and he was perfectly right as long as we look for ends only within the bounds of experience. This amounts to saying that the categorical imperative does not prescribe this end to man—at least not directly. But no more does the categorical imperative prevent me—as has just been shown—from treating this end as one which is naturally common to all human beings. The categorical imperative *abstracts from all ends* because, in deriving from it an absolute demand as such, I cannot rest my case on any end that I presuppose; but this does not mean that the categorical imperative demands a will *that has no ends at all* and so wills nothing. It abstracts from all ends—that is, in the present case, it does not say with the utilitarians: 'You must help others in need because by this you will promote your own happiness'. Rather it says: 'You must help them, whether this promotes your own happiness or not, since to will the maxim of indifference as a law is in contradiction with your inevitable and permissible end, namely, to receive help from them'. When therefore the empiricist E. Becher asserts that if there is no question of consequences, I can will any arbitrary maxim whatever as a law, he must be told that he is a victim of the loose expression 'there is (for Kant) no question of consequences'. If we make this expression precise, it runs as follows: In deciding the unlawfulness of the maxim 'Never help any one in need' there is no question of consequences so far as these concern the *possibility of attaining my own happiness as an end* if this maxim is followed by myself and others. But in coming to this decision there is indeed a question of consequences so far as these concern the possibility *of taking my own happiness,* and consequently my own rescue in distress, *as an end,* if I will the maxim of hard-heartedness as a law. Inability to distinguish these two points of view is the secret—to use the language of John Stuart Mill—of the almost grotesque failure of those who have attempted to criticise Kant's deductions of particular moral duties. The reason why I cannot will the maxim of indifference as a law is not that by so doing I should stand in the way of my own happiness. Whether my chance of happiness will be improved or impaired by freeing every one, and consequently myself, from all obligation to help others depends on circumstances about which there can never be any *a priori* decision. But I can indeed decide *a priori*, as in the case of every analytic truth, that if my will includes a will to be left without help in need, I cannot possibly take happiness as my end and consequently must be able to will my own unhappiness.

With the help of this analysis we must try to penetrate a little more deeply into the seemingly paradoxical mechanism which makes it possible for a will to fall into contradiction with itself by willing that a maxim it can have should be a law. The decisive consideration here is obviously that the will is viewed in a situation where the object of its volition can itself be a volition. I do will my own happiness—there is no further problem in that. I *can*, secondly, will the happiness of others. But, in the third place, in willing my own happiness, I also will on the principle that others should will my happiness. Now if on my side I do *not* will the happiness of others, I cannot (without willing contrary to my own volition) will that my maxim should be acted on by others, and consequently I cannot will that it should be a law. Hence if the categorical imperative is valid, there follows from it *as a definite command* of duty that I must include within my end of happiness the happiness of others.

With this we conclude our discussion of one *example* by which Kant has illustrated the possibility of deriving particular precepts from the categorical imperative. I cannot hope that this discussion will be enough to show in a new light the world-wide practice of talking as if philosophy were not in a position to tell men quite precisely what they ought to do and ought not to do. But perhaps it will be enough to raise doubts about the reliability of those who want to dismiss Kant's moral philosophy and its categorical imperative as a *causa judicata*.

If this is the situation, would it not be better to refrain

from dragging questions of philosophy into regions where there may enter even a stray breath of political passion? When Dewey imagined he could find in Kant's moral philosophy a preparation for those outrages against the rights of man by which a crazy political movement has shocked the whole world, he failed to observe that he was talking about Kant exactly as the Janizaries of the tyrant had also talked. So far as I am concerned, I do not think it the function of philosophy to engage directly in man's battle for the rule of law. All that philosophy can do is to bring the struggle of opinions to a theoretical agreement on rational grounds. Even so, the service it renders to mankind is beyond price; for there can be no assurance of a possible peace among men so long as the division of opinion on ultimate matters cannot be settled. Such a settlement is possible only if those who come to these affairs with reasons can have their reasons heard. The task I had set myself was to make it plain that as regards the reasons Kant puts forward in his doctrine of duty he has not been adequately heard and has not been understood at all.

KANT'S EXAMPLES
OF THE FIRST FORMULATION
OF THE CATEGORICAL IMPERATIVE

JONATHAN HARRISON

I do not know of any commentator who has given an accurate account of all of Kant's examples of the first formulation of the categorical imperative, and though some have
given an accurate account of some examples, there are other
examples of which no-one has given an accurate account. Accounts of the first formulation of the categorical imperative
have frequently been vitiated by the assumption that what he
says in dealing with one of his examples—a different one in
the case of different commentators—can be taken as showing,
without consideration of the other examples, what Kant
meant by the first formulation of the categorical imperative.
Commentators have frequently been misled in their account
of Kant's argument in the examples not only because they
have assumed that Kant always does what one would expect
him to do from what he says about the categorical imperative
generally, but because they have found a certain argument in
one of the examples, and then seen it when it was not there
in one or more of the other examples. Kant's treatment of his
four examples is extremely wayward and sometimes inconsequential, and each one of them must be considered independently both of the others and of Kant's remarks about his
own programme.

Kant divides duties into perfect and imperfect duties, and
into duties to self and duties to others. If you combine these
two divisions, four classes of duty result, (*a*) perfect duty to

Reprinted with permission of the author and of the editors from
Philosophical Quarterly, 7 (1957), 50–62.

self, (b) perfect duty to others, (c) imperfect duty to self, and (d) imperfect duty to others. Kant gives one example of each of these four classes. It does not appear to me that there is any noticeable difference between Kant's treatment of duties to self and duties to others. There is obviously, however, a great deal of difference between his treatment of perfect and imperfect duties. It is alleged to be *impossible* for everybody to adopt the maxim which I adopt when I infringe a perfect duty. It is not impossible for everybody to adopt the maxim which I act on when I infringe an imperfect duty; it is merely impossible for me to will that everyone should adopt this maxim. Before going on to a detailed consideration of Kant's four examples of the application of the first formulation of the categorical imperative, there are some general comments I wish to make.

(1) In the first formulation of the categorical imperative, Kant was attempting to put forward the supreme principle of morality, and in this respect the first formulation of the categorical imperative is similar to the principle of utilitarianism. He is not just telling us that what is right for me is right for any similar person similarly placed, which would not tell me what was right for me; nor is he laying down certain conditions (for example that they should be of unrestricted generality) to which a principle must conform if it is to be a moral principle, from which, of course, no moral principle could be deduced. These are things which Kant takes for granted, but they are not what he is trying to prove. To hold that this is all that Kant is saying is to replace views which are exciting and important, if erroneous, by certain harmless platitudes, which would make ridiculous the fanfare of trumpets with which Kant heralded them.

(2) Kant did not use the first formulation of the categorical imperative to test whether certain alleged moral principles really were moral principles, or even to test whether they were acceptable moral principles. He does not use it to test the morality of moral principles at all, but the morality of maxims. For the same reason, it cannot be held that Kant is dealing with a problem which has received a good deal of attention recently, the problem of the universalisation of moral judgments and the universalisation of moral reasons.

It has been held, I think rightly, that any moral judgment gives rise to a moral principle, on the ground that if a particular moral judgment is true of a given action, then the same moral judgment must apply to all similar actions performed in similar circumstances, and it has also been held that if a certain statement is a good reason for coming to a certain moral conclusion, then the same statement must give rise to the same moral conclusion in all similar cases. Kant is not, however, discussing the universalisation of moral judgments or of reasons for moral judgments, but the universalisation of maxims, e.g. he does not consider the moral judgment 'It is right for me to borrow this money, though I know I cannot pay it back' but the maxim 'Whenever I believe myself short of money, I will borrow money and promise to pay it back, though I know that this will never be done'. Nor is he saying that if a maxim is right for me, it is right for everyone, but that if it is not possible for everyone to act on it (or not possible for me to will that everyone should act on it) it is not right for me to act on it.

The following points about maxims should be noted: (*a*) A maxim is a subjective principle of action, that is, a principle on which a man in fact acts. It seems to me that by this it is meant that a maxim is a rule which a man makes for himself. If I make it a rule to rise at seven, then to rise at seven is my maxim. If I make it a rule to make promises which I cannot keep, whenever I need a service which I cannot obtain in any other way, then to make such promises is my maxim. (*b*) Maxims can be formulated, but what the words which formulate them express cannot properly be said to be true or to be false. My maxim will be expressed in words such as 'to turn the other cheek' or 'always to declare my full income'. It does not make sense to say that 'to turn the other cheek' expresses a truth or a falsehood. (*c*) Maxims may be 'legislated'. In more ordinary English, maxims are rules which I make for myself, and I may make it a rule to turn the other cheek, or I may not. Whether I make this my rule or not is something which I personally decide. (*d*) Maxims are not moral principles, as has already been said. It may well be a valid moral rule that the other cheek ought to be turned, but my maxim or rule is not that the other cheek ought to be turned, but to turn the other cheek. Maxims or rules can be 'made', but moral principles cannot. I can make it a rule to declare my full income, but I cannot make it a rule that men ought to declare their full incomes. To talk of making this a rule does not make sense. (*e*) Though maxims are not identical with moral principles they can accord or fail to accord with moral principles. My maxim always to tell the truth conforms with a moral principle if it is in fact the case that the truth ought to be told, whereas, on the same hypothesis, my maxim to lie when it suits me does not. (*f*) Maxims apply only to the person who makes them. I can make it a rule for myself always to rise at seven, but I cannot make this a rule for Jones, or, if I do—let us suppose I am Jones's wife—the rule I make for Jones is not a maxim, but some other sort of rule.

(3) Kant holds (*a*) that a maxim is not morally acceptable and must not be adopted (ought not to be adopted) if it cannot be universalised; (*b*) that it may be adopted (it is false that it ought not to be adopted—not to be confused with saying that it ought to be adopted) if it can be universalised. He may also have thought (*c*) that a maxim must be adopted (ought to be adopted) if what I shall loosely call its 'contradictory' is not universifiable. (*a*) and (*b*) are logically independent of one another. (*c*) would follow from (*a*) together with the additional premise, which I see no reason to cavil about, that if it is our duty not to do A, then it is our duty to do non-A.

(4) A maxim is not universifiable if (*a*) it is impossible for everyone to act on it, or (*b*) it is impossible for anyone to will that everyone should act on it. When formulating the categorical imperative, Kant only mentions the impossibility of willing that everyone should act on a given maxim. Perfect duties, therefore, would only fall under Kant's first formulation of the categorical imperative if we can assume that, if it is impossible for everyone to act on a given maxim, it is impossible for anyone to will that everyone should act on it. I shall assume that what Kant means by saying that we cannot will that a maxim should become a universal law is that, if it were within our power to bring about a state of affairs in which everyone acted on our maxim, we could not bring ourselves to do it, or, what comes to the same thing, that if, as a

result of our acting on a given maxim, it became a law of nature that everyone acted on that maxim, we would not act on it. The statement that, if it were within my power to bring about a state of affairs in which everyone acted on a maxim which infringed an imperfect duty, I could not do it, is a hypothetical proposition with a false antecedent, and there are difficulties enough about these. The statement that, if it were within my power to bring about a state of affairs where everybody acted on a maxim which infringed a perfect duty, I could not do it, is, on Kant's view, a hypothetical proposition with a logically false antecedent; for if it is logically impossible for everyone to act on a given maxim, it must be logically impossible for me to have the power to will that they should. I do not know how one decides what one could or could not bring oneself to do in the event of some state of affairs being realised, the realisation of which is logically impossible.

(5) There is no logical difficulty whatsoever in deducing whether or not a maxim is morally acceptable from Kant's first formulation of the categorical imperative, as there would be if he were merely saying that what is right for me is right for anyone or that moral principles must be unrestrictedly general. We simply argue syllogistically as follows: A maxim is not morally acceptable, if it is either impossible for everyone to act on it or impossible for the person whose maxim it is to will that everyone should act on it; it is either impossible for everyone to act on this maxim or impossible for me to will that everyone should act on it; therefore this maxim is not morally acceptable.

(6) There certainly are maxims which it is logically impossible for everyone to act on. For example, I may make it a rule to be first through every door, but not everybody could successfully make this their rule. I am not convinced that there are any maxims which I could not, if I made a supreme effort, will that everybody should adopt (supposing this to be in my power) but there certainly are maxims which I would be unlikely to act on, if I knew that as a result of my acting on them everyone else would adopt and act on them. I may make it a rule to consume without producing, but I should be unlikely to make this my rule if I knew that, as a result

of my making this my rule, everyone else would make it their rule.

The first maxim the universalisation of which Kant considers is one which enjoins suicide. Kant states the maxim as follows: 'From self-love I make it my principle to shorten my life if its continuance threatens more evil than it promises pleasure', but he is quite wrong to state it in this way. The phrase 'From self-love I make it my principle' has nothing to do with my maxim, but only with the motives which cause me to adopt the maxim. These words should be omitted, therefore, in which case my maxim will be simply 'to shorten my life if its continuance threatens more evil than it promises pleasure'. It is perhaps a little odd to speak of this as a rule—I have maintained that to adopt a maxim is to make so-and-so a rule. It is a little odd to say that I make it a rule to commit suicide, for I can only do this once, but this limitation does not spring from the nature of my maxim, but from matter of fact extraneous to it, so perhaps it can be ignored.

What, then, is the contradiction which would result if this maxim were to be universally adopted? There must be such a contradiction, of course, because suicide is alleged to be a perfect duty, not an imperfect one. It is natural, I think, to suppose from what Kant says in other places—he says, for example, that it is inconceivable that a maxim which infringes perfect duty should be universalised—to look for a contradiction in the conception of everybody's acting on this maxim: to look for a contradiction in the bare statement that everybody is acting on it. It is obvious to the meanest intelligence, however, that there is no contradiction whatsoever in the idea of everyone's committing suicide if they would be happier dead, and, what is more, Kant makes no attempt whatsoever to show that there is such a contradiction. What he does try to show is, not that the statement that everybody acts on this maxim is self-contradictory, but that it contradicts another statement, a statement of fact, namely that the purpose of self-love is 'to stimulate the furtherance of life', which I shall take to mean—I don't think it affects my argument if I am wrong—that the purpose of self-love is to prevent people from committing suicide.

Either something can have a purpose which it usually does not fulfil—as my watch usually does not fulfil its purpose of telling the time—or it cannot. In the first case, there is obviously no contradiction between the statement that self-love usually prompts people to commit suicide, and the statement that the purpose of self-love is to stop people from committing suicide. Is there a contradiction in the second case? Perhaps there would be if the universal adoption of my rule to commit suicide if I should be happier dead would mean that self-love usually led people to kill themselves, but it does not mean this. My rule—and Kant almost seems to forget this—is not simply to commit suicide, but to commit suicide if I should be happier dead. Since it is not unreasonable to suppose that those people who would be happier dead are in a minority, the universal adoption of my maxim would not mean that people usually committed suicide, and not mean, therefore, that self-love usually (or even frequently) caused people to commit suicide.

It is not sufficient, of course, for the statement that everybody acts on my maxim to commit suicide if I shall be happier dead to contradict the statement that the purpose of self-love is to stimulate the furtherance of life. It is also necessary for this to be a true statement. To consider whether it is a true statement or not, however, is not a problem for a moral philosopher.

Let us now pass to Kant's second example—one of perfect duty to others. The maxim the universalisation of which he considers is this: 'Whenever I believe myself short of money, I will borrow money and promise to pay it back, though I know that this will never be done'. Kant argues that, though it is possible for me to adopt and act on this maxim, it is not possible for everybody to adopt and act on it; for, were they to do so, no-one would trust anyone who made a promise to keep it, hence no-one would be able to obtain a service by making a promise, hence no-one would make any promises, hence no-one would be able to act on the maxim in question.

On this argument I have the following comments to make:

(1) Kant is obviously not considering the universalisation of the maxim he says he is considering, which concerns only

obtaining money by promising to pay it back. The universal-isation of this maxim would not lead to a cessation of promise-making in general, but only to a cessation of promising to pay back loans. However, I see no reason why we should not be charitable to Kant in this, if in no other, instance, and substitute for the maxim he states the more general rule to promise anything to obtain any service, even when I know I cannot keep my promise.

(2) Kant claims that the statement that everybody acts on this maxim is self-contradictory, 'that this maxim can never rank as a universal law and be self-consistent'. He has not shown that this statement is self-contradictory, however. He has at most shown that it is impossible for everyone to act on my maxim to obtain services by making promises which I know I cannot keep, given that certain contingent statements are true. The contingent statements in question include at least the following: (*a*) People frequently find themselves in circumstances when they need a service which they can only obtain by making a promise they cannot keep. Unless this statement were true, the universal adoption of my maxim would not lead to much dishonest promise-making, and so promise-making would not cease to be a human practice. (*b*) People usually remember when in the past other people have made promises they cannot keep. If people always forgot this, then people could quite happily go on obtaining services by making promises they could not keep, and promises would not cease to be made. (*c*) People are sufficiently egotistical not to provide a service for someone, in return for a promise to perform a future service, unless they think there is a reasonably high probability that the promise is one which can be kept. I am not disputing the truth of any of these statements. What I am doing is pointing out that they are contingent statements, and that if the universalisation of my maxim is only impossible given the truth of certain contingent assertions, its universalisation is not logically impossible.

(3) I am willing to grant that if everyone acted on the maxim in question, promise-making would die out. This, however, does not mean that it is impossible for everybody to act on my rule to obtain services by making promises I know I cannot keep. For my rule is hypothetical: If circumstances

arise in which you can obtain a service by making a promise
which you know you cannot keep, make that promise—and
there is a perfectly good sense in which everybody can make
this their maxim, even if, as will be the case if everybody
does make it their maxim, circumstances never do arise in
which they can obtain a service by making a promise they
know they cannot keep.

(4) You would expect Kant's treatment of promise-making
to be parallel to his treatment of suicide, since they are both
cases of perfect duty. They are not parallel, however, as they
would be if he said something like 'Everybody cannot make
promises they know they cannot keep, for the purpose of
some motive, e.g. enlightened self-interest, is to prevent people making such promises.'

I shall now depart from the order in which Kant considers
his examples, and consider the fourth before the third, for a
reason which will be apparent later. The third and the fourth
examples, of course, are examples of imperfect duties, so
there is no impossibility in my maxim's being universally
adopted. What is impossible is that I should be able to will its
universal adoption, or that I should be able to act on the
maxim, if I knew that as a result, by some queer freak of
nature, it would be universally adopted.

Kant states his fourth maxim in an extremely rhetorical
way, which I shall not repeat. It appears, however, that the
maxim or rule in question is 'Never to help others in distress'.
Kant argues that, though I can adopt the maxim, I cannot will
its universal adoption, and the reason why I cannot will its
universal adoption is that, if it were universally adopted, no-
one would help me when I was in distress.

Again, I have the following comments to make:

(1) It has often been alleged that Kant is appealing to
self-interest in this particular example. This is not the case.
He does not argue that it is wrong to adopt the maxim of not
helping others in distress, because as a result no-one would
help me when I was in distress, which would consist in an
appeal to self-interest. It is not the consequences of my adopting the maxim which are contrary to my interest, but what
would happen if everybody adopted it. Since there is no sug-

gestion that my adopting the maxim would actually cause others to adopt it, (i.e. the condition in the hypothetical statement, 'if everyone adopted my maxim, no-one would help me when I was in distress', is unfulfilled) there is no suggestion that the action is wrong because it has unfortunate consequences for me.

(2) The reason why it is wrong for me to make a rule never to help anyone in distress is that, if I were to will that everyone acted on this maxim, my will would be at variance with itself. I take this to mean that, though there is a motive for willing the universal adoption of my maxim, for if my maxim were universally adopted, I should not have the disagreeable task of helping others in distress, there is also a motive against, for I would in this case not have the agreeable experience of being helped by others. I am not sure whether or not it is Kant's view that it is the same motive which militates both for and against the universal adoption of my maxim, or whether it may be one motive which militates for, and a different motive which militates against. Nor am I sure that Kant's view is not that there would be motives for and against the universal adoption of my maxim, but that the same motive which would make me want to adopt the maxim myself would make me want it not to be universally adopted. Or perhaps his view is that, though there is a motive for adopting the maxim myself, there is some other motive for not wanting it to be universally adopted.

(3) It should be pointed out that to say that a will which willed the universal adoption of my rule not to help others in distress would be at variance with itself, is not to say that it is impossible for me to will the universal adoption of my maxim. I often do things in spite of motives impelling me not to do those things. From the fact that my will would be at variance with itself if it willed the universal adoption of my maxim it does not follow that I cannot will the universal adoption of my maxim. All that does follow is that I cannot will it wholeheartedly.

Kant's third example, which I am taking last, of a maxim which cannot be universalised is 'neglect to develop my natural gifts'. The reason why, though a man can adopt and act on this maxim himself, he cannot will that everyone should adopt and act on it, is that 'as a rational being he necessarily wills that all his powers should be developed, since they serve him, and are given him, for all sorts of possible purposes'.

My comments are as follows:

(1) The reason why I took the fourth example before the third was that I wanted to point out a lack of similarity in Kant's treatment of the two cases. If Kant's treatment of the third example had been analogous to his treatment of the fourth, what he would have said, presumably, would have been that, though I can act on the maxim 'neglect my talents' myself, I cannot will that everyone should make this their maxim, for in that case I should be deprived of any benefits accruing to me from other people's developing their talents. It is obvious that I do benefit from other people's developing their talents. However, what Kant in fact says is, not that I cannot will the universalisation of my maxim because other people's talents are useful to me, but that I cannot will the universalisation of my maxim because my talents are useful to me.

(2) If the fact that a man's talents are useful to that man is not sufficient to prevent him from neglecting to develop them—as it obviously is not, for people do neglect to develop their talents, in spite of the fact that these are useful to them —it is not going to stop him from willing the universal neglect of talent-developing. For Kant's argument to have any sort of plausability, it would have to be the case that the fact that my talents were useful to me was a better reason for not willing that everybody should neglect their talents than for not willing that I should neglect my own talents. The case is quite the opposite, however. That my talents are useful to me is a much better reason for not neglecting my own talents than it is for not willing universal neglect of talents.

(3) I am somewhat at a loss to know what is the import of the phrase 'as a rational being' in 'For as a rational being he necessarily wills that all his powers should be developed. . . .' This statement cannot be equivalent to the statement which you would get if you omitted the phrase in question, which is 'He necessarily wills that all his powers should be developed'. For it is absolutely obvious that this statement

is false, and Kant must have known that it was obvious. Perhaps 'As a rational being he necessarily wills that all his
powers should be developed' means 'If he were a completely
(instead of a partially) rational being, he would necessarily
will that all his powers be developed'. The most this statement would prove would be that a completely rational being
could not will neglect of his own talents. It would not prove,
what Kant claims he is trying to prove, that I, who am not a
completely rational being, cannot will universal neglect of
talents. In any case, as has often been pointed out, if 'rational
being' means 'being who always wills what is right', you could
not deduce that talent-neglecting was wrong from the fact
that a rational being could not will it. All you could do would
be to deduce that a rational being could not will talent-
neglecting from the prior fact that it was wrong.

I now want to make some general comments relevant to
Kant's four examples of the application of the first formulation of the categorical imperative:

(1) Only in one case, the third, does Kant make any mention of the actual consequences of my adopting a given maxim
in order to show that it is one which ought not to be adopted.
In dealing with the third example, Kant does point out, as we
have seen, that my talents are useful to me, i.e. that adopting
the maxim of talent-neglecting would have bad consequences
for myself. Only this is not a utilitarian argument, for Kant
is not saying that my adopting the maxim would be harmful
to society as a whole, but that it would be harmful to me,
the agent. Furthermore, this is not held to be the reason why
my maxim is a wrong one. The reason why it is wrong is that
I cannot will its universal adoption, and that it has harmful
consequences for me is—allegedly—the reason why I cannot
will its universal adoption.

(2) Not only is there no appeal to the actual bad consequences of my adopting a given maxim, alleged to be wrong;
there is no appeal to the fact that the consequences of everyone's adopting the same maxim would be bad. There is, of
course, mention of what would happen if everyone were to
adopt my maxim, but this is not the same thing as an appeal
to the bad consequences of what would happen, if everyone

were to adopt my maxim. It is quite clear, of course, that, in all the four cases Kant considers, the universal adoption of the maxim in question would be bad; but Kant never appeals to this as a reason for thinking the maxim a wrong one. Furthermore, it is sometimes the case that the adoption of a given maxim by *n* people would be more than *n* times worse than the adoption of this maxim by one person alone. In such cases some philosophers have argued that I ought to take account of the bad consequences of the universal adoption of the maxim as well as or instead of the bad consequences of the adoption of the maxim by myself only. I should like to point out that in the case of Kant's second example, concerning the making of promises, the consequences of the adoption of the maxim 'Obtain services by making promises you know you cannot keep' by *n* people would quite clearly be more than *n* times worse than the consequences of the adoption of this maxim by one person. In the case of suicide and talent neglecting it is arguable that the same would be true, though they are less obvious cases. Only in the case of not helping others in distress does it seem pretty clear that the consequences of the adoption of the maxim by *n* people would not be more than *n* times worse than the adoption of the maxim by one person. These, however, are just facts about Kant's examples. Kant himself makes no use of them, though the theory that does has a distinctly Kantian flavour.

(3) There is an occasional reference to purpose in Kant's examples. In his third example, Kant says that our talents are given us for all sorts of possible ends, though this is not alleged to be the reason why it is wrong not to develop them, but to be the reason why, as a rational being, I cannot will that everyone should neglect to develop them. In Kant's first example there is a reference to the purpose of self-love, which is said to be to stimulate the furtherance of life, though, again, this is not held to be the reason why it is wrong to commit suicide, but to be the reason why it is impossible that everyone should act on my maxim enjoining suicide in certain circumstances. In Kant's second example there is a reference to the purpose of promising, but I interpret this not as being a reference to the purpose of promising itself—compare 'the purpose of the liver'—or to the purpose

some transcendent being has for promising, but to ordinary human purposes in making promises. On these references to purposes I shall allow myself one brief comment. If Kant were arguing—and I have just pointed out reasons for thinking he is not—that suicide from self-love and talent-neglecting are wrong because this is to use self-love and talents for purposes other than those which they have, or for which they were intended, then, if this argument were valid at all, its conclusion would follow immediately, without any reference to the universalisation of suicide from self-love or to the universalisation of talent-neglecting.

(4) There are a number of maxims which are such that what might be termed the 'natural' or 'normal' purpose—though not just any purpose—of anyone's adopting them would be defeated if they were adopted by everybody. It is clear that the maxims Kant considers in his last three examples are all of this sort. If my purpose in making it a rule to make promises I cannot keep is to obtain services from others without doing anything in return, my purpose will be defeated if everyone adopts my maxim. If my purpose in making it a rule to neglect my talents is to live on the fruits of other people's labour without myself contributing anything, my purpose will be defeated if everybody adopts my maxim. If my purpose in making it a rule not to help others in distress is to benefit from the help of others without doing anything in return, then my purpose will be defeated if everyone adopts my maxim. This is not true of suicide, however. My purpose in making it a 'rule' to commit suicide if circumstances arise in which I shall be happier dead will not be defeated if everybody makes this a rule. Furthermore, only in the case of neglecting to help others in distress does Kant actually use this as a reason for thinking that I cannot will the universal adoption of my maxim. In the case of talent-neglecting we could scream with frustration and bafflement because he does not argue in this way. He may be arguing in this way, in the case of making promises you cannot keep, and this may be what he means when he says 'the universality of a law, that everyone believing himself to be in need may make any promise he pleases with the intention not to keep it, would make promising, *and the very purpose of promising,*

itself impossible. . . .' Only this is a case of perfect duty, so Kant should be trying to prove that the universalisation of my maxim is impossible, not that I cannot will it, though, of course, there is no reason why he should not try to prove both.

(5) Up to now I have considered the relation between the categorical imperative and the morality of maxims. So far, however, I have not said anything at all about the morality of individual actions. Let us suppose, for the sake of argument, that Kant has provided us with a satisfactory criterion for deciding upon the morality of maxims. It is quite clear to me that Kant thinks that, by doing this, he has automatically also provided us with a criterion for deciding upon the morality of actions. For example, he seems to think that, from the fact that my maxims or rule to commit suicide if I should be happier dead cannot be acted upon by everybody, it follows that the action of committing suicide, which would be performed on this maxim, is wrong. I think this is a howler. A maxim may be wrong, although an individual action performed upon it is right. Let us suppose, for example, that a promise is extracted from me by means of force. I may make it a rule to break promises which it is inconvenient for me to keep, and so break my promise. It is arguable that it is impossible for everybody to act on this maxim, and pretty clear that the maxim is a wrong one, whether it is possible for everybody to act on it or not. But the fact that my maxim was wrong would have no tendency whatsoever to show that my action, of breaking a promise extracted from me by means of force, was wrong. To suppose that it does is to commit a fallacy analogous to that of denying the antecedent in the *modus ponendo ponens*. If my maxim is right, it will follow that every action performed upon it is right, but if my maxim is wrong, it will not follow that every action performed upon it is wrong. In other words, the relation between the morality of maxims and the morality of actions is more complicated than Kant seems to have supposed. I am inclined, fairly tentatively, to say that a maxim is right if and only if every action it could conceivably enjoin is right, and is wrong if some action it could conceivably enjoin is wrong. It does not follow that because a maxim enjoins a right action it is right, nor does it follow that because a maxim is wrong, the action

which it enjoins is wrong. (I should also add that for every right action there is at least one, and possibly more than one, right maxim which would enjoin it, and that for every wrong action there are a large number of wrong maxims which would enjoin it.) In other words, you may have: maxim right, action enjoined right; maxim wrong, action enjoined wrong; maxim wrong, action enjoined right; but you cannot have: maxim right, action enjoined wrong. This suggests that, instead of arguing that, because my maxim cannot be universalised, the action it enjoins must be right. In this case, done better to argue that, because my maxim can be universalised, the action it enjoins must be right. In this case, though an action is shown to be right if a maxim can be found for it which can be universalised, it is not shown to be wrong because a maxim can be found for it which cannot be universalised. It is only shown to be wrong if every maxim which would enjoin it cannot be universalised. Is it the case that, if an action is wrong, no maxim which would enjoin it can be universalised? Against this there is a very formidable objection, which I am not sure can be answered. It is this: Given any wrong action, you can find a maxim for it which is so specific that it enjoins that action and no other. For example, my action of killing my mother-in-law would be enjoined by my maxim to kill anyone with purple hair (we will assume my motives are aesthetic ones). If she is the only purple-haired person, it would seem that my maxim can be universalised, in Kant's sense, without contradiction. It is, nevertheless, very wrong of me to kill my mother-in-law.

I want to end by making some very brief remarks on some of the ethical theories which a consideration of Kant's examples of the first formulation of the categorical imperative might suggest.

(1) I have a slight inclination to agree that, if my maxim is such that not everybody can successfully act on it, then it is a wrong maxim—though, as I have pointed out, it does not follow that every action it enjoins is wrong. I do not know how to prove this, however, and I am very far from being sure that it is true. There is an alleged proof of a different statement, namely that, if a maxim is such that not everybody can

successfully act on it, it cannot be a maxim on which it is my *duty* to act. The proof is as follows: If it is everybody's duty to act on a maxim, it must be possible for everybody to act on it. Hence if it is not possible for everybody to act on a maxim, it cannot be a duty for everybody to act on it. What is not a duty for everybody is not a duty for anybody. Therefore it cannot be anybody's duty to act on a maxim on which everybody cannot act. I must confess I have some doubt about the premise: What is not a duty for everybody cannot be a duty for anybody, which I suspect some philosophers have confused with the different statement that what is not a duty for me cannot be a duty for anybody else in the same circumstances. I am inclined to think that 'What is not a duty for everybody cannot be a duty for anybody' really means 'What is not a duty for anybody, if everybody else is doing the same, is not a duty for anybody, even where not everybody else is doing the same'. This is not self-evident, for, from the fact that it is not anybody's duty to do something in one set of circumstances, it does not follow that this is not anybody's duty in another different set of circumstances.

(2) I have very little tendency to agree that, if I should be more reluctant to will the universal adoption of my maxim than to adopt it myself, this shows that the maxim in question is wrong. A murderer who was also a hangman might be very reluctant to will that everybody should make it a rule to hang murderers, but this would not show that the maxim is a wrong one, though it might be wrong for other reasons. I make one exception to this expression of disagreement with Kant, however. If the reason why I am reluctant to will the universalisation of my maxim is that I should be horror-struck at the spectacle of everybody's acting on a wrong maxim— Kant nowhere says that this is the reason—then the fact that I feel this horror does indicate that the maxim in question is wrong. But I do not think you can argue from the fact that I would feel horror at the universalisation of my maxim to the fact that it is wrong—though you can argue from this to the different fact that I think it is wrong—for unless I first thought it was wrong, I should not feel horror at its universalisation, and if I mistakenly thought it was right, I should feel no such

horror, and hence contemplating its universalisation would not enable me to correct my mistake.

(3) Lastly, I am very strongly inclined to think that the fact that my maxim would have bad consequences if everybody were to adopt it would show it was wrong, even if my adopting it alone had no bad consequences, but this view has enormous difficulties, with which I have no space to deal adequately. Perhaps the worst of them, however, has already been mentioned. If I make my rule sufficiently specific, so specific that it enjoins simply one action, which itself has no bad consequences, then no bad consequences would result from its universalisation. I should like, if I can, however, to get over the difficulty in the following way. If my maxim is to break my promises, where this has no bad consequences, provided that I happen to be a person with webbed feet—we will assume that I have webbed feet, and that I am the only person who has—everybody else could adopt this maxim without harm resulting. But not everybody could adopt this sort of maxim without harm resulting, for if I can argue that I may break my promises where promise-breaking has no bad consequences because I have webbed feet, someone else may argue that he may break such promises because he is over nine feet high, and someone else that he may break such promises because he is unique in having blood-group Z. But if everyone argued in this sort of way, harm would result. The problem is: What is the difference between arguing in this sort of way, which is not admissible, and arguing in other sorts of way, which are? But I hope I have already said enough to show that, though Kant's theory is not tenable as it stands, there are implicit in it numerous suggestions which it would be profitable to consider at greater length on another occasion.

KANT'S EXAMPLES OF THE
CATEGORICAL IMPERATIVE

J. KEMP

In his article on *Kant's Examples of the First Formulation
of the Categorical Imperative*[1] Mr. Jonathan Harrison has
combined an exegesis of some of Kant's views with a criticism
of them. My purpose here is to express certain doubts about
his exegesis; the criticisms will be referred to only incidentally.

The difficulties begin with the title: what *is* the 'first
formulation'? It would be natural to suppose that it is what
Paton, in *The Categorical Imperative*, refers to as Formula I:
"Act only on that maxim through which you can at the same
time will that it should become a universal law".[2] But this
formula has, in the *Grundlegung*, no examples at all; and
the examples which Harrison discusses all belong to what
Paton calls Formula Ia: "Act as if the maxim of your action
were to become through your will a universal law of nature".
Nor is this just a piece of pedantry, for the two formulae
differ in meaning and in the method by which they are ap-

Reprinted with permission of the author and of the editors from
Philosophical Quarterly, 8 (1958), 63–71.

[1] *Philosophical Quarterly* (January 1957), 50–62 [pp. 228–45 of
this volume.—Ed.].

[2] *Grundlegung* 52. It is highly desirable that agreement should be
reached on a systematic way of referring to Kant's works. The simplest procedure, here adopted, is to follow the practice of Kemp Smith
with the *Critique of Pure Reason* and of Paton with the *Grundlegung*,
and quote the pages of the original editions, where necessary denoting the first and second editions by 'A' and 'B' respectively. In cases
where the use of this method alone might cause difficulties, I have
added a reference to the pages of an easily accessible English translation, although my quotations are not always taken from the translations referred to.

plied. The 'universal law' of Formula I is a law (of freedom, not of nature) to the effect that everyone ought to, or may, act in a certain way: the 'universal law of nature' of Formula Ia is a law to the effect that everyone necessarily does, or is able to, act in a certain way. And the arguments in Kant's first, third and fourth examples,[3] at least, would not even begin to make sense in terms of Formula I; for they depend on the concept of nature, to which that formula makes no reference. The law of nature, in fact, is used by Kant as a 'type' or illustration of the moral law; "for if common sense did not have something to use in actual experience as an example, it could make no use of the law of pure practical reason in applying it to that experience".[4] The formula of the law of nature is thus intended as a practical criterion (or, more strictly, as the formal statement of a criterion which ordinary people actually use) for judging the morality of actions. Harrison is therefore in error in saying that, in this formula, Kant was attempting to put forward the supreme principle of morality.[5] Even in the *Grundlegung*,[6] Kant makes it clear that autonomy, not universality, is the supreme principle of morality; and in the *Critique of Practical Reason*, just before the passage quoted above, he states also that the comparison of one's maxims with a universal law of nature is not the 'determining ground' of one's will (as the supreme principle of morality would presumably be), but merely a useful example of a universal law which we can employ, by a kind of analogy, as a criterion.

Before he proceeds to discuss Kant's examples in detail, Harrison makes some preliminary remarks (mostly about maxims), one of which requires comment. "I shall assume", he says,[7] "that what Kant means by saying that we cannot will that a maxim should become a universal law is that, if it were within our power to bring about a state of affairs in which everyone acted on our maxim, we could not bring our-

---

[3] As for the argument of the second example, see pp. 151–52 below, especially n. 16 [pp. 152 of this volume.—Ed.].

[4] *Critique of Practical Reason* A 123, tr. Abbott, pp. 161–62.

[5] Page 50 [page 229 of this volume.—Ed.].

[6] Compare especially *Gr.* 87–88.

[7] Page 52 [page 231 of this volume.—Ed.].

selves to do it, or, what comes to the same thing, that if, as a result of our acting on a given maxim, it became a law of nature that everyone acted on that maxim, we would not act on it". Kant's conception of being able, or unable, to will that a maxim should become a universal law of nature is admittedly at first sight obscure—although some, at least, of the obscurity is due to the fact that the English verb 'to will' is used far less commonly and naturally than the German 'wollen'. But it is quite clear that Harrison's interpretation will not do. The inability to bring oneself to do something is quite irrelevant; a man may be unable, for various reasons, to bring himself to do his duty, but this neither means nor implies that he is unable to will it. Nor is the notion, contained in Harrison's interpretation, of a maxim becoming a law of nature as a result of someone's acting on it to be found in Kant.

It is clear from Kant's own arguments that the impossibility of willing certain types of maxim to be universal laws of nature is due to, or at least connected with, the fact that it would be irrational (not impossible) to set oneself to act accordingly. It is impossible for a man to will a universal law of nature that all men let their talents rust because "as a rational being he necessarily wills that all his powers should be developed, since they serve him, and are given him, for all sorts of possible ends"[8]—i.e. it is irrational to set oneself to produce such a state of affairs, because it is inconsistent with purposes which one necessarily has. And it is impossible to will a universal law of nature to the effect that nobody helped anybody else, because "a will which decided in this way would be at variance with itself (würde sich selbst widerstreiten)".[9] The essential point is that irrational willing, in this sense of the word, is for Kant a contradiction in terms; whereas setting oneself to act irrationally is always possible for human beings, but is, in his technical language, a manifestation of Willkür, not of Wille.[10]

[8] Gr. 55–56.
[9] Gr. 56.
[10] For this distinction see *Die Metaphysik der Sitten*, Introduction, AB 5, Abbott, p. 268.

As not infrequently happens, Kant expresses himself more clearly in the corresponding passage in the *Critique of Practical Reason*. He there argues that men do in fact use the formula of the universal law of nature as a criterion for judging actions: "People ask, 'If you belonged to an order of things in which everyone would allow himself to deceive when he thought it to his advantage . . . , would you assent of your own will to being a member of that order? (würdest du darin wohl mit Einstimmung deines Willens sein?)'".[11] This cannot of course mean 'Would you like, or enjoy, being a member of that order?'; for liking or enjoyment can never in Kant's view function as a criterion of morality. Nor can it mean 'Could you bring yourself to remain if you had the chance of leaving?'; for you might be able to bring yourself to remain, from love of pleasure or idleness, against your better judgment. The question is rather, 'Would you freely (i.e. rationally, independently of the pressure of your desires or other empirical factors) assent to your membership?'

We can now turn to consider Harrison's discussion of the examples themselves.

1. SUICIDE

Kant's explanation of the wrongness of suicide rests on a teleological assumption about the function of the instinct of self-love. A system of nature (eine Natur) in which everyone who felt tired of life was led by self-love to kill himself "would contradict itself and consequently could not subsist as a system of nature",[12] because the function of self-love is to stimulate the furtherance of life. Now this argument is obviously open to criticism in various ways; one might, for instance, object to basing any duty on a belief about the purposiveness of nature or, less sweepingly, one might say that Kant has failed to distinguish the instinct of self-preservation (a blind tendency to preserve one's life at all costs) from the principle of self-love (a calculated desire for pleasure

---

[11] *Critique of Practical Reason*, A 122–123, Abbott, p. 161.
[12] *Gr.* 54.

and aversion from pain). But Harrison's objection to the argument is different and is, I think, based on a misunderstanding of Kant's meaning. What Kant is trying to show, he thinks, is that the statement that everybody acts on the maxim of killing himself when the continuance of life promises more pain than pleasure contradicts the (true) statement that the purpose of self-love is to stimulate the furtherance of life. But this misses the point of Kant's argument. What is in question is not a mere statement to the effect that everyone acts on a certain maxim, but a law of nature to the effect that everyone necessarily acts on it, and this, Kant is saying, in effect, contradicts another law of nature according to which the function of self-love is to preserve life. This failure to distinguish between a statement that people as a matter of fact always, or usually, behave in a certain way and a law of nature to the effect that people necessarily behave in that way is at the root of Harrison's objections to Kant on this point. There are, he thinks, two possible interpretations of the contention that it is the purpose, or part of the purpose, of self-love to prevent people from committing suicide. (a) The purpose referred to may be one which is usually not fulfilled (as some watches usually fail to fulfil the purpose of telling the time). In this case, he says, "there is obviously no contradiction between the statement that self-love usually prompts people to commit suicide, and the statement that the purpose of self-love is to stop people from committing suicide".[13] This is true, but completely irrelevant to anything Kant actually says. (b) The purpose may be one which cannot remain as a rule unfulfilled. But on this assumption also, Harrison thinks, the contradiction alleged by Kant does not occur. "Perhaps there would be [a contradiction] if the universal adoption of my rule to commit suicide if I should be happier dead would mean that self-love usually led people to kill themselves, but it does not mean this. My rule—and Kant almost seems to forget this—is not simply to commit suicide, but to commit suicide if I should be happier dead. Since it is not unreasonable to suppose that those people who would be happier dead are in a minor-

[13] Page 54 [page 234 of this volume.—Ed.].

ity, the universal adoption of my maxim would not mean that people usually committed suicide, and not mean, therefore, that self-love usually (or even frequently) caused people to commit suicide". Once again, the connection of Kant's notion of universality with the word 'usually' is a mistake. It does not matter how many weary people commit suicide—it is as wrong for one as for a million, and as possible for a million, or for the entire human race, as for one. Kant is not saying that it is impossible for self-love to lead everybody to commit suicide, still less that it is impossible for it to lead all those who are weary of life to do so; what he *is* implying is that such a state of affairs could not form part of a system of nature which also contained the law that the purpose of self-love is to promote the furtherance of life. For a system of nature is *ex hypothesi* rationally ordered, and it would be irrational if one and the same principle or instinct could lead to diametrically opposed types of behaviour. (One might, of course, conceive of a system of nature which included beings in whom some sort of death-wish was the guiding force, though they would obviously not form part of this system for long; but nature is not, in Kant's view, like that.)

2. FALSE PROMISES

Here the maxim which Kant considers cannot become a universal law of nature is "Whenever I believe myself short of money, I will borrow money and promise to pay it back, though I know that this will never be done".[14] "Kant argues", Harrison says, "that, though it is possible for me to adopt and act on this maxim, it is not possible for everybody to adopt and act on it; for, were they to do so, no-one would trust anyone who made a promise to keep it, hence no-one would be able to obtain a service by making a promise, hence no-one would make any promises, hence no-one would be able to act on the maxim in question".[15] But what Kant says is, not that it is impossible for everyone to adopt and act on this

[14] Gr. 54.
[15] Page 54 [page 234 of this volume.—Ed.].

maxim, but that a law that everyone is able[16] to do so would contradict itself; and thus the impossibility of everyone adopting the maxim cannot be a merely causal impossibility, as Harrison's version would allow it to be. But the chief error here, a not uncommon one, lies, I think, in a misunderstanding of Kant's statement that the universality of the maxim in question "would make promising, and the very purpose of promising, impossible". Kant's use of the word 'machen' here is taken by Harrison to indicate a causal relationship: if the maxim were universally adopted, then a causal consequence would be that the practice of promisemaking, or at least of making promises in connection with loans, would soon die out, because it would be seen to be pointless (Cf. Harrison, p. 55 "I am willing to grant that if everyone acted on the maxim in question, promise-making would die out"). And if this were Kant's meaning, the argument would indeed be as unsatisfactory as Harrison maintains. It may well be true, for instance, that if everyone cheated at bridge, it would soon result that no one would play it; but this result is in no way inconsistent with the universalised maxim to cheat whenever it is to one's advantage. For the maxim does not assert or imply that everyone plays bridge, but only that, if and when they play bridge, they will cheat whenever they think it is to their advantage.

What Kant actually says, however, is not that the maxim of making false promises could not exist as a universal law of nature for very long (which is what Harrison's interpretation amounts to, for there would obviously be a time-lag), but that it could not exist at all as a universal law of nature without contradiction. And if he really means this, it is clear that the relation designated by the verb 'machen' must be one of logical or quasi-logical, not causal consequence. The argument has the effect of a *reductio ad absurdum*. If, *per impossible*, there were a universal law to this effect, then there would not be and would never have been any prom-

---

[16] Paton here mis-translates 'könne' by 'may'; and also, presumably by an oversight, omits the phrase 'of nature' after 'I then see straight away that this maxim can never rank as a universal law', thus creating the misleading impression that Kant is talking about a law of morality, not a law of nature.

ises[17] (the 'if . . . then' indicating an entailment-relation); but the statement that there is such a law of nature also entails that there are promises. Hence it has contradictory implications—i.e. it is self-contradictory.

It is worth noticing that Kant is careful to distinguish the concept of self-contradiction from that of being self-defeating or self-destructive. In the passages of the *Grundlegung* under discussion, whenever a putative universal law of nature is rejected as being inconsistent with itself, Kant says (and, I have argued, means) that it is self-contradictory, using always the phrase 'sich widersprechen'. But when he wishes to say, of a putative universal law of morality, that it would be inconsistent with itself, he uses different terminology—such a law would annihilate itself, 'sich selbst vernichten' or 'sich selbst aufreiben'.[18]

3. DEVELOPING ONE'S TALENTS

Harrison here makes the mistake of supposing that Kant's argument to show that willing the universal neglect of talents is impossible involves a reference to prudential considerations. "If Kant's treatment of the third example had been analogous to his treatment of the fourth, what he would have said, presumably, would have been that, though I can act on the maxim 'neglect my talents' myself, I cannot will that everyone should make this their maxim, for in that case I should be deprived of any benefits accruing to me from other people's developing their talents. It is obvious that I do benefit from other people's developing their talents. However, what Kant in fact says is, not that I cannot will the universalisation of my maxim because other people's talents are useful to me, but that I cannot will the universalisation of

---

[17] People might have used the expression 'I promise', but they could not (logically) have used it for the purpose of making a promise; for you cannot (again logically) make a promise if nobody will believe you. Although you could say 'I promise to repay the money', it would be only a statement of intention, not a promise, which requires the existence of a promisee as well as a promisor.

[18] Compare *Kritik der praktischen Vernunft* A 50, Abbott, p. 115.

my maxim because my talents are useful to me".[19] In this
last sentence, as in some other places, Harrison says 'says'
when he means 'means'; but even as an interpretation of
what Kant means it is, to say the least, hazardous, for there
is nothing in the *Grundlegung* to suggest that the ends which
the development of my talents may help me to achieve are
selfish ones. This interpretation is, indeed, hardly consistent
with Kant's original description of the situation, in which he
refers to a man with a talent, the cultivation of which "would
make him a useful man [*not* "would be useful to him"] for all
sorts of purposes".[20] In the *Metaphysik der Sitten*, when
Kant comes to expand his views on the development of talents and faculties, he expresses himself quite unmistakably.
Man's duty to develop his faculties, he there says, is not dependent on any advantage their development may bring him;
indeed, the advantage might turn out to be in favour of
Rousseau's noble, but uncultivated, savage. "On the contrary,
it is a command of morally practical reason, and a duty of a
man towards himself, that he should cultivate his capacities
(one rather than another according to the diversity of his objectives), and be a man who, from a practical point of view,
is well adapted to the purpose of his existence".[21]

The key to the understanding of this third example lies in
its last sentence: "For as a rational being he necessarily wills
that all his powers should be developed, since they serve him,
and are given him, for all sorts of possible ends".[22] What
chiefly distinguishes man from the rest of creation, according
to Kant, is his possession of freedom; this in turn depends
on his possession of reason, not in the sense that he is capable
of theoretical activity, but in the sense that he can set ends
or purposes before himself (whereas the rest of creation can
merely fulfil passively the purposes of nature).[23] And this

[19] Page 57 [page 238 of this volume.–Ed.].
[20] Gr. 55.
[21] MdS *Tugendlehre* A 111, tr. Semple, 3d ed., pp. 261–62. (This
translation of Semple's is full of inaccuracies and should be used with
great caution.)
[22] Gr. 56.
[23] Compare *Critique of Judgment*, B 399, tr. Bernard, p. 361.
"Only in man, and only in him as subject of morality, do we meet

gives its point to the expression, which Harrison finds obscure, "For as a rational being he necessarily wills . . .". Whatever a man's private aim or purpose in life may be, the fact that he has such a purpose is a sign of his rationality, even though all men, being imperfectly rational, have some purposes which they would not have if they were perfectly rational, and fail to have some which they would then have. Now any human purpose requires the exercise of some talent or capacity for its fulfilment; for a talent or capacity just is the ability to take appropriate means to given ends. Man's ability to conceive of purposes would be of no value, and his freedom would be incomplete, if he were not also endowed with the capacity for discovering and adopting the best means for the attainment of those purposes. Hence to refuse to develop *any* of one's talents would be irrational; it would be failing to take rational means to the achievement of any of one's aims or purposes, and all of us must have some such aims or (as we should more naturally say) desires. But why, it might be asked, should I not restrict my efforts to developing those talents which will enable me to live a more pleasant life; why should I worry about developing my moral capacities or increasing my ability to help others? Because, Kant would reply, you are a man and a rational being, and to restrict the development of one's capacities to those which provide an increase of pleasure for oneself is to put oneself on a level with the beasts, to behave in an inhuman and irrational way. It is because of this that a man cannot rationally assent to being a member of an order of nature in which self-development was universally neglected. Moreover, the use of reason, as manifested in the deliberate cultivation of one's talents, in order merely to promote one's own happiness is unlikely to be successful, human nature being what it is: "the more a cultivated reason concerns itself with the aim of enjoying life and happiness, the farther does man get away from true contentment".[24]

---

with unconditioned legislation in respect of purposes, which therefore alone renders him capable of being a final purpose, to which the whole of nature is teleologically subordinated."

[24] *Gr.* 5.

4. HELPING OTHERS IN DISTRESS

All that need be said under this head is that Harrison
once again seems to misunderstand Kant's use of the words
'Wille' and 'wollen'. He points out that people sometimes do
things in spite of motives impelling them not to, and concludes "From the fact that my will would be at variance with
itself if it willed the universal adoption of my maxim, it does
not follow that I cannot will the universal adoption of my
maxim. All that does follow is that I cannot will it wholeheartedly".[25] But although it does not follow that I cannot
set myself, whether wholeheartedly or not, to achieve its universal adoption, it does, in Kant's terminology, follow that I
cannot *will* its universal adoption; for the notion of a will at
variance with itself is self-contradictory, even though the notion of human efforts at variance with one another is not.
'Wille' and 'wollen' always include the notion of rational
effort; and inconsistency, whether of judgment or of volition,
is a sign of irrationality.

Harrison concludes his article with some more general
comments. Of these, the only one I wish to discuss concerns
the relation between the morality of maxims and the morality
of actions. Kant is alleged to have committed a howler in
supposing that his criterion for deciding upon the morality of
maxims automatically provides us with a criterion for deciding upon the morality of actions; in supposing, for example,
that the impossibility of willing that the maxim of committing suicide if one would be happier dead should become a
universal law entails that the action of suicide in itself is
necessarily wrong. Even if a maxim is wrong, Harrison thinks,
some individual actions performed in accordance with it may
be right. "Let us suppose, for example, that a promise is extracted from me by means of force. I may make it a rule
to break promises which it is inconvenient for me to keep, and
so break my promise. It is arguable that it is impossible for

[25] Page 57 [page 237 of this volume.—Ed.].

everybody to act on this maxim, and pretty clear that the maxim is a wrong one, whether it is possible for everybody to act on it or not. But the fact that my maxim was wrong would have no tendency whatsoever to show that my action, of breaking a promise extracted from me by means of force, was wrong".[26]

Now the whole question of the relation between actions and their maxims is somewhat obscure, and Kant does not give us as much help in elucidating it as we should have liked: serious difficulties, in particular, arise from the fact that we can apparently extract maxims from actions at varying levels of generality. And if I have performed an action, and tell someone what its maxim was, it is easy to imagine a situation in which he might wish to challenge my statement, but not at all easy to formulate the grounds on which such a challenge might be supported or resisted—disagreement about the maxim of an action is not the same as, though it may be connected with, disagreement about its motive. Nevertheless, I do not think that Kant has committed a 'howler' in this instance, however obscure, and perhaps mistaken, his general account of maxims may be. Harrison's impression that he has done so seems to be due to the misleadingly abstract sense in which he, in contrast with Kant but in common with most contemporary British philosophers, uses the word 'action'. For Kant, the use of the principle of universality is to test, by examining the nature of its maxim, the totality consisting of action-on-this-maxim; whereas Harrison argues as if examination of the maxim will provide a criterion of the action, even when this action is considered quite independently of the maxim examined, i.e. as if the wrongness of action on a certain maxim entailed the wrongness of any action which, even though performed on a different maxim, was otherwise identical with it. In Kant's view, the assessment of actions in the narrower sense, considered independently of their maxims, concerns, not their morality, but their legality—quite a different matter.[27] The impossibility of universalising the maxim of breaking promises whenever it

[26] Page 60 [page 242 of this volume.—Ed.].
[27] For this distinction between Sittlichkeit and Gesetzmässigkeit see *MdS*, Introduction, AB 27, Abbott, p. 282.

is inconvenient to keep them shows, not that breaking promises is always wrong (if Kant had held that it did he would
have been mistaken), but that breaking promises just because it is inconvenient to keep them is wrong. It is true, of
course, that Kant took a very rigorous view of the obligation
to keep promises, as of that to avoid telling lies, whatever
the circumstances. But it is important to distinguish Kant's
personal opinions on moral matters from the principles of
his moral philosophy; for there are some of the former which
are not entailed by anything in the latter.

THE CATEGORICAL IMPERATIVE

JONATHAN HARRISON

I cannot hope to deal with all the points raised by Mr. Kemp[1] in his scholarly criticism of my paper; on the other hand, I cannot forbear from commenting on the following somewhat arbitrary selection.

ON 'WILLING'

Talk about whether or not we could will that our maxim should become a universal law is queer not, I think, because 'will' is an unusual verb, but because it is difficult to see what volitional attitude we could take up to something so utterly outside our power to achieve as the universalisation of our maxim. This is presumably the reason why some commentators use 'desire' and 'wish' instead of 'will', and it is why I talk about what we could choose, if we had the power, or what we would choose, if the universalisation of our maxim should by some miracle be the consequence of our action. Against Mr. Kemp's view that willing should be defined not simply in terms of choosing, but in terms of rational choosing, the following objections may be raised.

(1) The trouble with using what a rational being can or cannot will as a test of right or wrong is that in the ordinary sense of 'rational' rational beings are as capable of immorality as anyone else, and that in its technical, capital letter sense it tends to be a criterion of a Rational Being that he never chooses immorally; hence you have to know what is immoral

Reprinted with permission of the author and of the editors from *Philosophical Quarterly*, 8 (1958), 360–64.
[1] [Pp. 246–58 of this volume.–Ed.]

first in order to know what a Rational Being would choose, and so cannot deduce that it is immoral from the fact that a Rational Being would not choose it.

(2) Kant (19) states that I can will to lie, and clearly means decide or choose to lie.

(3) In the passages we are discussing there is an obvious antithesis between the *objects* of my choice, i.e. the action and its universalisation. According to Mr. Kemp, there is also an antithesis between two sorts of choice, ordinary choice and rational choice (willing). If this were correct, we would expect to see Kant contrasting being able to *choose* an action with being unable to *will* (rationally choose) it, and being able to *choose* the universalisation of our maxim with being unable to *will* it; in fact he never does this. On my view, the contrast between being able to choose the action but unable to will its universalisation is a straightforward antithesis between two different objects of choice. On Mr. Kemp's view, it is a clumsy because simultaneous contrast of object of choice and nature of choice, i.e. between being able to choose the action, but unable rationally to choose its universalisation.

ON 'LAW' IN FORMULA I

If Mr. Kemp is right in thinking that 'law' in Formula I means 'moral law', Formula I may mean one of (at least) two things. (A) Act only on that maxim which you could cause to become a moral law, if you had the power. (B) Act only on maxims which you are satisfied accord with moral laws.

(1) A would be the most natural interpretation of Kant, given that 'law' means 'moral law'.

(2) B would have the advantage of being true; I surely ought to consider whether my maxims accord with moral law before I adopt them. B has the disadvantage, however, that it does not tell me what the moral law is to which my maxims ought to conform.

(3) On neither A nor B is Kant right in supposing Formula I equivalent to Formula Ia, for they mention my atti-

tude to laws on which people ought to act, whereas Formula Ia mentions my attitude to laws which describe how people actually do act. There might be many things that I could will to be a law that people ought to act on, so long as I thought that it would not become a law (of nature) that they act on them, e.g. the debtor of the parable might well be able to will it to be a moral law that everyone ought to imprison their debtors, but unable to will it to be a law of nature that everyone did imprison their debtors.

(4) On A, however, consideration of what it would be like if my maxim became a law of nature might be one of my motives for deciding whether or not to make it a moral law. Perhaps I cannot will it to be a moral law that no-one ought to help others in distress (or should the moral law be that anyone may refrain from helping others in distress?), because in that case no-one would help anyone else in distress, and then no-one would help me. And perhaps there are other maxims which I could not make moral laws had I the power because, as a legislator, I must wish to make practicable moral laws, and the worst sort of impracticability in a moral law is the logical impossibility of its being acted upon by everybody.

(5) On this view, of course, I am not subject to laws which I make, but subject to laws which I could have made, had I the power.

(6) What, on this interpretation of Kant, I am asked to do, (i.e. consider what moral laws I could make, had I the power) must not be confused with something different, (i.e. considering what positive laws I could make, had I the power). The notion of making moral law is such a very odd one, that I think anyone trying to put himself in the former position is likely to succeed in putting himself only in the latter. The difference is important, for there might be many things that he might wish to make illegal, which he did not wish to make immoral (and, perhaps, *vice versa*).

(7) In deciding what moral laws one could make, I think it would be important to avoid moral considerations. Of course, if one were considering what positive laws to make, it would be natural and proper to allow moral arguments to weigh with one—e.g. if one were considering whether to make

homosexual intercourse illegal, one would naturally, though I hope not exclusively, be influenced by whether or not one thought it immoral. But I think that in imagining oneself as a moral-law giver, one cannot properly do this, for if one has to decide what the moral law is *via* a consideration of what moral laws one could legislate, one must not suppose it to be already determined what it is, in order to decide what moral laws one could legislate.

(8) If I am right in supposing that the only reason why one could not will one's maxim to be a moral law would be consideration of what would happen if this moral law were acted upon (i.e. consideration of what would happen if one's maxim became a law of nature), then if there are immoral maxims which one could will to be laws of nature, one could also will them to be moral laws, so any difficulties with Formula Ia would also be difficulties with (A) above.

(9) It must not be supposed that 'law' in Formula I must mean 'moral law' because Ia mentions the law of nature explicitly. It could mean (as I had supposed it did) 'law in general' (i.e. that of which moral laws and natural laws and logical laws are all species). If it does, Formulas I and Ia are much more nearly equivalent than if it means 'moral law', for a law of nature is a species of law in general, though it is not even a species of moral law.

SUICIDE

(1) I take it that to say a system of nature contradicts itself is to say that the statements involved in its description are contradictory, nor do I know what it means to say that *laws* contradict one another if it does not mean that the statements which formulate these laws contradict one another. Mr. Kemp himself finds the contradiction which he thinks is involved in the universalisation of promise-breaking in a contradiction between statements.

(2) To point out that the universality of suicide among *men who would be happier dead* does not even imply that suicide is usual among *men* (without restriction) is no more

to misunderstand what is meant by universality than is to point out that men are not usually hanged to fail to appreciate that murderers always are.

FALSE PROMISES

(1) Mr. Kemp accuses me of attributing to Kant the view that the universal making of promises which one has no intention of keeping is only causally impossible; what I actually say is that though Kant thought it was logically impossible, it is in fact (at most) only causally impossible—and not even this in a universe where people's memories are very short.

(2) Mr. Kemp agrees with Kant that the universal making of promises one has no intention of keeping is logically impossible, for, if the maxim in question became a universal law, then there would both be and not be promises. Three questions arise: (i) Would the universalisation of Kant's maxim entail that all promises were false promises? (ii) If all promises were false promises, would this entail that no promises would be "believed"? (iii) If no promises were believed, would this entail that there were no promises?

(i) Even if we ignore—as I believe we may—the fact that Kant's maxim relates only to promises to obtain money, and substitute the maxim 'make false promises when it suits me', the universalisation of this maxim does not entail that all promises are false promises, unless we add the additional dubious premise that it never suits me to make any promises except false promises. If we drop the qualification 'if it suits me', the result is a maxim which is absurd, and does not in any case entail that I never make any other sort of promises. The maxim which would entail that all promises were false promises, '*Only* make false promises', is not Kant's, and would not in any case entail that there *were* promises, which is a necessary step in Mr. Kemp's argument.

(ii) That all promises are false promises does not in itself entail that no promises are believed, but only in conjunction with certain other empirical propositions about people, e.g. that they are all possessed of a certain (admittedly low) degree of acumen, not given to superstitions about the integrity of certain limited classes of people.

(iii) It is certainly not necessary that any given promise should be believed, either by the promisee or by anybody else. Why then should it be necessary that at least one, or a good many, *other* promises should be believed? I suspect that the truth is that uttering the words 'I promise' (or an equivalent) cannot accomplish the making of a promise if they are greeted with open ridicule by the promisee. The proposition that if no promises were believed, all promises would be greeted with open ridicule by the promisee is an empirical proposition. I do not know whether or not it is true.

DEVELOPING ONE'S TALENTS

(1) My concern was not to criticise Kant morally (for appealing to self-interest, which I don't think he does), but logically for seeming to suppose that the effects of my talent-neglecting on my interest, which are features of an individual case of talent-neglecting, were reasons for my being unable to will the universalisation of talent-neglecting. Mr. Kemp may be helping Kant's character, but not his logic, by suggesting that he regarded my talents as something useful to everybody, for that my talents are useful to everybody is just as much a feature of the individual action as that my talents are useful to me, and so no better a reason for being unable to will the universalisation of talent-neglecting than that my talents are useful to me.

(2) Mr. Kemp's positive interpretation turns on taking 'talent-neglecting' to mean 'neglecting to develop one's capacities for achieving any of one's purposes'. That talent-neglecting does not mean this is shown by the fact that the South Sea Islanders neglected to develop their talents; yet I understand they cultivate their capacities for achieving some ends quite assiduously. The contradiction found by Mr. Kemp (between having purposes but not developing one's capacities for achieving them) has nothing to do with universalisation, and would make Kant's mention of this irrelevant.

HELPING OTHERS IN DISTRESS

(1) Surely there is nothing in the least irrational about willing things—one's duty, for example—in spite of having motives impelling one not to will them.

(2) I am inclined to think we are both wrong in the meaning we attribute to 'at variance with itself'.

KANT'S HOWLER

Mr. Kemp's remarks raise questions too general to be considered here. I call the fallacy I attribute to Kant a howler, because it is analogous to the fallacy of denying the antecedent. It does not follow that if a rule is wrong—because there are some cases in which it would lead one astray—it has led one astray in this case.

THE COPERNICAN REVOLUTION IN ETHICS: THE GOOD REEXAMINED

JOHN R. SILBER

I. THE PRIMACY OF THE MORAL LAW IN THE DETERMINATION OF THE GOOD

Kant's predecessors generally believed that ethical enquiry should begin with the definition of the good from which the moral law and the concept of obligation are to be derived. But from his revolutionary point of view, Kant saw that this was precisely the source of

> all the confusions of philosophers concerning the supreme principle of morals. For they sought an object of the will in order to make it into the material and foundation of a law; . . . instead they should have looked for a law which directly determined the will *a priori* and only then sought an object suitable to it.[1]

Reprinted with permission of the author and of the editors from *Kant-Studien*, Band 51 (1959), Kölner Universitäts-Verlag, in which it was first published.

[1] *KdpV*, p. 71: Beck, pp. 172–73.—In order to simplify references, I have abbreviated the titles of the books cited as will be shown below. I have usually cited both the German text and an English translation. Unless otherwise indicated translations are my own.

IKW	*Immanuel Kants Werke*, ed. Ernst Cassirer, 11 vols.
KdrV	*Kritik der reinen Vernunft, IKW*, III
Kemp Smith	Kemp Smith, A *Translation of Kant's Critique of Pure Reason*
KdpV	*Kritik der praktischen Vernunft, IKW*, V
Beck	Beck, *Critique of Practical Reason and other Writings in Moral Philosophy*
Gr	*Grundlegung zur Metaphysik der Sitten, IKW*, IV
Paton	Paton, *The Moral Law or Kant's Groundwork of the Metaphysic of Morals*

The "analytic" of the *Critique of Practical Reason* demonstrates that all attempts first to define the good as the object of the will and to derive from it the moral law and duty make the good into a material concept, and that all material principles are incapable of grounding the supreme principle of morality.[2] Kant's argument is not systematic; it comes in odd places and from many vantage points; sometimes it is implicit and at other times repetitiously explicit. But the argument is presented and it is capable of systematization.

At this point a few basic definitions will help to clarify Kant's argument. First, we must understand what Kant means by a practical principle. "Practical principle" is a generic term referring to the class of all propositions which contain a general determination of the will.[3] The will is the power of a rational being to act in accord with its *own idea of law* rather than in mere conformity to law.[4] This idea of law in terms of which the will acts is the principle of the will, that is, a practical principle. A being possessed of will in an act of willing does not simply respond to a stimulus; rather he consciously projects an intention. This intention is again the practical principle. But practical principles may be of two kinds: either subjective, in which case the principle of volition is regarded by the subject as valid for himself alone, or objective, in which case the principle is regarded as valid for all subjects. The subjective sort of principle is called a *maxim*, whereas the objective sort is called a practical law.[5]

We must also bear in mind Kant's distinction between "formal" and "material" as these terms relate to concepts and

MdS	*Die Metaphysik der Sitten*, IKW, VII
Abbott	Abbott, *Kant's Critique of Practical Reason and other Writings on the Theory of Ethics*
Rel	*Religion innerhalb der Grenzen der blossen Vernunft*, IKW, VI
Theorie und Praxis	*Über den Gemeinspruch: Das mag in der Theorie richtig sein, taugt aber nicht für die Praxis*, IKW, VI
Greene	Greene and Hudson, *Religion Within the Limits of Reason Alone*

[2] *Ibid.* pp. 47, 119: pp. 152, 214.
[3] *Ibid.* p. 21: p. 130.
[4] *Gr*, p. 270: Paton, p. 80.
[5] *KdpV*, p. 21: Beck, p. 130: *Gr*, p. 257n: Paton, p. 69n.

knowledge. Knowledge, or a concept, is material when it refers to some object; it is formal when it refers merely to the form of understanding and reason, that is, when it refers only to "the universal rules of thinking as such without regard to differences in its objects".[6] Thus, the presence or absence of reference to a specific object determines whether or not concepts and knowledge are formal or material.

It follows analytically from these definitions that the traditional concept of the good is a material concept. A formal concept is one which makes no reference to an object. But the traditional concept of the good, defined prior to the moral law, is the concept of an object for which the will is to strive. Hence, because of its reference to an object, the good is a material concept.

Kant's insistence that the moral law and duty can never be grounded on material concepts does not follow analytically, however, from these definitions. As Kant sees it, the problem is this: for the good to be a meaningful ethical concept it must be related to the moral agent as the obligation of the agent to embody the good in the practical principle of his will.[7] But the good as a material concept cannot be related to the will in this fashion. For if it is related to the will at all, then the good will be related to the will either empirically and contingently, and hence without obligation; or it will be compulsive upon the will as the natural cause of the effects of the will, and hence the freedom of the will, and thereby the will itself, will be destroyed. Thus, the attempt to ground the principle of morality on a previously defined material concept of the good founders on this dilemma: *either* the good stands in no relation or in a contingent relation to the will *or* the good itself has the power to determine the will to action and thereby destroys the will. In neither case can the moral law be derived from the good and, therefore, no rela-

[6] *Gr*, p. 243: Paton, p. 55.

[7] Kant takes for granted that moral obligation is categorical, i.e. necessary, inescapable obligation. And he also holds that obligation presupposes freedom of the will. We will assume these points for the present and hold that a sound moral theory must give an account of obligation on these terms.

tion of obligation can be effected between the good and the will.

Kant's argument in support of this position is provided in connection with his exposition of the theorems of *The Critique of Practical Reason*. Suppose one defines the good as the object (material) of the faculty of desire. The good then becomes an object whose reality is desired. As such the good stands in relation to the will[8] as that which the will desires. The practical principle of the will then expresses the desire of the will for the desired object, namely the good. But in this case, the practical principle can never be an objective practical law for all wills but only the subjective maxim of the particular will as it empirically encounters a desire within itself. The relation of the will to the good, therefore, is contingent because the decision of the will either to pursue or not pursue the good

> consists in the conception of an object and its relation to the subject, whereby the faculty of desire is determined to seek its realization. Such a relation to the subject is called pleasure in the reality of an object, and it [this pleasure] must be presupposed as the condition of the possibility of the determination of choice.[9]

But in defining an object as the good we cannot know *a priori* that it will be "associated with pleasure or displeasure or will be merely indifferent".[10] Thus the theory of ethics which defines the good in this fashion offers no rational foundation for the relation of necessity between the good and the will, and hence cannot derive the concept of duty from the idea of the good.

Furthermore, the will that is related to the good by the fact that it happens to desire it will be acting under a principle which is merely a subjective maxim and not an objec-

---

[8] We must remember that for Kant the will is both practical reason and the faculty of desire (*KdpV*, p. 9n: Beck, pp. 123–24).

[9] *KdpV*, p. 24: Beck, p. 132. Beck translates *Willkür* as "choice." It seems to me that Abbott's practice of translating *Willkür* as the "elective will" is a sounder one, because it stresses the fact that the *Willkür* is a genuine part of the faculty of will and not merely one of its activities.

[10] *Idem.*

tive moral law. Since the practical principle of the will is determined by the pleasure or aversion of the faculty of desire in regard to the good as its object, the practical principle is inevitably determined subjectively. There is no object sufficiently determinate to arouse the desire of even one person which can likewise arouse the same desire in all persons. Hence a practical principle cannot be an objective (universal) law if it is based on a choice which is determined by reference to pleasure or displeasure in regard to an object. The principle is *in fact* binding on the will of the person who actually desires the good, who actually takes pleasure in its reality. But it is only hypothetically binding on him as the maxim of a subject who happens to take a particular delight in this particular object. To sum up then the consequences of a theory in which the good is so defined, we find that the good is either unrelated to the will or is only contingently binding upon it. And even if, as the result of a felt desire, it happens to be binding on the will, it is only binding on a particular will as his subjective maxim and is in no wise binding upon all wills as a practical law or even upon his at all times.[11]

From this argument we can confidently deduce theorem I: "All practical principles which presuppose an object (material) of the faculty of desire as the determining ground of the will are without exception empirical and can furnish no practical laws."[12]

Some moralists prior to Kant saw this difficulty and sought to avoid it by distinguishing between a higher and a lower faculty of desire. The distinction was made on the basis of the origin of the pleasures entertained by the faculty of desire. Accordingly, pleasures belonged to the lower faculty of desire if they had their origin in the senses, whereas they belonged to the higher faculty of desire if they had their origin in the understanding. Now, it was argued, if the good as the object of the will were related to the will through the higher faculty of desire, that is by means of a pleasure of the understanding, then it could be related to the will as a law.

[11] *Idem*. Cf. *ibid*. pp. 29–30, 42: pp. 137, 148.
[12] *Idem*.

But Kant finds that this attempt to solve the difficulty is unsuccessful. We must note at once that even with this modification the good is still related to the will contingently; the good is binding on the will only if *in fact* there is a felt desire on the part of the will to attain the reality of the good. And this desire will be present only if the faculty of desire, whether higher or lower, encounters within itself pleasure in the anticipation of the reality of the good. Thus the concept of duty cannot be derived from the definition of the good even though the good is made the object of the understanding as the higher faculty of desire.

Furthermore, we find that this distinction between higher and lower faculties of desire does not enable us to regard objects of the higher faculty of desire as laws. Whether or not an object of the will stems from the understanding, whether or not the good is defined in terms of sense or in terms of the understanding, whether or not the good is defined rationally or empirically, the consequences on this point are the same. If the only way in which the good can determine the choice of the will is by means of desire, then the principle of the will which is so determined will be subjective. No matter how one defines good,

> However dissimilar the conception of the objects, be they proper to the understanding or even to the reason instead of to the senses, the feeling of pleasure, by virtue of which they constitute the determining ground of the will (since it is the agreeableness and the enjoyment which one expects from the object which impels the activity toward producing it) is always the same. This sameness lies not merely in the fact that all feelings of pleasure can be known only empirically, but even more in the fact that the feeling of pleasure always affects one and the same life-force which is manifested in the faculty of desire, and in this respect one determining ground differs from any other only in degree.[13]

Since the determining ground of the will is always desire, whether from higher or lower faculty, the practical principle

[13] *Ibid.* pp. 25–26: p. 134. Mill's failure to heed this passage points graphically to the importance of the history of philosophy as a guide and measure for fruitful philosophical inquiry.

of the will so determined can never be a practical law. As we saw earlier, felt desires or aversions are individual, and practical principles which are based upon them can only be subjective maxims.

When we add to our conclusion the reminder that Kant calls the principle of choice which is based upon the desire for that which is pleasant the principle of self-love or the principle of personal happiness, the deduction of the second theorem becomes clear: "All material practical principles are, as such, of one and the same kind and belong under the general principle of self-love or one's own happiness", and its corollary: "All material practical rules place the ground of the determination of the will in the lower faculty of desire, and if there were no purely formal laws of the will adequate to determine it, we could not admit [the existence of] any higher faculty of desire."[14]

Kant's first Theorem seems obvious enough for no one can responsibly argue that the good can be defined merely as the object of actual desire if one hopes to give meaning to moral obligation. But Kant's second theorem and its corollary cut much more deeply, since they strike down not only the claims of moralists like Hutcheson and Shaftesbury, those who ground the moral law on the moral feeling directed toward the good, but also strike down the claims of Wolff, the Stoics, and theological moralists who ground morality on the idea of perfection. The empiricism of the first group exposes its weakness. But since the latter group base their theories on the rational idea of perfection, it would seem that by defining the good in this manner they would have escaped the difficulty besetting the others. The difficulty remains, however, for when the concept of perfection is used in its practical sense it does not refer to the perfection of a substance, whether of a particular substance or of being in general. When used in the practical sense, the idea of perfection re-

---

[14] *Ibid.* pp. 25–26: p. 133. Here Kant does not distinguish the higher faculty of desire from the lower on the basis of desire but on the fact that the higher faculty of desire is determined by principles and not by desires. The truly higher faculty of desire is not determined by either sensible or intellectual desire but has a desire produced in itself by a principle.

fers to the sufficiency of an act or a being to a given end. The perfection of a knife, for example, is determined by its competence for cutting. Until the end is given, however, one cannot give meaning to the practical concept of perfection. The idea of perfection, even though it is developed by reason, cannot determine the will to action, nor even guide much less obligate the will, unless ends are antecedently given in terms of which perfection is to be judged. The concept of perfection cannot serve to relate the will to an end which must be given prior to the concept itself. Hence we face once more the problem of relating the end to the will. And as we have already seen, an end

> as an object which precedes and contains the ground of determination of the will is, if taken as the determining ground of the will, only empirical; it could thus serve for the Epicurean principle in the happiness theory but never as a pure rational principle of ethics and duty. Thus talents and their cultivation, because they contribute to the advantages of life, or the will of God, if agreement with it (without any practical principle independent of this idea) be taken as an object of the will, can be motives only by reason of the happiness expected from them.[15]

If the concept of perfection, which can indeed be defined by reason, could be given practical significance apart from the antecedent determination of an end, then it might be possible to sustain a theory of ethics which did define the good as perfection. But perfection has no meaning as a practical concept unless it specifies the degree of sufficiency of an object or act or person to a given end. Hence, if the will is not already related to some end as its object, it cannot be judged by the norm of perfection (whether human or divine perfection). But if the will is already related to some object, then we face our original difficulty of relating the will to the object in a way that makes the object normative for the will. But thus far we have found that the object is either irrelevant to the will or that it determines the principle of the will through natural desire, with the consequence that the con-

[15] *Ibid.* p. 47: pp. 151–52.

nection of the will to the object is empirical and contingent and that the principle of the will so related to the object is subjective.

Throughout this discussion, however, an assumption has been made which must be questioned. We may fairly ask why the good, as the object of the will, must be related to the will by means of desire at all? Granting the soundness of the objection to relating the will and the good in this manner, this objection does not become overwhelming until it has been shown that when the good is defined prior to the law as the object of will, desire provides the *only way* of relating the good to the will. Kant's answer is contained in Theorem III: "If a rational being can think of its maxims as practical universal laws he can do so only by considering them as principles which contain the determining grounds of the will formally and not materially."[16] As Kant states and defends this theorem it is not clear that his argument moves beyond Theorems I and II. In his demonstration of it Kant says:

> The material of a practical principle is the object of the will. This object either is the determining ground of the will or it is not. [If it is not, then the object (the good) is irrelevant to the will.] If it is, the rule of the will is subject to an empirical condition (to the relation of the determining notion to feelings of pleasure or displeasure), and therefore it is not a practical law.[17]

Here Kant seems to be assuming the very point at issue. Actually, however, he is not, since he bears in mind the nature of the will. We have noted previously that the will is the faculty of a rational being to act in accord with its own idea of law, rather than in conformity with the laws of nature. That is, the will is itself "a kind of causality" and *"freedom* would then be the property this causality has of being able to work independently of determination by alien causes".[18] The will must be unconditioned, independent,

16 *Ibid.* p. 30: p. 138.
17 *Ibid.* pp. 30–31: p. 138. The sentence in brackets is my explication of a tacit part of Kant's argument.
18 *Gr*, p. 305: Paton, p. 114. Cf. *KdpV*, p. 38: Beck, p. 144.

capable of being the cause of actions without itself being the product of alien causes. In short, the will must be capable of responsible action. Its presence in a person must mark that person as a moral agent, as a being "whose actions are capable of imputation".[19]

Bearing this in mind, suppose now that such a will is related to an object in such a way that it is determined by that object. When this is done, the will is conditioned by that object. But the will cannot be free and responsible unless it is unconditioned, capable of acting apart from external determination by an object. Hence if the good as the object of the will is related to the will in this fashion it is indeed related by law and with necessity, but it is not related to the will of a moral person. For in being related to the subject as its causal determinant, the good destroys the freedom of the subject, and hence the subject is no longer a moral person. If on the other hand, the will is related to the good as its object in such a way as to retain its power to act undetermined by that object, then the freedom and moral significance of the will as well as its relatedness to the good can be maintained.

But now we must inquire as to the nature of the relation between the will and the good as its object. The good does not condition the will. It does not reduce the will to an effect of external causation. But apart from this negative statement, what can be said about its relation to the will? If prior to the determination of the moral law the good is presented to the will as an object and yet is not made the causal determinant of the will, the good in no way binds the will. The relation between them is either non-existent, or, if present at all, is empirical and contingent. If the good so defined is to be related to the will at all, without destroying the freedom of the will, it can be related only by the agency of the will itself. That is, the will must freely elect the good as its object. But this election of the good as a previously defined object is contingent and empirical. The will may or may not elect this object. If the object appeals to the will, arouses in the will a

[19] *MdS*, p. 24: Abbott, p. 279; cf. *ibid*. p. 28: p. 283; *Gr*, p. 303: Paton, p. 111; *KdpV*, pp. 105–7: Beck, pp. 202–3.

desire for its realization, the will and the object are, in fact, related. But if the will does not happen to desire the object, then no relation obtains between them. Since the object is defined prior to the moral law, the moral law cannot serve to obligate the will to the object. There is simply no principle or law, or universal condition, which can be called upon to relate the will to this object so long as the freedom of the will is maintained. Hence, the good so defined cannot be related to the will either as a law or as an obligation, but only perchance as an object of desire.

Thus, bearing in mind Kant's definition of the will, we see the force of his demonstration of Theorem III.[20] If the rational being thinks of his maxims as being voluntarily conditioned by a subjective relation between himself and the good as his object as a result of the attraction the object has for him, then he cannot think of his maxims as universal laws.[21] If the rational being seeks to act on maxims which are practical laws while preserving the unconditioned quality of his freedom, he must relate himself to an object by means of the practical principle itself which must determine the will formally and not materially by reference to the previously defined object. If in his practical principle the rational being has abstracted all consideration of the object and makes the mere form of universality itself the determining ground of the will, then the will is indeed determined. But in being determined the will is not conditioned. Its act is free and unconditioned because, by abstracting from all consideration of the object, the will disassociates itself from "every induce-

[20] And it is perhaps worthy of note that this examination of the will provides us with the demonstration of Theorem IV which, because it is presupposed in the demonstration of Theorem III necessitated this detour into Kant's constructive theory. In light of our previous discussion, we can, without further examination, accept Theorem IV: "The autonomy [freedom] of the will is the sole principle of all moral laws and of the duties conforming to them; heteronomy of choice [conditioned choice] on the other hand, not only does not establish any obligation but is opposed to the principle of duty and to the morality of the will." (*KdpV*, p. 38: Beck, p. 144.) (The words in brackets are my additions. They are often used by Kant, however, as substitutes for the terms preceding them.)

[21] *KdpV*, pp. 39, 65, 69 ff.: Beck, pp. 145, 167, 171 ff.

ment that might arise for it (the object)".[22] When this is done, the will can be related to the object only by reference to the practical principle of the will itself, that is, by reference to its own idea of law which through the universality of its form is beyond all conditions and, hence, can serve as the ground of the determination of the will without conditioning it.[23]

Thus, in summary, we see the force of Kant's insistence that to define the good prior to the law as an object of the will makes it impossible to relate it to the will except by desire. By moving on from Kant's criticism of his predecessors to his positive view of freedom and the will, we can see the justification of the alternative he presents in Theorem III. When we consider the character of freedom, when we recognize that freedom presupposes unconditionedness, we see that an object can be necessarily related to the will only if it is related formally from the side of the law and not materially from the side of the object. The good as an object cannot be related to the will materially, that is, by reference to its nature as an object, unless the good as an object conditions the will either (1) by forcing itself upon the will as the causal determinant of the will's action or (2) by happening to be of such a nature that the will is impelled to determine itself to seek the attainment of the object. Now, if the object conditions the will in the first way, it destroys the will. Hence, no moral theory can take this course in relating the good to the will. If, on the other hand, the object conditions the will in the second way by virtue of the action of the will itself, then the relation of the good to the will is both contingent and subjective and obtains or not according as the will happens to desire or not desire the good as its object. Hence, no moral theory can take this second way in relating the good to the will, since no moral law or obligation can be derived from such a relation. And since neither course can relate the good

[22] *Gr*, p. 258: Paton, p. 70; *KdpV*, p. 39: Beck, p. 145.

[23] Of course Kant insists, and most of Kant's interpreters have ignored this point, "It is certainly undeniable that every volition must have an object and therefore a material; but the material cannot be supposed for this reason to be the determining ground and condition of the maxim." *KdpV*, p. 39: Beck, p. 145; cf. *ibid*. p. 40: p. 146.

to the will in a manner required by sound moral theory, that is, in a manner which preserves the freedom of the agent while obligating him necessarily by the moral law, the hopelessness of this procedure in ethical thinking is revealed.

Thus Kant has succeeded in showing that when the good is defined prior to the moral law as the object of the will, the good is either (1) in an indifferent relation to the will or (2) is related to the will contingently through a decision of the will that is based on the subjective conditions of desire, or (3) determines the will and thereby destroys its moral significance. In showing so much, Kant has demonstrated that the classical tradition can never relate the good to the moral agent with the necessity of law and obligation. He has shown therefore the error of the method most commonly employed in moral philosophy: that moralists who begin by defining the good prior to the moral law can never succeed in endowing their concept of the good with moral significance, and hence can never hope to offer a sound theory of ethics.

II. THE HETEROGENEITY OF THE GOOD

Kant's case against the classical tradition does not rest, however, on these theoretical difficulties alone. As a result of defining the good prior to the moral law, the classical tradition emerged with a homogeneous concept of the good, a concept in which no distinction was made between moral and non-moral good. This conclusion has serious consequences for ethical theory even if we ignore the devastating objections already mentioned: happiness and virtue can not be distinguished, freedom of the will is denied, and the experience of obligation is impossible. Since on this view the good is defined prior to any consideration of the moral law, this concept can be brought into effective relationship with the moral agent (allowing for the sake of the argument that the conditions of moral agency are not destroyed) only by making the good itself compulsive for him. It must, therefore, be defined as the object of the agent's desire. But when this is done, the good becomes a homogeneous concept whose relation to the will can be measured by the agent's desire.

Although an ethical theory based on this conception might begin with a distinction between what is desired and what ought to be desired, this distinction can not be maintained. The good is related to the agent only by desire, and there is no distinction *in the faculty of desire* between good desires and bad desires.[24] Desires are not quelled simply because they are illicit in terms of this concept of the good; for the only means whereby the good can influence the will is through the fact of desire or aversion itself! Hence, the independence of the good from desire (which is essential if the good is to be normative for desire) can be achieved only at the price of the irrelevancy of the good. In spite of the finer sensitivities of the authors of such theories, the good becomes a homogeneous concept which sanctions all desires or is merely silent.

The classical ethicists were aware of this problem to some extent, since their theories culminated in moral paradoxes which they were hard pressed to explain. Socrates found that his theory led to the paradoxes that a man would *prefer* to suffer injustice than to do it; that he would be *happier* than the man who was unjust with impunity; that the unjust man is the most miserable of men while the just man, however mistreated, is a happy man. The Epicureans were led to the paradox that the happy man is a virtuous man. And the Stoics shared with Socrates the paradox that the virtuous man even in misery is a happy man.

But Kant insists that these are not unavoidable paradoxes of the moral life. They are the *reductio ad absurdum* of ethical theories based upon the mistaken analysis of the good as a homogeneous concept. Nothing is more obvious, Kant thinks, than that we do not make a man good by making him happy. Nor do we live in so blessed a world that we can fail to see men brought to ruin as a direct result of their fidelity to duty.[25] It is unfortunate, Kant adds, that philosophers so often strive "to overcome essential differences in principle, which can never be united, by seeking to translate them into a conflict of words and thus to devise an apparent unity of

[24] *KdpV*, pp. 25–26: Beck, p. 134.
[25] *KdpV*, pp. 40 ff., 137–38: Beck, pp. 146 ff., 230; *passim*.

concepts with other terms".[26] Nothing can be gained but absurdity and the decay of all moral sensitivity from the habit of "digging up an identity between such extremely heterogeneous concepts as those of happiness and virtue".[27]

Surely, Polus, Callicles, Thrasymachus, and Kant are right in thinking that it is silly to appeal to a man's *self interest*, to his *desire for happiness*, in order to persuade him to be blinded, castrated, and then buried alive in punishment for a crime he has committed.[28] Socrates can answer, of course, that one's self interest and one's happiness are not to be understood merely in terms of bodily appetites and physical health. He can insist, rather, that they must be understood in terms of the health of the soul. But when Socrates does this he falls into an inconsistency. He predicates this distinction on a genuine heterogeneity in the concept of the good. He makes justice (or the moral law) the basic ethical principle in terms of which the good and happiness are defined. By this tack, Socrates reveals the genuine confusion in his ethical theory. When he says that one should seek justice as the health of the soul and suffer injury to the body rather than incur a disease of the soul, he identifies morality with the welfare of the soul and prudence with the welfare of the body. But Socrates then blurs this important distinction by saying that one can genuinely pursue his happiness, his self-interest, by permitting injury and even destruction to his body when the health of the soul cannot otherwise be maintained. Instead of sustaining his distinction between prudence and morality by going on to distinguish happiness from moral contentment, Socrates combines these two mental states under the term "happiness" and, as a result, falls into direct conflict with human experience.[29] Fortunately, it is not completely foreign to human experience for a person to be aware of having refused to violate the dictates of his conscience even though this refusal has resulted in great personal misfortune. Such a person, in the midst of his misfortune, may be possessed of a certain self respect in that he has

---

26 *Ibid.* p. 122: p. 216.
27 *Idem.* Cf. p. 101: p. 198; pp. 137–38: p. 230.
28 Plato *Gorgias* 473, cf. 522. See *KdpV*, pp. 43–44: Beck, p. 149.
29 *KdpV*, pp. 126 ff.: Beck, pp. 219 ff.

been faithful to the moral law which is the law of his personality. But, Kant insists, "this comfort is not happiness, not even the smallest part of happiness; for no one would wish to have occasion for it, not even once in his life, or perhaps even would desire life itself in such circumstances".[30] The Kantian analysis of the awareness of having fulfilled one's duty thus appears to comport better with moral experience than the Socratic analysis.

One might argue that if the Socratic analysis were sound, if Socrates were genuinely happy in drinking the hemlock, why would not people so order society that great numbers of them could share this fate? If happiness were a simple concept referring to the mental state of a person whose action comports with a homogeneous concept of the good, why should men so overwhelmingly prefer quiet death in bed to death in the execution chamber? We cannot avoid the embarrassing consequences of the Socratic analysis of the good and of happiness by arguing that Socrates was not *positively* happy while drinking the hemlock but that he would have been very unhappy had he avoided this draught by escape. Socrates would not have been unhappy choosing the alternative of escape unless *prior to* his acceptance of the good as the object of his desires he had accepted the moral law not merely as the descriptive law of his desires but as the prescriptive law of what he should desire—and made his happiness and the satisfaction of his desires contingent upon the fulfillment of this law. As Kant states it,

> One must already value the importance of what we call duty, the respect for the moral law, and the immediate worth which a person obtains in his own eyes through obedience to it, in order to feel satisfaction in the consciousness of his conformity to law or the bitter remorse which accompanies his awareness that he has transgressed it. Therefore, *his satisfaction or spiritual unrest cannot be felt prior to the knowledge of obligation, nor can it be made the basis of the latter.*[31] Only the virtuous person, or one who is on his way to becoming so, is

[30] *KdpV*, p. 97: Beck, p. 194. Cf. *ibid.* p. 129: p. 122.
[31] *KdpV*, p. 45: Beck, p. 150 (italics are mine). Cf. *ibid.* pp. 126 ff.: pp. 220 ff.

capable of this pure moral dissatisfaction (which does not stem from consequences of the action in question which are disadvantageous to him, but from the action's very opposition to the law). Accordingly, *the dissatisfaction is not the cause but the effect of the fact that he is virtuous;* and the motivation to be virtuous cannot be derived from this unhappiness (if one so wishes to call the pain resulting from such a misdeed).[32]

Socrates, consequently, could not claim to have done his duty (the good) because it made him happy nor that he was happy because he had done his duty without doing violence to human experience. The fulfillment of one's duty could not be recognized as an essential condition of one's spiritual contentment unless there were a prior recognition of the moral law. Similarly, the avoidance of mental discontentment could never be the motive for the fulfillment of duty, since there would be no mental discontentment at all were not the law respected antecedently and for its own sake.

When the principle of one's action is a form of self-love —prudence or happiness—one's action is determined according to a principle which is fundamentally different from that by which action is determined according to duty. The principle of happiness or self-love, or indeed any single principle, is insufficient to account for such a common human experience as that of delighting in having won a prize while despising oneself for having cheated to do so. For when one has to say to himself, "I am a worthless man, though I've filled my purse," he must have a different criterion of judgment than if he approves himself and says, "I am a prudent man, for I've enriched my treasure."[33] A philosopher who lumps these extremely disparate judgments together by saying "the man is simply unhappy" contributes only to confusion. "So distinct and sharp are the boundaries between morality and self love that even the commonest eye cannot fail to distinguish whether a thing belongs to one or the other."[34]

The classical tradition was not mistaken in regarding the desired objects of self-love as good. But it was imperceptive

[32] *Theorie und Praxis,* p. 366. Italics are mine.
[33] *KdpV,* p. 43: Beck, p. 149.
[34] *Ibid.* p. 41: p. 147.

in failing to see that the concept of the good is complex and that it has a moral as well as a natural usage.[35] The ancients did much sound work in defining the natural concept of the good. Such programs for the harmonious realization of natural values as that which is recommended in the *Republic* are among the greatest achievements of thought. But a philosophical system must not seek simplicity at the cost of making impossible the very experience which it is trying to articulate. Moral experience is far more complex than the account given of it by the classical tradition. Man is a being with many natural desires such as the desire for health, food, companionship, sex, or the summation of all natural desires-happiness. But he is likewise a rational being capable of taking an interest in the enactments of his free moral nature which may often be attained only at the expense of his natural desires. The object of man's intention in this case is the moral good as opposed to the natural good.[36]

It is, thus, in the moment of moral decision that the confusions of traditional philosophical analysis fall away. The moral individual finds himself torn between that which he *desires* to do and that which he *ought* to do and *ought to desire* to do. He does not behold the good as the homogeneous object of his faculty of desire. Instead, he frequently encounters the good as disastrously heterogeneous such that he is unable to fulfill the moral good apart from the sacrifice of the natural good, or vice versa.[37]

When, in the moment of moral decision, the heterogeneity of the good is recognized, the naïveté of the Socratic thesis that to know the good is to do it is clearly seen. In order to develop with consistency the consequences of his assumption that the good is homogeneous, Socrates did not even try to give an account of obligation and of the apparent freedom of the will to rebel against that which it knows to be good. In-

[35] *Ibid.* pp. 137–38: pp. 229–30.
[36] *Ibid.* pp. 95–96: p. 193.
[37] *KdpV*, pp. 68–69: Beck, p. 170; *Gr*, p. 311: Paton, p. 119. To indicate this difference in kinds of good, Kant thinks it is wise to refer to the natural good as *"das Wohl"* and the moral good as *"das Gute"*, to natural evil as *"das Ubel"* and to moral evil as *"das Böse"*. (*KdpV*, p. 67: Beck, p. 168).

stead he rejected such views as the mistaken opinions of the multitude.[38] From the assumption of the homogeneity of the good it follows, as we have seen, that virtue and happiness are identified and are realized together in the attainment of the good.[39] Since all men seek happiness, and since virtue and happiness are realized together, all men seek virtue; hence, there can be no motive or occasion for evil action. On this view, with the good so defined as to comprise the greatest self-interest of the individual, ignorance alone could lead a man to act in opposition to the good; therefore, Socrates concludes consistently, and with the assurance consistency brings, that if a man knows the good he will do it.

But Socrates' assumption regarding the good deceived him. While he held fast to this assumption it was impossible for him to observe the facts of the moral situation which his theory needed to explain. He was thus not able to see the untenable consequences of his assumption because the assumption itself reduced all the evidence which could refute it to erroneous opinion. It is this characteristic of the assumption of the good's homogeneity, namely, that it blinds one to contravening evidence, which undoubtedly has accounted for its staying power.

Once, however, this assumption is questioned long enough to permit an uncensored look at the moral situation, its plausibility vanishes. In this situation, we confront the good in the experience of *obligation*, not in the experience of simple *self-fulfillment*. In the moment of moral decision a man not only knows the good, he knows two different goods. In the moment in which he recognizes the natural good as his personal advantage, he also recognizes the moral good as his duty. He is not groping for knowledge of the personal utility of the moral good. If the moral good were to be understood in these terms, he would never encounter it at all except as a redundant expression for the natural good of which he is already aware. The moral agent does not seek a Socratic or Stoic argument to prove either that the health of his body and mind is of no consequence to him or that his

[38] Plato *Protagoras* 352b ff., *passim.*
[39] Plato *Republic* 392b, *passim.*

moral well-being is the condition of worthiness to have physical and intellectual well-being. He knows the first proposition to be false and the latter to be true; otherwise, he would never have experienced the temptation to reject the moral good. His awareness of duty testifies to the reality of the *goodness* of both the natural good as happiness and the moral good as the condition of his worthiness to attain happiness. The Socratic concern for knowledge in the moment of moral decision is a misguided concern resulting from his mistaken view of the good. The crucial concern of the moral agent is to find the strength of will to do that which he knows to be his duty (and the moral good) even though he knows that to do his duty may cost him his happiness and self-fulfillment (which he knows to be good also). To be sure, the moral agent needs to know the good, both in its moral and natural dimensions. But this problem of knowledge precedes the moment of moral decision which is a moment not of speculation but of action.[40] If this knowledge of the good is not attained prior to the moment of decision then the conditions for moral decision are not met. It is the knowledge or awareness of the good in its heterogeneity that poses the moral problem for the will. In confronting the good as heterogeneous, the moral agent confronts—in addition to the good as the object of desire—the moral law. In this encounter, the moral law does not tell him what he must do as a member of the natural world; it tells him what he ought to do as a self-legislating member of the intelligible world.[41] In this experience the moral law relates itself to the will "under the name of *obligation*"[42] and thereby reveals to the moral agent both his duty and his freedom "which without the moral law would have remained unknown to him".[43]

[40] *Gr*, pp. 261, 315: Paton, pp. 73, 123; *passim*. We note Kant's statement: "On the other hand, practical reason is not concerned with objects in order to know them but with its own capacity to make them real (according to knowledge of them)." (*KdpV*, p. 98: Beck, p. 195.)

[41] *KdpV*, pp. 33–36: Beck, pp. 140–43.

[42] *Ibid*. p. 36: p. 143.

[43] *Ibid*. p. 34: p. 142; cf. *ibid*. p. 4n: p. 119n; *Gr*, p. 319: Paton, p. 127.

To recapitulate: We now see additional objections to the method of ethical inquiry which begins by defining the good prior to the moral law as the object of the will. We have seen that when the good is defined in this way, it becomes a homogeneous concept and is related to the will at the object of its desire. But if the good is the object of desire the good is always sought, and virtue and happiness become identified since to the extent that one attains the good he is both virtuous and happy. Furthermore, since the good is naturally the object of the will, the will is not free; it merely does that which it believes to be the good. Hence there are no moral problems: there is no awareness of conflicting goods, no awareness of temptation, no awareness of obligation, no awareness of freedom. To know the good then becomes the critical problem in ethics since the good, by its very attractiveness, determines the will to strive after it once it is known. On this view we seem to be living in the best of possible worlds where all men strive after the good, whether with knowledge or in ignorance, and where those with knowledge strive to teach those in ignorance, and where all that ought to be done is done. When, having traced out all these consequences, we confront this theory with the facts of moral experience which a sound ethical theory is obliged to explain, we find that, far from explaining the facts of moral experience, this theory either faces paradoxes and falls into inconsistencies or explains *away* the data of moral experience as the erroneous opinion of the multitude.

The crux of the problem is this: The good must be heterogeneous in order to account for the awareness of obligation and freedom. But so long as the good is defined prior to the moral law, the good must remain homogeneous, because it is the moral law, as the *ratio cognoscendi* of freedom, which provides the principle of distinction between the two basic types of good that together constitute the good in its heterogeneity. That concept of the good (or evil) which is defined prior to the moral law is the concept of the natural good (*das Wohl*), whereas that concept of good (or evil) which is defined subsequent to and by reference to the moral law is the concept of the moral good (*das Gute*). The moral good unlike the natural good can never be defined apart from the moral law. It must be the object of human striving; yet it must be related to the agent in such a way that his freedom is not destroyed. We have seen that the attempt to define the moral good in independence of the moral law results in both the denial of freedom and the confusion of virtue and happiness, since apart from the moral law it was impossible to relate the good to the moral agent except by means of desire. Kant concludes, therefore, that the genuine moral paradox is this:

> "that the concept of the good and evil is not defined prior to the moral law, to which it would seem, the former would have to serve as the foundation; rather the concept of the good and evil must be defined after and by means of the law."[44]

III. THE GOOD AS THE OBJECT OF THE MORAL LAW

Although Kant rejected the approach to ethics which began with the definition of the good, because he saw that this procedure destroyed the very possibility of morality, he nonetheless recognized the responsibility of the ethicist to define the concept of the good. He recognized that the will must have an end, that "every volition must have an object"[45] for "since there are free actions, there must also be ends to which as an object those actions are directed".[46] Kant's problem therefore was to find an object for the moral will which, while standing in a necessary relation to the will and serving as a guide to moral action, would not destroy the freedom of the moral agent. In order to preserve the freedom of the agent while introducing an object as the guide to his volition, Kant

[44] *KdpV*, p. 70: Beck, p. 171.

[45] *KdpV*, p. 39: Beck, p. 145. Cf. *idem*. ff.

[46] *MdS*, p. 194: Abbott, p. 295. Consider also Kant's statement that "rational nature separates itself out from all other things by the fact that it sets itself an end. An end would thus be the matter of every good will". (*Gr*, p. 296: Paton, p. 105; cf. *ibid.* pp. 271–72: pp. 82–83; *MdS*, pp. 189 ff.: Abbott, pp. 290 ff.; *KdrV*, B 836: Kemp Smith, pp. 637–38; *Theorie und Praxis*, p. 362; *Rel*, pp. 142–43: Greene, p. 4.)

saw that the object of the will must be determined by the
will itself rather than the will by the object. If the object
were not determined by the will, the will would be conditioned by the object and its freedom would be destroyed.
But to have moral significance the will must be free and
therefore the will must determine the object. Furthermore,
Kant saw that since the obligation of the will to the object
must be categorical the object must be one that the will
necessarily determines for itself. If the object is conditional
the will's obligation is subject to that which conditions the
object. The will, then, must have an object of volition, and
that object must be determined by the will, and it must be
unconditional so that the obligation of the will to that object
is likewise unconditional.[47] But free will alone has the property of being unconditioned. It alone is undetermined and
unqualified by anything external to it. Therefore, only the
free will can be the unconditioned object of the will. And
since free will is unconditioned and free only in relation to
itself and not in relation to other free wills, which by virtue
of their own freedom condition themselves in independence
of outside wills, the only object that a particular will can determine for itself unconditionally is its own free willing.
Now to this object, its own free willing, the will can be related without being conditioned or without having its freedom destroyed. For this object is determined by the will
itself. And in determining itself to this object the will determines itself merely to be free, that is to be unconditioned.
Its unconditionality is maintained in the act of willing only
if it wills according to the universality of law, thereby tran-
scending the conditioning effects of subjective inclinations.
Willing according to law is ingredient, therefore, in the act
of free willing in which the freedom of the will is not con-

[47] "Amongst these ends", Kant says, "there must be some which
are at the same time (that is, by their very notion) duties. For if
there were none such, then since no actions can be without an end,
all ends which practical reason [the moral law] might have would
be valid only as means to other ends, and a categorical imperative
would be impossible; a supposition which destroys all moral philosophy." (*MdS*, p. 194: Abbott, p. 295.) The moral law must command
"categorically because it is unconditional". (*KdpV*, p. 36: Beck, p.
143.)

ditioned but is actively maintained in its unconditionedness. Thus free willing itself, the good will, is the sole unconditioned object to which the will can be related unconditionally without destroying either the unconditionality of the object, or the unconditionality of the will, or the unconditionality of the will's relation to the object. And since moral obligation requires the unconditionality of both the will and the object in addition to the unconditionality of the relation between them, the good will is, therefore, the sole moral good, the sole object that can be given with necessity by the moral law.[48] To restate the argument: the moral good must be unconditionally good; the moral good must be the moral will itself projected as its own object since only the will, by virtue of its freedom, has the requisite unconditionality when projected as its own object.

> If something is to be, or is held to be, absolutely good or evil in all respects and without qualification (which is essential to the moral concept of the good), it could not be a thing, but only a manner of acting, i.e. it could only be the maxim of the will, and consequently the acting person himself as a good or evil man.[49]

We see, then, how Kant proceeds to define the good. He rejects the attempt to begin with the good as a previously defined object to which the will must be related. This method, he finds, can never relate the object (the good) to the will as an obligation. Such a concept of the good is not merely related to the will irrelevantly, contingently, or compulsively, and is thus unable to account for the theoretical conditions of obligation—namely, for the freedom of the will and at the same time the necessitation of the good upon it. The good when so defined is, in addition, a simple, homogeneous concept and thus makes impossible the human experience of obligation in which duty is encountered in the

[48] *KdpV*, pp. 65, 67: Beck, pp. 67, 69.
[49] *KdpV*, p. 67: Beck, p. 169. We see, therefore, that morality "has for its object not nature but freedom of choice". (*MdS*, p. 17: Abbott, p. 272.) Or again, "For analysis finds that the principle of morality . . . commands nothing more or less than precisely this autonomy." (*Gr*, p. 299: Paton, p. 108; see also *ibid*. pp. 287, 305: pp. 96, 114.)

tension between the natural and moral aspects of the good. Consequently, Kant, in keeping with his critical method, begins his ethical inquiry with an examination of the experience of obligation. By searching for the conditions of the possibility of this experience he discovers that the good must be heterogeneous and that the moral concept of the good, instead of being defined prior to the moral law, must be determined by that law and posed by it as the object of the will. As the object of the will, the moral good may indeed conflict with the natural good as the object of personal desire. The good is thus encountered in its heterogeneity. By following his original method of inquiry in ethics, Kant thus succeeds in determining the good in such a way that he can account for the moral experience from which he began.

THE CONCEPT OF MAN AS END-IN-HIMSELF

PEPITA HAEZRAHI

"Now I say man and generally every rational being exists as an end and must never be treated as a means alone."[1] Thus Kant's proud assertion. We might be inclined to sympathise prompted by some obscure feeling of its sublimity, did not Kant fall back from this emotional vantage to a particularly unsatisfactory piece of reasoning in lieu of proof.

"This position", writes Kant "that humanity and every intelligent being is an end in itself is not established by my observation or experience, as is seen, first, from the generality by which we have extended it to every rational being whatsoever; and second because humanity was exhibited not as a subjective end of mankind [i. e. not as an object which it stood in their option to pursue or decline] but as their objective end, which whatever other ends mankind may have, does as a law constitute the supreme limiting condition of such subjective ends and which must consequently take its rise from reason *a priori* . . ."[2]

And in proof he advances: "All mankind must of necessity thus conceive to themselves their own existence and to this extent it is a subjective principle of conduct." But "in the very same way all rational beings thus conceive their own existence by force of the same grounds of reason which determine man to think so" and therefore "the above [i. e. 'Every intelligent nature exist as an End in itself'] is likewise an objective principle . . . from it as the supreme practical position all laws of the will must be capable of being de-

Reprinted with permission of the editors from *Kant-Studien*, Band 53 (1962), Kölner Universitäts-Verlag, in which it was first published.

[1] *Grundlegung zur Metaphysik der Sitten*, zweiter Abschnitt.
[2] *Ibid.*

duced . . ."[3] This argument, it seems to me, begs the question at the crucial point. In order to substantiate this contention, it must be remembered that for Kant (at his point of his critical philosophy) the concept of human dignity as defined in the moral domain only. I regard myself as possessing dignity, as being of infinite value, solely on the ground and to the extent to which I also regard myself as capable of moral action, i. e. as a rational being whose will is capable of determining itself in accordance with and for the sake of the moral law. The certainty which characterises my direct and immediate experience of my moral responsibilities assures me that the view I have of myself as possessing dignity is fully justified. Supposing that we concede the plausibility of an argument, based on analogy and inductive reasoning, which from the fact that I regard myself as possessed of dignity on certain grounds draws the conclusion that other rational beings when regarding themselves so (i. e. as possessed of dignity) will probably do so on the same grounds. In other words, that the same complex of circumstances and conditions which assures me of the certainty of my own freedom and moral responsibility, assures other rational beings of *their* freedom and *their* responsibility. Yet, as we must stress, no point in this argument necessarily implies an assurance for men of each other's freedom and moral capacity. In other words, the inductive assumption, or even an established fact that each rational being regards himself as possessed of dignity, on the same ground and for the same reasons that all other rational beings regard each himself as possessed of dignity, does not involve a logical necessity for rational beings to regard *each other* as possessed of dignity. This, however, is the decisive test for a general recognition by rational beings of the universal application of the dignity of man.

More explicitly: (a) The proposition "all men *qua* men are possessed of dignity" cannot be deduced from the concept (of human-dignity) itself since universal validity in the distributive sense is not an essential qualification of the concept and therefore not implied in it. Hence, (b) the complex and synthetic concept "the objective universality of the dignity

[3] *Grundlegung zur Metaphysik der Sitten*, zweiter Abschnitt.

of man" is not a self-evident concept, i. e. immediately perceived by reason. Therefore, (c) the validity of the synthesis it performs is in need of proof. This proof, I submit, Kant's formalistic argument fails to supply.[4]

In Kant's defence it must be said that he treated the whole matter rather casually. He did not in fact intend to convince anyone by this argument, since he did not think that any man, in his capacity of rational agent, would need to be convinced by what his own Reason would tell him most plainly should he but stop to reason. All one needed to do was to make men stop in the pursuit of their desires—and make them reason. This is done by the Categorical Imperative. In his argument, Kant only meant to retrace what happens when men *do* stop to reason. That is, Kant thought he was merely formulating in precise terms what men think in their own slovenly way, when they declare: "Other men are human beings too." According to Kant, the moment someone sets up a Categorical Imperative for himself and submits to it, he is governed by Reason. And being governed by Reason, when Reason is no longer the servant of his desires but their master, he imposes certain limitations on himself. He asks himself whether he could wish other people to act in the way in which he is just proposing to act. By doing this he already assumes other men to be possessed of rationality,

---

[4] It may be interesting to point out that Professor Paton was very much aware of the dubious nature of Kant's professed proof for the objective validity of man-as-an-end-in-himself, and the in consequence necessary universal acknowledgment of man's status as an end. But he tried to patch things up by offering another possible deduction pieced together like a jigsaw puzzle from different *loci* in Kant's ethical writings. The end of the good will, he argues, cannot be less perfect than the will. Let us therefore look for something that is not less perfect than the good will. There are for instance ends which are also duties like performing moral actions for the sake of duty. (*Metaphysik der Sitten*, Tugendlehre, Einleitung, 111, iv.) But products of moral actions are not absolutely good, and morally good actions are not absolutely good, such supreme goodness belonging only to the will. (*Kritik der praktischen Vernunft*, 62–182.) Now since the end cannot be less perfect than the will, therefore only rational agents as far as they are possessed of a will itself capable of being a good will actuated by the idea of the law, can be the Ends of a Categorical Imperative (viz. H. J. Paton, *The Categorical Imperative*, pp. 166–72).

of free will, in short, of a will which can be determined by
the moral law. So that when he decides that a certain maxim
will not do, he implies at the same time that other people,
did they but stop and think, would reject it too. He acts
against the background of a moral universe.

On this view Reason is common to all men.[5] When not
forced into the service of one man's particular desires, correctly reasoned conclusions are valid for all, and would be
reached by all who considered the same problem. If one man
becomes aware that rational beings are ends-in-themselves, by
representing to himself the moral law, this awareness being
rational is implicitly valid for all men and accessible to all
men. It is therefore enough if men stop to reason, to make
them realise that other men are ends-in-themselves. The main
difficulty for Kant lies in making men also *act* by the light
of their reason. It never occurred to Kant that men could, on
rational grounds, refuse to treat other men as ends.

To our generation however this possibility *has* occurred,
indeed the question has been brought home to us with great
emphasis. We can no longer afford to be casual about it but
must seek a more stringent answer to the question: How can
a universal application of the concept of man-as-an-end-in-
himself be rationally vindicated?

Let us briefly trace this concept in the different phases of
the development of Kant's ethical thought. In common with
most of Kant's other basic ideas this concept originated in
what I have termed on another occasion the "humanitarian

[5] In this argument Kant most closely follows the Stoic Doctrine as
expounded by Marcus Aurelius, in *Eis Heavton* Book IV. ch. iv: "If
the faculty to reason is common to us [i. e. all human beings] then
Reason itself, by and through which, we are rational, must be our
common possession. If that be so, then also the Reason which prescribes what ought and what ought not to be done is common [to all
human beings]. If that be so, then the law too is common [i. e. valid
for all human beings]. If that be so, then we are citizens. If that be
so, we take part in some commonwealth. If that be so, the Universe
itself must be in a way, a commonwealth. For in what other commonwealth, could anyone claim, that the whole of the human race take
part as citizens? Thence then, from this commonwealth in which we
all have part, we hold our very faculty of reasoning, and our rationality, and our being subjects to laws; or whence (else could we
hold it)?"

superstitions" of the eighteenth century, and is moreover strongly coloured by Rousseau's version of these ideas. Now according to Rousseau the intrinsic worth of a human being *qua* human being, which for short we shall term the dignity of man, is part of man's innate nature. By an innate qualification of their nature human beings are endowed with freedom of will and hence are capable of virtue.[6]

Man's innate capacity of virtue[7] is, objectively speaking, the reason for the worth and dignity of human beings. Subjectively it is recognised by a corresponding sentiment, itself innate in human nature: the natural love of man for humanity.

In his pre-critical writings Kant followed Rousseau very closely: "True virtue", he writes, "can be grown only on principles; the more universal these principles the nobler and more elevated the virtue. These principles are not speculative rules of reason, but the awareness of a feeling which dwells in every human heart and which is more than mere pity and helpfulness. I think this sentiment is best described as a feeling for the Beauty and Dignity of human nature . . . *Das Gefühl von der Schönheit und Würde der menschlichen Natur*".[8]

To be capable of virtue, according to Kant, one must possess this feeling. This feeling, however, is innate and therefore universal. 'Beauty and Dignity' are also innate qualities of human nature as such. But in distinction from Rousseau, Kant holds that this 'Beauty and Dignity' are grounded primarily in the rational quality of human nature. Kant also holds, that what we call the 'Beauty and Dignity of Human

[6] «La liberté morale . . . seul rend l'homme vraiment maître de lui, car l'impulsion du seul appetit est esclavage et l'obéissance à la loi qu'on se presente est liberté . . . la vertu n'est que la liberté morale.»

[7] It is only a capacity for "virtue" i. e. to be pursued in the face of objection, for according to Rousseau, the actual natural goodness of man has been vitiated by the impositions of culture, and needs to be reinstated by perseverance in merely virtuous actions "until perfect artificiality becomes nature again." (Rousseau, *Lettres sur la vertu et le bonheur*.)

[8] Kant: *Beobachtungen über das Gefühl des Schönen und Erhabenen* (1764), ch. II, p. 4.

Nature' refers to and comprises more than the sole capacity
for moral virtue, namely capacities for scientific research,
philosophical speculation, artistic creation, religious inspira-
tion, etc. At this particular point in Kant's philosophical
evolution neither the concept of the 'dignity of man' nor its
(assumed) universal validity present any difficulty. Both are
contained in the definition as an inherent, innate part of human nature indissolubly bound up with the rational qualities
in their various activities and modifications (in the Arts,
Sciences, Philosophy etc.) which thus provide the main *raison
d'être* of human dignity. The universal validity (in its distributive sense) of human dignity, on the other hand, is vindicated on the basis of an universal participation of human
beings in the rational, this being by definition an essential
quality of human nature.

Later, in his critical writings, Kant had to change his
ground for reasons of method. In view of the requirements of
the transcendental method of deduktion,[9] Kant had to abandon his former view of moral virtue as grounded in an innate
natural sentiment. In accordance with his new method Kant
grounded moral virtue, which he now calls the good will, in
its determination by the categorical imperative, that is in the
determination of will by reason.[10] The possibility of a will
determined by reason, he deduced from the *presupposed*
possibility of freedom. On the other hand, he viewed Human
Nature as split in two parts, one irrational and sensual, and
one rational part. Inner worth and dignity are made conditional on the domination and determination of the irrational
part by the rational. That is ultimately on the freedom of

[9] Transferring the problem of objectivity from the *Critique of Pure
Reason* to Ethics, Kant formulates his question thus: "Whether in
Ethics too there might not be a pervading lawfulness, which does not
depend on the material content, or the material differences and vari-
ations of what is willed, but determined solely by the manner in
which it is willed, i. e. the particular modality of the will itself which
thereby provides this lawfulness with objectivity in the transcendental
sense of the word, i. e. provides a ground for the necessary and universal validity of ethical values." Cassirer, *Kants Leben und Lehre*,
p. 266.
[10] Thus receding further away from Rousseau by grounding both
virtue and its recognition in reason.

the human will which enables man to determine himself in accordance with the dictates of his reason and regardless of his sensual desires and impulses. In short, the dignity of man is made to depend on the ability of man to perform moral actions[11] and bear moral responsibilities, that is in the last instance, on the freedom of the will.

In this new framework, the demonstration of the objective reality of the dignity of man, and the vindication of its objective universality are rendered extremely difficult, perhaps impossible altogether. For on closer inspection Kant's deduction is seen to move in a circle: He presupposes the freedom of the human will as a necessary condition for the possibility, i. e. existence and reality of moral obligation and responsibility; and then attributes dignity to men because they have free will, i. e. are morally responsible. Now a categorical judgment cannot be deduced from two hypothetical judgments. The objective reality of the dignity of man cannot be deduced from the hypothetical reality of freedom, much less can the universality of its application be so deduced. But nothing less than such *objective reality* is demanded by Kant for this concept. Nor, to judge from the way in which he first introduced this concept ("*Nun aber sage ich—Now I say* man and every reasonable agent *exists as an* end in himself . . ."[12], or to judge from the vital function and crucial importance of this concept for Kant's system of ethics, could he admit of less.

Nor is it any help that there exists in fact one point at which we can break through the circle of Kant's deduction and touch reality. Namely the point reached in our immediate moral experiences as a datum of so vivid a certainty that it excludes all doubt. "A higher certainty than that which assures us of our moral self, our autonomous personality, is not conceivable."[13] But this experience is as we have seen of necessity limited to my own person. It can therefore assure me of my own freedom, my own moral responsibility, and

[11] Thus oddly enough re-approaching Rousseau, by relating Human Dignity solely to the moral sphere.

[12] *Grundlegung*, zweiter Abschnitt.

[13] Kant: *Kritik der praktischen Vernunft*; Teil 1, Kap. 5.

therefore of my own dignity and worth, but not of the dignity of others. It is, however, the *dignity of others that is in question* if I am to limit my own freedom out of a respect for theirs.

Moreover the *dignity of others* must not be demonstrated solely from my sense of moral responsibility and obligation and from my voluntary self-limitation, for then it would be dependent entirely on my pleasure whom I wished to honour in this way, and who are to be the recipients of a dignity conferred by me. This is a possibility Kant most certainly would have rejected as detrimental to the moral rightness of an action. From a Kantian point of view it is most unsatisfactory and unacceptable that man should acquire moral dignity by being treated *as though* he possessed it. From a Kantian point of view, man must be treated as being possessed of moral dignity because he *is* so possessed. A corroborating reason for this position derives from Kant's view that moral worth and dignity cannot be acquired by an outside grant but must be acquired by inner effort.

Some sort of objective justification and vindication is therefore desperately needed at this point if the autonomy and the very meaning of ethics in Kant's sense is to be saved.

Kindred problems have been faced, to name but a few, by Rousseau in the idea of «la volonté générale», by J. S. Mill in his idea of "The general happiness" and Sartre in his proposition «l'acte individuel engage toute l'humanité». A brief survey of the respective arguments and their respective solutions might conceivably be of some help in indicating how our solution may be found.

Taking Rousseau first, we find that he has the easiest stand.

«Les engagements qui nous lient au corps social ne sont obligatoires que parce-qu'ils sont mutuels; et leur nature est telle qu'en les remplissant on ne peut travailler pour autrui sans travailler pour soi. Pourquoi la volonté générale est-elle toujours droite, et pourquoi tous veulent-ils constamment le bonheur de chaqu'un d'eux si ce n'est parce qu'il n'y a personne que ne s'approprie cet nom chaqu'un et qui ne songe a lui même en votant pour tous? Ce qui prouve que l'égalité de droit et la notion de justice qu'elle produit derivent de la préférence que chaqu'un se donne et par conséquence de la nature de l'homme».[14]

Men, according to this argument, respect each other's persons and attribute dignity to each other, because this is the only *practical* way to pursue their own ends in comparative safety and security. By a voluntary self-limitation, they secure a similar self-limitation in others, indeed the one is the condition of the other. «Ils ne sont obligatoires que parce qu'ils sont mutuels»; and this self-limitation in retrospect confers rights and privileges and dignity on the members of the *contrat social*. In other words, this dignity depends on the willingness, or the enforced willingness to self-limitation (enforced by the very circumstances of human existence and its natural dangers). But if there should be a man, or a group of men whose 'préférence' for themselves need not, thanks to accidental circumstances, be limited in order to assure its own success (for instance the near extermination of the red races in North America); then there is no power in the world which can force those men to attribute dignity to the others, and therefore these others will not possess dignity. Rousseau's argument does not safeguard the objective universality of the dignity of man. It provides for a comparative generality inside closed societies only, more or less in the sense of Lindsay "other people's behavior is necessarily an assumed background to ours . . . different social atmospheres compel us to act differently . . . If one knows that people are willing to co-operate one acts differently even if one's purpose is not allowed to alter . . . Moral rules . . . are no use unless they are generally kept and form an *effective* moral code, i.e. most men are ready to keep them and enforce their keeping. . . ."[15]

Rousseau's argument is mainly valuable as a reminder that we must not allow the dignity of man to be reduced to a conditional status for fear of finding our system of ethics disintegrate into relative and ephemeral moral codes. For the objectivity and autonomy of ethics—and without such objec-

[14] J. J. Rousseau, *Le Contrat Social*, Part II, ch. vi.
[15] A. D. Lindsay, "*The Two Moralities*", pp. 21–22.

tivity and autonomy whatever else it would be it would no longer be ethics—is indissolubly bound up with the absolute validity of the dignity of man and unrestricted universality of its attribution.

J. S. Mill's famous argument on general happiness runs:

"The sole evidence it is possible to produce that anything is desirable is that people do actually desire it . . . No reason can be given why the general happiness is desirable except that each person so far as he believes it to be attainable desires his own happiness. This however being a fact we have not only all the proof which the case admits of, but all which it is possible to require that happiness is good; that each person's happiness is a good to that person and the general happiness, therefore a good to the aggregate of all persons."[16]

If analysed this argument proves a mine of problems each of which had had its day as a *cause célèbre* of philosophical disputation. The only points which need concern us here are (a) the argument (given the relationship what is desired is desirable, what is desirable is good and therefore what is desired is good) from the goodness of each person's happiness for himself to the goodness of general happiness for the aggregate of persons and (b) the argument from the fact that each person actually desires his own happiness, to the alleged fact that general happiness is desired by all (i. e. desirable to all). It has often been pointed out that the validity of Mill's argument hinges on the definition of general happiness. If the general happiness is a sum of particular happinesses, then each individual desires it to exactly that degree to which his own happiness is involved. Thus, if, for instance, I desire to regain my coat from a cloakroom in which hang many other coats desired by many other people, it is possible to define the concepts of all the coats, all the people, and all the desires of all the people for all their coats. Now my desire for my coat, though definable as part of the general desire for all the coats in the cloakroom is neither increased nor diminished nor affected in any other way by being part of a general desire. Nor is my coat affected in any way by hanging together with

[16] J. S. Mill, *Utilitarianism*, ch. IV.

other coats. But if to regain my coat I have to queue up so as to avoid a scramble in which all coats including mine are liable to be damaged, then my desire is no longer a mere item in the sum total of all desires but enters into some co-ordinated system with them limiting its own intensity and accommodating itself to all the others somewhat in the manner described by Rousseau in the *contrat social*. My desire is now modified in its activity by the collective desire of which it is a part, but it still is a desire for my own coat and for nothing else, though my coat gains a relative safety from damage. I can however envisage the possibility that my desire for my coat enters into some combination with the other people's desires for their coats. Thus, by joining in with other people, I am able to pay an attendant to guard it whilst I'm away, brush it, and mend it, a thing beyond my means if I were on my own. My desire forms a collective system with all other desires, by which my coat is actually benefited. Still my desire is centred on my own coat, and if through this organic relationship other people's coats benefit as well as my own, this is as far as I am concerned of secondary importance, a mere accidental by-product of the situation. In other words, though my happiness be an organic part of the general happiness, i. e. increased, modified, even changed in its content by the whole of which it is a part, and though I be a tireless worker for the improvement and enrichment of general happiness, I am basically concerned only with my own happiness, and with general happiness only insofar as it is the precondition of my own. At no point in the rational argument leading from my own happiness to general happiness had I any reason to entertain a disinterested regard for other people's happiness. At no point was I confronted by a rationally necessitated demand (arising from the argument itself) to desire general happiness for itself and regardless of my own. In other words, at no point was I given the opportunity to exercise the generosity which is Mill's ultimate intention.

We must therefore conclude that the fact that general happiness is desired by all people, or even the proposition that it ought to be desired by all people, are not sufficient to cover Mill's ethical meaning. To it must be added a demand that it be desired for its own sake, for the sake of the

regard I have for other people, and regardless of any satisfaction that might accrue to me in the process. This must be
so if I am to put the consideration of general happiness above
the consideration for my own in case of conflict—as Mill
taught. This demand however is implied in none of the concepts which appear in the original argument (my happiness,
general happiness, my person, the aggregate of persons, good
for me, good for all etc.), nor in the relations defined to hold
between them. From the given fact of my desire for my happiness for its own sake, the process of reason can at the outside lead me to a concept of general happiness as the ultimate
warrant and supreme condition of my own happiness. It can
never furnish me with the idea of general happiness as being
desirable for its own sake, nor confront me with a demand
to desire it for its own sake. This demand is not justified by
the preceding argument, nor indeed definable without a certain forcing of the concepts with which Mill operates. It must
therefore be regarded as an intruder from some other domain, a heterogeneous eruption which, from the point of view
of the argument, gratuitously breaks up the cohesion of the
argument. Besides, in the given context, this demand defeats
its own ends for if all people acted on the maxim that one
ought to desire and pursue general happiness at the expense
of one's own happiness, nobody would be happy at any time,
and general gloom and misery the sole effect. To sum up, we
may say that a pursuit of Mill's argument in vindication of
the idea of general happiness as a *moral* duty has shown that
the moral obligation so defined (i. e. a regard for other people's happiness and, *a fortiori*, a regard for their persons) cannot be deduced from the explicit tenets of Mill's utilitarian
system of ethics. On the contrary this idea having been, as it
were, injected into the system by some heterogeneous force
and being antagonistic to the general tenor of his philosophical theory disrupts its inner cohesion.

   The profit of this lesson for our study of the Kantian theory
is this: Though the idea of the unconditional regard we owe
to other people's persons as the core of all our moral obligations, is not as an idea incompatible with the general tenor
of the Kantian theory of ethics, analogy from Mill's argument
brings home the suspicion that in Kant's case too, the idea in

question may have been injected into the system by the eruptive and non-rational force of some intuition, rather than be the rationally demonstrable deduction from rationally valid concepts Kant took it to be. In short, what Kant had taken to be a simple case of *intellectus quaerens intellectum*, is really another case of an *intellectus quaerens fidem*, and as such likely to be disappointed in its quest.

Let us see what we can learn from Sartre's argument in vindication of his proposition, «l'act individuel engage toute l'humanité» which runs thus: To choose is to affirm the value of that which we choose, because it is always the good that we choose. Nothing can be good for us without being good for everybody. Hence to choose for oneself is to choose for everybody.

Sartre interprets both the proposition and its proof in two different senses, a metaphysical sense and a moral sense. I intend to show that the two do not accord and that the moral interpretation rests on a supplementary intuition of the intrinsic worth of human beings, which is alien to the basic metaphysical tenor of Sartre's existentialist thought and superimposed on it. Moreover the argument (quoted above) which could just pass in its metaphysical setting becomes plainly fallacious if a moral interpretation is attempted.

To expound the first interpretation of Sartre's argument we must briefly sketch in its metaphysical background. Sartre's fundamental tenet is that God does not exist. Since God does not exist, man's freedom is absolute and he can never escape it. No objective truth, no moral principle, no religious conviction, no intrinsic value exist apart from man's choosing to believe in them. Thus man is responsible for the truth he believes in as well as for providing the proofs in its favour. Man is responsible for his very experiences, since the respective significance and interpretation of experiences are determined by the selection he makes. Man thus selects the manner of being he chooses to become. In consequence freedom is not simply an attribute of man, but his very essence (la liberté est l'étoffe de son être), and any action, thought, impulse, which denies this freedom is an act of bad faith. Any attempt to appeal to a moral principle, an intrinsic value, a religious conviction, when faced with a choice, is an

action smacking of insincerity, cowardice, and «mauvais-foi».
It is a deplorable and moreover *futile* attempt to evade and
shift one's responsibilities. Whatever man chooses to do or to
be, he must choose in the consciousness of his absolute liberty
and full responsibility. This is the only possible *right* choice
(la choix au nomme de la liberté) and in choosing to choose
so, man sets it up as an objectively right principle of action.
Thus in choosing the right way for himself, he *ipso facto*
chooses the right way for others. Man is compelled (by the
logical necessity of his metaphysical situation) to choose the
freedom of others when he chooses his own. It is factually
impossible for man to pursue his own liberty without pursuing at the same time the liberty of others.

Two unavoidable consequences follow from this metaphysical theory. The first, which need not concern us further for
the moment, is that seen against this stark metaphysical background the implications of «l'act individuel engage toute
l'humanité» become truly terrifying. For it means that man,
in whatever he chooses to feel, think, or do, moulds the whole
of humanity in his own image. The second, which is of the
greatest importance for us, is that the regard for the liberty
(i. e. the persons, as liberty is the essence of the human person) of others is a necessary result of a regard for my own
person and therefore an automatic not a voluntarily sought
consequence of this regard. As such it is morally irrelevant.
The only *moral* duty, which can be defined within the bounds
of Sartre's metaphysical assumptions, is a duty to oneself.[17]

This however does not suit Sartre's purpose at all. He intends to establish a moral code where such a code ought to be
established, namely in the relation between one man and
another, in the intrasubjective sphere. Sartre proceeds to do
this in the following manner: He asserts that the sole datum
which can be immediately and directly experienced is the
reflective consciousness expressed in the declaration 'cogito
ergo sum'. At the same time, through this same primary expe-

---

[17] In this connection it is of no consequence whether choosing for
oneself implies also choosing for others, since it is one's own salvation one works out, and in which one is primarily interested. The
salvation of others is an inevitable, though not undesirable corollary
to one's own.

rience I gain an intuitive knowledge of the existence of 'l'autre': «Je decouvre l'autre comme une liberté *posée* en face de moi qui ne pense, qui ne veut *que pour ou contre moi*.» However we may regard this affirmation of a primary and intuitive perception of the "other", and the assertion that this intuition is part of the very first 'cogito',[18] it is enough for our purpose that Sartre admits it to be the yield of a primary intuition wholly unconnected with the preceding considerations of his metaphysical theories.

The point we wish to make is that the yield of this intuition is not only wholly unconnected with the above theories, but directly contradictory to them, and indeed overthrows them at every point. For the astonishing thing about this suddenly revealed 'other' is that he is not identical nor indistinguishable from the I; nor is he compelled to live in harmony with the I. He is free to choose for or against the I. Therefore the I must be free (from the point of view of the other) to choose for or against the other. That is, what the I chooses for itself (for itself it chooses only the good), it does not necessarily choose for the other. In other words, "To choose for oneself is to choose for others" is a moral injunction, not a law of human nature (i. e. metaphysical human nature). Therefore the proposition «L'act individuel engage toute l'humanité» must be classified *as a moral injunction*[19] to regard all one's actions 'as though' they were obligatory for all mankind, and not as a statement that they are. Hence the metaphysical and the moral interpretations of Sartre's theory of choice, action and responsibility, are mutually exclusive.

The disturbance occurs at the very point where the intuitive perception of the other as a free and therefore dangerous being breaks the train of the argument. The 'other' is no longer something which I mould in my own image every time I make a choice; he is a person for himself, who makes his

[18] Descartes affirmed that in this experience and through it the I gains knowledge of the existence of God. Both affirmations however seem the expression of some separate intuition, separate from the perception of the I, that is, rather than inferences from the primary datum of the 'cogito'.

[19] Equivalent to Kant's categorical imperative: Act only on that maxim which is also fit to become a universal law of nature.

own choice irrespective of and uninfluenced by the choice I make for him. «il veut pour ou contre moi» He therefore possesses the dignity of a free person, and as such I ought to respect him even as he ought to respect me. That is, we both ought to choose to respect each other's persons though we are not by virtue of our very nature *compelled* to do so. Thus and thus only *moral* decisions and acts can be defined.

Let us illustrate this point by re-examining Sartre's proposition: «L'act individuel engage toute l'humanité» and the argument which is supposed to vindicate it. The first step of his argument: to choose for oneself is to affirm the value of that which one chooses is factually correct and moreover a self-evident proposition if only value be defined loosely enough i. e. not restricted to moral value. Similarly we can accept the second step that it is always the good which we choose,[20] if the concept of the good be also defined loosely enough to cover all possible values. The third step "nothing can be good for us without being good for all" on the other hand seems highly questionable. There is no reason on earth why something should not be good for me, or why I should forego something that seems good to me simply because it may not be good for everybody.

Moreover, it seems to me, that most of one's desires and purposes insofar as they have not yet been subjected to the categorical imperative and adjusted to the requirements of the moral law[21] represent primarily choices for us against others. If our wills are directed towards concrete ends, toward material possessions, it is the exclusive rights in these possessions which we covet most.[22] Even in the pursuit of spiritual ends and rational achievements where exclusiveness of possession has no real meaning, since the same spiritual content

[20] Viz. Nihil appetimus nisi sub ratione boni, nihil aversamur nisi sub ratione mali.

[21] I. e. subsequently cut to the moral measure.

[22] The more desires for material things accord and agree with each other, the fiercer their battle against each other, viz: the pun attributed to Francis I and cited by Kant: "was mein Bruder Karl will, das will auch ich (nämlich Mailand)". The bigger the difference in what we desire, the greater our chance of not getting in each others way. But differences in what is desired entail a mutual negation of the value of what is chosen.

can be pursued, attained, and its possession enjoyed by many men at the same time without loss to its inner richness, exclusiveness of possession is nevertheless highly valued. In the latter case, the value of exclusiveness refers to the personality of him who possesses rather than to what is possessed. We are wont to cherish the belief in the exceptionality of our persons and our pursuits,[23] and this alone is reason enough to make any choice, which is a choice for ourselves at the same time a choice against others.

In consequence it seems fairly safe to conclude that the act of "choosing for oneself" does not *de facto* involve an act of "choosing for all". On the other hand considered as a moral exhortation "choose for all what you would choose for yourself!" appears highly unsatisfactory, since not I but they must choose for themselves what they consider of value and of goodness. Even the injunction to "make the freedom of others your end at the same time that you make your own freedom your end" (freedom in the sense Sartre gave to the word)

[23] I think this is why, if by chance upon people whose ideas and pursuits completely resemble our own we are both pleased and displeased. However great our joy in finding kindred souls, a joy which is nourished chiefly by the praise implied in such agreement, the annoyance at finding our most cherished "exceptionalities" duplicated is far greater, for such duplication devalues our exceptionality: Unless of course one marries the duplicator and continues to be exceptional à deux. Compare Goethe's: "Lebt man denn wenn andere leben" (*West-östlicher Divan*) and Thomas Mann, who also ends by quoting this line of Goethe's: "From Switzerland came the two volumes of Hermann Hesse's *Das Glasperlenspiel*. In far Montagnola my friend had achieved his difficult and beautiful novel, of which until this moment I had known but the introduction . . . I often said of this introduction that its style was so near to me 'als wär's ein Stück von mir'. Enabled to take in the whole in one comprehensive view, I felt almost terrified to see how similar it was to what had occupied me so intensely these last years. The same idea of a fictional biographer, and the same overtones of parody, which this form permits. The same emphasis on music. The same criticism of our age and our culture though more dreamy and utopian than my own . . . still, there were similarities enough—more than enough, and the entry I made in my diary: 'to be reminded that one is not alone in the world is always annoying', bluntly expresses this facet of my feeling. It is but another version of Goethe's: 'Lebt man denn wenn Andre leben?' " (Th. Mann, *Die Entstehung des Dr. Faustus* [Amsterdam, 1949], p. 68.)

proves vain simply because such a pursuit would be selfcon-tradictory and meaningless inside Sartre's theory. For if the right choice for man is the choice made in the full conscious-ness of his absolute liberty and accepting full responsibility for it, the liberty of another man which I make my own end is not his choice, and therefore cannot represent a right use of his essential liberty. In other words other people's liberty (in the metaphysical sense) cannot be an end for my will for I cannot bestow liberty on other people. Moreover, any attempt on my part to do so would be tantamount to a denial of their liberty. But the liberty of others cannot be denied at all since it is according to Sartre a reality perceived by an immediate and decisive act of intuitive perception. The intuitive percep-tion of the 'other' as an independent entity, endowed with the power 'to choose for or against me', faces each one of us with a demand to respect the liberty of the other on a plane of mutual engagements. This is however, tantamount to a de-mand, that men should respect the persons of all other men.

Once again we watch the impetuous idea of the dignity of man *qua* man, injected into a recalcitrant and incompatible system of thought by the force of some irrational intuition, play havoc with the consistency and coherence of that system.

Summing up what we have learned from the case of Kant, Rousseau, Mill, Sartre, we can say that what looked at first blush like rationally arguable demonstrations of the dignity-of-man-in-others—by inductive reasoning from the data of one's own experience,[24] have proved but a barrage of words designed to hide the mental jump performed under their cover. This mental jump is occasioned by the intrusion of a logically always gratuitous,[25] at times inimical idea[26] into the argument. With its appearance previously used concepts acquire a new meaning, and a new validity. But as the words[27] denoting such concepts are usually not replaced by others or qualified by an epithet to evidence the inner change in content, the fallacy of seeming to prove what has really

---

[24] That is in Kant and Mill, *not* in Sartre.
[25] In Kant and Sartre.
[26] In Mill.
[27] I.e. 'general happiness' in Mill's, 'liberté' in Sartre's argument.

been accepted[28] without proof (namely the intrusive idea) is made possible.

Let us now try to examine this intrusive and troublesome idea of the 'infinite worth of the human person' on its own merits and apart from these diverse systems. Let us agree to give it the form of a proposition couched in Kantian terms: "All men *qua* men are endowed with dignity" and examine possible proofs for its validity.

Then in the first place we must say that this proposition is not an analytic proposition as Kant attempted to show. For from the bare concept of man, only his rationality can be deduced with any certainty as to its universal validity. But the quality of rationality does not entail (by logical necessity) the quality of moral goodness nor does it entail the possession of dignity. The proposition "all men *qua* men are endowed with dignity" must therefore be a synthetic proposition.

It is however not synthetic proposition *a posteriori* for the following reasons: (1) I can experience only my own dignity as a moral being, since I can be certain only of my own freedom and my own capability of moral action. (2) Since morality lies in the manner of willing, and since it is beyond my power to see into the hidden motives of another man, I can never actually be certain that they perform moral actions and are capable of performing moral actions. (3) I am on the other hand continually faced with the sight of people who disregard the moral law and who therefore definitely do *not* perform moral actions. (4) Any judgment from myself upon others is therefore not warranted by experience. But even if it were so justified inductive reasoning could never supply sufficient certainty for the objective and absolute necessity of this synthesis. We must however have sufficient certainty, nay absolute certainty in this matter.

The proposition 'all men *qua* men are endowed with dignity' if it be at all objectively necessary, must therefore be an *a priori* synthetic proposition.

Now it seems to me that if any rational necessity can be said to exist for the synthesis in question, it is not of the same

---

[28] I use 'accepted' rather than 'assumed', because intuitions and postulates, if based on intuition, possess a greater compelling power than assumptions.

kind of rational necessity as the rational necessity in which
the synthesis between will and freedom finds its justification.
There is no necessity to conceive all men as *eo ipso* endowed
with dignity, similar to the necessity to think of the will as
being free. In other words, the extension of the attribute of
dignity to all men *qua* men (i. e. to conceive of dignity as a
prerogative natural to all men) is not a category of reason.
But perhaps a rational justification for the *a priori* synthesis
between man as such and dignity can be found in some
middle term, in which as pre-condition common to both, both
could be grounded? Now if such a term could be found, the
composite concept of the dignity of all men, would derive
from this term, and therefore be dependent on this term. It
would be a conditioned, a hypothetical synthesis. This would
lead to Ethics itself (as a discipline) being dependent on the
same middle term. Ethics would thus be reduced to a heteronomy dictated by that term. Therefore all attempts to vindicate the proposition "all men *qua* men are endowed with
dignity" by the authority of the scriptures, a metaphysical
doctrine inclusive of a teleological view of the universe, or
man's biological qualification, must be repudiated as damaging to the unconditional validity of human dignity as such,
and by implication, to the autonomy of ethics. All attempts
to vindicate the proposition "all men *qua* men . . ." by individual and outstanding[29] qualities must be repudiated as
pernicious to the universal attribution of human dignity. All
attempts to vindicate the proposition "all men *qua* men . . ."
by a mutual agreement to accord each other this dignity (a
contrat social) must be repudiated as damaging to the reality
of dignity.

Finally the necessity of performing the synthesis between
"human being" and "dignity" is not grounded in an emotional
compulsion[30] innate in all human hearts. As a matter of fact,

[29] As Kant did by making dignity dependent on moral capacity.

[30] Viz. Rousseau's view, and also Kant's view in his precritical
writings, especially in *Beobachtungen über das Gefühl des Schönen
und Erhabenen*, quoted above. Kant's latter occasional loose references to the heart as the seat of morality, must not be interpreted
to mean that he had given up the view that morality is exclusively
grounded in reason. He uses the term "heart" to cover those decisions prompted by *reason* and *commonsense* but not fully understood

very few people actually *feel* that all people are endowed with dignity. Mostly the innate emotional regard for other people's persons embraces a restricted and definite group (who are thought of as endowed with dignity in virtue of their class, profession, nationality, etc.). Almost always the purely emotional respect for other people's persons excludes certain groups on more or less defensible rational reasons, or on irrational, sometimes even unconscious, grounds.

The synthetic proposition "All men-*qua*-men are possessed of dignity" is therefore incapable of any proof whatsoever, including the transcendental proof for the objective necessity of categories. Since it is also very rarely the object of an intuition, in the usual sense of intuition, it can only be classified as a *postulate* which because of the uniqueness of its nature and position can only be described by comparison. Like the postulate of freedom it is wholly implied in the given datum of moral experience and represents the ultimate reason for this experience. In another sense it resembles the postulate of the existence of God in its (i. e. the latter's) structural rela-

---

in their theoretical demonstration. At no time does he oppose heart (the irrational) to reason (the rational). He opposes heart (rational reason, Eingebung des natürlichen Verstandes) to mind (of which at times in speculative deliberation one can make unsound and incorrect use). I believe passages like the one on Herr Garve ought to be interpreted in this sense: "Hr Garve remarks (about the difference which I define between the discipline that teaches us how to become happy and that which teaches us how to be worthy of happiness) are: 'For my part I must confess that though I can understand this division of ideas with my *head* I cannot find this division in my *heart*. I cannot even comprehend how anyone can be sure that he had isolated his desire for happiness to such a degree, that his actions were indeed done for duty's sake only'. . . . In spite of Hr Garve's confession that he does not find the division (or rather separation) aforementioned in his *heart* I do not hesitate to contradict him and defend his heart against his head. He, the upright man has indeed found (this division) in his heart (i.e. in the determination of his will), but he could not adjust it in his head to the usual explanations according to psychological principles (which are all of a physical causal nature) so as to understand what cannot be understood or explained, namely the possibility of a categorical imperative and in order to speculate on this imperative . . ."
Kant: *Über den Gemeinspruch: Das mag in der Theorie richtig sein, taugt aber nicht für die Praxis* (1793), Part II.

tionship to religious experience, for it can be taken for the effective real cause of moral experience as well as for its ultimate reason (formal cause). That means that moral experience, though it is our only means of discovering this postulate, is not to be treated as though it were the cause or the ground of the postulate. On the contrary, the postulate is to be treated as though it were the cause and the ground of moral experience, on the justification that moral experience can be explained completely only by this postulate. (Note the close analogy to the postulate of the existence of God in religious experience). In short, the postulate is to be treated not like a postulate. It is to be treated in all respects and to all purposes, like a statement of fact, the statement of an ultimate, irreducible, unquestionable fact. Now it so happens that the irreducible and unquestionable fact the postulate is supposed to state is not a very probable fact. It is indeed 'a fact' denied and invalidated by the greater part of our experience and knowledge. It therefore resembles those tenets of our convictions of which it can be truthfully said: *credo quia absurdum*. An act of faith, and a gratuitous act of faith at that, is needed for its acceptance. Moreover it has a peculiar quality of its own, the power of challenging the will. Its challenge is that the will by electing to treat the postulate as though it were a statement of fact, will in the end prevail by creating the fact, whose statement it was supposed to be.

To sum up: the postulate that all men *qua* men are endowed with dignity fulfils the following four simultaneous functions:

a) It functions as a necessary hypothesis without which moral experience would be neither possible nor explicable.

b) It is a statement of fact (i. e. a statement of existence) and as such is the real and efficacious cause of moral experience.

c) It is an affirmation of faith in the face of clear evidence to the contrary.

d) It is a challenge to our wills, i. e. a regulative idea.

Since it fulfils all those functions simultaneously, each of the four propositions correctly defines one facet of its nature.[31] All facets play definite and decisive rôles in moral theory and practice, so that their separate description might not prove altogether useless.

The significance of Kant's assertion: "Now I say that man exists as an end in himself", must not be obscured or diminished by would-be and impossible proofs of its validity. It should rather be gauged in the sense of Rudolf Otto's perceptive if somewhat sentimental annotation: "It is with great inner emotion that we look upon this eruption of a deep and independent intuition, for we are privileged to witness the birth of the mightiest and most significant of all ideas that were ever pronounced in the domain of ethical enquiry: The idea of a concrete, existent value-in-and-for-itself, an idea moreover which reason can accept and respect."[32]

[31] It is interesting to note that Kant explicitly uses b first part; c; d; but never a, and would probably reject b part two, for reasons of method.

[32] R. Otto, Notes to Kant's *Grundlegung* . . . , p. 199.

WHAT DOES KANT MEAN BY
'ACTING FROM DUTY'?

PAUL DIETRICHSON

Kant claims that our *pure* reason (our reason in that mode of its operation which is not conditioned by *empirical* factors) has not only a speculative use, but also a practical use. Its practical use—which is to provide grounds for performing moral action, as distinguished from grounds for developing merely abstract speculative thinking in terms of unschematized *a priori* categories—involves two closely related functions.

Our pure reason's *first* practical function (which I shall not attempt to analyse in detail in this paper) is to make us cognizant of the moral law: the paradigm of universalizability to which maxims of objectively correct actions would conform. The volitional dimension of our being is not determined exclusively by reason. It is guided by our pure practical reason, but it is also affected by sensuously conditioned impulses and has an innate propensity to evil. In short, our being is such that we, as distinguished from a holy being, do not unavoidably act in conformity with the paradigm of completely rational action. When we through pure practical reason become aware of the moral law concerning universalizability of maxims, we therefore inescapably come to regard it as a *prescriptive* law of our sensuously affected and temptable being. That is to say, we come to recognize that we in any empirical situation ought so to act that we, at any time, could consistently want the maxim of our action to be raised to the

Reprinted with permission of the author and of the editors from *Kant-Studien*, Band 53 (1962), Kölner Universitäts-Verlag, in which it was first published.

status of a universal law of nature.[1] The hypothetical law of nature that I according to the typic should envisage as becoming modeled on my maxim is a universal causal law of voluntary behavior: a hypothetical causal law according to which every person would, in the same type of circumstances as mine, act invariably on the same subjective rule as the one I in fact decide to act on in that type of circumstances. We satisfy the "legality" requirement of the categorical imperative if and only if our action is such that we could at any time

[1] By having included in the above sentence the words 'of nature', I have expressed the principle of the categorical imperative, not in the abstract form in which we *originally* apprehend it through our pure practical reason, but in the manner in which we, for our practical purpose, have to restate that principle in the form of the *"typic"*. In this particular paper there is no need to make a thorough examination of the nature and justification of the typic of pure practical reason. (I have done that in a paper on Kant's universalizability criterion.) A few words about the typic will suffice for the present discussion.—My pure practical reason commands me to act always in such a way that I could consistently want the maxim of my action to hold as a universal law. I cannot make any practical use of that completely abstract categorical imperative as a standard for appraising my material rules of action in the phenomenal world, however. Because when I ask: '. . . hold as a universal law' *of what?*, I find that no answer is forthcoming from that abstract formula of duty. I therefore have to restate it in a symbolically concrete manner. The only way I can do so is to restate the principle of that imperative so as to make it include reference to the idea of a purely *hypothetical* world of *nature*. The kind of natural world I have to envisage, and envisage as though I were a part of it, is one that would have to be assumed to be capable of being arranged according to purely hypothetical *causal* laws, namely universal causal laws that are to be modeled on my maxims of action in the actual phenomenal world and would hold for all persons of that counterfactual system of nature, of which then, I am to envisage myself as though I were a part. Having expressed the abstract principle of the categorical imperative in terms of the idea of a sensory world capable of being arranged in such a hypothetical manner, I can use that principle of imperativeness as a practical criterion for appraising my empirical maxims of action in the actual phenomenal world. The *typifying* of the categorical imperative is, in other words, a necessary but merely heuristic mediation-device, a substitute for a schematism of the abstract categorical imperative. That kind of heuristic mediation-device is—at least implicitly—being used in common sense moral judgments every day, according to Kant.

consistently want a universal causal law of voluntary action to become modeled on the principle of our maxim of action.— So much for our pure reason's *first* practical function, namely that of making us aware of the categorical imperative and making it concretely applicable as a practical standard for appraising our material maxims in respect to the requirement of legality.

Our mere awareness of the principle of the categorical imperative as expressed in the typic does not, however, constitute a sufficient condition for deciding to act in conformity with it. We also need a stimulus, an affective-conative impetus, an incentive to act, namely *a subjective interest in obeying the objective unconditional command of our pure practical reason.* Kant points out of course that even if the incentive by which we decide to motivate ourselves should happen to be devoid of moral worth, our maxim (subjective rule of voluntary action) might still be in objective conformity with the moral law and thereby satisfy the legality requirement. He speaks of such actions as conforming to "the letter of the moral law" without conforming to "the spirit of the moral law", or as proceeding "according to duty" but not "from duty". Our actions are of that type when we motivate ourselves by merely natural (empirically conditioned) inclinations, e. g. by purely *prudential* interests that happen to prompt us to conform to the objective requirement of the moral law. An example would be when a merchant abstains from cheating his customers because, and only because, he thinks cheating would be too risky for him. But Kant insists that any human being who can properly be called a person knows his actions should satisfy, not only the requirement of legality (objective correctness), but also the requirement of morality (subjective worthiness).

Our pure reason must therefore have a practical function in. addition to that of enabling us to apprehend the paradigm of objectively correct behavior, i. e. a function over and beyond the type of practical function that has been referred to so far. That *second* practical function of our pure reason must be to elicit from our conative-affective nature an *interest,* an incentive which is in kind different from any natural (empirically conditioned) interest, namely, a purely *moral* interest in obeying the law of objectively correct behavior. Such a strictly moral interest in complying with the paradigm of objectively correct action is, according to Kant, based on a feeling of a unique kind. The feeling is unique in that it is not a "pathological" feeling (a passional response elicited by outer or inner *empirical* stimuli) but a *"pure"* feeling, namely our spontaneous emotional response to nothing but the moral law—the categorical imperative—which we impose on ourselves through our *empirically unconditioned* reason alone. That purely rationally elicited feeling response is of course what Kant speaks of as "respect for duty, reverence for the moral law".

If we were not capable of being tempted, we could not come to regard the moral law as a standard obligating us. Kant argues that because we are sensuously conditioned beings with an innate propensity to evil, and are therefore temptable beings, it is *impossible* for us to apprehend the moral law without coming to stand in awe of and feel reverent respect for it. Our pure practical reason commands us to attain moral worth by obeying its law in the face of any tempting natural inclinations to disobey it. We realize that we would not attain any moral worth by adopting the rule of obeying the letter of the moral law only in those cases where doing so would happen to satisfy our natural inclinations. The law will therefore inevitably be felt by us as imposing a painful check on our selfish inclinations and as deflating in a painfully humbling manner any moral self-conceit or moral arrogance we might have a tendency to develop. We could not experience negative feelings of that kind, however, unless we in the first place had a positive feeling of reverence and respect for this self-imposed (or at least self-approved)[2] law that thwarts our selfish inclinations, exposes our propensity to moral conceit and gives us a prospect of achieving moral dignity. That feeling of reverent respect elicits in us a purely *moral interest* in obeying the law of our pure practical reason. We are free to adopt

[2] If that demanding type of normative law were imposed on us by some other being, and were *not endorsed* by our *own* pure reason, we could not feel reverence and respect for it. We would instead probably feel as we normally would if someone were to tyrannize us, i.e. we would probably feel nothing but anger or disgust or indignation.

that interest as an *incentive* for acting in conformity with the legality requirement of the categorical imperative, and our own pure reason makes clear to us that we should do so whether we want to or not. But we can of course deliberately (and immorally) refuse to do so, according to Kant. We might, e. g. decide to satisfy the legality requirement of the moral law when and only when that type of action happens to satisfy our self-interest.

I have found Kant's critics and commentators surprisingly inattentive to one important point pertaining to the nature of the moral incentive and to the requirement to act "from duty". What I have in mind is his insistence on and explanation of the type of partial epistemological opaqueness that we inevitably encounter if we try to determine whether we in a given case motivate ourselves *exclusively* by our interest in obedience based on our feeling of reverent respect for the moral law. The commentators and critics that I am familiar with say explicitly or by implication that we, according to Kant, have a duty to adopt our reverent respect for the moral law as our sufficient incentive for obeying the universalizability requirement of the law. I shall attempt to show that interpretation to be a gross misinterpretation.

Kant maintains that it is possible for us, at least in certain types of conflict situations, to know whether we do or do not adopt our morally pure interest in obedience (based on reverent respect for the categorical imperative) as an incentive-factor in our total motive. Suppose, then, we recognize that we in certain situations acted in accordance with the categorical imperative (satisfied the legality requirement), and also recognize that our actions had moral worth in the sense that we, when we satisfied the legality requirement, motivated ourselves at least partly by our interest in obedience springing from reverent respect for the imperative. However, when it comes to determining whether we in any situation of that kind succeeded in adopting our incentive of reverent respect for the moral law in such a wholehearted and decisive manner that that incentive served as our *sufficient* subjective reason for obeying the letter of the law, we find that it is impossible for us to become absolutely certain. Some ignorance concerning the *degree* of moral purity of our motives is simply inescapable, according to Kant. The more diligently and honestly we search the deeper motivational patterns of our minds, the more apt we are to find—or at least to come to suspect very strongly—that certain of our "pathological" impulses (e. g. our desires for such-and-such sensuous satisfactions, or our desire to appear good in the hope of being respected or praised or admired or rewarded, or our fear of disapproval or retaliation or punishment, or sentiments of pity and sympathy that happened to well up in us) cooperated with our morally worthy disposition by inciting us to satisfy the objective requirement of legality, and that we to some degree *motivated* ourselves by such pathological impulses. How, then, are we ever to know that we adopted our purely moral incentive as a sufficient spring of action in the sense that we would have satisfied the letter of the moral law even if none of our natural inclinations had to any extent incited us to do so? That type of question can of course be pressed further. If *all* our natural inclinations—the clearly felt ones as well as the more concealed ones—had incited us strongly to act *contrary* to the paradigm of objectively correct behavior, would we still have decided to act in objective conformity with that paradigm? In such a situation it would not have been possible for us to have bolstered our purely moral disposition by adopting into our pattern of motivation certain of our natural (amoral) inclinations, because any one then would have prompted us to act contrary to the legality requirement of the moral law. In order to have satisfied the objective requirement of legality (the letter of the moral law) in such a difficult situation, we should have had to have willed to keep *all* our natural inclinations in check and to have decided to act *exclusively* from our pure (empirically unconditioned) interest in obeying the moral law, namely from our interest in obedience based on nothing but our rationally elicited feeling of reverent respect for the moral law.

It is important to keep in mind at this point that Kant does not say it is impossible for us to know that our interest based on pure respect for the categorical imperative is in certain cases a *part* of our motivation. As I see it, his point is simply that we in such cases can always find that certain of our natural inclinations *also* prompted us to act (or at least did not strongly prompt us not to act) in conformity with the moral law, and that it is therefore possible that we would not have acted according to duty if the pattern of our natural inclinations had been different from what it in fact happened to be.

So even though our actions in certain cases might be such that we know our purely moral interest in obeying the categorical imperative was *a* motivating factor, it does not follow that we can determine with complete certainty to what *extent* our motive was of that morally pure kind. It is obvious that many people in a number of cases act "according to duty" (i. e. in conformity with the letter of the moral law). But is there even a single case where a person who acts according to duty adopts his purely moral incentive (reverent respect for the moral law) with such a firm resolve that he not only would have managed to have acted according to duty without motivating himself in part by certain natural (amoral) inclinations, but would have resisted his natural inclinations even if *all* of them should have happened to have incited him strongly to act *contrary* to the moral law? Could a person ever be justified in claiming to know that he in some situation adopted his purely moral interest in such a wholehearted manner that he made it operative as his *sufficient* incentive for satisfying the legality requirement (the letter) of the moral law? Kant's answer is unambiguous: ". . . it is not possible for a human being to see so far into the depth of his own heart that he could ever be completely certain about the purity of his moral purpose and the disinterestedness of his disposition in even *one* action, even if he has no doubt whatever about the legality of the action. Weakness, which might dissuade a person from the daring enterprise of a crime, often comes to be regarded by him as virtue (which gives the notion of strength). And how many may have led a long and blameless life, who are only *fortunate* in having been spared so many temptations. *How much*[3] of pure moral value might have belonged to the

[3] 'How much' italicized by me.

disposition of each deed remains hidden even from themselves."[4, 5]

The conclusion that follows from the above considerations might be surprising to a number of Kantian scholars: according to Kant, the requirement to act "from duty" *does not mean that we are obligated to motivate ourselves exclusively by our interest in obedience based on reverent respect for the moral law.* The reason for this has already been indicated and is quite simple. Since it is absolutely impossible for us to see so far into the depth of our own hearts as to *be* certain that we even in a single case motivate ourselves exclusively by our interest based on our reverent respect for the moral law, we can of course not have an obligation to *make* certain that we motivate ourselves exclusively by that interest. That is to say, we cannot be *obligated* to perform an inner action of a type we could never *know* we perform. An obligation to make sure that one performs an inner action of such a kind would simply be incongruent with human ability and would therefore be an absurd obligation—which is to say, we do not have such an obligation at all. Kant stresses that point: "consequently, the law . . . does not command the action itself . . ."[6] The obligation to act "from duty" must therefore be of a *wider*—i. e. less demanding, less rigorous—type.

In respect to motivation, our pure practical reason can meaningfully demand of our volitional nature no more than that we, with all our power, should *strive*, should *endeavor*, to make our pure interest in obedience based on reverent respect for the moral law serve as a sufficient incentive for satisfying the universalizability requirement (the letter) of the law. According to Kant, *striving* of that type is not a striving *for* purity of heart; it *is* purity of heart. So that very

[4] The passages cited from Kant in this paper are my own translations based on the 11 vol. Ernst Cassirer edition of Kant's works—*Immanuel Kants Werke* (Berlin, 1912–1922), I–XI. (I use italics where extended type is used in the original.)

[5] *Die Metaphysik der Sitten,* zweiter Abschnitt: "Metaphysische Anfangsgründe der Tugendlehre", IKW, VII, 202.—Cf. Thomas K. Abbott's tr., *Kant's Critique of Practical Reason and Other Works on the Theory of Ethics* (London, 6th ed., 1909, reprinted 1954), p. 303.

[6] *Op. cit.* p. 202 (Abbott, p. 303).

type of *striving* is what *constitutes* purity of heart, good will, obedience to "the spirit of the moral law", fulfillment of the requirement to act "from duty".

As far as motivation is concerned one is, then, as a decision-making agent, commanded by one's own pure reason merely "to *seek*[7] the ground of obligation, not in sensuous inclinations (advantage or disadvantage), but exclusively in the law . . . So this duty to appraise the worth of one's actions, not merely by their legality, but also by their morality, is, then, only of a *wide* obligation (nur von *weiter* Verbindlichkeit). The law commands only that in actions that are conformable to duty (*pflichtmässigen*), all *efforts* should be *aimed*[8] at making the thought of duty itself a *sufficient*[9] incentive (Triebfeder)."[10] So our duty is not to succeed, but merely to *strive* to succeed in making our reverent thought of the moral law a sufficient incentive for acting in conformity with the legality (universalizability) requirement of that law.

We have seen, then, *one* sense in which the duty to appraise the moral worth of one's action by its incentive, by its mental disposition (Gesinnung), is only a *wide*, i. e. somewhat *indeterminate*, type of duty. Our duty only to strive to satisfy—to aim at satisfying—a regulative ideal which in itself *transcends* our ability, namely the transcendent (unattainable) ideal of making absolutely *certain* that our interest in obedience based on reverent respect for the moral law is adopted by us as our sufficient incentive for obeying in our action the legality requirement of that law.

Kant's text suggests however that there is also a *second* sense in which the duty to appraise the moral worth of the motives from which we act is only a wide (somewhat indeterminate) type of duty. That second sense, which (like the first sense) is contingent on a cognitive limitation, pertains to the assertion that we are obligated, not only to aim, but to aim *with all our power* to satisfy the transcendent motivational ideal of pure practical reason. If the phrase 'with all our power' were to be interpreted in the strictest conceiv-

---

7, 8, 9 'seek', 'aimed', and 'sufficient' italicized by me.
[10] *Ibid.* p. 203 (Abbott, p. 303).

able manner, it would follow that we at any time can know precisely the limit of our capacity to strive and that we at any time are obligated to utilize our capacity to that very limit when we aim at the transcendent motivational ideal of pure practical reason. But *can* we at any time know the limit of our capacity to strive to attain that motivational ideal? Kant is, in my opinion, open to the criticism that he has not developed his answer to that important question as explicitly and fully as he ought to have done. But various parts of his writings suggest quite strongly what he would take to be the correct answer. At the risk of proceeding somewhat beyond the confines of Kant's own view, but in the hope of formulating explicitly what he has in mind, I shall elaborate on the basis of his suggestions.

According to Kant, "our abilities would probably for the most part have remained unused if we were not supposed to be resolved to exert our power to produce an envisioned object until we had assured ourselves of the sufficiency of our abilities to produce that object. For we usually learn to know our powers only by trying them out".[11, 12] The limit of my capacity to strive to attain the transcendent motivational ideal of pure practical reason cannot be determined in an *a priori* manner. There is therefore no rigidly determinable criterion available in this domain. I must at any time rely on my more or less tentative practical judgments based on my inner experience. Only by actually striving on a given occasion to fulfill the motivational ideal do I come to know that I have the capacity to strive to (at least) *that* extent.

[11] *Kritik der Urteilskraft*, IKW, V, 211n.—Cf. J. C. Meredith's tr., *Immanuel Kant, The Critique of Judgment* (Oxford: Oxford University Press), 1952, pp. 16–17n.

[12] Kant makes that point in several places, but his particularly forceful statement of it in the above cited footnote from the Third *Critique* was brought to my attention by a reference in John R. Silber's article "Kant's Conception of the Highest Good as Immanent and Transcendent" (*Philosophical Review*, Vol. 68, No. 4, October 1959). The topic of Professor Silber's article is quite different from the topic of the present article, but I have found his emphasis on Kant's conception of the transcendence of the highest good helpful in my attempt to indicate the second sense in which our motivational duty is only of a relatively wide (indeterminate) kind, according to Kant.

Let us assume that at a certain time I honestly believed that I
on a given occasion did my utmost in aiming to fulfill the
transcendent motivational ideal of pure practical reason and,
therefore, believed I had on that occasion satisfied *completely* the requirement to act "from duty". It is still possible
that by further retrospection of that act, or by comparing
it with later choice situations that tested my moral strength
more severely, I might come to believe that I on that former
occasion fell short (perhaps far short) of actualizing the moral
capacity I had. I might come to be convinced that when I
satisfied the legality requirement of the moral I did so to a
large extent because I deep down found that line of action
to my own advantage, in the sense of satisfying certain of
my natural (amoral) inclinations. According to the requirement to appraise the morality of my motives, I must therefore
develop my intellectual faculties, especially my capacity for
introspection, attempt to approximate more and more closely
the transcendent motivational ideal of pure practical reason,
search my heart with unflinching honesty and in good faith be
willing to modify my previous appraisals of my moral character. In future conflict situations subjecting my moral fibre
to more demanding tests I might come to manifest to myself
hitherto unknown and perhaps even unsuspected capacities
for developing purity of heart. If I appraise my moral character in good faith, I will hope to have occasions to discover
such manifestations of greater strength in the future.

My only partially self-transparent complex rational and
sensuously conditioned nature being what it is, I am not likely
to come to believe and remain believing in full honesty that I
on some occasion strived to the very *limit* of my capacity to
develop purity of heart. But even if I should honestly come
to hold such a belief—it would be belief rather than knowledge—I would still have no occasion for relaxing my effort.
Because my pure practical reason would then obligate me to
re-appropriate that purity of heart, namely by commanding
me to act from the same pure motive in future situations involving moral choices.

The transcendent but regulative motivational ideal of
pure practical reason is to make certain that one always

adopts one's pure interest in obedience based on reverent respect for the moral law as one's sufficient incentive for acting in conformity with the legality requirement of the moral law. The duty to strive *with all one's power* to attain and preserve purity of heart is, then, a duty to strive *continuously* in good faith to approximate that transcendent ideal more and more closely.

Such a requirement to act "from duty" might seem forbiddingly harsh and unduly severe. It might seem that, according to Kant's view, there is no rest for the virtuous. Kant does not deny, however, that such striving has its profound satisfaction.[13] When a person's action has at least a degree of moral worth, he will experience a purely rationally elicited feeling of peaceful *self-contentment* (*Selbstzufriedenheit*) accompanying his consciousness of virtue. That feeling is not a feeling of gratification or happiness in response to one's inner or outer empirical conditions and is not dependent on mood and fortunate circumstances (Cf. the "aesthetic" level as described by Kierkegaard). It is rather a peaceful contentment with one's very *existence* and is dependent on nothing but virtuous striving, which is a matter, not of mood, but of volition—willingness to act as one's pure reason demands. Being a feeling of peaceful contentment with one's very existence (rather than with the empirical conditions of one's existence) it is of a unique quality, and can easily be distinguished from any feeling of natural (amoral) well-being (happiness) and from any feeling of self-indulgent joy and even from purely aesthetic joy. It is symptomatic of nothing but a virtuous disposition. It can therefore be regarded as a (unique type of) feeling which *confirms* that one is in the process of developing purity of heart. A malevolent person, or a merely prudent person, or a person appraising his character in bad faith will not experience that peaceful contentment with his very existence.—Someone might then calculate that it might be quite prudent for him to act so as to attain that feeling of contentment with his existence. His calculation would be a miscalculation, however. If one were to attempt

[13] As will be seen later, he even maintains that it will in the long run elicit a *love* of duty.

to act virtuously *in order to attain* that enjoyable feeling, i. e. if the desire for that satisfying emotional *consequence* of a virtuous disposition were one's *motive* for obeying the legality requirement of the moral law, one's pure practical reason would make one recognize that that very motivational disposition would not *be* virtuous, but impure—heteronomous. (Instrumentalistic morality is futile, then, according to Kant.) The feeling—peaceful contentment with one's very existence—that one would (illicitly) be seeking would therefore not *arise* because it is an accompaniment of a *virtuous* disposition only.[14]

To a person who seeks to appraise his own moral character in good faith there is always the sobering, humility-inspiring but at the same time also constantly *effort-inspiring* thought that he might not even in a single one of his actions thus far have reached the limit of his capacity to approximate the transcendent regulative motivational ideal of his own pure practical reason. (That *same* thought, which by a man of good faith is considered humbling and constantly effort-inspiring, might of course by a man of a different disposition be focused on and used as an excuse for self-complacency and moral laxness. A person who has allowed himself to slide into a habit of appraising his own moral character in bad faith, would be seeking self-excuse for his own moral laxness by *capitalizing on an obscurity*, namely by capitalizing on the recognized fact that he can never *know*—he can never be absolutely *certain*—that he has done all he can to approximate the motivational ideal of pure practical reason. He finds it to his own interest to have a rather cynical attitude towards belief. His attitude would be somewhat like this: 'Our appraisal of our motives has to be based on mere belief[15] and feeling. Belief is subjective and hence notoriously tenuous. Our motive patterns are complex, changing and intertwined, and we are by no means self-transparent beings. There are no rigidly precise criteria for appraising

---

[14] Cf. *Kritik der Praktischen Vernunft*, IKW, V, 125–29. Abbott, pp. 211–15; Lewis W. Beck's tr., *Immanuel Kant: Critique of Practical Reason and Other Writings in Moral Philosophy* (Chicago, 1950), pp. 219–22.

[15] Such a person would emphasize 'mere' rather than 'belief'.

the moral worth of one's disposition. The evidence is, even at best, of a rather flimsy type. Since there is in this domain no unambiguous distinction between genuine insight and pathological fantasy, one ought to have a relaxed—perhaps even a very, very relaxed—attitude when one attempts to appraise one's moral worth. One should be careful not to get lost in futile aspirations, and one should avoid producing what might after all be groundless self-reproach and guilt feelings.')

According to Kant, then, we have a duty to subordinate any motivational rule of self-love to the motivational rule of striving—striving (in the sense described previously) to the best of our ability—to approximate the *transcendent* regulative ideal of pure practical reason: making certain we obey the legality requirement of the moral law from, and simply from, reverence and respect for its command. Various of Kant's readers might criticize him for providing only a somewhat loose and indefinite procedure for determining to what extent one's actions proceed "from duty". Kant could only answer that man's combined sensuous-and-rational nature and its capacity for introspective and retrospective apprehension being what it is, no more precise procedure of an applicable kind could possibly be found—regrettable though that might be. He would maintain, then, that his inability to formulate a more sharply delineated procedure for appraising the moral worth of our actions by their mental disposition is not a shortcoming of his philosophy but simply a consequence of the fact that man's nature happens to be structured the way it is.

A few words need to be said about Kant's conception of the relationship between moral striving and the ideal of holiness, and his conception of the relationship between moral striving and the feeling of love.

According to Kant, the moral law is not, in its own nature, a prescriptive law. It is a *descriptive* law, namely a paradigm to which a completely perfect (holy) volitional being would in fact inevitably conform in every act. That we come to regard the moral law as subjecting *us* to an unconditional *imperative* is not due to the nature of the law as such. As suggested previously, it is only due to the contingent fact that our nature happens to be so structured that we are not simply rational beings but also sensuously conditioned beings with a propensity to evil, and hence, temptable beings. Because we have a pure reason that can be practical, we are capable of apprehending the formal paradigm of a completely perfect moral volition. That is to say, what we initially apprehend through our pure practical reason is the following descriptive law: every maxim of a completely perfect volition is founded exclusively on reason and is capable of being consistently thought and consistently willed to hold as principle of a universal lawgiving. In other words, we recognize the paradigm of moral holiness. Because we—in addition to our purely rational faculty—have needs that are sensuously conditioned, however, we realize clearly that we are not holy (morally incorruptable) agents. We also see that we cannot *attain* moral holiness, i. e. perfect ourselves as voluntary agents so as to reach a level of existence where it would be absolutely *impossible* for us to act contrary to the moral law. But by apprehending the paradigm of perfect volition we come to realize that we, whether we happen to *want* to or not, *ought* to act on the same kind of maxims as that on which a holy being would *unavoidably* act. "The moral law is in fact for the will of a completely perfect being a law of *holiness*, but for the will of every finite rational being a law of *duty*, of moral constraint (Nötigung) and of the determination of his action through *respect* for this law and from reverence for his duty. Some other subjective principle must not be adopted as *the*[16] incentive. For otherwise the action might indeed turn out to be as the law prescribes, but since it then, admittedly, proceeds according to duty but not from duty, the disposition (Gesinnung) to do the act is not moral. The disposition, however, is what really matters . . .".[17]

But even though we are finite and sensuously affected agents, and therefore incapable of attaining holiness by our efforts Kant maintains that we have a duty to progress constantly towards holiness in the sense of inculcating in ourselves a *habit* of striving, against any tempting natural inclina-

---

[16] Italicized by me.
[17] *Kritik der Praktischen Vernunft*, pp. 90–91. (Abbott, p. 175; Beck, p. 189.)

tion, to obey the universalizability requirement of the moral law from an incentive based on pure reverence and respect for its command. (Kant's view is reminiscent of Pelagius' view.) The more thoroughly we inculcate such a habit, the less we become susceptible to temptations. His point is that by so doing we will come to develop, as a "second nature", a more or less spontaneous *inclination* to obey the legality requirement of the moral law; we will come to fulfill our duties to others and to ourselves more and more from a feeling of *love*.

The emergence of a strong spontaneous and enduring *inclination* to obey the moral law (i. e. to act benevolently) can therefore be considered a *sign* that virtuousness has been developed to a high degree. On the other hand, the *absence* of that type of inclination can be taken as a sign that one is far from having developed the moral character one can and should develop. A motivational disposition in the form of such an *inclination* to benevolence, acquired through volitional striving, might be very dependable but would not be completely incorruptible. In its most developed form it would be the closest finite approximation towards moral holiness, and might appropriately be called 'saintliness'.

"Love is a matter of feeling, not of volition, and I cannot love because I *will*, still less because I *ought* . . . ; hence *a duty to love* is an absurdity (ein Unding). *Benevolence* (*amor benevolentiae*), however, can as a mode of action be subject to a law of duty. . . . so when it is said: you should *love* your neighbor as yourself, this does not mean: you should immediately (in the first place) love, and by means of this love (in the second place) do him good; but: *do good* to your neighbor, and this doing of good (dieses Wohltun) will develop in you a *love* of men (as a *settled habit* of *inclination*[18] to benevolence in general)".[19] That passage alone (which is one among an abundant number of other passages to the same effect in Kant's works) should serve to discredit, once and for all, the persistent criticism that Kant is a pedantic legalist myopically concerned with volition and patheti-

[18] 'love,' 'settled habit,' and 'inclination' italicized by me.
[19] *Die Metaphysik der Sitten*, pp. 211–12. (Abbott, pp. 312–13.)

cally insensitive to the important role that both habit and the feeling of love can come to play in moral behavior.

My criticism of certain standard interpretations of what Kant understands by the requirement to act "from duty" has been made, not in an attempt to advocate, but merely in an attempt to elucidate his doctrine concerning the nature of moral motivation.

KANT AS CASUIST

W. I. MATSON

In this paper I shall mean by casuistry that species of deductive argument having as conclusion the assertion that a
particular person is morally obliged to perform a certain act,
and having as premises (*a*) statements of fact about the person and the act and (*b*) a philosophical theory of moral
obligation, or at least one or more general statements deduced from such a theory.

This definition accords with one dictionary sense of the
word casuistry. But the other sense, which is the one meant
by the word in the English language in all its occurrences
except rare technical usages, is highly pejorative: casuistry is
synonymous with sophistry and quibbling. This is odd to the
point of singularity, for engineering, art criticism, medicine,
bookkeeping, and the like, which are the analogues of casuistry, are honorific. We are told that the word acquired this
sense on account of outrage at the alleged disingenuousness
of the Jesuit casuists; but this cannot be the whole story, for
in English-speaking countries at least the activity is held in
as much disesteem as the word. The plain man is impatient
of all attempts to exhibit obligations as following from theories. One is supposed to know what one's duties are; if there
is any doubt, it is taken for granted that the doubt arises
from insufficient factual information. Hence plain ethical argumentation is carried on wholly in factual terms, and any
introduction of moral theory—with the one significant exception of what is implicit in the rhetorical question "What if
everybody did that?"—is considered redundant at best.

It is not improbable that Kant's reputation as a moralist

Reprinted with permission of the author and of the editors from
Journal of Philosophy, 51 (1954), 855–60.

has suffered among his English critics from this circumstance. For the Kant who in the first *Critique* scorned examples as "go-carts of philosophy" was by no means so niggardly with illustrations when he wrote on moral philosophy. The result has been that a moral theory which is very much *à l'anglais* has been generally rejected because of dissatisfaction with what Kant asserted to be its casuistical consequences.

Serious criticism of the Kantian ethics on the basis of this dissatisfaction is of two sorts: first, that the supposed casuistical consequences do not really follow from the theory; second, that the consequences really follow and, since these consequences are to the effect that certain kinds of acts are obligatory which in reality are not obligatory, the theory has thereby been reduced to absurdity by its author. Let us consider the second kind of criticism first.

The criticism rests on two assumptions regarding the relation of ethical theories to practical consequences: (1) That ethical theories, like scientific theories in general, do have observable consequences which verify or falsify the theories —the consequences, in the case of theories of obligation, being claims that certain particular acts are obligatory; (2) That ethical theories, again like scientific theories, are meaningful only if their consequences are knowable independently of the theories. For example, a theory in psychiatry that a certain treatment will cure a certain psychosis would not be acceptable if the theory implicitly defined "cure" in such a way that only one holding the theory could know that a cure had been effected. Similarly, a theory of obligation according to which some action could not be recognized as obligatory except in terms of the theory, would be under suspicion.

The only question that can be raised about the first assumption concerns the sense in which the consequences of an ethical theory can be said to verify it; and this question is best discussed in connection with the second assumption.

The second assumption, which at first glance seems obvious and innocent to the point of triviality, is actually crucial to almost every ethical theory. If a theory of obligation is meaningful only if there are means, independent of the theory, for deciding whether certain acts are obligatory or not, then the means in question must either be based on some other theory, or on none. If the means depend on another theory, then the same point can be raised with respect to that theory; and, in the end, there must be a method for recognizing the property of moral obligation independently of any theory, i.e. in the last analysis the only tenable "theory" of moral obligation is Intuitionism, viz. the denial of the possibility of any ethical theory amounting to more than a cataloguing of intuitions. Furthermore, if two persons in possession of the same facts honestly intuit differently, there can be no possible means of deciding who is right, so Relativism also follows. Hence, to return to Kant, his theory must be false, because Relativism (*alias* Emotivism) is true. This is the most concise proof of Intuitionism-Relativism-Emotivism that I know of; I venture to say also that it is very plausible. I believe, however, that it is fallacious, and that its fallacy can be exposed by Kantian methods.

It is not amiss to note, as Plato did in the *Theaetetus*, that theories of this sort refute themselves, for most people intuit that they are false. In modern times, no one has stated the case for Intuitionism more clearly than H. A. Prichard. "If we do doubt whether there is really an obligation to originate A in a situation B," he wrote at the end of his paper "Does Moral Philosophy Rest on a Mistake?,"[1] "the remedy lies not in any process of general thinking, but in getting face to face with a particular instance of the situation B, and then directly appreciating the obligation to originate A in that situation." But common experience plainly teaches us that in general the very *least* reliable way of determining whether an obligation exists, in any situation that is at all complicated, is to consult our own moral intuitions when we are actually in that situation; for even moral philosophers by profession sometimes have their judgment overthrown by bias when they are intimately involved in a moral predicament.

So much for the argument *ad hominem*. The real strength of Intuitionism lies in the undeniable fact—pointed out by Plato's Protagoras—that in the great majority of cases that we encounter we do not find it difficult to intuit moral obligations; moreover, society expects us, and rightly so, to have

[1] *Mind*, n. s. 21 (1912), 21–37.

the proper intuitions. Society does not expect us, however, to be moral philosophers. Hence the conclusion that moral judgment is independent of theory, i.e. that casuistry is useless, or even impossible.

This conclusion, of course, does not follow. Granted, as we must grant, that in very many cases "the sense of obligation to do . . . an action of a particular kind is absolutely underivative or immediate,"[2] we are by no means compelled to conclude that there are no cases at all of moral puzzlement in which a "process of general thinking" may be essential for the solution of our difficulties. No more must we conclude that there cannot be a general theory from which even those obligations which we sense underivatively or immediately can be shown to follow as deductive consequences.

This is clear from the parallel case of mathematics. In elementary arithmetic and geometry we can sense intuitively the correctness of the theorems; and if we were not able to do this, we should never have been in a position to develop any systematic mathematical theories. Nevertheless, the theories, validated in the first instance by their agreement with our numerical and spatial intuitions, go far beyond those intuitions, and in many cases can even serve to correct erroneous "intuitions." For example, it is not intuitive that the diagonal of a square is incommensurable with the side; if anything in the situation is "self-evident," it would seem to be the proposition that *all* quantities are commensurable. All the same, the Pythagoreans were consistent enough to admit incommensurability when it was proved, declining to take the easy common-sensical way out, of rejecting the theory when its consequences shocked not only their intuitions but their most cherished metaphysical preconceptions.[3]

A further consequence for ethics of the mathematical analogy is that *only* an a priori ethical theory can meet the intuitionist's objection that moral obligation must be knowable independently of theory. Any a posteriori theory, to the effect that all actions having the property of being morally obligatory also (as a matter of fact) have some other prop-

2 Prichard, *op. cit.* p. 27.
3 Bishop Berkeley was apparently the first philosopher to plump for common sense in this field; cf. *Philosophical Commentaries*, B 264.

erty, must fail whenever it is shown that some act has, in fact, the one property and not the other. But a theory according to which obligation *entails* the existence of another property is safe against the intuitionist's objection as long as the theory does not conflict with really self-evident moral intuitions; and the number of really self-evident moral intuitions is perhaps smaller than it is sometimes thought to be.

These considerations are sufficient to show that a moral theory of the Kantian type is capable of meeting the intuitionist's objection.[4] We must next determine whether even so Kant has not reduced his theory to absurdity by his casuistical examples.

We shall consider only the two most crucial examples: (1) the wrongness of suicide (*Foundations of the Metaphysics of Morals*, Second Section), and (2) the wrongness of lying to save an innocent man from death ("On a Supposed Right to Lie from Benevolent Motives").

(1) It has often been pointed out that there can be neither a logical nor a "volitional" inconsistency in a man, contemplating suicide, willing also that all men, in like circumstances, should put an end to their lives. Moreover, it has been remarked that there is a scarcely covert appeal to consequences in the words: "One immediately sees a contradiction in a system of nature, whose law would be to destroy life by the feeling whose special office is to impel the improvement of life. In this case it would not exist as nature." Granted that such a system could not exist as a "system of nature," one still needs the premise that existence is better than non-existence, which is presumably what the would-be suicide denies.

I regard these objections as well taken. Do they then disprove the Kantian theory? Not if we are prepared to admit that there is no general moral obligation to refrain from suicide. And I do not see why we should not admit this. Whether there is or is not such an obligation, there is no immediate intuition that suicide is always wrong. Kant, in effect, has made things worse for himself by attempting, as so many

[4] They also show how preposterous is the usual classification of Kant as an ethical intuitionist.

moralists do, to show that his theory has as consequences the whole system of received *mores*. But this should not be the function of a rational moral theory; on the contrary, its most important function should be the discrimination of valid moral insights from mere taboos.

(2) There have been philosophers—Plato is the most notable example—who lived too long. It is regrettable that the repellent fanaticism and casuistry-in-the-bad-sense of the essay "On a Supposed Right to Lie from Benevolent Motives" forces us to place Kant in this category. Surely no one will undertake to defend Kant's conclusion. Hence if that conclusion really follows from his theory, then that theory is convicted of absurdity or worse; for there cannot be any more clear-cut case of an incorrigible ethical intuition than that it is wrong to contribute, by whatever avoidable means, to the murder of an innocent man.

Fortunately, however, it is equally clear that Kant's conclusion not only does not follow from his theory, but is in direct opposition to it. The case presented is one of conflict of duties. This is a problem that Kant nowhere adequately discussed, but it can be rather easily resolved in Kantian terms. There is a duty to tell the truth, and there is a duty to preserve the lives of the innocent. Which takes precedence? What would happen if it were a universal law of nature that every case of truth-telling resulted in someone's undeserved death? If everyone told the truth only once, the human race would be annihilated, and truth-telling with it. This would be as self-defeating as universal lying, to say the least. The only thing that can be said in Kant's defense is that the duty to tell the truth is subject to fewer qualifications than the casuistry of his day and ours would indicate, and Kant's reaction, though excessive, was in the right direction.

Thus, while Kant's own essays in casuistry were sometimes disastrous, it does not follow that his theory was at fault; nor does it follow that his theory does not afford a sound basis for the rehabilitation of rational casuistry—a discipline that could conceivably have some good effects in this wicked, because irrational age.—Provided, of course, that it be suitably re-named.

PART THREE

DISCUSSIONS OF
KANT'S AESTHETIC THEORY

PERCEPTION AND PERFECTION
IN KANT'S AESTHETICS

INGRID STADLER

Obscurity is painful to the mind as well as to the eye.
[David Hume]

Not since the Hegelians has anyone attempted to present the "critical" synthesis in all its grandeur. There is not apt to be another Caird. Nevertheless, there may be another way to tie the end of Kant's three-part Critique to the beginning. The sentence in Hume's *Enquiry* cited above suggests one way to knot one strand or maybe two. I am not inclined to think that what Hume says is so, nor do I wish to argue that it prompted Kant's queries or guided him in his inquiries. But I do think that pondering Hume's remark enables one to understand some little appreciated features of the Kantian system: in particular, how seemingly independent, even apparently conflicting passages scattered through the first and third Critiques are linked with one another. And I shall argue that once the passages that deal with matters pertaining "to the eye" are seen to be thus related, it should become apparent that they are all parts of one coherent undertaking that aims at elucidating and qualifying a view not unlike Hume's about the painfulness of things obscure. Part of my object, then, will be to show that it is possible to trace two lines of argument in which Kant focuses attention on problems that arise when one considers what is accessible to our (human) eye. The other will be to establish my claim that these two should be (although they seem never to have been) treated or critically examined as parts of one whole. For these purposes I have chosen to look upon Kant's arguments as attempts to justify a pair of dis-

tinctions that make common-sense sense: the first, the distinction between primary and secondary qualities; the second,
that between secondary or sense-qualities and the qualities
we tag aesthetic. This paper is accordingly divided into two
main parts. In each I shall rely on the assumption that Kant's
critique of such distinctions is a critical inquiry into certain
relevant types of concepts and capacities and that this inquiry is, among other things, meant to set out and justify
the criteria we implicitly rely on in drawing the distinction
in question. If I succeed, I will have shown that this justification ends by being an illuminating critique of the belief
that "obscurity is painful to the mind as well as to the
eye".

I should like to clarify a few things at the outset. The first
is that what follows is not, in its present form, properly a
contribution to Kant scholarship, and is not meant to be.
Although it contains references to familiar interpretations of
Kant's philosophy, I make no claims for the justice of my
representations of their author's views, nor shall I attempt
to support or contest the details of their reasoning. I shall
simply use these views as anchors for my own. The second
is that I ought to speak in terms of what *a* Kant (rather
than of what Kant) would argue about a given point. The
reason is that I shall be taking for granted a great deal about
Kant's actual position on a number of broad and basic issues, and consequently, in discussing various passages that
deal with the relatively specific and less central issues on
which I wish to focus, I shall be saying only what someone
holding Kant's *sort* of view would find perplexing with respect to the matter at hand, would wish to argue or maintain,
etc. I hope that the Kant that emerges is recognizably the one
and only Kant; though it would be foolhardy to try and prove
it here. Thus, all I am entitled to claim for my thesis, is
that it helps one see how much one may learn from Kant's
scattered discussions about the three types of qualities implicated in the distinctions "primary/secondary" and "sense/
aesthetic" if one regards them as all being parts of a single
project. My thesis is that this project consists of the attempt
to formulate a theory about the perfection of conception and
the perfection of perception (the "mind" and "eye" of

Hume's remark): a theory that will elucidate these twin notions and indicate what makes it reasonable to operate with the distinctions associated with them. (Indeed, Parts I and II of this paper might have been headed: "The Perfection of Conception" and "The Perfection of Perception".) Third, I should like to mention that I have found it useful to distinguish at various places between two approaches to the problems that give shape to the pattern of my argument, which I have labeled "logical" and "epistemological." Without explaining these labels at length, I think it can be shown that I use the term "logical" as Kant uses it in his *Lectures on Logic*; and that the difference in approach I have in mind is in keeping with the rationale for example of Kant's including both a "metaphysical" and a "transcendental exposition" of the ideas of space and time in the "Transcendental Aesthetic," and both a "metaphysical" and a "transcendental deduction of the categories" in the "Transcendental Analytic" of his first Critique.

Finally, I should like to shield this paper against some objections to which I know it to be vulnerable: in particular, the charge that I have cursorily, at times even cavalierly, treated issues that deserve something better. My defense is simply that I am here primarily concerned to argue for a relatively broad (possibly too broad) thesis and that detailing each step of the over-all arguments would make it impossible to attain my principal objective.

I. PRIMARY/SECONDARY QUALITIES

I.o. Refinements apart, the classical philosophical doctrine of primary and secondary qualities (which I shall call for short "the two quality doctrine") is a doctrine that purports to establish that there are two radically different kinds of qualities, that judgments concerning for example a thing's shape or size differ radically in status from judgments concerning for example its color, taste or smell.[1] The doctrine

[1] Unfortunately all this was written before I had an opportunity to read Jonathan Bennett's incisive and thoroughly impressive "Sub-

may take many forms. It has provoked discussions and debates on a variety of levels and in a variety of modes of discourse, and a good many of these have been carried on in the name of Kant: many evidently suppose that Kant subscribes to the doctrine, while others charge that he fails to take an unambiguous stand. By examining these discussions, it should be possible to clarify some of the problems engendered by the doctrine and to indicate what may be learned from Kant's attempts to grapple with them. This is what I attempt to do in I.1–4.

It is, however, in many ways a vexing business, in part because the major problems raise further, not always smaller ones, which raise other problems still, and also because there is no clear, obvious place to start, and little, if anything, to take for granted or as generally accepted. Even so it seems worth leaping in. Besides, when one reflects with care upon the tradition of discussions or the traditional discussions a few guidelines emerge. One of these connects with the fact that, to my knowledge, no one has said that Kant plainly did not subscribe to anything like the classical two-quality doctrine; another with the fact that it would clearly be wrong to suppose that Kant could consistently subscribe to the letter of that doctrine as expressed by Galileo when he said that

> tastes, smells, colors, and so on, regarded as the properties of objects are mere names: their true location is, rather, in the sensitive body [of the observer]—so that if every living thing were taken away, all these qualities would vanish and be destroyed.[2]

For it is surely one of the cornerstones of the Critical System that we literally cannot be said to know anything about the world as it would be if "every living thing were taken away." And finally it seems to me safe to assume that if

---

stance, Reality, and Primary Qualities," *American Philosophical Quarterly*, Vol. 2, No. 1 (January 1965), 1–17. As it stands, my paper relies heavily on what was said in a seminar led by Paul Grice a number of years ago.

[2] S. Toulmin and J. Goodfield, *The Architecture of Matter*, New York, 1963, p. 175.

Kant does subscribe to a version of the two-quality doctrine[3] it must be one that preserves the point of Galileo's and Descartes' and Locke's distinction between the so-called primary and secondary qualities, but (*a*) cancels the sceptical implications of Locke's remarks about the "something I know not what" to which the primary or scientifically determinable qualities are "presumed to belong," and (*b*) does not entail that all our concepts of spatio-temporal things, or of the entities that form the subject matter of (Newtonian?) science, are *mere* constructs, merely convenient fictions. In sum, I shall take it that there is some truth in what has traditionally been said about Kant's position and something to be learned from the controversies that center on the question: Does he or does he not make plain where he stands and what makes it right to stand just there? But in considering this question I shall be little concerned with the evidence that has been adduced in support of one answer or another. I shall instead focus attention on something toward which the traditional critical discussions rightly point, viz.: that Kant was genuinely troubled by the doctrine and not prepared to make a simple pronouncement about its truth or falsity. This is, I think, amply borne out by his writings: by numerous passages in the first Critique (*K.R.*), and by many in the *Critique of Judgment* (*K.U.*),[4] and in the latter perhaps most conspicuously by the passages that virtually repeat what is said in *K.R.* about the ideals of science and clearly echo what is said in the *Lectures on Logic* about "the perfection of conception." The thesis I shall try to establish is that Kant inclined toward accepting a transformed version of the classical doc-

[3] I nowhere try to specify which qualities are which. That colors, smells, etc. belong on one side, and mathematical determinations of weight, shape, etc. on the other is all I need for my argument.

[4] I have used the following abbreviations: for *The Critique of Pure Reason*, K.R.; for *The Critique of Aesthetic Judgment*, K.U. All references to Kant's works are based on the following standard English translations. When I have used my own revised translation, I have so indicated.

Critique of Aesthetic Judgment, tr. J. C. Meredith, Oxford, 1911.
Critique of Pure Reason, tr. N. Kemp Smith, London, 1950.
Introduction to Logic, tr. T. K. Abbott, London, 1963.
Prolegomena to Any Future Metaphysics, New York, 1951.

trine after raising and trying to answer two basically different
sorts of questions about it and, as a sort of corollary, that
one of these—a question whose double-facetedness seems to
have gone largely unnoticed—seems to underlie most of the
traditional discussions of Kant's views.

I.1   Much traditional discussion of whether Kant deems the
two-quality distinction "critically" respectable, that is, deems
it to rest on a sound foundation, has centered on the topic:
Are qualities like colors, tastes, or smells, "subjective"? I, too,
shall consider it, but not because I am convinced that to
ask whether Kant is a "subjectivist" about secondary qualities (or "sense qualities," after Paton) is *the* central or even
a good question. Indeed it should become quite clear that
I do not think it a good question, or that I consider it good
only because of its flaws. But the many remarks about Kant's
"subjectivism" in the literature provide some justification for
taking this allegation as the starting point in a re-examination
of his views about perceptible qualities, in particular, about
sensorily detectable or discernible ones. Locke's arguments
especially in Book II of the *Essay* also lend some support.
For Locke probably did more than anyone else to put the
two-quality doctrine on the philosophical map and devoted
virtually all his energies to making out a convincing case for
his thesis about the secondary ones, and his arguments to the
effect that there are no qualities *in* things "resembling" our
"ideas" of colors, tastes, etc. are one of the most conspicuous and problematical features of his legacy. Although I shall
not try to indicate why his arguments might aptly be described as arguments for "subjectivism," what I want to get
at in Kant can be reached by considering the reasons why
one might think it a label that fits Kant. Further, by focusing
attention on this leg of the distinction, it should be possible
to bring to light the transitions about which I am primarily
concerned and to develop my thesis that Kant's K.R. arguments about sense qualities invite disputations of the sort I
shall consider—and that they do so partly because K.R. leaves
some questions dangling; understandably, if one sees the first
Critique in its entirety as an attempt to raise and answer
questions about the powers and limitations of the Human

Understanding (or, as I am tempted to put it here: as devoted to matters pertaining to the perfection of cognition, and not, or only secondarily to the perfection of perception). If I am right, the K.R. account does not tell the whole Kantian story. I do not, however, mean that there is nothing of schizophrenia in the first Critique chapter of that story, to which I shall now turn.

Something about the first Critique must make it fairly plausible to maintain that it was Kant's view that "sense qualities are purely subjective and [can] in no sense be attributed to objects."[5] Paton is not an unsympathetic reader and statements like his recur throughout the Vahinger-Kemp Smith tradition and may be found as well in more recent books, for example in Weldon and in Körner.[6] Paton evidently thinks that Kant held such a view owing to his acceptance of the classical two-quality doctrine which, in Paton's words "has been forced upon men's minds by the success of the sciences, and especially of physics".[7] Kemp Smith's infamous "patchwork thesis" is directly implicated in his charge that Kant "wavers," takes "alternative," even conflicting stands;[8] but in his *Commentary* on K.R. allegations of "subjectivism" seem less intimately tied to a conception of the

[5] H. J. Paton, *Kant's Metaphysic of Experience*, London, 1936, p. 73.
[6] N. Kemp Smith, *A Commentary to Kant's Critique of Pure Reason*, London, 1929. Cf. esp. pp. 83, 121–22, 146–48, 306. But he throughout stresses the "waverings" in Kant's statements about the objectivity of the things we may be said to know. Cf. T. D. Weldon, *Kant's Critique of Pure Reason*, Oxford, 1958, esp. pp. 182, 289; S. Körner, *Kant*, Hammondsworth, 1955, esp. pp. 48 ff.
[7] Paton, p. 60. But in the next paragraph he says: "[Kant's] own Critical doctrine, however, is that we must distinguish, not two things but three: (1) the secondary qualities which depend on our individual sense organs and on our position in space; (2) the primary qualities, which are objective and common to all men . . . ; (3) the thing-in-itself, which is what it is independently of the human mind. . . ."
[8] Cf. Kemp Smith, *passim*, but esp. pp. 101–3, 121–22, 272–80. His attempt to draw a distinction between what he calls "subjectivism" and "phenomenalism" may further confuse the whole confusing issue. I hope that by not availing myself of his distinction I shall not end by creating chaos. I rather think not.

philosophical significance of Newtonian science. Körner seems ready to diagnose ambiguity in Kant's pronouncements, but does not merely chime in with his commentary-writing predecessors. His conclusions seem to result from attempting a rational reconstruction of Kant's theory of meaning to make it make sense to Körner's, and our, non-historically minded contemporaries, which may give these conclusions quite a different sort of significance and mean that if they are wrong, they are wrong for quite different reasons. What reasons are there for saying that Kant retains, even that it never occurred to him to doubt, the then-current view about the subjectivity of sensations?[9] What evidence exists for construing what he says as an attempt to show that the so-called secondary qualities should be distinguished from the primary because they are "subjective" or "purely subjective" or "private"? There have been attempts to defend what I shall now call the Subjectivity Thesis (S.T.) on the grounds that sensation is "dependent on the nature of our sensibility"; but that falls very far short of defending the familiar version of the primary/secondary quality distinction, as Berkeley partly saw, and as G. E. Moore may help one to see more clearly.[10] Nor does it help to be told that for Kant "the objects apprehended through sense are real, only not in their sensuous form": for this, if I understand it rightly, is simply false.[11] There are

[9] Kemp Smith, *passim;* L. W. Beck, *Studies in the Philosophy of Kant,* New York, 1965, p. 20; Körner, p. 165.

[10] It might be useful to recall the arguments adduced by G. E. Moore in his "Refutation of Idealism," in particular the one he uses to explain why the proposition *"Esse* is *percipi"* involves, or appears to involve, a contradiction if it is taken as expressing an analytic truth,—e.g. that the proposition "Yellow can never be apart from the sensation of yellow" amounts to "Yellow can never be other than yellow"—since one is, in formulating that proposition, implying that the sensation of yellow is distinguishable from the quality (G. E. Moore, *Philosophical Studies,* New York, 1922, esp. pp. 1–17). Moore is surely right regarding the ambiguity of that proposition. What he says about construing the Idealist formula as analytic should keep one from reading the proposition(s) here under discussion as being analytic. Kant's repeated warnings about the role of definitions in a philosophical argument are probably more to the point.

[11] Cf. Kemp Smith, pp. 88 ff. It does seem to be one of the alternatives he thinks worth taking seriously.

passages in K.R. that may seem to substantiate S.T. for example:

> The taste of wine does not belong to the objective determination of the wine . . . but to the special constitution of sense in the Subject tasting it. Colors are not properties of the bodies to the intuitions of which they are attached, but only modifications of the sense of sight, which is affected in a certain manner by light. . . .
> [A 28–29]

One might even say that Kant argues for it quite explicitly in saying that

> Sensations of colors, sounds and heat, since they are . . . mere sensations . . . do not of themselves yield knowledge of any object. [B 44–45]

And there are other similar, although more ambiguous passages: for example at *Prolegomena* #13, Remark II, #49; in the argument of the fourth Paralogism; at K.R. A 320=B 376. But to suppose that citing passages like these will suffice to establish S.T. is an enormous blunder, since the question S.T. is meant to answer is not unlike "When did you stop beating your grandmother?" To accept it as straightforward is virtually bound to land one in the mud. For there are at least three distinct things that one may be calling into question when one asks: "Are colors, tastes, etc. 'subjective'?" And Kant has something not always clear or simple to say to each. Roughly, the three I have in mind and shall take up in I.2–4 may be put thus:

1. Do things genuinely have, for example, colors, tastes, etc.?

2. Do things genuinely have the colors, tastes, etc. they appear to us to have?

3. Does noting or telling about the color something is or has genuinely enlighten us about it?

There may well be relationships among these three questions, or among the consequences of answers to them. But the linkages between them are not such that considerations central in answering one logically force the issue respecting some other, and Kant did not, in an obvious way, fail to

keep separate what is separable. Indeed, when one looks at
the over-all layout of K.R., the broad divisions in the text,
the order and the way topics are taken up and dropped and
taken up again (e.g. the discussion about space in the Transcendental Aesthetic; the remarks about "the concept of space"
in the opening sections of the Transcendental Deduction of
the categories, viz. that the "[pure concepts of the under-
standing] . . . owing to their tendency to employ the concept of space beyond the conditions of sensible intuition
. . . render it ambiguous" (A 88=B 121); the arguments
about the idea of space in the Antinomies; etc.), there is
reason to suppose that the scattering of passages relevant to
the primary/secondary quality distinction is not random; that
the rationale underlying it becomes intelligible when one
considers the differences among questions ##1–3. But
there is yet a fourth and radically different type of query:

4. Does noting or learning about a thing's color(s) afford
reasonable grounds for modifying or altering our concept of
a thing of that kind?

About this, which I shall tag the "logical" question, and
which has not, to my knowledge, been discussed in the better
known interpretations of Kant's position, I shall have a good
deal to say. Of questions ##1–3, #1 may, I think, be
safely set aside a while, as it points in an un-Kantian direction. In I.2 I shall take up #3, construing it as questioning
the importance of judgments concerning sense qualities; that
is, their importance as contributors to our knowledge of the
world of spatio-temporal things. Question #2, which I take as
an instance of a typical "critical" question of the sort Kant's
Transcendental Deductions are, among other things, meant
to answer, is the concern of I.3.

I.2   If S.T. is interpreted as being, albeit covertly, a thesis
about the value or importance of noting or telling about
colors, tastes, or smells, the passages from K.R. cited in I.1
become directly relevant, especially: "Sensations of colors
. . . do not of themselves yield knowledge of any object."
It certainly looks as though Kant is there saying that he would
not be prepared to accept as genuinely informative my stating

for example that something is yellow. Since one might independently of Kant think this a reasonable stand, and expect a Kant to argue that such judgments are not in general capable of really contributing to any normal adult's knowledge or understanding of the world of his everyday experiences, one might find a yet stronger claim implicit in his words, viz. that to see or note something's color is not to see or note anything that should be accounted a proper fact about it. One might, however, discern an error in proceeding from the seemingly innocuous premise "It is not illuminating to be told of something that it is yellow" to the conclusion "To tell what color something is, is not to state a (proper) fact about it." A (Kantian) paralogism? Does it not exploit an ambiguity in the word 'something' (which is used as a mere dummy term or place-holder; and also as shorthand for "some thing, i.e. some physical or material thing")? One would be right, I think, to object on such grounds, although they may strike one as sophistical. In any event there is another more roundabout but more convincing way to show where such an argument goes wrong.

Consider the alleged conclusion, "To tell what color something is . . ."; and compare what it appears to signify with what Kant says in several places in *K.U.* There is, for example, his remark that "The green color of the meadows belongs to objective sensation, as the perception of an object of Sensibility," and the fact that it occurs right after a paragraph in which he argues, quite explicitly, that what one apprehends when one apprehends a color *is* "available for cognition."[12] Elsewhere he says, "The referent of any idea, even one of sensation, may be objective . . . save only that of a feeling of pleasure or displeasure, which designates nothing in any object. . . ."[13]

[12] *K.U.*, #3, 1. 206–7.

[13] The first passage cited here is reminiscent of Vahinger's by now legendary praise for the greatness that shows itself in Kant's lack of concern about self-consistency; the second is suggested by Kemp Smith's endorsement of the "patchwork theory" and by some of Beck's remarks about the changes in Kant's position between the writing of the first Critique and that of the second; the third seems a natural extension of Körner's observation that "a comparison be-

The tone of the passages from which these quotations are taken is *not* calculated to leave one with the impression that Kant is here concerned to establish the claim that seeing or noting a color cannot ever tell anyone anything about any something whatsoever. (What someone's color description may tell about his "inner" or mental state is not here in question.) And unless one wants to argue, as I do not, that Kant changed his mind about the relevant issues in the years between the writing of his first and third Critiques, or that he uses the key terms 'objective' and 'subjective' with significantly different meanings in the two,[14] it seems that on the interpretation of S.T. as a thesis about the importance for our knowledge of various specifiable classes of descriptions, K.U. makes it obvious that the Kantian version of S.T. should not be described along such lines as: Judgments or propositions in which terms for Lockean secondary qualities function as predicates are to be adjudged "subjective" because they are inevitably uninformative. And if such a description is unpermissible it would also be incorrect to infer from the passages in the K.R. Aesthetic that Kant is maintaining that we should never be justified in regarding such a judgment as competent to convey what we should call a fact.

Two sorts of considerations may help clarify this last sug-

---

tween practical and theoretical objectivity lacks any even moderately precise standard." Cf. Kemp Smith, *passim*; Beck, p. 20; Körner, p. 178.

[14] There is doubtless no such thing as *the* "subjectivist theory" of anything. Sometimes that label is used to cover any putative definition of a term in the statement of which a reference is made to the psychological state, condition, or to the attitudes or feelings of some human being. Thus, e.g. when it is argued that "*x* is good" just means that I, or you, or most of us, or everyone, or the right sorts of people, like *x*. I take it that what is being argued for may be called a subjectivist theory about the good, or the expression "is good," or about the relevant concept. It is something like this that commentators and critics of Kant appear to have in mind when they talk about the subjectivity of sense qualities. There are far more problems here than I would dream of trying to tackle. But I shall use the label anyway. But cf. fn. 10 above, for Kant does not confound sensation (the mental process, act) with the sense-quality (the "object" sensed, or apprehended).

gestion. For neither need one go beyond the K.R. Aesthetic: one is found in the many places where Kant speaks of sense-qualities ("Sensation" = sensa) as the "matter" of, or as supplying the "materials" for, knowledge; the other in the "General Observations on the Transcendental Aesthetic." It is particularly noteworthy that in these Observations one finds Kant observing that several "common" distinctions, for example, between what is "essentially inherent in . . . [and] belongs only accidentally to [an] intuition" (A 45=B 62), between illusory and veridical perception (B 70), are "merely empirical" and "pragmatic." These are I take it "common" not so much because they are common-sensical but because they are philosophical commonplaces. Inasmuch as they are, as "commonly" understood (by Kant's mostly English-speaking predecessors or mentors), knotted up with the rationale underlying the two-quality doctrine, it seems reasonable to suppose that Kant would say of the primary/secondary quality distinction what he says of the others, viz. that for it to be significant it must have some basis in actual experience. In that event the criteria we implicitly rely on in deploying that distinction become relevant.

But when one reflects on the relevant practices, it becomes apparent that no simple formula will succeed in expressing the basis for that distinction. Consider, for example, what we should say about a proposition of the form "That is yellow," uttered by S. (*a*) when hypnogic imagery is known to be occurring, (*b*) when there is a barely visible clump of grasses in the distance, (*c*) when S. is looking at a screen on which he knows that someone else is projecting mingled red and green lights. It would surely be a distortion to maintain that we would adjudge that proposition to have o information-power in all three circumstances. And would it not also be a distortion to maintain that we are incapable of discerning an ambiguity in the propositional function "that *x* is yellow" that we do not distinguish between cases where the value for *x* or the range of *x* is something identifiable as the object of thought, and ones where it is restricted to physical or material things? I think so. Hence if Kant regarded the primary/secondary quality distinction as being on a par with the appearance/reality distinction and the others he explicitly mentions, it would be absurd to suppose that he would categorically debar color descriptions and the like from being competent to convey facts. Indeed on the supposition that he would be prepared to accept the point of my three examples, the seeming conflict between the *K.R.* and *K.U.* pronouncements vanishes. That is, it vanishes if one takes the *K.R.* Kant to be talking about the sorts of situations in which a remark about a thing's color is made by way of reply to a question about a thing's physical properties and sets the *K.U.* pronouncements into the context of a discussion about how something looks (thus, e.g. a meadow may look green all over even when there are variously colored weeds among the grasses, but on a sunny summer day a distant isolated clump of grasses may appear yellow to persons of normal eyesight, etc. *ergo*: a color may, as Kant puts it, "belong to objective sensation" (*K.U.*), even though for someone sharing the central concerns of *K.R.* it would make sense to say that seeing something's color "does not as such contribute to knowledge"). I shall return to this in II, below. But here one rider should be added, given the opening remarks about what Kant means by "appearance" (his term for "the undetermined [or indeterminate] object of empirical intuition" [A 20=B 34]), and the claim that "the manifold of sensibility" is what we strive to understand. For in the light of this it is highly unlikely that Kant would deny, even in the context of *K.R.*, that comparing the colors of two insects' bodies and noting that one is all yellow and the other not entirely so, enables one to tell the hornet from the bee, or would refuse to assent to the proposition that in suitable circumstances pointing out *differences* in color contributes to someone's knowledge of [material, physical] objects," or counts as being genuinely informative about them. (Cf. e.g. A 266=B 322 where it is said that "'matter' signifies the determinable in general, ['form'] its determination.")

I.3 I have been attempting to indicate reasons why one need not assume that Kant is committed to the view that descriptions in terms of colors, tastes, etc. are of no genuine cognitive value. It would be advantageous to complete a list of such reasons, in that it would quash the idea that, if it is the notion of absolute lack of information power that is involved in by dubbing Kant a "subjectivist" about sense qualities, he clearly is one. But doing so would not show that there are no counterindications, and indeed there are counterindications; the most forceful appear in the various passages giving a foothold to the by now legendary ideas about Kant's reverential attitude toward Newton. That foothold may appear the stronger when one remembers that by Kant's time the physical sciences could be formulated as a system of mathematical equations relating such quantities as force and momentum. One may then leave the "Analytic of Principles" feeling pretty much convinced that Kant would have wished that we expunge all mention of Lockean secondary qualities from serious theorizing about physical reality. Or, to put it slightly less fancifully: one might, after pondering the first two Kantian Principles, the "Axioms" and "Anticipations," be left with the impression that in Kant's ideal universe, the Enlightened would agree that terms for Lockean secondary qualities are strictly dispensable. For the "Analogies" *are* intimately connected with "the laws of general dynamics" (B 202) as has often been noted. And the first two Principles, the "mathematical" ones, are supposed to justify the description of qualitative differences in quantitative terms. Moreover, by calling them "mathematical" (as distinct from "dynamical"), and "constitutive" (as distinct from "regulative"), Kant apparently means to point up the dual aspect of the thesis that they express, viz. not only (*a*) that they concern the philosophical consequences of the measure of success with which scientists describe perceptible phenomena in mathematical terms, but also (*b*) that we are entitled to claim to know in advance of any possible "experience" that it admits of being thus described (and he seems to make no such claim for colors and the like). It is also relevant that this dual thesis serves to elaborate on the Kantian assertion that "knowledge is a whole in which representations stand compared and connected." In light of this the argument of the Principles carries the implication that only what has been expressed in mathematical propositions or equations can be incorporated into that whole which is the whole of knowledge. This, in its turn, implies that it was Kant's view that ideally there need be no mention of Lockean secondary qualities in the mansions of science; hence that whatever explanatory or descriptive power the propositions of science have is absent from ordinary "qualitative" propositions. But to conclude that *therefore* propositions of the latter sort are somehow inherently defective or uninformative *simpliciter* would clearly be a mistake (tempting as it might seem). Such a conclusion would confuse Kant's idea about the possible value of translating a non-scientific proposition into the accepted symbolism of science with a thesis about the possibility of transforming, without change in meaning, any non-mathematical "qualitative" description into a scientific (=mathematical) one.

To argue this point in detail falls outside the scope of this paper. I should, however, like to inject a few comments that may help silence some unfortunate, even foolish, objections that are too often raised in connection with the second of the mathematical Principles, the "Anticipations of Perception," where Kant argues that "intensive magnitudes" admit of measurement; cf. esp. A 166–172=B 208–214. Kant may have been wrong in supposing, if he did, that e.g. brightness is a function only of the intensity of light falling on a given region of the retina at a certain time; that is, wrong in supposing that there is a simple 1:1 correlation between phenomenal or directly apprehended brightness and intensity. We now know that light intensity is not the only determining factor; that such things as the state of adaptation of the eye, various relatively complex conditions determining the contrast between a given object or patch of light and what surrounds it are also involved; that brightness may be a function of color [e.g. the so-called spectral-luminosity curve, which shows that if presented with lights of different colors but the same intensity, one will see those in the middle of the spectrum as brighter], etc. But even so it is surely not silly to argue, as Kant does, that qualitative differences of the sort he terms differences in "intensive magnitude" are correlatable with numerically describable ones. Further, even if one finds scientific explanations, e.g. of the relation between the so-called phenomenal or directly apprehended brightness and the physical objects producing these visual experiences couched in a terminology invoking the relational concepts "is similar to," "corresponds to," etc. and even if one should expect or find a Kant unflinchingly accepting such formulations, this need not mean that he is distrustful of Lockean "ideas of sense" for Lockean reasons; nor does it follow that he is thereby (logically) committing himself to the so-called "double-affection" theory. Some of this may become clearer below.

What bears more directly on my immediate goals is the fact that there are no compelling textual grounds for viewing the over-all argument of the Principles as an argument primarily purporting to establish that if one wants a just, informed assessment of the illumination-power of qualitative descriptions, it is requisite that one contrast them in this respect with the propositions or judgments that, so to speak, reside in the inner quarters of science proper. By proceeding in this way the contrast may become sharpest. But the relevant point is that, even at its most dramatic, it hardly warrants anything but a conclusion couched in comparatives. That descriptions of one sort, or in one symbolism or language, are better (more enlightening, informative, etc.) than some others does not entail that they are good (or perfect) *simpliciter*, nor that the others are worthless (or, in an absolutistic tone of voice, ". . . of minimal value"). If Kant had wanted to establish that conclusion he would have needed different grounds. He may have thought that he had such grounds. But it may also be that the conclusion for which he meant to marshal arguments is not this one, but similar by virtue of being suggested by reflection on some salient features of the fundamental propositions of Newtonian science. I shall now turn to these arguments and to that interpretation of S.T. that I think associated with them. (I shall have to be brief and therefore must presuppose considerable familiarity with the deservedly notorious "windings and twistings of the Transcendental Deductions," the mastery of which Paton has likened to the exhausting task of "crossing . . . the Great Arabian Desert".[15] Controversies

[15] Quoted in T. D. Weldon, *Kant's Critique of Pure Reason*, Oxford, 1958, p. 152.

about significant differences between the Deductions in A
and B will also have to be put to one side.)

I suggested earlier that S.T. may be addressed to a typically
"critical" question about the justification for, or philosophical
implications of, our doing certain things we may rightly be
said to do. Thus I said that S.T. is interpretable as a thesis
concerned with what one should call into question in our
being entitled to claim to know e.g. that something has the
color it appears to have. In I.1. I suggested that it may be
important to distinguish the meaning of three questions. #2
is the one for discussion here, viz. Do things genuinely possess
the colors they appear to us to have? Although perhaps helpful there, that formulation of the question may prove misleading here; hence I prefer not to stress it. To reformulate
it as I have just done may make it seem superfluous to argue
that such questioning calls attention to an issue that should
have concerned Kant, or that it helps make manifest one
aspect of the problem(s) generated by the two-quality doctrine as this presented itself to Kant. The truth is rather that
it proves too simple or too complex (*ergo* the parenthetical
comments above). A compromise may suffice: merely to say
that there is textual support not only in the Principles and
in "The Amphiboly of Concepts of Reflection," especially in
the passages purporting to point to the respects in which
science (on sound "critical" principles) improves upon
our everyday non-scientific picture of things (cf. esp.
A 285=B 351, also B 273 and 521); and to indicate the relevance of some passages in the Deductions. One that chiefly
concerns me is the following in which Kant says that

> if cinnabar were sometimes red, sometimes black . . .
> my empirical imagination would never be capable of
> bringing to mind heavy cinnabar when I see something
> red.   [A 101]

Eventually we will see how this connects with Kant's later
statement that

> Anyone who has familiarized himself with these distinc-
> tions [including that between "empirical and pure con-
> cepts [Begriffe]" and between these and "an idea [Idee]

or concept [Begriff] of reason [Verstand]"] must find it intolerable to hear the representation [Vorstellung] of the color red called an idea. It should not even be called a Notion (concept of understanding [Verstandesbegriff]).

> [A 320=B 377. The brackets are mine;
> the parentheses, Kant's.]

But in I.3 I should like to restrict the focus of attention to the Kantian remark about cinnabar, which becomes significant when one examines it in the light of the crucial Deduction statement that

> the object is [to be] viewed as that which prevents [was dawider ist, dass] our cognitions [Erkäntnisse] from being haphazardly or arbitrarily . . . determined, inasmuch as, if they are to have reference to an object they must have that harmony [Übereinstimmung], i.e. that unity, which constitutes the concept of an object. [A 105. Kemp Smith's translation is somewhat different. Mine, although not a lesser barbarism, accords with the German text and may be less apt to obscure
> its spirit.]

To guard against misapprehensions, it should be mentioned first that the context in which Kant's cinnabar story occurs makes it evident that it is primarily intended to help make a point about the orderliness of nature. What chiefly matters for the present argument is not the (simple) fact that cinnabar is red, but the (complex) fact that it is not at one moment red and then at some other time some other color. And this latter matters insofar as it exemplifies a truth Kant seems to think we may be tempted (in philosophy?) to belittle or ignore, viz. that we all must in some sense know that there are regularities in nature, that it would be inconceivable that everything "in the course of nature" might change randomly (Was Hume guilty of this? cf. the *Enquiry*, especially IV). Of the other things that might be said about it, two seem to be of particular interest. The first is tricky because the exegetical procedures on which it relies are open to criticism. By the choice of this particular example a covert reference to Newton's published writings is imported into the Critique argument. That may of course be a mere accident, or it may have occurred simply because Kant was up on some then-current scientific discussions about what Newton termed the "elective-attractions" among atomic particles. But in speculating about this process, Newton does refer to the possibility of extracting mercury from cinnabar by the addition of quicklime, saying that it exemplifies the process (the quicklime "'by a stronger Attraction' detaches the sulphur from the cinnabar, and so 'lets go the Mercury'").[16] I do *not* want to argue that the Newtonian echo is brought in by design, or that it should have a direct bearing on one's assessment of the argument as presented in *K.R.* But it does seem not totally irrelevant for *understanding* what Kant may have been driving at and may at least be of value as a check against possible *mis*understandings. Specifically it may be not only symptomatic of a general uneasiness about the two-quality doctrine but an indication of a constructive attempt to show that color attributions should be accorded the same status as descriptions of things in terms of their shapes or measurable sizes. In saying what he does, Kant does seem to be licensing support of a claim that one can class or identify something by pointing to its color. If Körner's avowedly "rough outline" of Kant's derivation of the Categories and of the "procedure" for distinguishing between "judgments of perception" and "judgments of experience" is even roughly right, one should expect exactly this and should be able to explain it without appeals to extratextual authority (I have, I admit, also been assuming that Newton knew that cinnabar is used to make a color pigment, vermilion). In connection with what he terms Kant's "procedure" Körner writes:

> For example, by subtracting 'This is a substance with accidental properties' from 'This stone is heavy' or 'This is a heavy stone' we get the perceptual judgment 'This seems a heavy stone to me'.[17]

And when he remarks elsewhere in his book that

> Kant sees the difference between merely subjective perceptual judgments and objective empirical judgments in

---

[16] Toulmin and Goodfield, pp. 189–90.
[17] Körner, p. 56.

the fact that the latter involve, as the former do not, the application of the Categories.[18]

he is, I believe, taking it for a fact that that "merely subjective perceptual . . ."/"objective empirical . . ." dichotomy is at work in K.R. as well as in the *Prolegomena* even though the relevant *Prolegomena* distinction does not appear in K.R. A detailed critique of Körner's picture would be out of place here (and since a penguin is a penguin might anyway prove a bit unfair), but the general picture is worth considering because if it is right my thesis is plainly false, and the problem I see in Kant is simply not there. Unlike Weldon who in a kinder mood tries to help Kant out, saying that his

> epistemological vocabulary . . . is far too simple to do the job he requires of it. He just has not enough words with which to draw the distinctions within 'perceiving' which he must draw in order to expound his concept of the 'object of perception',[19]

Körner faces the issue squarely, and by slashing the class of all empirical judgments in two with a few bold strokes should make it painfully obvious that the *Prolegomena* distinction, if that is the *Prolegomena* distinction, will not do. Is "That is red" exactly like "This stone is heavy"? Surely not in all significant respects. One relevant difference is reflected in the fact that "How heavy?" is not as like or as unlike "How red?" as it may seem. But this feature of the Körner distinction is not now of principal concern; I mention it chiefly for the sake of things to come, when I shall insist that we ought to protest (even if Kant did not) that the two propositions "This stone is heavy" and "That is red" are not obviously on a logical or philosophical par. More to the point at this juncture is that if Körner's sharp dichotomy adequately represents the pattern of Kant's argument, what Kant is saying when he points out that it is not the case that cinnabar "is sometimes red, [and] sometimes black" poses no problem for the Critical philosophy and makes traditional proponents of S.T. out to be thoroughly misguided insofar as they maintain that

[18] Körner, p. 100.
[19] Weldon, p. 127.

Kant does not want to defend the claim that color attributions are objective. I feel reluctant to dismiss that thesis quite
so readily. One way to see that this version of S.T. may have
some textual basis is by considering the following: Is one, by
acknowledging that its deep red color is one of the identifying
"marks" of cinnabar, thereby committed to maintaining that
the proposition "That (It) is red" should be accounted objective on any occasion provided only that normal conditions
obtain, i.e. (roughly) normal illumination, normal distance,
a normal observer with normal color vision and a normal interest in getting it right? I think that a ready "Yes" may be-
speak a confusion, and that Kant would not only not reply
"Yes" but that he is concerned about distinguishing two sorts
of relevant consideration. I shall now deal with half this
claim. The other half is taken up in I.4 supplemented by a
major portion of II.

Suppose it is agreed, in the abstract as it were, that a deep
red color is one of the identifying "marks" (Kant's term; we
should probably say "criterion") of cinnabar, at least partly
because this is *ex hypothesi* one of its relatively stable properties. Suppose it is also agreed, also in the abstract, that
cinnabar is a source of mercury. Now consider the following
situation. Having identified a chunk of stuff as cinnabar, A
replies to my question about how he knows it is by saying "It
is red"; B, in similar circumstances, says "We can extract
mercury from it by introducing quicklime." And now suppose
that C, having given an A-type answer, being a philosopher,
asks himself: "No one objects to my calling it red, but is it?",
while D, a similar creature, gives a B-type answer and queries:
"No one objects to my saying that introducing quicklime
causes the freeing of the sulphur, but is the quicklime (more
precisely for Kant: the introducing of the quicklime) the
cause . . . ?" C's and D's queries may seem to be of radically
different stripes. With the right sort of stress on "cause,"
D's takes shape as a typically Humian query, a sceptical query
of the sort Kant explicitly set out to answer and for the
answering of which the whole of his Categorical machinery is
allegedly required. C's, on the other hand, is apt to awaken
thoughts of Locke and my question #1 from I.1, viz. "Do
things genuinely have colors?" It might nowadays also pro-

voke an objection to the effect that *C*'s "No one objects to my calling it red, but is it?" is senseless or misguided because (roughly) something just is red if it is unobjectionable to call it red; this is what the expression 'is red' means. I agree that it is probably correct to regard both as sceptical queries, and probably historically correct to see Hume in *D*'s and Locke in *C*'s, but do not agree that by accepting *C*'s query one is inevitably led to the sort of scepticism Berkeley thought he found in Locke. In any event it seems to make sense to look on *C* as expressing a doubt about the objectivity of the proposition "It is red" (expressed also in *A*'s reply), and on *D* as harboring a similar doubt about the proposition "We can extract mercury from it by introducing quicklime" (also expressed by *B*). As for the objection that *D*'s is not a genuine query, it should be sufficient to indicate that Kant would not have rejected it on such grounds: to suppose he would have involves mistaking him for an "ordinary language" philosopher, which he is not. But even leaving Kant to one side, something is seriously amiss with that objection, for it is a necessary, but not a sufficient, condition for rightly deeming something red that it be linguistically correct to speak of its looking red to someone.[20]

What, then, could one say to assuage *C*'s and *D*'s sceptical doubts? Perhaps one should begin by reminding both that it would not seem unreasonable of either *A* or *B* to expect the assent of others, and that both judgments would normally be understood by others as intended for general acceptance. On these counts, they could both be called "objective," even to Kant—at least to the *Prolegomena* Kant who seems to be the Kant Körner's account chiefly relies on (cf. especially *Prol.* ##18, 19).[21] But how should one proceed if one means to point up a disparity between the two, to explain why *A* and *C* are somehow on less solid ground than *B* and *D* —which is the point of introducing these sceptics into the argument? To get at this, consider what would happen if *A*'s and *B*'s expectations failed. How should they cope with

[20] I *think* I owe this formulation to Grice, but cannot trace the source.

[21] G. Bird, *Kant's Theory of Knowledge*, London, 1962, p. 143. I owe this point about the *Prolegomena* argument to Bird.

a non-paranoiac doubting-Thomas or an outright denial?
There are two types of cases to consider: doubt or denial addressed to the truth of the propositions "It is red" and "We
can extract mercury . . ."; doubt or denial addressed to the
wisdom of A's and B's putting these propositions to the use
they do. A detailed rehearsal of the things that could go wrong
with each proposition in each type of case would prove illuminating, but it would fall outside the scope of this paper.
The following observations, however, are necessary here: (*i*)
When one examines "It is red" and "We can extract mercury . . ." with a view to setting out the truth conditions for
such propositions, it quickly becomes obvious that specifying
the acceptable procedures for testing the truth value of propositions of the latter sort is a considerably easier task; (*ii*) *i*
seems to connect with the fact that there is simply a larger
number of such procedures in connection with B's sort of
proposition, which makes it possible to go quite a long way
without bringing in considerations that are as obviously
person- or situation-dependent as are those requisite for as-
suring oneself that, for example, the stuff is in fact the color
A says it is. As regards the cogency of answering in A's fashion or in B's (the second type of case mentioned above), the
principal point that emerges is, (*iii*) that the seemingly inconsequential fact that we rarely classify things on the basis
of their colors has at least one potentially significant philosophical consequence. (There are some counterexamples but
not many: white and red wine, yellow for jonquils as distinct
from narcissi?, yellow-backed wasps versus golden, yellow,
brown striped-backed honey bees? . . . Picasso's "blue period"? . . . something's "tell-tale gray.") What I am driving
at is this: the truths in these quasi-oracular pronouncements
all seem to point to the conclusion that there are after all
grounds for holding the status of color attributions suspect,
and for not readily accounting them objective. But considerably more important is the fact that Kant's Deduction argument bears traces of the lines of reasoning I have been sketch-
ing. Hence I feel confident that by pursuing them it becomes
possible to understand why he was, and with reason, unpre-
pared to maintain that color attributions are logically on a

par with other sorts of judgments that convey facts about spatio-temporal things.

Put in the shortest way, the point of the foregoing comes to this: It would be irrational to fly in the face of science, but not irrational in the same way to deny a color attribution. Thus we should be more apt to think you irrational for withholding assent from the proposition: "We can extract mercury from it by introducing quicklime; so it is cinnabar" (after telling you a few things about chemical displacement, and explaining some relevant experiments, procedures, etc.), then we should if you persisted in not assenting to the proposition: "It is red, so it is cinnabar" (after you had been given a color chart, told to look again, etc.). That this is owing both to facts about the propositions taken separately and to some facts about them in the context of their use as supports for the claim that a chunk of stuff is cinnabar is, I think, important in understanding the source of Kant's struggle. For it seems to be characteristic of him to start with the more complex and then scrutinize the "elements" with a view to determining what they contribute: that is, to start by claiming that "knowledge is a whole in which representations stand compared and connected" and ask whether, for example, "is red" should be licensed a contributing member of the "unified" whole of knowledge, of which the conception of cinnabar forms a part. It is the relevance of this whole consideration of the availability of reasons and the attendant possibility of reason*ing* that I have been trying to bring into the foreground. To present a tighter and more obviously Kantian sort of argument for its importance would require a thorough re-examination of the Deductions. But something short of that will serve if one is prepared to rest content with a conclusion of this form: one reason for distinguishing some qualities as "secondary" from others as "primary" is to emphasize that the latter are pre-eminently suited for use in judgments or propositions that we account "objective." For if one confronts the Deductions with the question: "What makes it right to adjudge a judgment 'objective'?" An answer emerges straightforwardly from Kant's attempt to elucidate the notion of objectivity and particularly from the crucial step he takes in a passage cited earlier, viz. the claim that the notion of "an object corresponding to, but distinct from our cognitions" serves to keep "our cognitions" from becoming "haphazard or arbitrary" since

> insofar as they are to relate to an object they must have that harmony . . . that unity which constitutes the concept of an object.

The implication here is that a principal criterion for assessing the objectivity of particular descriptions of spatio-temporal physical things is the descriptions' compatibility with other possible descriptions of the same things (or other sufficiently like them to be classed as the same species). And this connects with one of the primary objectives of the Deduction argument, which is to defend the thesis that although we understand the notion of "an object of representations" as referring to something distinct from our "experiences," it does not refer to something that is totally inaccessible through those "experiences." Its referent is rather both a process and its product, that is the specifiable principles we ought to employ in assessing claims to objectivity and the conception of physical reality produced thereby. Alternatively, we might say that the philosophical notion of "the object" that Kant inherited is, in the Deductions, transformed into the notion of the product of the various procedures we should follow in our attempts to perfect our conceptions of the object. That the Kantian elucidation of these ideas relies heavily on a claim about the unifying function of concepts may help clarify their bearing on my Sceptic story (cf. especially A 104–106, but also A 79=B 105, A 141, and A 647=B 702). (Because they stress Kant's stating that "a concept is something universal that functions as a rule," the recent discussions by Wolff and Bird also help considerably.[22] But for ears attuned to fashionable slogans relating meanings and linguistic rules it may in any case be perspicuous.) In any case what Kant says in these Deduction passages points to the conclusion that (*a*) to look upon ordinary empirical concepts through Kantian eyes is to see them as supplying us with "rules" for the objective determination of what we appre-

22 Bird, esp. ch. IX. R. P. Wolff, *Kant's Theory of Mental Activity,* Cambridge, Mass., 1963, esp. pp. 130–36.

hend, (*b*) that it is questionable whether a judgment like A's "It is red" can be said to conform to the "rules" associated with the concept "cinnabar," and (*c*) this is so because it is at any rate not obvious that the Kantian compatibility criterion for objectivity will work with judgments of that type (or will work with them as readily as it will with judgments like B's). One may of course object that there appear to be ways of making that criterion work in connection with color attributions, for example, the so-called discrimination-curve, which compares differences in wave lengths of light with the smallest observable differences in perceptible hue. But that sort of objection *may* be beside the point since it leads not to the conclusion that particular color attributions (like A's) are to be adjudged objective, but to the conclusion that if one concentrates on procedures for comparing color descriptions with one another, one makes use of criteria for assessing the objectivity of judgments about material things similar to the Kantian compatibility one. I do not think the latter conclusion proves any more than that there is something of interest in comparing judgments of the two types. (I deliberately refrain from pursuing the suggestion that facts about psychophysical measurements should be brought in at this juncture; cf. my earlier remarks about correlations.)

In sum, I have been arguing as follows: Negatively, it would be wrong to represent Kant as maintaining that color attributions are either clearly objective or subjective. They are not clearly objective because the facts that they can be cast in non-personal form ("It is red" as distinct from "It looks red to me") and are intended for general acceptance are surely not sufficient conditions for objectivity ("It is repulsive" is *not* for Kant objective; cf. II). That these may not be even necessary conditions is the whole point about "It is red." (I shall deal with that problem more fully below. But here it may not be out of place to point out that there is evidence of Kant's worries about the status of such judgments even in *K.U.*, especially ##7 and 14.) The error in the view that they are, for Kant, clearly subjective may well be that of misconstruing his compatibility criterion, viz. deeming it both necessary and sufficient for objectivity. (If it were that, the line separating Kant from some nineteenth-century Ideal-

ists would disappear.) On the positive side, I have suggested
that Kant may have held that the primary/secondary quality
distinction would be justified or made "critically" respectable
if it could be shown that the so-called secondary qualities
are rightly so called because they deserve a secondary place
in the domain of objective judgments by virtue of their failure to measure up to the criteria on which we rely in our attempts to perfect our understanding of physical reality. And
it appears to be Kant's view that one should have succeeded
in showing this if one could show that secondary qualities,
unlike primary ones, cannot be framed or tested in accordance with antecedently explicable "rules" for reasoning about
that which our judgments purport to be about (i.e. the judgments he came to label "determinate" and in *K.U.* distinguishes from "reflexive" judgments).

I.4   I turn now to the last of the four questions mentioned
in I.1 as possible bases for the formulation of the classical
two-quality doctrine, and as possible prompters for allegations of S.T.: viz. Does noting or learning about a thing's
color(s) afford reasonable grounds for modifying our concept
of a thing of that kind? This question raises some important
issues for the "critical" philosophy that Kant, seriously and
quite successfully, grappled with. Because this question has
not, to my knowledge, been considered by writers on Kant
except in passing (with, of course, the exception of Paton[23]
who at one point edges up for a close look but then with-
draws, pleading ignorance about the relevant issues), and because raising it pays real dividends, especially in connection
with *K.U.*, I hope I shall be pardoned for my fumblings and
for devoting this whole section to little more than an exposition of some relevant portions of the texts.

   In referring to the fourth as the "logical" question I mean
that it is not concerned with matters having to do with the
truth conditions of propositions of various types, but with
the sorts of issues Kant discussed under that heading—judge
by his *Logic* and by what is said concerning essentially the

[23] Paton, I, ch. ix, #4 *passim*. Cf. esp. p. 194, fn. 6, and p. 195,
fn. 6.

same topics in his "critical" writings, especially in the Amphiboly of K.R., and in the section headed "Definition" in the "Transcendental Doctrine of Method," ch. 1 (A 727–733=B 755–761). (Some might find it helpful to think of the question as speculation about what Chomsky meant in speaking of the "formal" and "substantive" claims embodied in a universal grammar.)[24] I shall therefore dub "logical" Kant's inquiry into the nature of our concepts: an inquiry in which he attempted, among other things, to distinguish among various types of concepts, to set out the various reasons why some types should be deemed defective, and to spell out the procedures appropriate to this assessment. More specifically my object will be to indicate the philosophical significance Kant attached to some of the theses emerging from this inquiry, first, to those that appear to have had for him a fairly direct bearing on aspects of the problem presented by the two quality doctrine that we too might dub "logical" or "formal."

To see how what I am about to say connects with my earlier arguments it may prove useful to ponder the following: It is possible to make sense of someone's qualms about saying that ". . . is red" is on all fours with ". . . is a source of mercury"; even to make sense of his temptation to say that the proposition, "That stuff is red and a source of mercury," involves a Rylean "category-mistake." That it is possible may be explained on grounds similar to those that led Kant to conclude that whereas, for example, "is mercuric sulphide" or "is a source for mercury" expresses concepts (or a concept), "is red" does not. (Cf. the remark cited earlier concerning "the representation of the color red" [A 320=B 377].) That Kant arrives at this conclusion is clear. The challenge is to understand the rationale, and then the consequences.

One line of reasoning leading to this conclusion may be seen at work in K.R.; specifically in the passages where arbitrary, would-be empirical concepts are discussed (I put it this way to evade issues raised by Kant's statements about mathematical concepts, with which I cannot deal here). Kant

[24] N. Chomsky, *Aspects of the Theory of Syntax*, Cambridge, Mass., 1965. Cf. esp. pp. 29 and 64–69.

explicitly cites instances of two types: (*a*) the concept of a ship's clock (A 729=B 757), and (*b*) the concepts of fate and fortune (B 177). He also suggests that there may be a third, (*c*), when he speaks of "the somewhat absurd and far from edifying" attempts of novelists to depict a moral idea or ideal in their novels (A 570=B 598). This last proves in many ways the most intriguing and suggestive. Since it belongs more properly to II, I shall put off discussing it in detail. But this much is to the point here, viz. what makes it right to speak about the novelists' representation of "the wise man of the Stoico" in the same breath with arbitrary concepts is connected with the fact that, as Kant puts it, "it is determined by no specifiable rule . . . and yields none that admits of being explained or tested" (A 571=B 599). The implications of this correction for Kant's main tenets about ordinary empirical concepts should be obvious. His comments about the other two types combine to strengthen and clarify his outlook. His point in calling the concepts of fate and fortune "usurpatory" is probably familiar, viz. that they are *taken into use* as though significant by "almost universal indulgence" which, in the somewhat picturesque terminology of *K.U.* (Intro., III), signifies a sacrifice of the "distinctive" and "rightful authority" of concepts that depend for their meaning on the *K.R.* Categories. The "almost universal indulgence" is apparently a function of our almost universal aversion to the exertion that would be required for doing away with them altogether and finding explanations of the phenomena that they, as it were, provide pseudo-explanations of. But what Kant would give as the reason for deeming them arbitrary (rather than, e.g. just useless) is not altogether clear. Is it their lack of explanatory value, or is it because there is no way to delimit the circumstances in which it would and those in which it would not be significant to invoke them? Perhaps it does not matter, and the two possibilities may be only different aspects of a single one.

The point exemplified by (*a*), the concept of a ship's clock, is at the outset more troublesome. For one thing, both clocks and ships are artifacts, and one may believe that when Kant says "empirical concept" he means a concept of a natural kind, and so suspect that he might regard any concept of an artifact as somehow arbitrary. For another, there is the lurking suspicion that what struck Kant about this particular concept struck him only because he knew little about ships' clocks. But neither of these thoughts seems to me worth pursuing. For even though he says no more about the matter, it seems perfectly plausible that what he wanted to explain in terms of this example has to do with the fact that not all concepts are, like this one, built up out of others, and hence mere constructs or reflections of what we have observed or found convenient to distinguish (so e.g. Englishmen call ice hockey what we call (just plain) hockey; and that, I suppose, tells us something about the differences between life in England and in New England).

The lessons one can learn from these brief comments regarding Kant's conception of our ordinary empirical concepts are borne out by what is said about mathematical concepts for example at A 128, A 137=B 176, B 166, and *Logic* VIII, 1–5. None of these lessons may seem startling (although, surprisingly, one surprised Paton).[25] But they do seem instructive, and since they are of considerable help in understanding some extraordinarily taxing discussions in the *Logic* and in *K.U.*, they are well worth spelling out. The principal point is that our ordinary empirical concepts are, although artifacts of sorts, not arbitrary. And from this it follows that they have some explanatory power; that is, that they reflect or embody our con-ceptions of things, our way of understanding how various items in our "experience" relate to one another, our way of unifying and so ordering in an intelligible fashion what is directly presented to us. In sum, it amounts to this: that Kant wisely sees our concepts as functioning in the same way as hypotheses and inductive generalizations, and, like them as capable of being tested and corrected and responsive to the same sort of factual and reflective pressures. This is clearly indicated by the discussions in K.R. cited above, and confirmed by Kant's remarks about "Definition," which elaborate on the same theme. Thus, for example,

[25] Paton, p. 197. Perhaps his surprise stems from an Idealist streak in his philosophical upbringing. But Kant, unlike Bradley, does not worry about whether it may prove insuperably difficult to explain how our concepts get purchase on the world of our experience.

Kant remarks that to define a term for an empirical concept is not a determina*tion* but a determin*ing* of its sense, since further observations may "remove some properties and add others" and that "their [precise] limits" cannot be assured (A 728=B 759). And elsewhere in the same connection he remarks that in explicating the meaning of an arbitrary term I may succeed in explaining "what I intend . . . but should not say that, in explaining this, I have explained the nature of a real thing" (A 729=B 760).

To see the import of all this for the primary/secondary quality distinction (or, more precisely, for Kant's conception of the formal aspect of the problem it presents), one needs to take a further step (one that makes little sense unless one confronts it via an issue that becomes central in *K.U.*). It is a consequence of a claim adumbrated in the above, but one that hovers uneasily between turning out trivially true or plainly false, unless one tortures one's way through the intricacies of Kant's critique of the Baumgarten thesis that "truth is the perfection of conception" (which has as its seemingly less awe-inspiring aesthetic counterpart that "beauty is the perfection of perception"). For the claim amounts to this: that our empirical concepts are perfectible, not perfect. To make it turn out trivially true one need, I think, only construe it as a claim setting out the fundamental difference between our ordinary class concepts and the concepts of mathematics, as understood by Kant. And it would prove plainly false if construed as a thesis to the effect that each of us in his own way is making our concepts better every day. In fact the extremes seem barely worth the mention since Kant makes it painfully apparent that his claim is tied by intricate lines to a complex of considerations about what should be accounted reasonable grounds for adjudging a given concept defective in "internal-" or "external-distinctness," and these considerations quite plainly are ringed by restrictions that both of the above constructions would violate. The main guidelines for correctly interpreting Kant's thesis lie in three propositions: (*i*) that our empirical concepts are "partial conceptions of a merely possible total concept"; (*ii*) that they are not and cannot be "internally complete"; and (*iii*) that they can, and progressively do, approximate an ideal of "external completeness" that Kant seems to equate with "external distinctness" (cf. *Logic* VIII, esp. 1–5). When Paton observes that, for Kant, empirical concepts are not "adequate to our intuition of individual things falling under" them,[26] he is, I take it, alluding to *i*. Unfortunately, he says no more about it. Beck seems to be thinking of *ii* and *iii* when he says that "any attempt to state [a definition of terms associated with such concepts] fails to meet the requirements of definition, with respect either to completeness or precision."[27] But he, too, fails to explain what I think needs explaining. Yet they seem to agree, and I agree with them, that it would be contrary to the spirit of Kant's words to suppose that he would take Russell's well-worn little story about the creature encountered in Australia that looked and acted for all the world exactly like a swan—except that it happened to be black—as an illustration of the sort of thing that should make us alter and thereby perfect the concept of a swan. To say why this should be so is easy enough: distinctness, not clarity, says Kant, is what we want. But there remains the task of showing that our obtaining the desired distinctness is primarily dependent on eliminating obscurity which is, as Kant not very kindly puts it, "too easily palmed off as depth or as originality" (*K.U.* #47); and that obscurity *is* eliminable, as he seems to think, by dint of more precise and more sustained reflection.

II. SENSE/AESTHETIC QUALITIES

If the foregoing proves anything it is that Kant's uneasy peace with the two-quality doctrine affects not only his answers to certain questions that we have come to regard as typically Kantian (especially those about the justifiability of

---

[26] Paton, p. 195.

[27] Beck, p. 67. But his entire discussion seems curiously old-fashioned. Thus he finds that although Kant distinguishes nominal from real definitions, "he does not draw this distinction as between the definition of a word and the definition of a thing; because he regarded the concept, rather than the thing or word, as the *definiendum* . . ." And this, unfortunately, raises many questions that are left without answers.

certain claims), but also has repercussions in his attempt to clarify the ideal of the perfection of conception, which is a conspicuous part of his Rationalistic legacy. That Kant addressed himself to the task of elucidating that notion in his *Lectures on Logic* and again in his *Critique of Judgment* (thoughts about it also emerge in various places in *K.R.*) supports the view that it was closely tied to his central concerns. That I find it difficult to set out his ideas on this topic in lucid terms may tell more about me than about Kant, but it also means that something about these issues is extraordinarily difficult to get into focus. I nevertheless propose to pay particular attention to the tantalizing portions of the *K.U.* argument that deal with them, as these are the passages that show why *K.U.* is most profitably read as an attempt to elaborate on themes central to the *Critique of Pure Reason*. Clarifying the *K.U.* contentions should make it possible to cast some retrospective light on the argument of *K.R.*

In the interests of getting the principal links into view, I shall begin with one of Paton's comments, viz. that our (empirical) concepts are not "adequate to our intuition of individual things falling under them" (cf. I.4 above). For in saying this, he is perhaps unknowingly but nonetheless dramatically, pointing toward those portions of the *K.U.* argument that lead to Kant's perhaps most suggestive but also most widely misunderstood contentions: that beauty is "the expression of aesthetic ideas" (*K.U.* ##49, 50), and "that there is no science of the beautiful but only a critique" (*K.U.* #59). In explicating the arguments that bear directly on these claims I shall keep more or less to the format of I, but there will be these differences: Because I am concerned to pursue the "logical" sort of question left dangling in I.4, I shall pass hastily through the lines of inquiry—interesting though they are—raised by the analogue of the question posed in I.3. The analogue of the question in I.2 is taken up last, since it provides the occasion for summing up what can be learned from the importance Kant attached to instructing us about aesthetic qualities.

II.0.   Once again a few preliminary observations would seem to be in order. Among the points I should like to bring into the open but set aside for another discussion are the following:

A. That there is a genuine and philosophically significant distinction between 'sense qualities' and 'aesthetic qualities' is nowadays a philosophical commonplace. The distinction was not a common one in Kant's day, and hence his attempt to draw it marks him as something of a revolutionary. That Kant did want to draw such a distinction and attached some importance to setting out the rationale for it is attested in several passages in the text, for example, *K.U.* ##3, 4, 38, 39; it is alluded to, as well, at *K.R.* A 569–572=B 597–600. And in roughly the same connection it is worth noting the remarks in the Introduction to *K.U.*, where Kant gives it to be understood that with the writing of his third Critique he felt he had brought his "entire critical undertaking to a close"; in *K.U.* he felt he had formulated and answered questions that arose from a consideration of his other two Critiques, and he therefore looked upon the third as "a means of connecting the two parts of Philosophy in a whole." It may also be worth noting that he remarks of the *Critique of Aesthetic Judgment* that its questions form an integral "part of the general problem of transcendental philosophy" (cf. *K.U.* #36). Since the notion of beauty looms large in these questions, and since this is a notion that it has become fashionable to shun (either out of humility or out of the conviction that it has somehow lost its centrality), I should also say here that there is good cause for its prominence in the argument of *K.U.* Some of Kant's points simply could not be made or understood without it, although there are others that would not be affected if one were to heed the Austinian plea for doing "field work in aesthetics" and *did* "forget a while about the beautiful and get down instead to the dainty and the dumpy."[28] But it may also be possible to reassure some injured sensibilities via the suggestion that "beauty" functions in *K.U.* as a sort of analogue for the *K.R.* Categories. For this means that Kant is claiming that the notion of beauty occupies as central a position in the cluster of concepts we

28 J. L. Austin, *Philosophical Papers*, Oxford, 1961, p. 131.

invoke when concentrating on matters aesthetic as does, for example, "cause" in our search for explanations or relations among phenomena (thus the interconnections among "substance," "cause," "change," "event," etc. in the Analogies). And in that case the onus seems to fall on the opponents of the notion, to show that we would be better off without it. I shall not argue that contention now.

B. It is unnecessary to fuss about whether Kant in *K.U.* takes back or happily contradicts his not unvenomous remark about "those Germans" (i.e. Baumgarten) who flagrantly abuse the Greek term "aesthetic" by using it to label their abortive efforts "to bring the critical treatment of the beautiful under rational principles . . ." (B 36). For it is Baumgarten's claim to have produced "a *science* of the beautiful" that is the bone of contention between them; and Kant does not change his mind about the error inherent in this claim.

There is however something well worth noting in the same connection, something that may, if not fully understood, prove a well-nigh insurmountable obstacle to appreciating the arguments presented in *K.U.* It concerns the significance of Kant's characterizing the K.R. Aesthetic as a "doctrine of Sensibility." This characterization will prove crucial, and on two main points needs to be perfectly clear. In presenting his "doctrine of Sensibility" Kant is clearly concerned to distinguish something from what might be labeled a "doctrine of Understanding." That the something in question is Sensibility, not Sense (or Sensory Apparatus, Mechanisms, etc.) is going to be the main point of my argument. But the basic ingredients are these: (*i*) the distinction between the "immediacy" of "intuition" and the "mediacy" of discursive (or conceptual) thought, and (*ii*) the distinction between the "ideas of Sensibility" and the "concepts of Understanding." Let me explain briefly: The task Kant sets himself in the Aesthetic is, as he puts it, to "isolate Sensibility," that is, to abstract from our ordinary apprehensions or experiences any element of thinking or conception that we may rightly be said to bring to bear upon them, and then to scrutinize what remains. What is left? Well, says Kant, whatever it is, it is something that should reveal the central facts about our "intuition" [Anschauung].[29] One of these "facts" is expressed in the claim that Sensibility is "the source of intuitions," as is Understanding of conceptual thought. But the other facts are concerned with the immediacy of intuition, and thus intuition, as "immediate cognitive relation," is contrasted with "conception" or "thought," characterized as a "mediate" cognitive relation to something (cf. A 19, A 20=B 34, A 42=B 60, B 132; *K.U.* Intro., vii). And this makes sense, for it amounts to a claim that in our ordinary dealings with the world we implicitly rely on what we have come to know about the things around us; we do not, as Ruskin picturesquely puts it, look on the world with a completely "innocent eye." If these dealings are then "mediated" by thought, why not call our relation to that which we think about "immediate"? The "immediate" then appears implicit in and logically prior to the "mediate," the relation that actually obtains between us and the world of ordinary things. N.B. Kant does not use the term "immediate" in connection with Sensation, but that does not preclude inferring that he distinguished between the objects of intuition and what is given to Sensation, that is, sensa or sense impressions [Eindrücke].[30] The warrant for such an inference is strengthened by the other claim that emerges from the Aesthetic, which connects with Kant's introduction of the term "idea of Sensibility" to contrast the objects of intuition with the objects of thought. When one compares the "ideas of Sensibility" with the objects of thought ("concepts"), it becomes

[29] I agree with Kemp Smith: There is some significance in the fact that Kant uses the term "intuition" (Anschauung) rather than the also available "sensation" (Empfindung). This is not explained, but should be fairly clear.

[30] He is not clearly consistent in this, but that may be owing to the genuine difficulty of finding the right words to formulate what he wants to explain. There may also be another problem: that Kant wants to avoid actually saying that in his terms, a "synthesis" is involved in any and every apprehension. But I am strongly inclined to agree with Paton who remarks that Kant's not explicitly saying it does not mean that he is not aware of it, or means to deny it outright (Paton, p. 289, p. 339*n*.). But there may be further complications here. Cf. e.g. B 160*n*.

apparent that both are what Kant would call "synthetic uni-
ties," that is, wholes of parts, which are the wholes they are
because they have the parts they do (for the full significance
of this, remember Kant's: "[it] must be intolerable . . . to
hear the representation of the color red called an idea . . ."
I shall return to this point.).[31] One principal respect in
which they differ is that, unlike concepts, "ideas of Sensibility" are ideas of wholes that are logically prior to their
parts (cf. especially A 23 = B 38); they are also ideas of individuals and not of particular members of a species or class.
This suggests that what is said here about the ideas of Sensibility relates (in perhaps surprisingly direct fashion) to some
of the claims Kant makes for his "ideas of Reason" several
hundred pages later. There certainly *seems* to be a connection:
for when he says that the ideals of totality, completeness, and
precision are not arbitrary because they are firmly rooted in
our experience, one hears echoes of remarks that could be
made in connection with the ideas of Sensibility; for example,
that but for our awareness of these wholes we could not be
aware that our conception of the individuals we come to know
are but "partial conceptions of a possible whole." And so one
is prepared for the possibility that Kant will be forced to
return once again to a study of Sensibility. But speculation
apart, the immediately relevant point is that the notion of
Sensibility operative in the Aesthetic stands ready to spill
over into the domain of what we should call Aesthetics. It is
both rich and vague enough to cover not only technical philosophical discussions of sense perception, but also discussions
of, for example, the Victorian sensibility. Remember Shake-
speare's punning "And shall all sensive things be so senseless
as to resist sense?"

[31] Paton expresses some doubts about this; cf. Paton, p. 289, and
p. 339*n*. There is support for my interpretation in several passages:
especially in the remark that to apprehend an individual something
involves "a synthesis of a manifold in one intuition"; cf. A 69 = B 93,
A 78 = B 103. It is implicit in Weldon's commenting, rightly, that
"spatio-temporal objects admit of indefinite analysis" (p. 299), for
on sound "critical" principles this could not be known but for a
prior awareness of that synthetic unity which is, in the terminology
of the Aesthetic, the object of Sensibility.

II.1.   It has been said that in *K.U.* Kant argues that

> Aesthetic judgments are purely subjective judgments, for
> they are not about the object but about our feelings
> about it.[32]

One also hears it said of Kant that he

> divorces the aesthetic experience from all content and
> meaning and transforms it into a 'no man's land' of de-
> tached and abstract feeling. His sole concern seems to be
> to establish *the identity of the aesthetic judgment with
> pure subjective feeling, dissociated from sensation*, also
> from the socio-ethical problems of life.[33]
>
> [My underlining]

That these summations are thoroughly misleading should become apparent before long. But because I propose to attack
them not straight on, but indirectly by way of an assault on
some difficult issues raised by Kant's Solution for the "Antinomy of Taste," it may be well to put these, as versions or
extensions of S.T., into their proper place, by noting first that
writers might have arrived at these conclusions by several
routes.

The more familiar approaches to *K.U.* follow roughly one
of two routes: (*a*) they see it as a development out of, and
systematic weaving together of, various eighteenth-century
attempts to characterize the distinctive "sense" or mode of
sensibility involved in the appreciation of beauty, for example, those of Hutcheson, Shaftesbury, Mendelssohn; or
(*b*) they look upon it as an attempt to characterize and argue
for the distinctive "logic" of the sort of aesthetic judgments
Kant calls "judgments of taste" (or, sometimes ". . . of reflective taste"). There are pitfalls and virtues in both.
Through the former, for example, it becomes possible to appreciate the intriguing problems raised by Shaftesbury's alleged discovery of a sense that is not in an ordinary way a
sense, that is, a "reflected sense" by which

[32] H. W. Cassirer, *A Commentary on Kant's Critique of Judgment*,
London, 1938, p. 145.
[33] I. Knox, *The Aesthetic Theories of Kant, Hegel and Schopenhauer*, New York, 1936.

there arises yet another kind of affection towards those very affections themselves [of pity, kindness, gratitude and their contraries] which have already been felt, and are now become the subject of a new liking or dislike.[34]

The views expounded in *K.U.* are indelibly marked by this idea. It becomes a challenge to trace the steps by which that Shaftesburian "reflected sense" is transformed by Kant into a reflect*ing* or reflex*ive* critical sensibility. (Failure to see that this does happen, makes it virtually impossible to understand some of Kant's oft-reiterated claims.) It now seems patent that eighteenth-century psychologizing about human "affections" provoked one of the big questions that Kant's *K.U.* claims about aesthetic reflective judgments are intended to answer. A question such as: "What makes it possible for us to dislike liking or to like some disliking? to delight in discovering that we are capable of liking or capable of disliking . . . ?" *does* underlie Kant's insistence that delight in beauty "strengthens and reproduces itself" (#12 and elsewhere). But it would surely be wrong to move from this to one of the summations cited earlier, to suppose Kant is arguing for a distinctive "sense of beauty" (*vide* e.g. ##28, 29, but especially 22), or that asking such a self-reflexive sort of question commits one to the conclusion that in adjudging something beautiful one is talking about himself or about his feelings about his feelings.

Discussions of Kant's claims about the distinctive "logic" of the judgments he calls "judgments of taste" focus on the considerations he deemed relevant for framing judgments about beauty, or for disputing those put forward by others. One of the pitfalls in this approach is that it is easy to confound two questions that Kant distinguishes, viz. (roughly): (1) "Am I, or can I be sure of being, right in deeming that thing beautiful?" and (2) "How is it possible to justify the very possibility of venturing judgments that purport to be right and final?" Unfortunately he buries the distinction in a brief paragraph leading up to the "Deduction of Judgments of Taste" (#38). And failure to notice it can prove fatal, for

[34] Shaftesbury, "An Inquiry concerning Virtue," quoted by Beck, p. 29.

unless one sees that Kant's *K.U.* question is only indirectly about the particular risk a particular person takes in judging a particular thing's beauty, one is virtually bound to misconceive the thrust of the whole "Analytic of the Beautiful", and see it as a doomed attempt to prove that certain persons' critical judgments are unassailable. But the "critical" or "logical" question to which *K.U.* is primarily addressed is a question such as (2). It concerns the very possibility of taking the sort of risk one takes whenever one says "She *is* beautiful," rather than taking a safer road with "She looks beautiful tonight, in this moonlight, in this particular setting," or (less grammatically) "She is, anyway, beautiful to *me*." That is, Kant's question is whether it makes any sense to take such risks, even to think that what we say might somehow prove to be wrong. (This at any rate seems to be the force of what he puts in terms of: What must be true of the distinctive *a priori* principle that reflexive judgment gives itself? [Cf. Intro., ##37–40. I shall discuss this more fully later.]

There are still other ways of reading *K.U.* so as to make it fit some "critical" version of S.T. One seems particularly worth mentioning. It starts by pointing to the Analytic and to the quite remarkable fact that in three out of the four part-explications of the idea of beauty presented there, one finds Kant bringing in the phrase "independently of any concept," and argues from this, via the *K.R.* claims about the relation between conceptual rules and objectivity, to the conclusion that since there appear to be no concepts and no rules, hence no accepted procedures for testing aesthetic judgments, such judgments should not be accounted objective. And if one accepts the argument, comparisons once again become relevant, especially the comparison of judgments of the form "That is beautiful" with the form "That is red, or green, or yellow." One could perhaps call again upon my example of the sceptics, this time giving them the passages in *K.U.* that explicitly deal with color attributions (e.g. the passage from #4, cited in I.2, but also the rather strange and ambiguous discussions in #14, where Kant seems to be worrying quite seriously about whether it makes sense to adjudge a color beautiful, and ends by warily suggesting that perhaps the significant condition is whether the color in question is "pure"). This exercise would yield its share of surprises (I suspect anyone who performed it would agree with one part of my conclusion, viz. that the quite distinctive "universality" and "necessity" Kant ascribes to aesthetic judgments prove the real stumbling blocks). But this may all be beside the point in the end. The fairly well-hidden concluding note of the Analytic suggests that there may be more fertile soil next door . . .

> Is taste . . . but an idea of a capacity . . . that is to be acquired by us, so that judgments of taste, with their demands for universal assent, are but a requirement of reason for generating . . . a consensus . . . and does the 'ought' . . . only bespeak the possibility of arriving at some sort of unanimity in such matters . . . ?
>
> [K.U. #22]

II.2. I have all along been proceeding on the assumption that questions about how to perfect our knowledge or understanding of our world should be distinguished from questions about the nature and possible perfectability of the concepts invoked in descriptions or explanations of it. Because the standards for measuring cognitive worth seem unsuited for measuring the worth of what we should call aesthetic judgments, it may be no wonder that discussions about whether aesthetic judgments should be accounted "subjective" begin to seem futile. At any rate I propose to turn from that matter to a question (to which I do not know the answer) of the latter, "logical" variety that has to do with how aesthetic concepts (and especially the concept of beauty) fit into our conceptual economy. I should like to slant that question in a particular way, for what I seek to understand is why a Kant should think that to fit those concepts into their rightful place, one must bear in mind that proud German who somehow got "aesthetics" thoroughly wrong and "perfection" at least partly right. As will appear below, the rough but ready perception/conception dichotomy has a considerable part to play here.

One way to begin is to compare the notion of beauty with those of space and time as set out in the *K.R. Aesthetic*. The reason should be fairly obvious: these notions are *prima facie* more alike than are, for example, the notion of beauty and that of cinnabar. They are alike in being ideas of wholes of parts, with the idea of the whole prior to that of the parts. That this can be said of space and time (and why they are tagged "ideas" rather than "concepts") is made quite plain in the "Metaphysical Expositions" referred to in II.o. That Kant means to make a similar claim in connection with beauty comes out most emphatically in the third and probably best-known segment of the *K.U.* Analytic, that is, the Third Moment from which is drawn the assertion that:

> Beauty is the form of purposiveness [or purposiveness of form? (Form der Zweckmässigkeit)] of an object insofar as that is apprehended independently of any idea [Vorstellung] of a [its?] purpose.

Surely to apprehend such purposiveness in the form of a thing involves being somehow struck by the apparent "zweckmässigkeit" of its elements, of their giving the impression of being "measured" each to each and to the whole. But would it make sense to speak of seeing them in this way did not the whole give that impression of its parts? Something like that is surely intended by Kant's words, and points up the similarity I have in mind. But it is certainly worth noting, too, the respects in which the *K.R.* ideas of Sensibility and the related *K.U.* idea differ. Here a consideration of the idea of perfection may prove of help. Would it be appropriate to invoke it in connection with the idea of space? I do not think so. Nor do the two become more similar when one remembers that it is part of the *K.R.* claim that from *knowing* what space is one *knows* something about the nature of its parts. A good deal more could be said about these differences, including that a Kant would surely say that the idea of beauty is clearly *not* constitutive of any and every possible sensory intuition. But the suggestions will serve here, and the penultimate indicates why the Kantian idea of the idea of beauty makes much of the differences between it and any "concept of experience." This is brought sharply into focus by the many passages in *K.U.* that are intended to explain why, as Kant puts it, there are no "examples" but only "exemplary cases" of beauty—no concrete spatio-temporal particulars of which it would make sense to say that we have in any ordinary way identified them as beautiful, none from which we can learn about what beauty is (as e.g. we can learn from an experiment about what chemical displacement is). Nor is our idea of beauty comparable to an hypothesis, in that it is perfectible as, on Kant's view, our ordinary empirical concepts are. And yet it should not be totally insulated against bombardments of our sensibilities; this is Kant's point in saying that we should "go to school" with the classics as someone in a court of law seeks out the precedents; should go to them "in order to learn from them how to avail ourselves of such sources," and because, as exemplary cases, they can "set others upon the track of seeking in themselves for the principles, and so of adopting their own, often better course" (cf. *K.U. #32 passim,* also #46). An idea of beauty is, then, correctible but not perfectible, tied to the past but loosely tethered.

Yet if it is not like a concept of the understanding, something that expresses a way of thinking about things or supplies us with rules for discriminating among phenomena, then what is it? One suggestion comes from a remark that follows in the *K.R.* text upon the heels of one I cited earlier in connection with Kant's claim about what makes empirical concepts arbitrary. It is this: although Kant thinks it absurd to suppose we could learn about moral virtue from a story book, he seems to think it not absurd but sensible and false to invoke the notion of an "ideal of Sensibility" in attempting to say what an artist is struggling to do when he sets out to do the impossible, that is, represent or depict a moral virtue (cf. I.4). If this sounds convoluted, so be it, for the convolutions lead, finally, to the concluding passages of *K.U.,* where Kant works the problem out. And what emerges there, via the claim that beauty may be said to be "the expression of aesthetic ideas" and, at the very last, "the symbol of the morally good," is that provided one does *not* claim to find in it the depiction of some otherwise specifiable notion of a moral ideal, one can get from a beautiful whole a forcible impression of totality, completeness, and precision that is the ideal toward which we should strive. Thus he also speaks of beauty as being an "inexponible representation of the imagination" (#57, Remark 1), meaning, I think, that it is to be contrasted sharply with an "exponible conception," which is "obscure" by virtue of "including an affirmation and concealed negation which an exposition makes apparent" (cf. *Logic*, #31). Together these three passages seem to be saying the following things: first, the idea of beauty is the idea of something in no way obscure. By adding that "no concept would be adequate to it," Kant evidently means to add that it functions for us as the ideal of a whole that is perfectly articulate, complete, and unique, and as such, stands as a reminder of what our "partial conceptions" can and cannot successfully capture. Second, there is the implicit claim that our ability to discern and take delight in contemplating beauty is one we ought to cultivate. This is the ultimate foundation of the Kantian claim that we are right to judge of beauty and to fault those who fail to agree (right, as he says, "to blame them," to "deny them taste," nonetheless demanding that they cultivate it, ##20–22). It seems to be in turn the consequence of two distinguishable claims that in judging of beauty all our mental powers are put to the test, the powers necessary for judging anything plus the extra sensitivity required for noting wherein individual members of a species or class differ discernibly from one another. And finally, that claim is a consequence of the thesis implicit in the question on which the Analytic account ends, viz. that the *sensus communis* that we must "presuppose" in judging or communicating our ideas is not something that now in fact exists, but something that we can create—but only if we persist in presuming that others may be brought to understand and agree.

BIBLIOGRAPHY

Aldrich, V. C., *Philosophy of Art*, Englewood Cliffs, N.J., 1963.

Austin, J. L., *Philosophical Papers*, Oxford, 1961.

Baumgarten, A. B., *Reflections on Poetry*, trs. K. Aschenbrenner and W. B. Holther, Berkeley, 1954.

Beck, L. W., *Studies in the Philosophy of Kant*, New York, 1965.

Bird, G., *Kant's Theory of Knowledge*, London, 1962.

Caird, E., *The Critical Philosophy of Immanuel Kant*, Glasgow, Maclehouse, 1889.

Cassirer, H. W., A *Commentary on Kant's Critique of Judgment*, London, 1938.

Chomsky, N., *Aspects of the Theory of Syntax*, Cambridge, Mass., 1965.

Kennick, W. E., ed., *Art and Philosophy*, New York, 1964.

Knox, I., *The Aesthetic Theories of Kant, Hegel and Schopenhauer*, New York, 1936.

Körner, S., *Kant*, Hammondsworth, 1955.

O'Connor, D. J., "Locke," in *A Critical History of Western Philosophy*, ed. D. J. O'Connor, New York, 1964.

Paton, H. J., *Kant's Metaphysic of Experience*, 2 vols., London, 1936.

Sibley, F., "Aesthetic and Nonaesthetic," *Philosophical Review*, Vol. 74, No. 2 (April 1965), 135–59.

Smith, N. Kemp, A *Commentary to Kant's Critique of Pure Reason*, 2d ed., London, 1929.

Strawson, P. F., *Individuals*, London, 1959.

Toulmin, S., and J. Goodfield, *The Architecture of Matter*, New York, 1963.

Warnock, G. J., "Kant," in *A Critical History of Western Philosophy*, ed. D. J. O'Connor, New York, 1964.

Weldon, T. D., *Kant's Critique of Pure Reason*, 2d ed., Oxford, 1958.

Wolff, R. P., *Kant's Theory of Mental Activity*, Cambridge, Mass., 1963.

Ziff, P., "Reasons in Art Criticism," in *Art and Philosophy*, ed. W. E. Kennick, New York, 1964, pp. 605–22.

KANT: THE AESTHETIC JUDGMENT

ROBERT L. ZIMMERMAN

The paradoxes which Kant pronounces in the section of the *Critique of Judgment* entitled "The Analytic of the Beautiful" can easily mislead the uncautious reader. On a superficial reading they appear as cryptic and inconsistent. How can an aesthetic state of mind be both disinterested and emotive? How can a proposition concerning beauty be both contingent and necessary? These and other questions come to mind as one works through the section and one feels helpless at the apparent lack of coherence.

However, the paradoxes disappear, or at least become meaningful, when they are seen against the background of the overall Kantian metaphysic. It is essential to bear in mind the metaphysical significance of aesthetic experience in order to make sense out of the so-called "four moments" of the aesthetic judgment. That is, it is necessary to bear in mind that aesthetic experience, i.e. the experience of natural beauty, is experience of the noumenal world as it filters through the phenomenal world, and, that in order to secure the experience of natural beauty, the human mind must act passively in receiving its contents and not actively in organizing them. Given the metaphysical significance of aesthetic experience, and given the condition that aesthetic experience be "pure" experience, the subjectivity and universality, the contingency and necessity of aesthetic judgments, and the emotive but disinterested state of mind in the aesthetic subject are seen as logical deductions. Or to be less verbose, once the *a priori* elements of aesthetic experience are revealed, clarified, and understood as deductively necessary elements of the Kantian

Reprinted with permission of the author and of the editors from the *Journal of Aesthetics and Art Criticism* (1962–63), 333–44.

system, the paradoxes become transparent and meaningful.

What is remarkable about Kant's analysis of the aesthetic judgment and the aesthetic state of mind is that despite the limits which his system places upon his thought he has called attention to certain central, indubitable truths. One would expect that such an *a priori* rendering of aesthetic experience would distort for purposes of rigor and consistency; but although one cannot deny the deductive nature of Kant's reflections, one cannot also deny the empirical truth of them. It is precisely the aim of this essay to demonstrate both these aspects of Kant's thought, i.e. the *a priori* deductive nature of it and the empirical truths couched within it.

The first deduction which Kant makes is that in aesthetic experience we are not concerned with an *object* but with the *representation* of an object in the subject's mind. It is the object as a perceived entity that produces the feeling of beauty. For example, when one perceives a sunset, aesthetic interest is awakened by the visual impression made upon the mind. The actual, physical object is not directly important; rather it is the peculiar visual sensations and patterns which strike the mind that result in aesthetic feeling. It is the object *as experienced* which exhibits beauty. Thus Kant says, "the judgment of taste is not a judgment of cognition, and is consequently not logical but aesthetical, by which we understand that whose determining ground·can be *no other than subjective*."[1] The aesthetic judgment concerns the subjective effect of the object on consciousness, i.e. whether or not it results in an undesigned harmony of the imagination and the understanding.

Kant does not assert that an object exhibits order and design in itself but that the representation of the object exhibits order and design. This distinction is crucial and is necessitated by the logic of Kant's system. For if he had asserted that an external object exhibits beauty, he would be contradicting his assertion that in aesthetic experience the mind is presented with contents from the noumenal world. No objects can be beautiful, i.e. reveal noumenal properties, since

[1] Immanuel Kant, *Critique of Judgment*, tr. J. H. Bernard (New York, 1951), p. 37.

as an object it has been determined by consciousness and no longer exists as a pure, in-itself entity. An object is an object insofar as, and *only* insofar as, it has been "objectified" to use Berdyaev's term.[2] "Objectification" is a primary mode of conscious determination. Thus, the only way Kant can assert properties of noumenal entities is to consider them prior to their having been determined by consciousness, i.e. to consider them phenomenologically, as non-conceptual appearances. If they are actual existent "objective" entities, they have necessarily already been altered by the knowing mind, they have been endowed with a derived phenomenal character.

Thus, when Kant asserts that the aesthetic object is a subjective existent, he is not impairing the significance of the aesthetic experience but rather making sure that it *is* significant. For if it were not the case that aesthetic experience was subjective, it could not be a pure, free experience. And this would mean that it could not be constituted by contents which were undistorted, contents which presented the real "in-itself" world; consequently that aesthetic experience could not serve as a means of bridging the cleavage between the world of science and the world of freedom. We might think that such a position would disturb Kant and force his aesthetic theory into a relativistic, subjectivistic doctrine; whereas, in fact, it is, from his point of view, a positive step, one which insured the more primitive requirement that aesthetic experience is the dimension which unites the two worlds. By forcing the emphasis from objectivity to subjectivity, Kant has secured the freedom of aesthetic experience and guaranteed its philosophical importance.

Once the object is substituted for it, the aesthetic attitude is changed. It becomes an attitude of indifference, a state of mind which is not in any way concerned with the object but only with the effect the object produces in the subject. Kant says, "Now when the question is if a thing is beautiful, we do not want to know whether anything depends or can depend on the existence of the thing, either for myself or for anyone

[2] N. Berdyaev, *The Beginning and The End*, tr. R. M. French (New York, 1957), ch. 1.

else, but how we judge it by mere observation."[3] And further on, "We easily see that, in saying it is *beautiful* and in showing that I have taste, I am concerned, not with that in which I depend on the existence of the object, but with that which I make out of this representation in myself."[4] If I am concerned with the beauty of something I am necessarily unconcerned about the existence of that something, I am concerned only with the manner in which it impresses me. My experience of it is not bound to the existence of it so that if it did not exist and was an illusion my judgment concerning its aesthetic quality would not be altered. The only condition is that I be impressed and have a representation. Whether this representation belongs to an external object is entirely irrelevant. It is relevant to practical and moral experience and that is why they *are* practical and moral. For if they dispensed with this concern they would become potential aesthetic experience. Only if an experience is completely free from conscious determination is it an aesthetic experience. Since being free from conscious determination means, at the very least, not being objective, aesthetic experience cannot be objective. Since, moreover, being free from conscious determination means not being the object of any conscious aim aesthetic experience must be indifferent experience.

Kant has enunciated an important truth. For it *is* one fundamental condition of aesthetic experience that the person having it see as if for the first time, i.e. perceive the contents without projecting into them the meanings which they have in everyday experience. Quite simply, the door is not an aesthetic object until I bracket all the meanings which have become part of the door and perceive it as a new unclassified thing. Things take on their function or their practical significance after a time and what they are becomes equated with what they do or have done. But the door is not just that which shuts the room from the world. It has, along with this existential property, a texture, a pattern and a character. These will not be experienced however, as long as the door is left within the network of conscious determinations which it

[3] *Critique of Judgment*, p. 38.
[4] *Ibid.* p. 39.

has accrued. We need fresh eyes to see it as an aesthetic object. We must dissociate it from its existence as a thing to open or a thing to close and experience it as a pure perceptual form of our awareness. Kant's way of saying this is to say that we must be indifferent to its existence since its existence has forced it into a stereotype and bars us from *really* seeing it. How often do we *look at* the door compared to how often we *use* it? Using it is, in one sense, dealing with it as existent. Looking at it is dealing with it as a visual phenomenon. Our everyday concern with it is an existential concern, our aesthetic concern with it is a phenomenological (as Husserl was later to call it) concern. There is therefore no paradox in this, but rather great insight.

The attitude of indifference then is a result of the shifting of attention in the aesthetic field from its objective to its subjective side, a shift demanded by the condition that the aesthetic experience be a free, pure experience so that *what* is experienced is an uncorrupted element of the noumenal world. There is a similar logic at work with respect to the emotion or satisfaction that occurs in aesthetic experience. The existence of such a unique aesthetic emotion is Kant's second *a priori* deduction. It is like no other emotion or satisfaction. Kant compares it to practical or appetitive feeling and moral feeling. He calls the former "gratification" and the latter "esteem or approval." He calls aesthetic feeling simply "pleasure." A more descriptive word would be more instructive. But it really doesn't matter. What is important is the quality of it and how it differs from the other satisfactions.

Kant explains the difference in an extremely compact and revealing passage. He says, "Pleasantness concerns irrational animals also, but beauty only concerns men, i.e. animal but still rational, beings—not merely *qua* rational (e.g. spirits), but *qua* animal also—and the good concerns every rational being in general."[5] That which gratifies appetitive satisfaction, gratifies because it fulfills an animal need, like hunger or thirst. That which is esteemed or is morally satisfying is esteemed because it fulfills a rational need, i.e. the consistency of a validity universalized maxim. That which pleases or is

[5] *Ibid.* p. 44.

aesthetically satisfying is pleasing because it fulfills a rational need but requires an animal element, i.e. the order and un-designed lawfulness of a representation unified by the imag-ination but originating from the organ of sight. The rational need in this case is for order and design, and its animal foundation lies in the role the sense organ plays. The moral feeling is tied to a purely intellectual process; the appetitive feeling to a purely animal process; the aesthetic feeling to an intellectual process which is impossible without an accom-panying animal process. It has often been claimed that Kant is a pure formalist and, as we shall see, to an extent he is, but his insistence on the necessity for a bodily, sensuous element in aesthetic experience indicates at least that his formalism is not asserted at the expense of the empirical facts.

Aesthetic pleasure then is neither appetitive gratification nor moral esteem or respect. It stands midway between the two. As a feeling it is neither purely animal nor intellectual, i.e. it is not satiation as when one eats when one is hungry or awe as when one sees the perfect consistency of a moral assertion or, to give a non-moral analogue, when one sees the answer to a difficult mathematical problem issuing almost magically. It has elements of the latter although it involves animal responses like the former. More important is the fact that its peculiarity is a result of the necessity that aesthetic experience be pure experience. For only such a "mid-way" feeling could square with the requirement that there be no concern for the existential object.

An appetitive satisfaction clearly demands the existence of its object. A moral satisfaction requires that what is esteemed be universally possible and become in fact a mode of be-haviour, i.e. that one act upon it. If a moral truth were not concerned with actual existence it would have no moral worth. The "oughtness" of moral judgments refers not to the fact that all men ought to believe the judgment, but that since it is consistent in its universalized form one ought to *act* upon the judgment. But an aesthetic satisfaction, being neither the result of a fulfillment of an animal need, nor the apprehen-sion of consistency and the possibility of the realization of the consistent statement in actual behaviour, is not therefore con-cerned with existence. It is indifferent whereas appetitive and moral satisfactions are predicated upon an interest in the objects or the maxims existential realization.

Aesthetic satisfaction is the awareness of the undesigned harmony between the imaginative representation and the understanding, i.e. that the former is ordered and designed in itself in accordance with the latter's standards. This satisfaction is a result of an internal harmony which strictly speaking, is not bound to any external existence whatsoever. For clearly the aesthetic emotion one feels before, let us say, some natural phenomenon like a mountain is not the feeling one feels when one is hungry and faced with a dinner, or the feeling one has when one is convinced of the rightness of an ethical decision. Although it is notoriously difficult to verbalize feelings at all, much less feelings so subtly different, one can at least roughly approximate the difference by calling attention to the pure bodily process in the first (the appetitive feeling), the pure rational process in the second (the moral feeling), and the rational-but-bodily-conditioned feeling in the aesthetic state. One could be more precise both analytically and poetically, but these Kantian distinctions, if nothing else, do create a vocabulary within which one could locate the difference and some way toward specifying exactly in what they consist.

The third deduction which Kant makes, i.e. the third *a priori* element of aesthetic experience, is that the aesthetic judgment is not a conceptual judgment. It does not involve or presuppose the concept-producing power of the understanding. Clearly the demand for pure experience excludes the possibility that the understanding function in aesthetic judgment. If it did function, i.e. if it placed a concept upon the imaginatively unified representation, it would be adding an impure element to the experience. Simply, it would *not* be granting the experience the freedom to be what it is, but rather, would organize or unify the manifold according to its cognitive aims. The aesthetic judgment is therefore conceptless, or less formally, not an intellectual judgment.

When one predicates the beauty of an object, one is not asserting that the object falls under a conceptual determination of the understanding; one is asserting that there is an immediate felt unique aesthetic satisfaction which accompanies the pure experience of the object. This is Kant's fourth deduction and follows from (1) the fact that all experiences of beauty pre-suppose aesthetic emotion and (2) the fact that beauty consists not in any conceptual determination, but in the appearance of the aesthetic emotion. Furthermore, when one predicates beauty of an object, one is asserting that every human subject would experience an immediately felt aesthetic satisfaction if they experienced the object freely. The judgment refers to *my* aesthetic feeling primarily, but it also refers to the universal quality of the situation, i.e. that the aesthetic feeling is an effect which would occur to all who experienced the object. For *my* aesthetic feeling is mine insofar as *I* feel it, but it is universal insofar as the process in me, which eventuated in the feeling, is a process that is not unique or private but a repeatable, universal process of consciousness.

To say ordinarily of some conscious state that it is *mine*, is to imply that the conditions of its occurrence could not be reduplicated in any other consciousness. It also means, of course, that the feeling is in principle not capable of occurring a second time, since such feelings have only one unique life. *My* feeling occurs in *me* and, therefore, it can never occur in anyone else. Kant, however, contrary to the entire Lockean tradition, claims that a feeling is private only if it rests upon some personal inclination or desire. Thus, if I am inclined to eat Roquefort cheese and my inclination has a history uniquely mine, my desire can only be mine. But if a feeling rests upon some event or process that in itself has no element of privateness or personalness about it, the feeling, in principle, is capable of any number of instances. Since aesthetic feeling rests upon the spontaneous "fittingness" of the imagination and the understanding, the imagination's free conformity to law, and since this phenomenon is a phenomenon that has nothing private about it, the aesthetic feeling is intrinsically universal.

Suppose one were to say that "The stove is hot." Now the meaning of the assertion would be, or could be, "I experienced a sensation of heat when I touched the stove," but, it could also mean, and generally does mean, "Anyone who touches that stove would experience a sensation of heat." What I mean by my assertion is (1) I felt hot and (2) the conditions are such that everyone with normal sense organs and brain *would* also feel hot. Such a declaration would go unchallenged because we believe that feelings which are the result of some factor whose existence is independent of a personal disposition will be feelings that are not *limited* to a single person. This same analysis would hold for Kant's understanding of the universality of aesthetic judgments. The feeling such judgments rest upon is the result of a process whose existence is independent of a personal disposition. That *my* imagination is in accord with *my* understanding does not mean that the accord is limited to *me*, since *we* all have minds that are equivalent. The Kantian mind is a universal mind, a transcendental unity of apperception which is mine or yours *not* because it is a different individual mind, but because of the different experiences which mine undergoes and yours undergoes. The Kantian mind is a delicately balanced machine which is individuated in this or that body and whose machinations are repeatable and duplicative even though they occur in different bodies.

Thus, when one predicates beauty, one is asserting that (1) one *felt* aesthetic pleasure when the object was experienced because of the harmony between the order of the imaginative representation and the order of the understanding, and (2) anyone would experience aesthetic pleasure since anyone's imagination would be ordered by the representation and would therefore result in its being in harmony with the order of the understanding. Quite simply, what one feels derives from a process which everyone can feel; therefore what one feels, although *one* feels it, is not private, but public. It is a conditional judgment. *If* one experienced object X freely, *then* one would experience aesthetic pleasure. Since aesthetic pleasure is based upon the spontaneous agreement of the imagination and the understanding, and since object X produced this in one person it would produce it in another, because its occurrence in one person is not dependent upon that person as a private person, but as a person having a mind. All those, therefore, who have minds, will experience aesthetic pleasure when confronted by object X *so long as* the confrontation is a pure confrontation.

The upshot of these reflections which, we should bear in

mind, are deductive inferences necessitated by the Kantian
system, is that the aesthetic judgment is based upon a subjective feeling but is a universal judgment. Kant says it has
"subjective universal validity" as contrasted with "objective
universal validity." The contrast is between a judgment which
rests upon reasons, (concepts) and a judgment which rests
upon feelings. The former is valid when the feeling is necessarily universal. The only kind of reasons which are necessarily
universal are, for Kant, *a priori* reasons or concepts of the
understanding. The only kind of feelings that are necessarily
universal are feelings which are not based upon personal desires, but upon objective states of mind. These latter could be
either moral feelings or aesthetic feelings, but since a moral
feeling is based upon *a reason* which implies a carry-over into
action, it must be excluded.

What remains is aesthetic feeling which is based upon the
natural harmony of the mental faculties. Thus, aesthetic
judgments are universal, and by analogous reasoning necessary, although one cannot give reasons for their universality
and necessity. One can only say, "If *you*, (meaning anyone)
have a free experience of the object, you will *feel* it as beautiful and your feeling must occur." This is Kant's meaning
when he says, "the judgment of taste itself does not *postulate*
the agreement of everyone . . . it only *imputes* this agreement to everyone."[6] Kant wants to maintain that what is revealed in aesthetic experience is the in-itself character of
Nature. Since this character is obviously not subjectively determined, it would be a contradiction for him to allow that
universality and necessity are inapplicable to the aesthetic
judgment. He therefore must find a way to guarantee universality and necessity but exclude all conscious determination—he does this by grounding aesthetic judgment in feeling
—and to hold onto universality and necessity—he does this by
grounding them in the notion of the objectivity of the process
which underlies aesthetic feeling. Kant's ingenuity is truly
extraordinary. But it is not simply ingenuity concerning logical consistency. It is also ingenuity at arriving at some clear
and important aesthetic insights while battling the stringen-

[6] *Critique of Judgment,* p. 51.

cies of his self-defeating system. For, again, Kant has unearthed some important aesthetic truths.

First, that our aesthetic judgments are *not* objective in that they simply refer to an objective property, but that they *are* objective in referring to the power which the art-object has of producing certain emotions in a normal subject. That is to say, the aesthetic judgment is not the same as an ordinary cognitive judgment like, "The table is cracked" or "The sky is cloudy." These, as it were, simply register entities in our experiential field and the properties such entities display. The aesthetic judgment does not simply record what is antecedently there in experience, it records what occurs in the interaction between what is there and the subject who experiences what is there. The reference is to the emotions of the subject so that the subjective pole of the experience is stressed and not the objective pole.

Of course, in some sense, the ordinary cognitive judgment also records what occurs in the interaction but this only secondarily. When I say, "The sky is cloudy" I mean directly *that* the sky is cloudy and indirectly that I *experience* the sky as cloudy. But when I say, "The sky is beautiful," I mean directly that I *experience* the sky as beautiful and indirectly that the sky *is* beautiful. The distinction might be a precious one, but the language which is ordinarily used to utter such judgments and talk about them seems clear. Thus, I say "The sky is cloudy" and someone says "Yes, that was predicted," but no one plausibly says "You mean *you* experience the sky as cloudy." However, when I say "The sky is beautiful" no one says "Yes, that was predicted," but someone could plausibly say "You mean *you* experience the sky as beautiful." There is an indubitable hidden reference in aesthetic judgments to the subjective pole of the field which is not implied in the cognitive judgment. I think, at the very least, this must be admitted. And this is what Kant is getting at. In aesthetic judgments we are not uttering the ordinary kind of object-referring statements—there is a subject-reference which is the most important part of its meaning.

Secondly, aesthetic judgments differ from moral judgments in that they have no reference to universal and necessary action, but only to universal and necessary assent. When I say,

"Lying is evil," I mean "One ought not to lie" and "All should not lie." But when I say, "The sky is beautiful," I mean only that all who experience the sky freely *ought* to assent to my judgment and nothing whatsoever is implied in terms of action. More specifically, moral judgments are concerned mostly with the behavioral, practical or, in those senses, objective side of life, whereas aesthetic judgments are concerned with the emotional, felt, or, in those senses, subjective side of life. Aesthetic experience is not geared to eventuate in action, but to produce states of feeling. That a beautiful object *does* produce action is not excluded, but that its *purpose* is to produce such action is excluded. Every moral judgment is in some sense propagandistic, every aesthetic judgment is neutral.

Thirdly, Kant's belief in the universality and necessity *without* reasons of the aesthetic judgment highlights the inevitable experiential and singular quality of beauty. For whatever else one could do to initiate someone into the realm of beauty, ultimately all talk must cease and the direct felt apprehension of beauty must occur if an aesthetic feeling is to be born. "If a man, *in the first place*, does not find a building, a prospect, or a poem beautiful, a hundred voices praising it will not force his inmost agreement."[7] "For though a man enumerate to me all the ingredients of a dish and remark that each is separately pleasant to me, and further extol with justice the wholesomeness of this particular food, yet am I deaf to all these reasons; I try the dish with *my* tongue and *my* palate, and thereafter (and not according to universal principles) do I pass my judgment."[8] "I must immediately feel pleasure in the presentation of the object, and of that I can be persuaded by no grounds of proof whatever."[9] Beauty ultimately is felt and no amount of reasoning concerning it can result in the same feeling as direct contact. There is no knowledge by description, only knowledge by acquaintance. Moreover, all aesthetic judgments state this. For the meaning of an aesthetic judgment, we have seen, is an if-then statement. That is, when I say, "The sky is beautiful" I mean, "If you were to experience the sky freely with no interference

---

[7] *Critique of Judgment*, p. 125.   [8] *Ibid.* p. 6.   [9] *Ibid.* p. 17.

from your intrinsically interfering mind, you would experience a felt aesthetic pleasure at the harmony with which the representation of the sky fits into the structural order of the understanding."

Finally, Kant's principle allows a way to handle aesthetic controversy, i.e. agreement and disagreement about beauty. For there is a "what," i.e. an easily verifiable phenomenon, that is common to all experiences of beauty, and a "why" it is common. There is also a procedure to follow which, in principle at least, can end disagreement. Let us take these in turn. The "what" that is common to those who agree in judging an object beautiful is the aesthetic pleasure which they sense in themselves. The reason why they experience this feeling is that a spontaneous agreement between the faculties of the mind has occurred. The undesigned coincidence of the imaginative representation and the understanding is felt as aesthetic pleasure. Further, when there is aesthetic disagreement there is a principle to follow which, in theory, can solve the conflict. For disagreement is usually reducible to either the one or the other party, either not approaching the art-object purely, or not realizing that beauty is to be found in aesthetic feeling. One may by searching for meanings, values, even patriotic symbols, or one may feel, but not be content with feeling and seek after rules, explanations, historical facts, or other conceptual criteria. The Kantian aesthetic provides a method whereby, through making the parties aware of *what* they should look for, and *how* they should look, disagreement can be overcome. Moreover, it also provides an explanation for continued disagreement. For as long as there is disagreement one party has not fulfilled the conditions. This continued disagreement need not signify that an art-object cannot be considered objectively beautiful, but rather that the conditions necessary to experiencing its beauty have not been met.

We mentioned above the fact that Kant is often termed a formalist. Before completing this discussion of the Kantian aesthetic theory, I should like to discuss to what extent, and in what precise sense, this assertion is true. Firstly, we have already seen that the peculiar aesthetic feeling is grounded in the rational demand for unity, order, and harmony. We also saw that this rational demand for unity, order, and harmony was linked to a non-rational agency, i.e. the body and in some way qualified by it. Therefore, on the basis of these considerations it is not correct to call Kant a formalist since formalism implies a stricter adherence to purely rational criteria. It is true however that Kant rejects all "empirical satisfactions," sensations, as qualifying properties of the beautiful. I shall argue that in rejecting these Kant was not inconsistent, i.e. he did not have to grant them aesthetic status, but that the reason he did reject them was *other than* a purely aesthetic reason. He was not against granting sense-elements aesthetic status for aesthetic reasons, but only because granting them that status would logically alter the philosophic importance of the aesthetic experience. And, as we have repeatedly seen, it is this fundamental thesis which, above all, Kant wishes to maintain.

We have seen that "contemplative pleasure or passive satisfaction"[10] is the necessary condition for keeping the aesthetic experience pure and thereby allowing it the status of being a window, so to speak, into the noumenal world. We have also seen in what this contemplative pleasure consists, the harmony of the imagination and the understanding or, as Kant says, "a mutual subjective harmony of the cognitive powers,"[11] in a "state of free play."[12] Let us look more closely into this subjective harmony.

Firstly, what is in the imagination? Presumably the "gathered together"[13] sensations. Now this "sense-entity" corresponds in some way to the understanding. But in what way? Suppose the "gathered together" sense-datum consisted in a group of red patches, each of which is half the size of the patch which preceded it. Would it be the "redness" of all or any of the particular red patches that corresponded? Clearly not, for it is absurd to say that there is an *a priori* "redness" in the understanding.

Supposing the red represented blood, i.e. the scene portrayed depicts a battlefield in which a great deal of blood is flowing. Would it be the idea of blood that corresponded?

[10] *Critique of Judgment*, p. 57.   [11] *Ibid.* p. 53.
[12] *Ibid.* p. 52.   [13] *Ibid.* p. 52.

Clearly not, for it is again absurd to suppose that there is an *a priori* concept of "blood" in the understanding.

What *would* correspond would be the order of the diminishing size progression. That is, the purely rational formula of half the first and half again, etc., is the rational schema which the understanding would have an affinity towards. Nothing that was material or specific could find an analogue in the understanding since it (the understanding) contains only immaterial and abstract entities. Only relationships—of a spatial kind which Kant calls "figure" or of a temporal kind which Kant calls "play"—could correspond to the immaterial nature and function of the understanding. A manifold of sensations gathered by the imagination could only harmonize with the understanding by virtue of the spatial relationships which they exhibited (their figure or geometrical shape) or the temporal relationships they exhibited (their play or temporal shape). The particular material elements or ideas are unimportant from this point of view since they have no counterpart or comparable pattern in the understanding. Only formal properties like geometrical relationships or temporal successions can have such counterparts or patterns. (It is significant, in this context, that Kant claims colors, which are purely material sensations, can be beautiful only insofar as they are simple and unmixed. In that state they signify purity and unity which are archetypal patterns of the understanding and therefore harmonize with the understanding.)

Clearly, then Kant's concern is not with *any* property which an art-object presents, but only in those properties which are common to both the imaginative entity and the understanding, i.e. some *common* characteristic which both the understanding and the imaginative entity display. This concern, moreover, is entailed by the entire metaphysical edifice Kant has constructed. He insists upon the harmony of the imagination and the understanding which means that only those aspects of the "gathered together" sense-image, which correspond to the immaterial nature of the understanding, are aesthetically significant. Since the understanding can have no material element, he must search for a formal element among the sensations to be the significant element. The figure and play of sensations are not sensations themselves but relationships among sensations. As relationships, they are rational entities and, as such, they can be compared to the understanding. And as relationships which express order, uniformity, design and purposiveness, they can harmonize with the understanding which imposes order, uniformity, design, and purposiveness.

Moreover, the fact that aesthetic judgments are communicable demands that aesthetic properties be formal and not material. For if I can communicate my feeling of beauty, it cannot be a feeling based simply on a sensed, material quality. My feeling on contact with a particular sense quality like "red" or "smooth" does not imply a similar or equivalent feeling on your part. This is arbitrary and too contingent. But my awareness of the harmony which exists between an ordered, purposive representation and an ordering, purpose-giving understanding does imply a similar awareness on your part since the elements contributing to this harmony are intrinsically universal. The faculties themselves are public since they constitute the transcendental mind and the object producing the representations is also an objective entity. Thus, the empirical fact that there is communicability of taste and agreement concerning aesthetic objects also leads to the conclusion that aesthetic properties must be formal properties, i.e. relations between sense-elements and not material properties.

Now, although Kant makes the above claim, and is to that extent a formalist, it is important to realize *that* he makes it because it is the only way to avoid contradicting his more important thesis concerning the philosophic significance of the aesthetic experience, i.e. that it displays the rational character of Nature. This rational character must be an order of purposiveness and design which obviously consists of intelligible, conceptual properties. But, although he holds this, he does not deny completely that material properties hold some aesthetic significance. He claims, for example, that such properties as decoration or ornamentation, and colors or sounds *can* enhance aesthetic perception by interesting the mind, or enlivening the object, or "because they make the form more exactly, definitely, and completely, intuitable, and besides, by their charm excite the representation, while they awaken and fix our attention on the object itself."[14] However, insofar as they lead the mind away from the formal properties they are negative, "they must only be admitted by indulgence as aliens."[15]

It appears then that sense-properties can enhance the aesthetic object by causing the formal properties to be more clearly apparent by throwing them into greater relief. For example, as when particular colored masses in a painting intensify the boundaries of the form and thereby render its relationship to other forms more overt and graspable. Or, when particular sound intensities throw the temporal succession of tones into a more recognizable light. However, when those material properties overstep their role as means and overshadow or obliterate the formal properties, they are no longer either significant or even indirectly useful.

Thus, while it is incorrect to call Kant a formalist, if one means by that an advocate of the complete elimination of material properties as aesthetically significant, it is equally as incorrect not to call him a formalist, since the only aesthetic significance which he grants material properties is as indirect stimuli which magnify the formal properties. Kant's position here is neither a formalism of the Baumgarten type (which he refutes), nor a sensationalism of the Humean type (which he also refutes), but a midway position which allows some aesthetic significance for sense-qualities but only insofar as they are directed to a larger aim.

This compromise position is readily recognizable in Kant's terminology. He calls the aesthetic judgment which is mingled with a sensuous element a "material aesthetic judgment" and the aesthetic judgment which deals only with the relationships between the sensuous elements "formal aesthetical judgments." The latter alone are "strictly judgments of taste." But clearly the former have *some* aesthetic significance for their very name involves the term "aesthetic." This paradoxical holding onto both sides of an apparently exclusive disjunction is characteristic of the Kantian aesthetic, as it is of the Kantian philosophy as a whole. We have seen it at work many times and have also seen, in the case of his aesthetic

[14] *Critique of Judgment*, p. 61.   [15] *Ibid.* p. 61.

paradoxes, that they are really inevitable consequences of the special role he grants to the aesthetic as that which "bridges" the fact-value dichotomy and the equally special role he gives the free or pure experience.

This can be seen even more clearly in Kant's discussion of the aesthetic significance of the content of a work of art. For again, in order to keep the experience pure, its content as ideas, meanings, etc., must be abolished and subordinated to its form as pure perceived representation. However, to deny an aesthetic significance to the content of a work of art is to deny obvious empirical facts. So some compromise must be worked out.

The compromise hinges on Kant's distinction between "free" and "dependent" beauty. "The first presupposes no concept of what the object ought to be; the second does presuppose such a concept."[16] Kant understands content here in the sense of the concept of the object, i.e. what it is. For example, in a painting of a church the painted object represents a church and since we have had innumerable experiences of churches, we inevitably *know* what a church is. Thus, the painted church is immediately correlated with the concept of church and is judged as to the degree of similarity. Our idea of what the painted object is supposed to be mingles with our experience of it. Now there is thus an element, namely, an idea of the church, interposed between the mind and its pure apprehension of a visual form. The visual form cannot be a unique form since we already have an idea of it which immediately, even unconsciously, structures our experience of it. Thus, we cannot judge its beauty *purely* since we are barred from experiencing it as pure visual form and without such experience beauty cannot be strictly predicated. As Kant says, "Flowers are free natural beauties" since "hardly anyone knows what sort of a thing a flower ought to be."[17]

As soon as an idea interposes itself into the aesthetic experience it destroys its purity. Only visual forms which "mean nothing in themselves"[18] can be proper objects of aesthetic contemplation. Examples are "delineations à la grecque, foliage for borders or wallpapers . . . what are called musical

[16] *Critique of Judgment*, p. 65.   [17] *Ibid.* p. 65.   [18] *Ibid.* p. 66.

fantasies (i.e. pieces without any theme), and in fact all music without words."[19] These are all phenomena which, having no intellectual content, present themselves for pure aesthetic judgment. They are instances of free beauty whereas the church or "a house, or a building (be it church, palace, arsenal or summer house) . . . is . . . adherent beauty."[20]

There is an easy transition from content in this sense, the concept of what the object depicted is, to content in a larger sense, namely, any *intellectual* idea or meaning which the object projects. And to the extent that an aesthetic object does suggest such ideas or meanings, it is not pure. For such a content will destroy the pure apprehension of the object and project into this ideal experience an element which is not relevant for aesthetic judgment.

Still, Kant cannot deny the obvious fact that much man-made art *is* concerned with projecting intellectual content. The reconciliation is accomplished firstly by classifying beauty as free and dependent. Dependent beauty is beauty insofar as the intellectual content *does not* destroy the formal structure of the presentation. When it arrests the attention, it outdoes itself and works against aesthetic satisfaction. It would be simply "talking" and not poetry if ideas were the sole subject matter of a poem. The point is that intellectual contents force the class of man-made artifacts out of the class of pure beautiful things, but this is not to say that those man-made artifacts cannot exhibit beauty. They do in a secondary sense to be sure, but they still do.

Moreover there is no reason why the intellectual contents cannot be projected in and through the form of the aesthetic object. The issue is between reason and feeling and since Kant *must* side here with feeling, he obviously cannot strictly speaking allow reason a role either as an idea in the art-work or as a conscious determination in art-appreciation. Nonetheless, insofar as reason is not given an independent function but is *tied* to feeling, it can still add somewhat to aesthetic experience.

In the same sense that ornamentation was allowed some aesthetic role as a means, so content is allowed some aesthetic

[19] *Ibid.* p. 66.   [20] *Ibid.* p. 66.

value insofar as it is not presented as idea but as a meaning
linked to the formal order of the object. For example, one
could simply state an idea in a poem or one, by a series of
metaphors and linked or associated images, could *suggest*
the meaning. One does not *state* it, but allows it to come to
the fore indirectly through the subject's feeling-state which is
controlled by the relationships holding between poetic images.
This is connected to Kant's notion of aesthetical ideas which,
as we saw, can present contents if these contents are projected
via a non-conceptual vehicle. The paradox then of form and
matter and form and content is presumably solved. Kant sides
always with form but never shuts the door on matter and
content. His formalism is a qualified formalism as his idealism is a qualified idealism.

From our point of view, it is enough to note that these
subtleties grow out of Kant's concern for the free experience
and the philosophical nature of the aesthetic. All his reason-
ings are controlled by these considerations. And, as we have
said earlier, the merit of the Kantian aesthetic is not solely
his remarkable dexterity in holding such apparently irrecon-
cilable elements together, as it is his ability to deal with the
empirical facts of aesthetic experience within the principles
of a system that threaten those facts. In the case before us, it
is clear that again Kant has drawn attention to an aesthetic
truth. The truth that the "what" of the art work is subordinated to the "how" of it. That is, on the one hand, the sense-
elements *qua* sense-elements are subordinated to the way in
which they are arranged and, on the other, ideas and meaning
which are expressed through an art-work are also subordinated
to the concrete perceptual entity which presents them. An
idea could be expressed in a declarative sentence and a sense-
datum as such is part of any physical experience. They are
significant insofar as they have been shaped, formed, balanced, colored, placed in a pattern, etc. What, for example, is
the aesthetic significance of a sound or a concept? These in
themselves, cannot be differentiated as aesthetic objects unless they are placed in some whole, concretized, designed, and
related in some ordered totality.

To some extent then Kant is correct in classifying these as
secondary. He does not eliminate them altogether, of course,

and again this is in accord with the facts of aesthetic experience. Kant's distinction between free and dependent beauty and material and formal properties points to the empirical fact that it is the art-object as perceived form which is uniquely beautiful and not as an intellectual statement or a trivial juxtaposition of sensations. It is the sensuously given as *arranged* and *designed* that produces the aesthetic effect, not the sensuous stuff itself or the author's ideas. Insofar as the stuff and the ideas contribute to or are presented by the formal relationships in the art-work, they are aesthetically significant. When they overflow and mar the primacy of these formal relationships they lose aesthetic significance.

In conclusion, let me summarize the main point of this essay. The Kantian aesthetic rests upon metaphysical principles. Primarily upon the notion that the aesthetic experience is not a second-rate phenomenon, but, rather a phenomenon of the utmost existential importance. Its importance lies in its being the only channel whereby men can apprehend the rays of the noumenal world filtering through the phenomenal world, or in a more up-to-date language, can see a unity of facts and values. Interpreted in this way, the aesthetic holds the key to the entire Kantian philosophy and it would be appropriate to say that it is the true culmination of the critical philosophy. Its ultimate consequence is moral, i.e. it bolsters faith in the morality of the hidden, postulated spiritual world by establishing some "feeling—understanding" of it. It provides some empirical grounds for maintaining the fundamental morality of reality. As Kant says, ". . . it interests reason that the ideas (for which in moral experience it arouses an immediate interest) should have objective reality, i.e. that nature should at least show a trace or give an indication that it contains in itself a ground for assuming a regular agreement of its products with our entirely disinterested satisfaction (which we recognize *a priori* as a law for everyone, without being able to base it upon proofs). Hence reason must take an interest in every expression on the part of nature of an agreement of this kind."[21] Instances of natural beauty are such expressions of Nature which show traces and give indica-

[21] *Critique of Judgment*, p. 143.

tions that our postulated idea of a spiritual and rational substratum has a counterpart in Nature. Clearly such a fundamental aim will be a basic driving force in Kant's reflections. I have tried to show how many of the specific aesthetic conclusions Kant reaches are necessitated by this metaphysical consideration. That they are so necessitated is one thing, that they are valid aesthetic conclusions is another. I believe they are and have also attempted to demonstrate this validity by squaring them with the empirical facts of aesthetic experience.

BIBLIOGRAPHY

BIBLIOGRAPHY OF WORKS BY AND ABOUT KANT

There is now a large library of editions of Kant's works in English, as well as a wide variety of commentaries and general works about his philosophy. The following suggestions may be of assistance to the student who wishes to pursue his interest in the Critical Philosophy.

I. EDITIONS OF KANT'S WORKS IN ENGLISH

1. The best translation of the *Critique of Pure Reason* is by Norman Kemp Smith, New York, St. Martin's Press. Although an earlier translation, by Max Müller, is available in paper, the Smith translation is so far superior that one should pay the extra amount for it.

2. A number of Critical works are available in Library of Liberal Arts paper editions, in good translations. Among them are: *Foundations of the Metaphysics of Morals*, tr. by L. W. Beck; *Prolegomena to Any Future Metaphysics*, tr. by L. W. Beck; *Metaphysical Elements of Justice*, tr. by John Ladd (Part I of the *Metaphysics of Morals*); *The Metaphysical Principles of Virtue*, tr. by James Ellington (Part II of the *Metaphysics of Morals*); *Analytic of the Beautiful* from the *Critique of Judgment*, tr. by Walter Cerf; and *Critique of Practical Reason*, tr. by L. W. Beck.

3. The extremely important *Inaugural Dissertation of 1770* is not in print, but many libraries will have copies of the early translation by Handyside.

II. COMMENTARIES AND SECONDARY WORKS

There are a great many books about Kant's philosophy by English and American authors. Rather than merely listing them, it might be more useful to mention only a few with some indication of their strengths and weaknesses. Following are some of the works I have found useful.

1. Norman Kemp Smith, *A Commentary to Kant's 'Critique of Pure Reason,'* 2d ed. rev. and enl., London, Macmillan, 1929. This is by far the best single work in English on the first *Critique*. It has several times reappeared in print, and any student who can obtain a copy should do so, even though it is now rather expensive. Don't expect to sit down and read this work through. It is to be used selectively, in conjunction with the text.

2. H. J. Paton, *Kant's Metaphysics of Experience*, 2 vols., London, Macmillan, 1936. A very useful book for beginning students, since it discusses in detail virtually every passage in the first half of the *Critique*. Paton has the unfortunate tendency, however, to tell the reader that Kant is clear and consistent, rather than showing how he is. Hence, for advanced students, Paton is likely to be not much use.

3. T. D. Weldon, *Kant's Critique of Pure Reason*, 2d ed., Oxford, Clarendon Press, 1958. Oddly enough, the first edition is better than the second, since in the later edition Weldon introduced some rather inappropriate linguistic philosophical jargon that was not successfully integrated into his commentary. For a few selected topics, Weldon is the best thing in English. He is especially helpful on the vexing problem of inner sense.

4. Robert Paul Wolff, *Kant's Theory of Mental Activity*, Harvard University Press, 1963. An interpretation of the Transcendental Analytic. The book is cast in the form of a textual commentary, and can be read either separately or in conjunction with the text.

5. L. W. Beck, *A Commentary on Kant's Critique of Practical Reason*, University of Chicago Press, 1960. A first-rate commentary on an oft-ignored Critical work. Beck's

mastery of the traditional Kantian scholarship is matched by his philosophical sophistication. The result is a very useful work which can be read as background to Kant's ethical theory in general, as well as in conjunction with the second *Critique*.

6. H. J. Paton, *The Categorical Imperative*, University of Chicago Press, 1948. A commentary on the *Groundwork of the Metaphysics of Morals*. Like his commentary on the first *Critique*, this work is extremely useful up to a point. Paton has managed to sort out the obscure and archaic psychological terminology in which Kant couches much of his argument. Consequently, the baffled reader will find considerable enlightenment in Paton's explanations of the text. Nevertheless, at the point that one begins to ask whether what Kant says is true or cogent, Paton ceases to be really helpful.

7. Mary J. Gregor, *Laws of Freedom*, New York, Barnes & Noble, 1963. A restrained but useful exposition of the *Metaphysics of Morals*. Mrs. Gregor's restatement and commentary provides a much-needed corrective to the distorted picture of Kant's ethical theory that one gains from the *Groundwork of the Metaphysics of Morals* alone.

SELECTED BIBLIOGRAPHY OF ARTICLES ON KANT, 1945 TO THE PRESENT

Addis, Laird C., Jr. "Kant's First Analogy," *Kant-Studien,* Band 54 (1963), 237–42.

Axinn, Sidney. "Kant, Logic, and the Concept of Mankind," *Ethics* (1957–58), 286–91.

———. "A Kantian Definition of Rationality," *Kant-Studien,* Band 51 (1959–60), 27–33.

Baumer, William H. "Kant and 'God is': A Reply to Mr. Engel," *Kant-Studien,* Band 55 (1964), 498–504.

Beck, Lewis White. "Die Kantkritik von C. I. Lewis und der Analytischen Schule," *Kant-Studien,* Band 45 (1953–54), 3–20.

———. "Apodictic Imperatives," *Kant-Studien,* Band 49 (1957–58), 7–24.

Blau, J. L. "Kant in America," *Journal of Philosophy* (1954), 874–80.

Bossart, W. H. "Kant and Some Metaphysicians," *Kant-Studien,* Band 55 (1964), 20–36.

Brown, Stuart M., Jr. "Has Kant a Philosophy of Law," *Philosophical Review* (1962), 33–48.

Castañeda, Hector. "'7+5=12' as a Synthetic Proposition," *Philosophy and Phenomenological Research* (1960–61), 141–58.

Cousin, D. R. "Kant on the Self," *Kant-Studien,* Band 49 (1957–58), 25–35.

Crawford, Patricia A. "Kant's Theory of Philosophical Proof," *Kant-Studien,* Band 53 (1961–62), 257–68.

Engle, S. Morris. "Kant's Copernican Analogy: A Reexamination," *Kant-Studien,* Band 54 (1963), 243–51.

Fackenheim, L. "Kant's Concept of History," *Kant-Studien,* Band 48 (1956–57), 381–98.

Friedman, Lawrence. "Kant's Theory of Time," *Review of Metaphysics* (1953–54), 379–88.

Gahringer, Robert. "The Metaphysical Aspect of Kant's Moral Philosophy," *Ethics* (1953–54), 277–91.

Grabau, Richard F. "Kant's Concept of the Thing in Itself: An Interpretation," *Review of Metaphysics* (1962–63), 770–79.

Gregor, M. J. "Kant's Conception of a 'Metaphysics of Morals,'" *Philosophical Quarterly* (1960), 238–51.

Haezrahi, Pepita. "The Avowed and Unavowed Sources of Kant's Theory of Ethics," *Ethics* (1961–62), 157–68.

Hall, Robert W. "Kant and Ethical Formalism," *Kant-Studien*, Band 52 (1960–61), 433–39.

Hancock, R. "A Note on Kant's Third Critique," *Philosophical Quarterly* (1958), 261–65.

——. "Kant and the Natural Right Theory," *Kant-Studien*, Band 52 (1960–61), 440–47.

Hanson, Norwood. "Copernicus' Role in Kant's Revolution," *Journal of the History of Ideas* (1959), 274–81.

Henle, Paul. "The Critique of Pure Reason Today," *Journal of Philosophy* (1962), 225–34.

Holmes, Eugene. "The Kantian Views on Time and Space Re-evaluated," *Philosophy and Phenomenological Research* (1955–56), 240–44.

Kaminsky, Jack. "Kant's Analysis of Aesthetics," *Kant-Studien*, Band 50 (1958–59), 77–88.

Kolenda, K. "Prof. Ebbinghaus' Interpretation of the Categorical Imperative," *Philosophical Quarterly* (1955), 74–77.

Mathur, G. B. "Hume and Kant in Their Relation to the Pragmatic Movement," *Journal of the History of Ideas* (1955), 198–208.

McRae, Robert. "Kant's Conception of the Unity of the Sciences," *Philosophy and Phenomenological Research* (1957–58), 1–17.

Meiklejohn, Donald. "Kantian Formalism and Civil Liberty," *Journal of Philosophy* (1954), 842–48.

Munitz, Milton K. "Kantian Dialectic and Modern Scientific Cosmology," *Journal of Philosophy* (1951), 325–38.

Nahm, Milton C. " 'Sublimity' and the 'Moral Law' in Kant's Philosophy," *Kant-Studien*, Band 48 (1956–57), 502–24.

Oliver, James Willard. "Kant's Copernican Analogy: A re-examination of a re-examination," *Kant-Studien*, Band 55 (1964), 505–11.

Paton, H. J. "An Alleged Right to Lie: A Problem in Kantian Ethics," *Kant-Studien*, Band 45 (1953–54), 190–203.

———. "The Aim and Structure of Kant's *Grundlegung*," *Philosophical Quarterly* (1958), 112–30.

Rees, D. A. "Kant's 'Physiology of the Human Understanding,' " *Journal of the History of Ideas* (1952), 108–9.

———. "Kant, Bayle, and Indifferentism," *Philosophical Review* (1954), 592–95.

Reiss, H. S. "Kant and the Right of Rebellion," *Journal of the History of Ideas* (1956), 179–92.

Robinson, Richard. "Necessary Propositions," *Mind* (1958), 289–304.

Rogers, Wiley Kim. "On a Comprehensive Principle in the Kantian Critiques," *Kant-Studien*, Band 52 (1960–61), 448–51.

Rotenstreich, Nathan. "Kant's Dialectic," *Review of Metaphysics*, (1953–54), 389–421.

Sacksteder, W. "Kant's Analysis of International Relations," *Journal of Philosophy* (1954), 848–55.

Schipper, E. W. "Kant's Answer to Hume's Problem," *Kant-Studien*, Band 53 (1961–62), 68–74.

Schrader, George. "The Transcendental Ideality and Empirical Reality of Kant's Space and Time," *Review of Metaphysics* (1950–51), 507–36.

———. "Kant's Presumed Repudiation of the 'Moral Argument' in the *Opus Postumum*: An Examination of Adickes' Interpretation," *Philosophy* (1951), 228–41.

——— and G. Clark. "Questions on Kant," *Review of Metaphysics* (1951–52), 473–80.

———. "The Status of Teleological Judgment in the Critical Philosophy," *Kant-Studien*, Band 45 (1953–54), 204–35.

———. "Autonomy, Heteronomy, and Moral Imperatives," *Journal of Philosophy* (1963), 65–77.

Schueller, Herbert M. "Immanuel Kant and the Aesthetics of Music," *Journal of Aesthetics and Art Criticism* (1955–56), 218–47.

Schwarz, Wolfgang. "Kant's Philosophy of Law and International Peace," *Philosophy and Phenomenological Research* (1962–63), 71–80.

Silber, John R. "Kant's Conception of the Highest Good as Immanent and Transcendent," *Philosophical Review* (1959), 469–92.

———. "The Context of Kant's Ethical Thought," *Philosophical Quarterly* (1959), 193–207, 309–18.

———. "The Importance of the Highest Good in Kant's Ethics," *Ethics* (1962–63), 179–97.

Singer, Marcus. "The Categorical Imperative," *Philosophical Review* (1954), 577–91.

Smart, Harold. "Two Views on Kant and Formal Logic," *Philosophy and Phenomenological Research* (1955–56), 155–71.

Stern, Alfred. "Kant and Our Time," *Philosophy and Phenomenological Research* (1955–56), 531–39.

Turbayne, C. M. "Kant's Refutation of Dogmatic Idealism," *Philosophical Quarterly* (1955), 225–44.

Wassmer, Thomas A. "Responsibility and Pleasure in Kantian Morality," *Kant-Studien*, Band 52 (1960–61), 452–66.

Williams, Forrest. "Philosophical Anthropology and the Critique of Aesthetic Judgment," *Kant-Studien*, Band 46 (1954–55), 172–88.